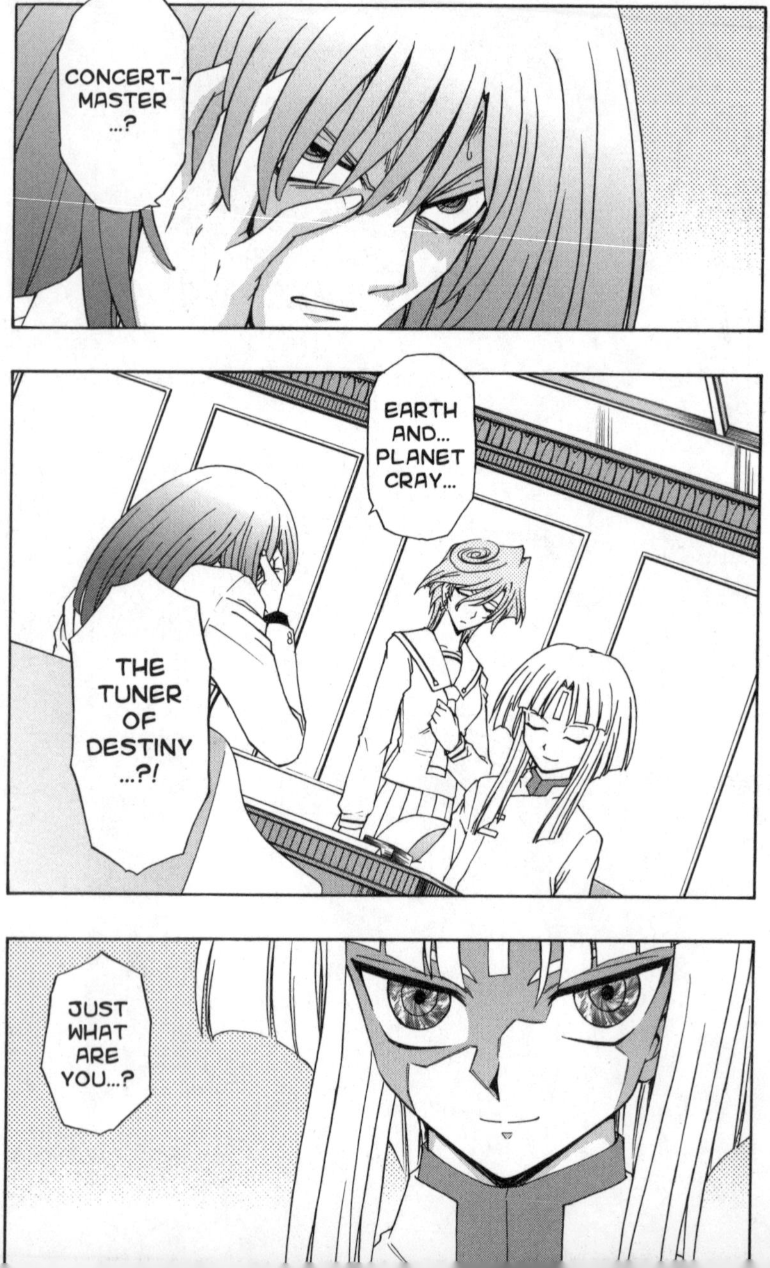
CONCERT-MASTER ...?
EARTH AND... PLANET CRAY...
THE TUNER OF DESTINY ...?!
JUST WHAT ARE YOU...?

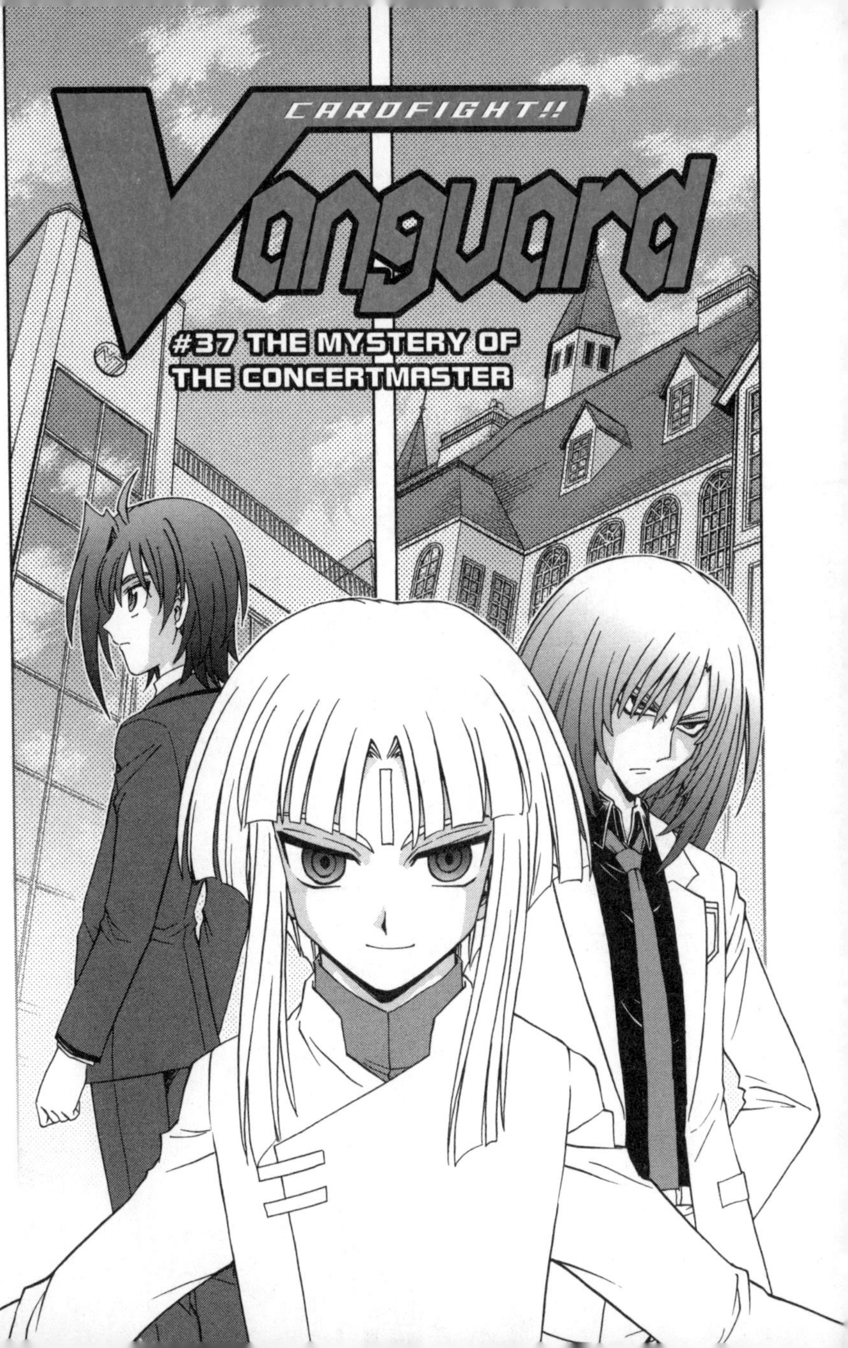
CARDFIGHT!!
Vanguard
#37 THE MYSTERY OF THE CONCERTMASTER

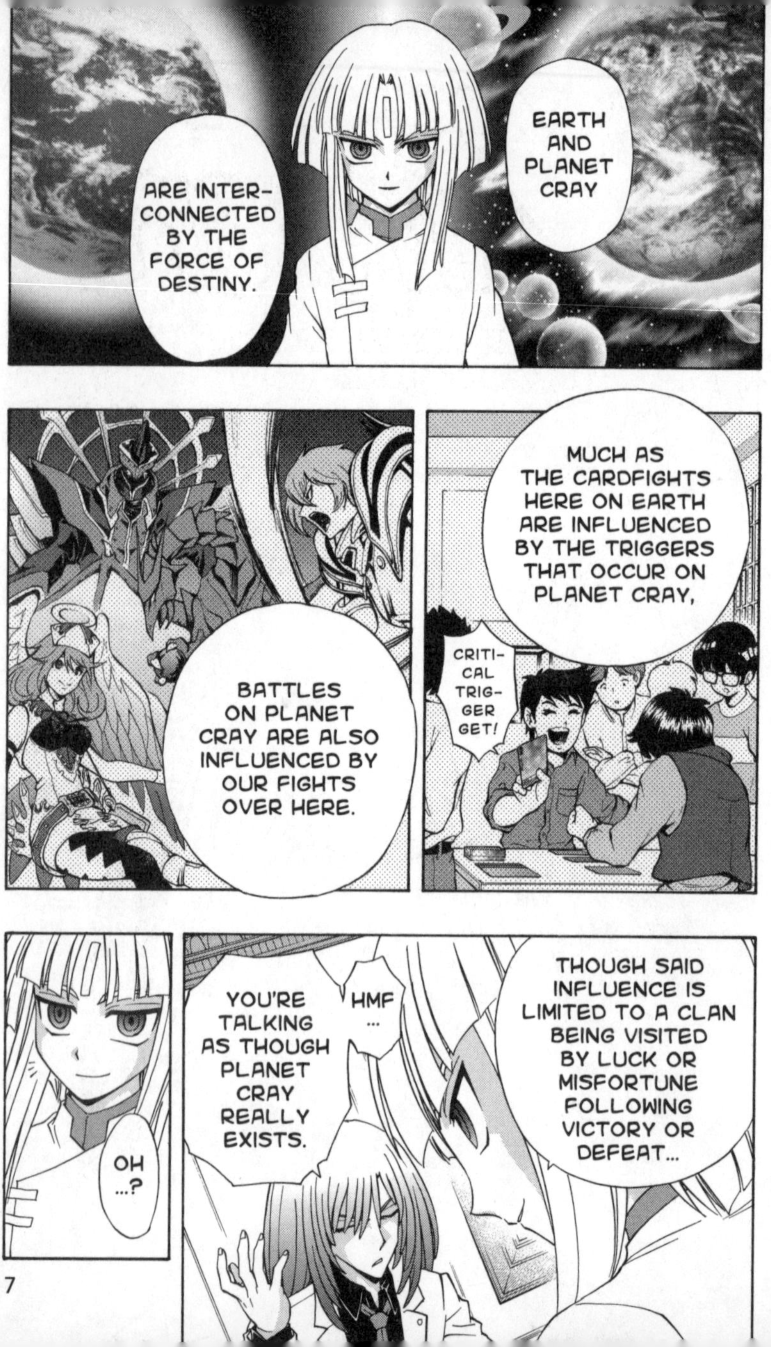
EARTH AND PLANET CRAY
ARE INTER-CONNECTED BY THE FORCE OF DESTINY.
MUCH AS THE CARDFIGHTS HERE ON EARTH ARE INFLUENCED BY THE TRIGGERS THAT OCCUR ON PLANET CRAY,
CRITI-CAL TRIG-GER GET!
BATTLES ON PLANET CRAY ARE ALSO INFLUENCED BY OUR FIGHTS OVER HERE.
THOUGH SAID INFLUENCE IS LIMITED TO A CLAN BEING VISITED BY LUCK OR MISFORTUNE FOLLOWING VICTORY OR DEFEAT...
HMF ...
YOU'RE TALKING AS THOUGH PLANET CRAY REALLY EXISTS.
OH ...?

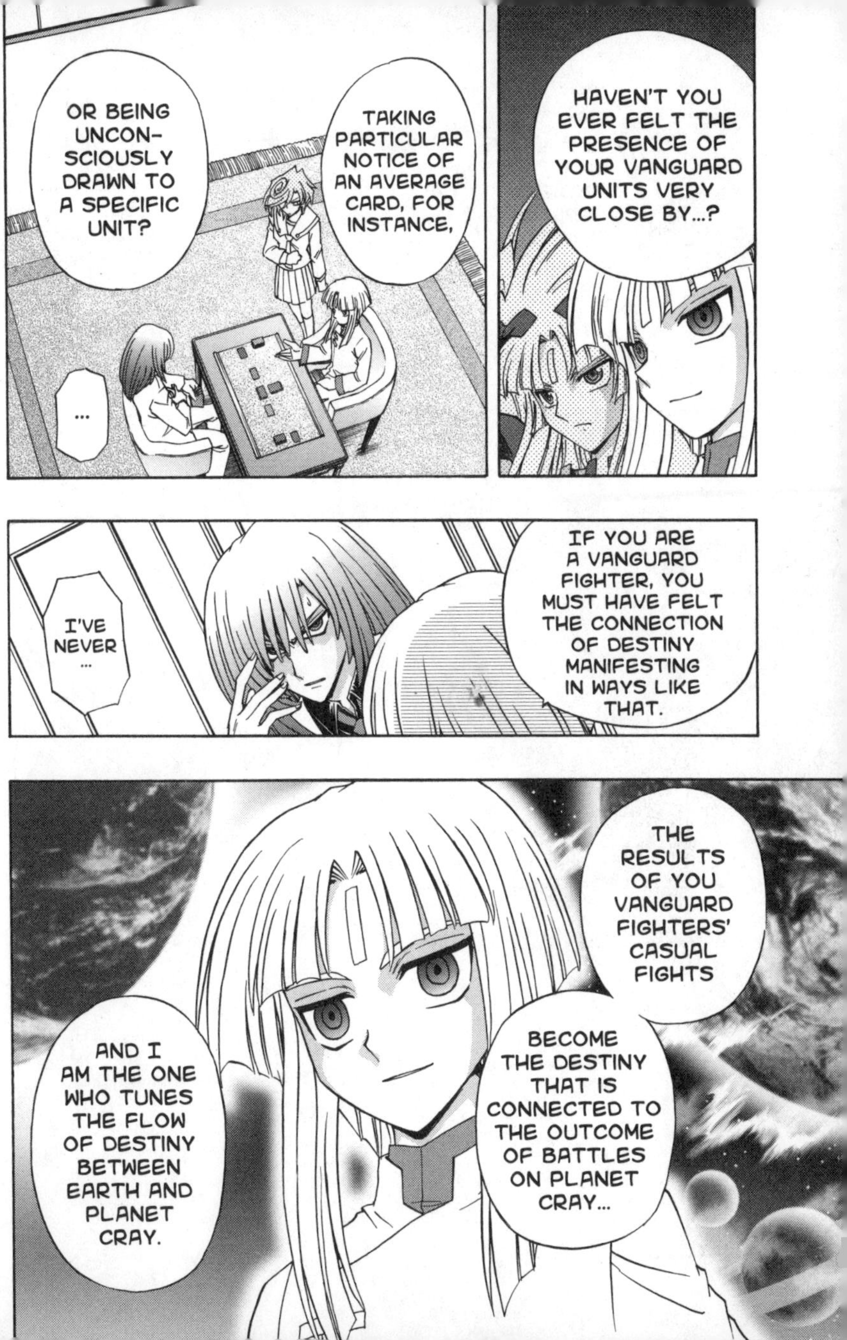
HAVEN'T YOU EVER FELT THE PRESENCE OF YOUR VANGUARD UNITS VERY CLOSE BY...?
TAKING PARTICULAR NOTICE OF AN AVERAGE CARD, FOR INSTANCE,
OR BEING UNCON-SCIOUSLY DRAWN TO A SPECIFIC UNIT?
...
IF YOU ARE A VANGUARD FIGHTER, YOU MUST HAVE FELT THE CONNECTION OF DESTINY MANIFESTING IN WAYS LIKE THAT.
I'VE NEVER ...
THE RESULTS OF YOU VANGUARD FIGHTERS' CASUAL FIGHTS
BECOME THE DESTINY THAT IS CONNECTED TO THE OUTCOME OF BATTLES ON PLANET CRAY...
AND I AM THE ONE WHO TUNES THE FLOW OF DESTINY BETWEEN EARTH AND PLANET CRAY.

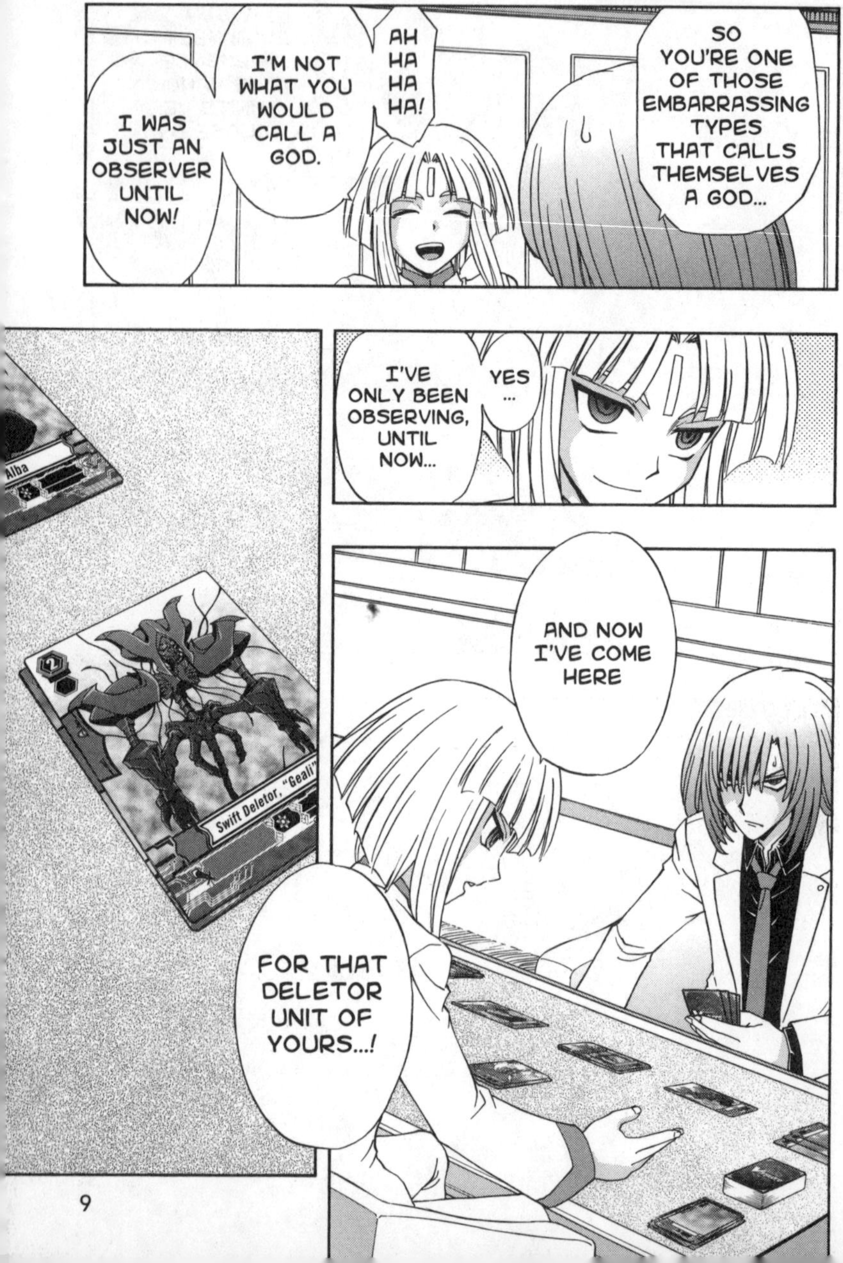
SO YOU'RE ONE OF THOSE EMBARRASSING TYPES THAT CALLS THEMSELVES A GOD...
AH HA HA HA!
I'M NOT WHAT YOU WOULD CALL A GOD.
I WAS JUST AN OBSERVER UNTIL NOW!
YES...
I'VE ONLY BEEN OBSERVING, UNTIL NOW...
AND NOW I'VE COME HERE
FOR THAT DELETOR UNIT OF YOURS...!
Swift Deletor, "Geali"

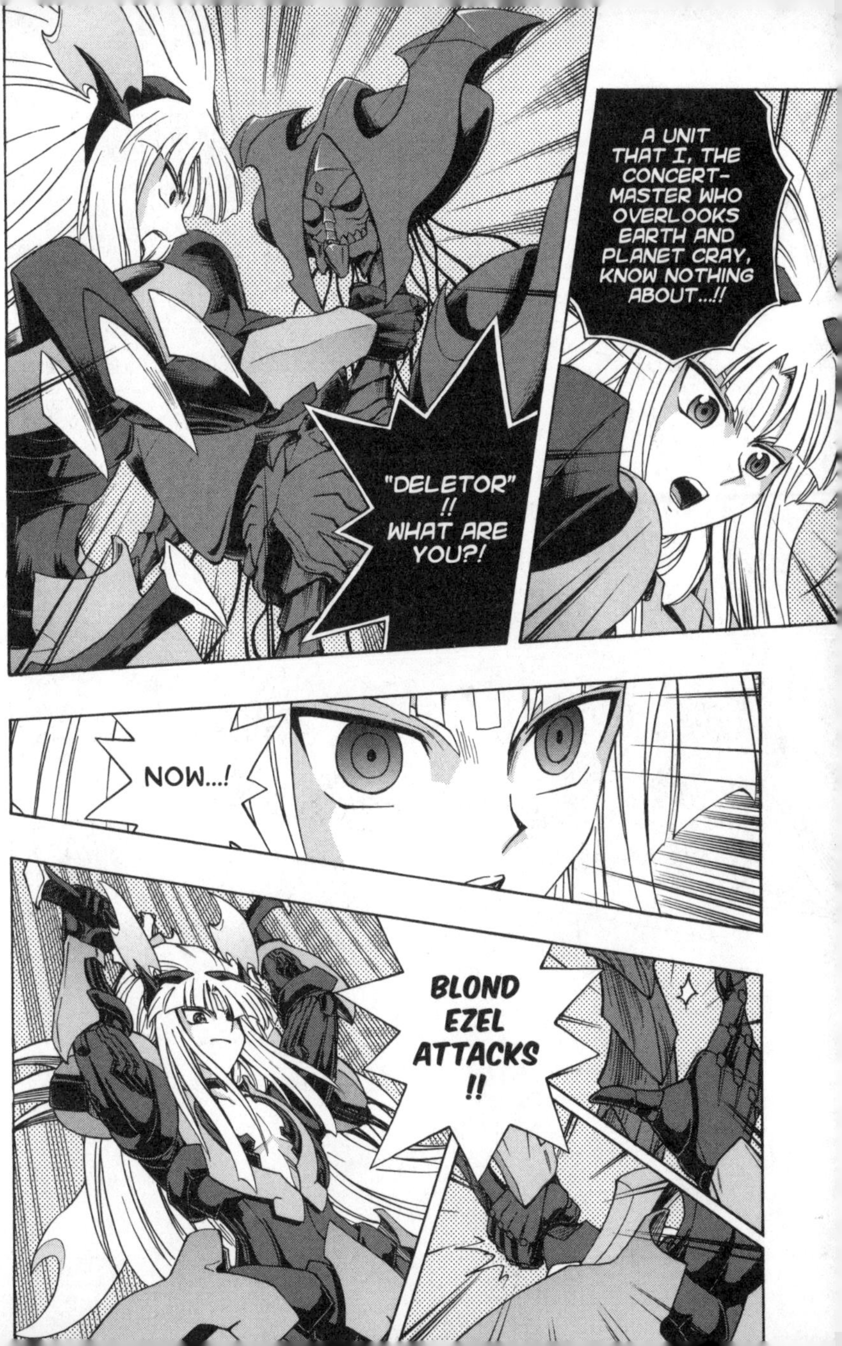
A UNIT THAT I, THE CONCERT-MASTER WHO OVERLOOKS EARTH AND PLANET CRAY, KNOW NOTHING ABOUT...!!
"DELETOR" !! WHAT ARE YOU?!
NOW...!
BLOND EZEL ATTACKS !!

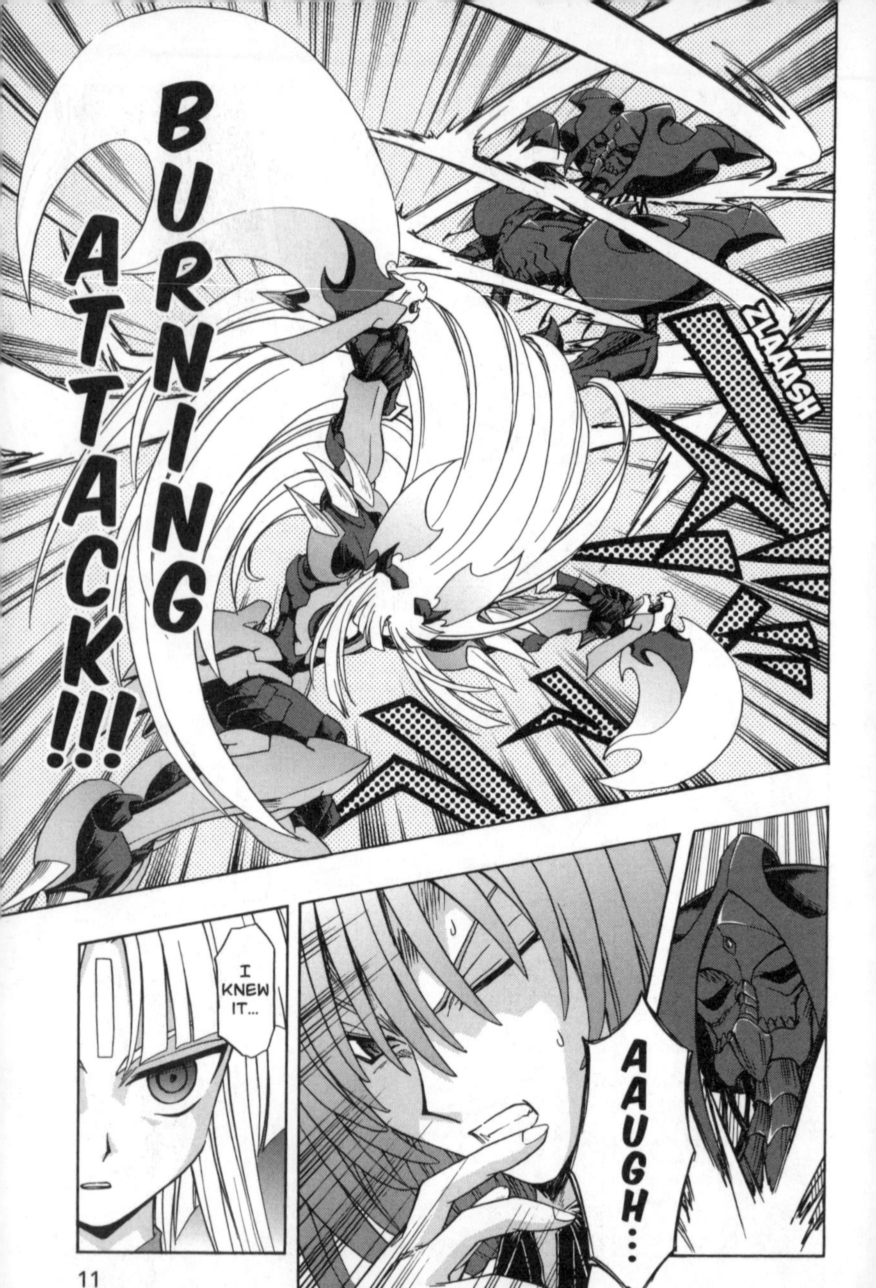
ZLAAASH
BURNING ATTACK!!!
AAUGH...
I KNEW IT...

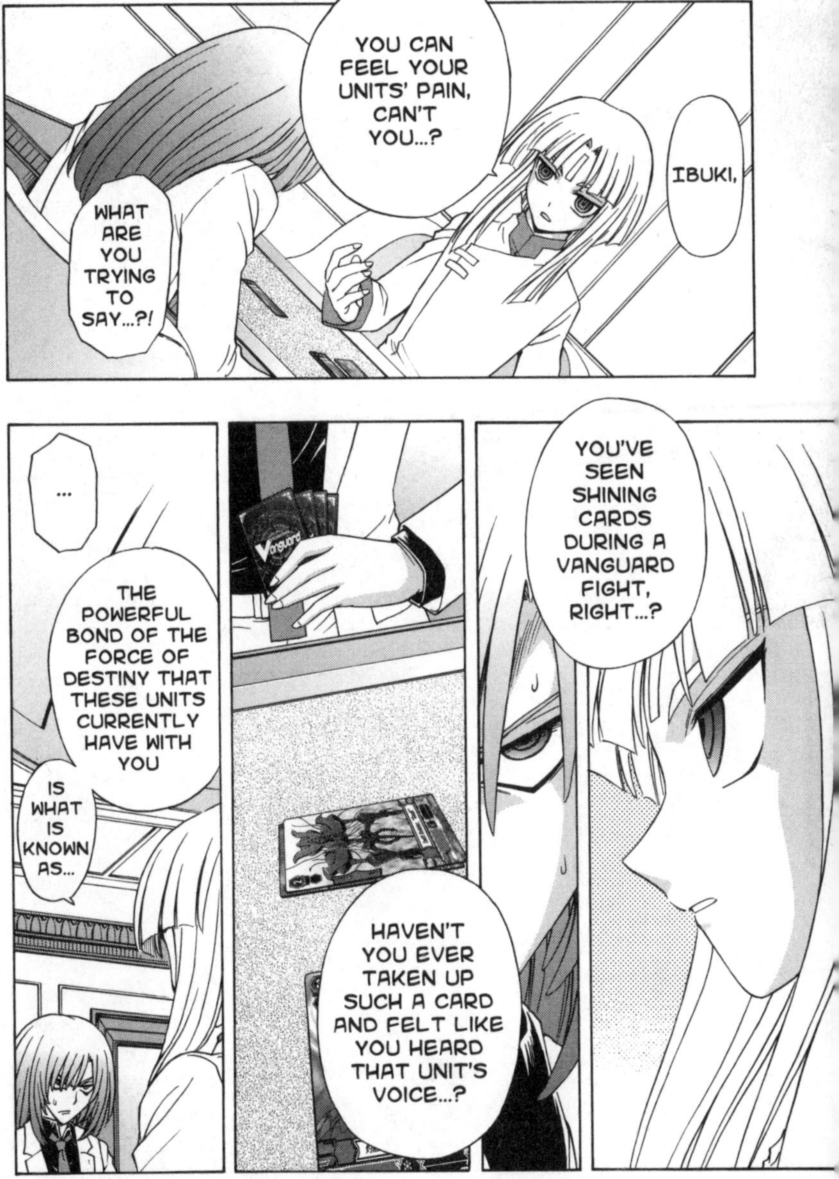
IBUKI,
YOU CAN FEEL YOUR UNITS' PAIN, CAN'T YOU...?
WHAT ARE YOU TRYING TO SAY...?!
YOU'VE SEEN SHINING CARDS DURING A VANGUARD FIGHT, RIGHT...?
HAVEN'T YOU EVER TAKEN UP SUCH A CARD AND FELT LIKE YOU HEARD THAT UNIT'S VOICE...?
...
THE POWERFUL BOND OF THE FORCE OF DESTINY THAT THESE UNITS CURRENTLY HAVE WITH YOU
IS WHAT IS KNOWN AS...

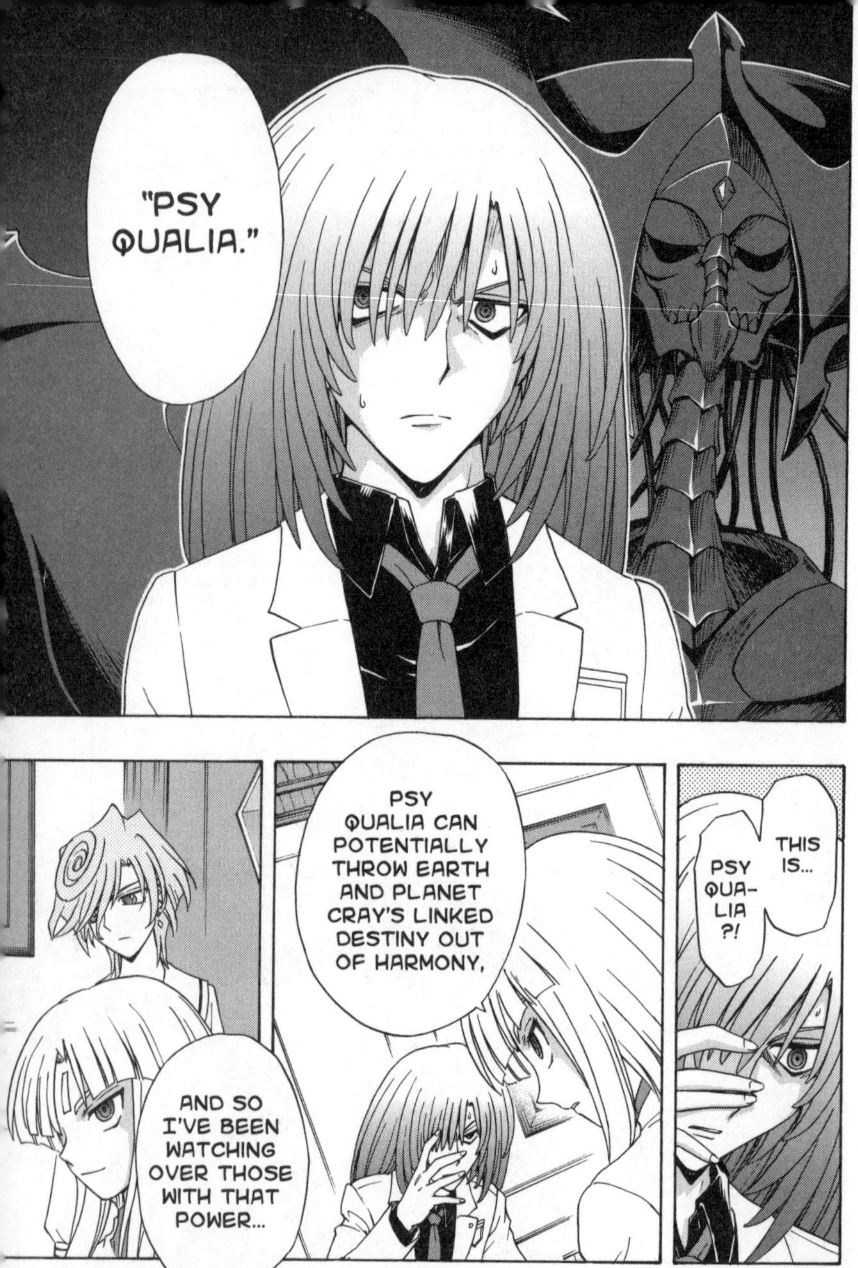
"PSY QUALIA."
THIS IS... PSY QUA-LIA ?!
PSY QUALIA CAN POTENTIALLY THROW EARTH AND PLANET CRAY'S LINKED DESTINY OUT OF HARMONY,
AND SO I'VE BEEN WATCHING OVER THOSE WITH THAT POWER...

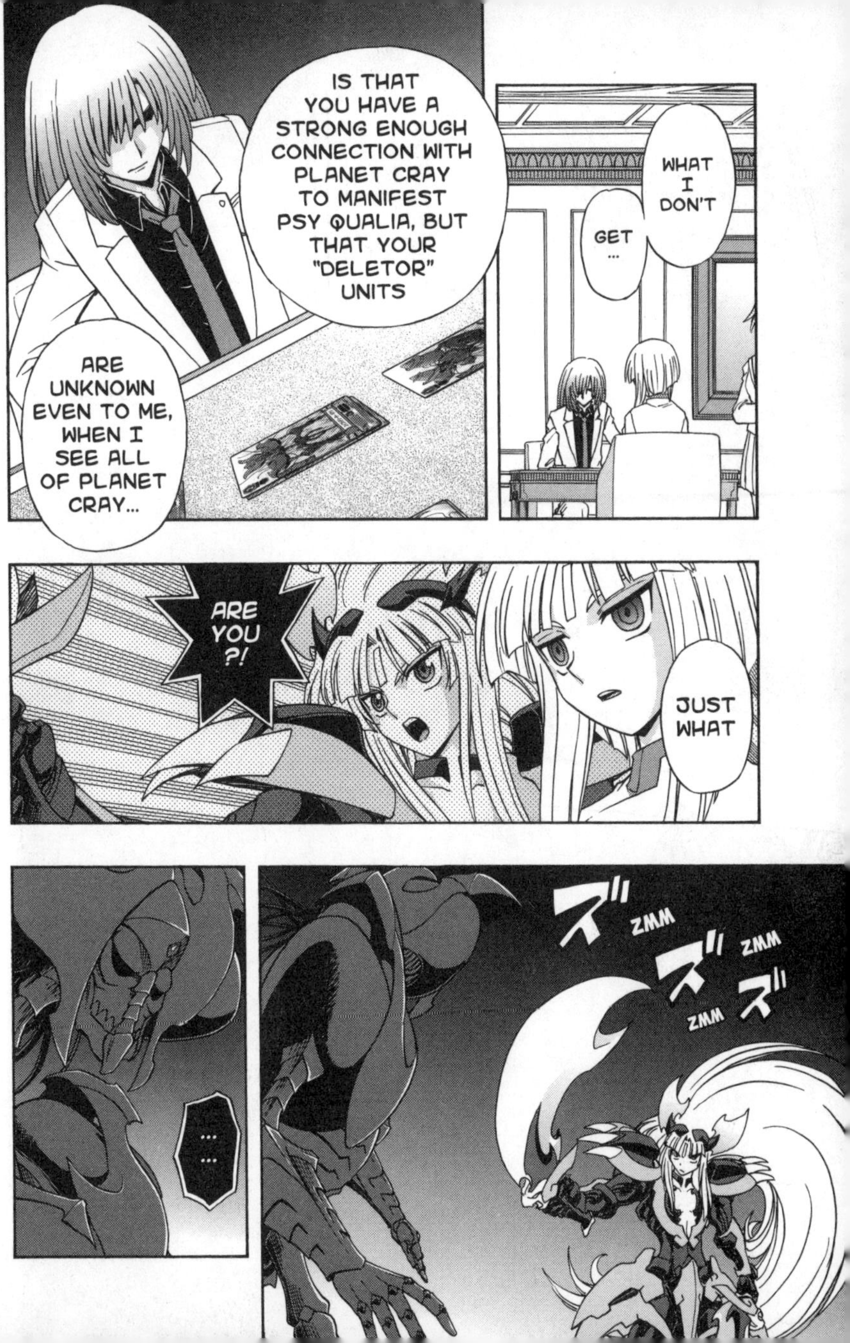
WHAT I DON'T
GET...
IS THAT YOU HAVE A STRONG ENOUGH CONNECTION WITH PLANET CRAY TO MANIFEST PSY QUALIA, BUT THAT YOUR "DELETOR" UNITS
ARE UNKNOWN EVEN TO ME, WHEN I SEE ALL OF PLANET CRAY...
JUST WHAT
ARE YOU?!
ズ ZMM
ズ ZMM
ズ ZMM
ズ
......

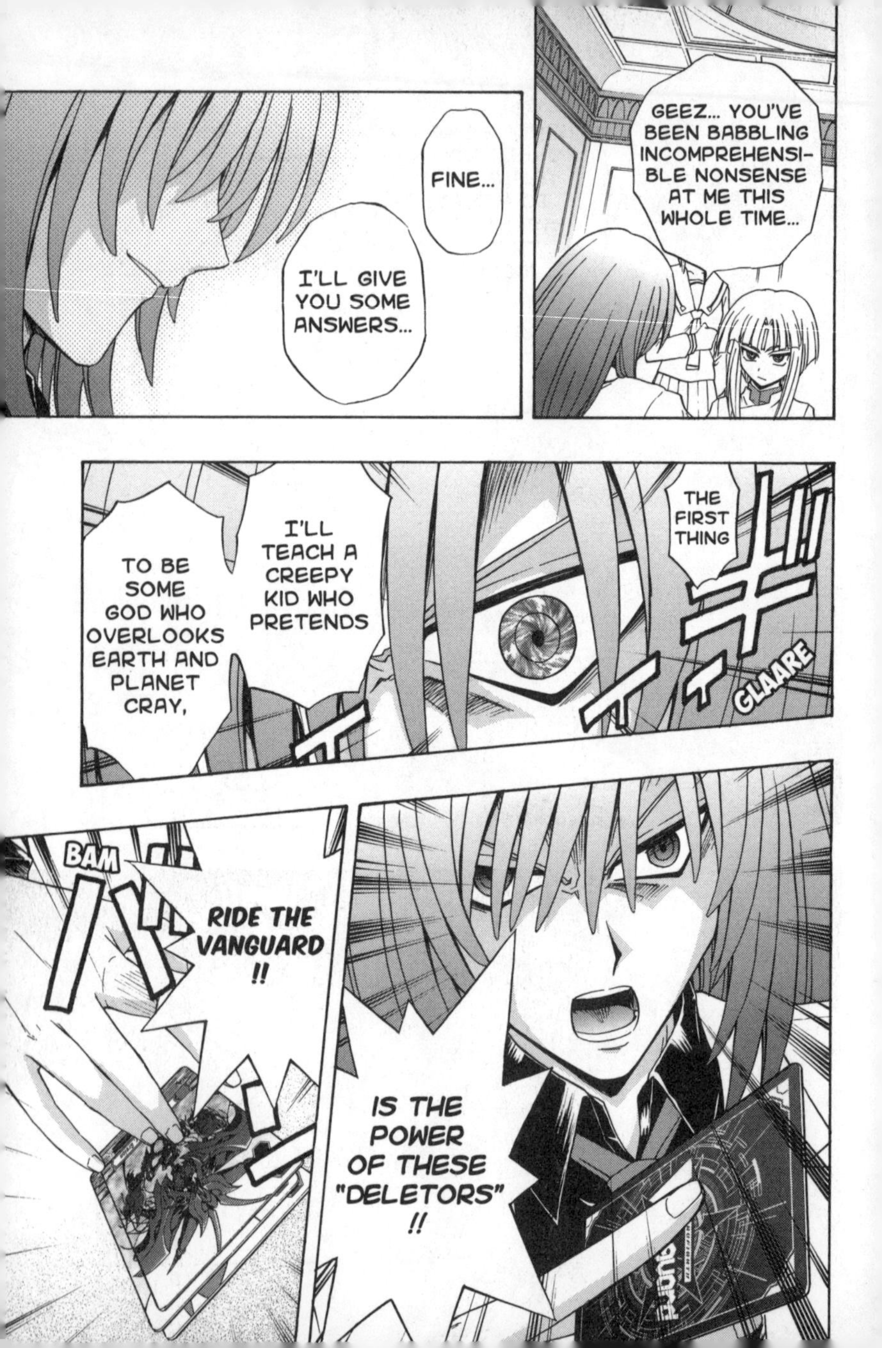
GEEZ... YOU'VE BEEN BABBLING INCOMPREHENSI-BLE NONSENSE AT ME THIS WHOLE TIME...
FINE...
I'LL GIVE YOU SOME ANSWERS...
THE FIRST THING
GLAARE
I'LL TEACH A CREEPY KID WHO PRETENDS
TO BE SOME GOD WHO OVERLOOKS EARTH AND PLANET CRAY,
IS THE POWER OF THESE "DELETORS" !!
BAM
RIDE THE VANGUARD !!

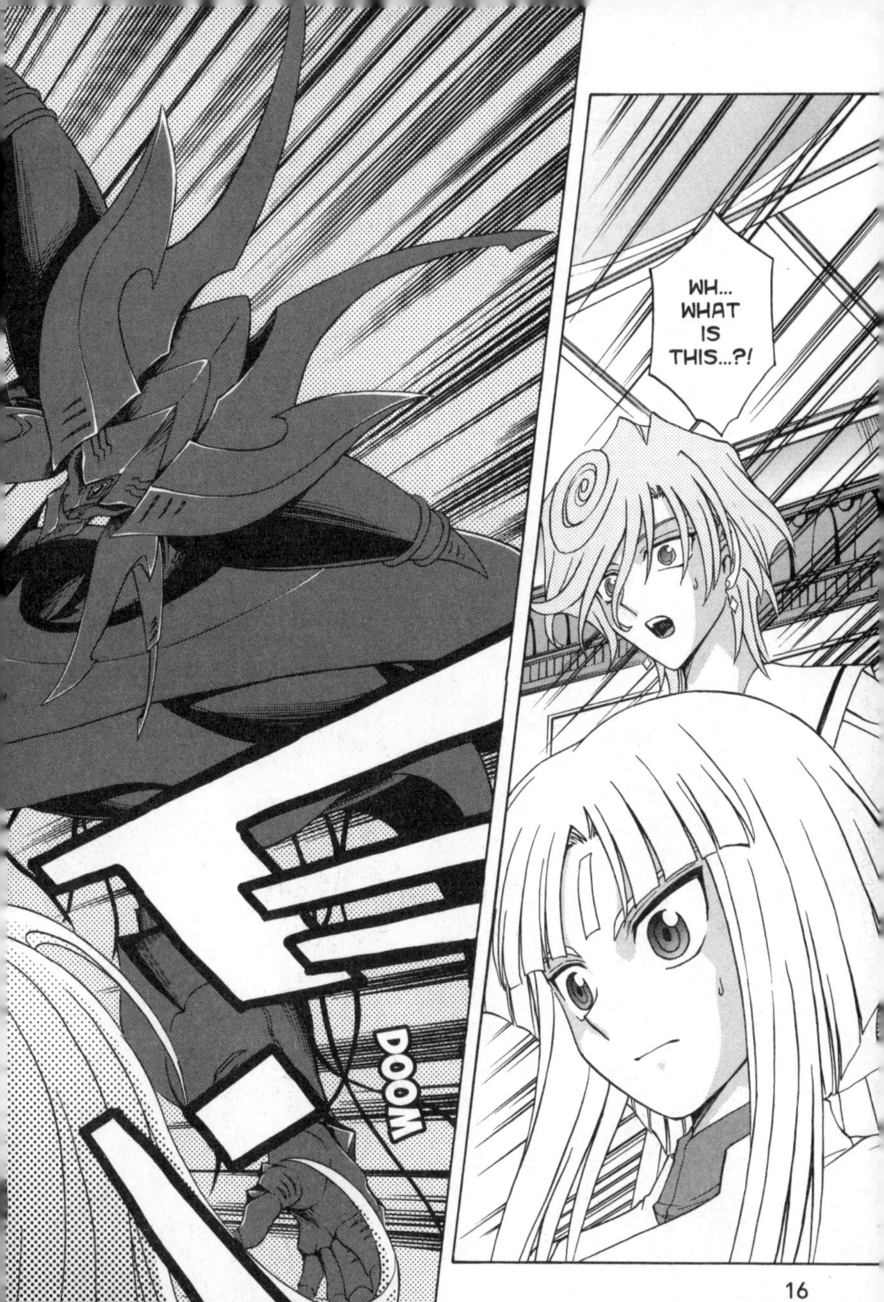
WH... WHAT IS THIS...?!
DOOM

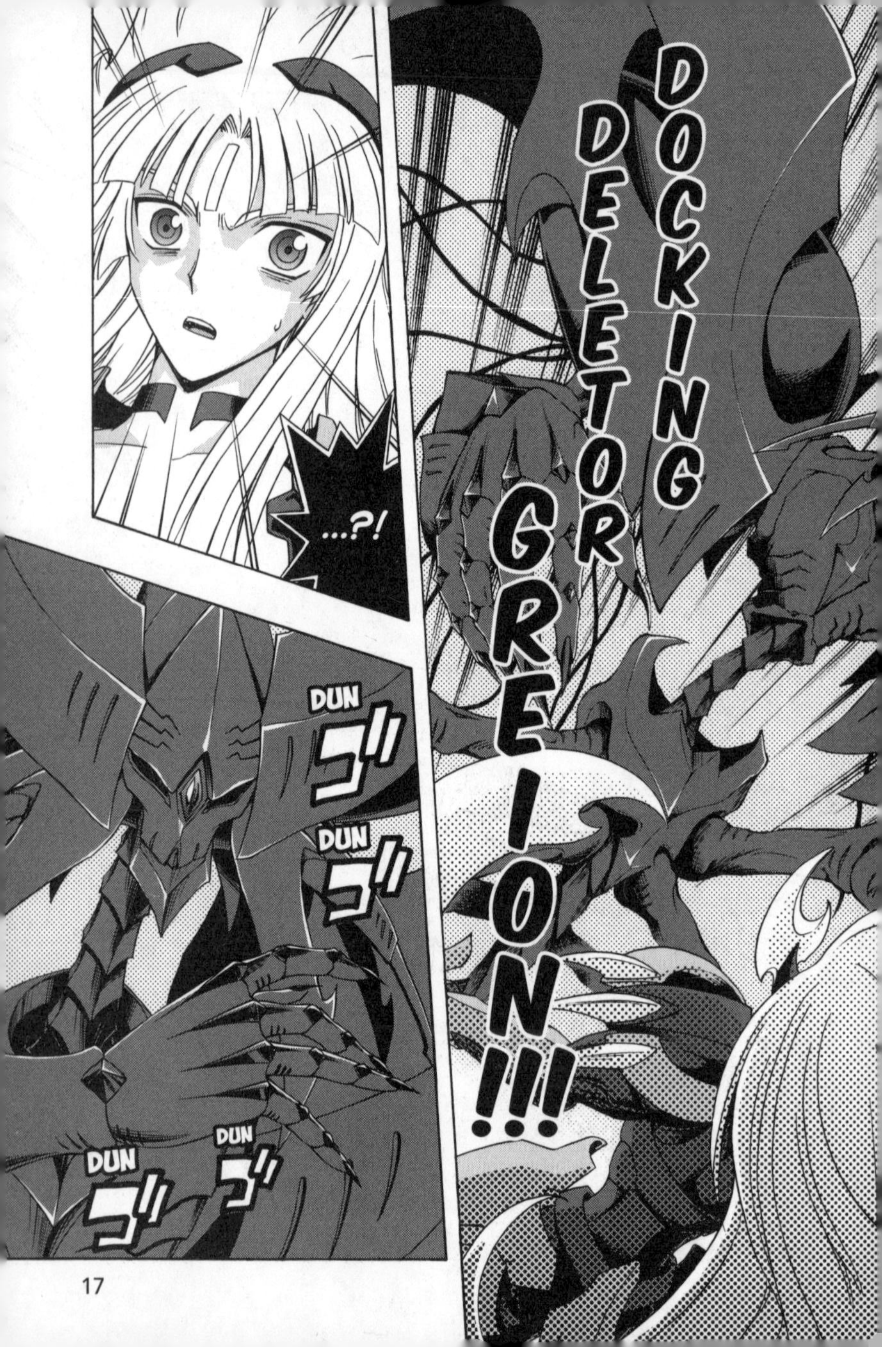
DOCKING
DELETOR
GREION!!!
...?!
DUN ゴ
DUN ゴ
DUN ゴ
DUN ゴ

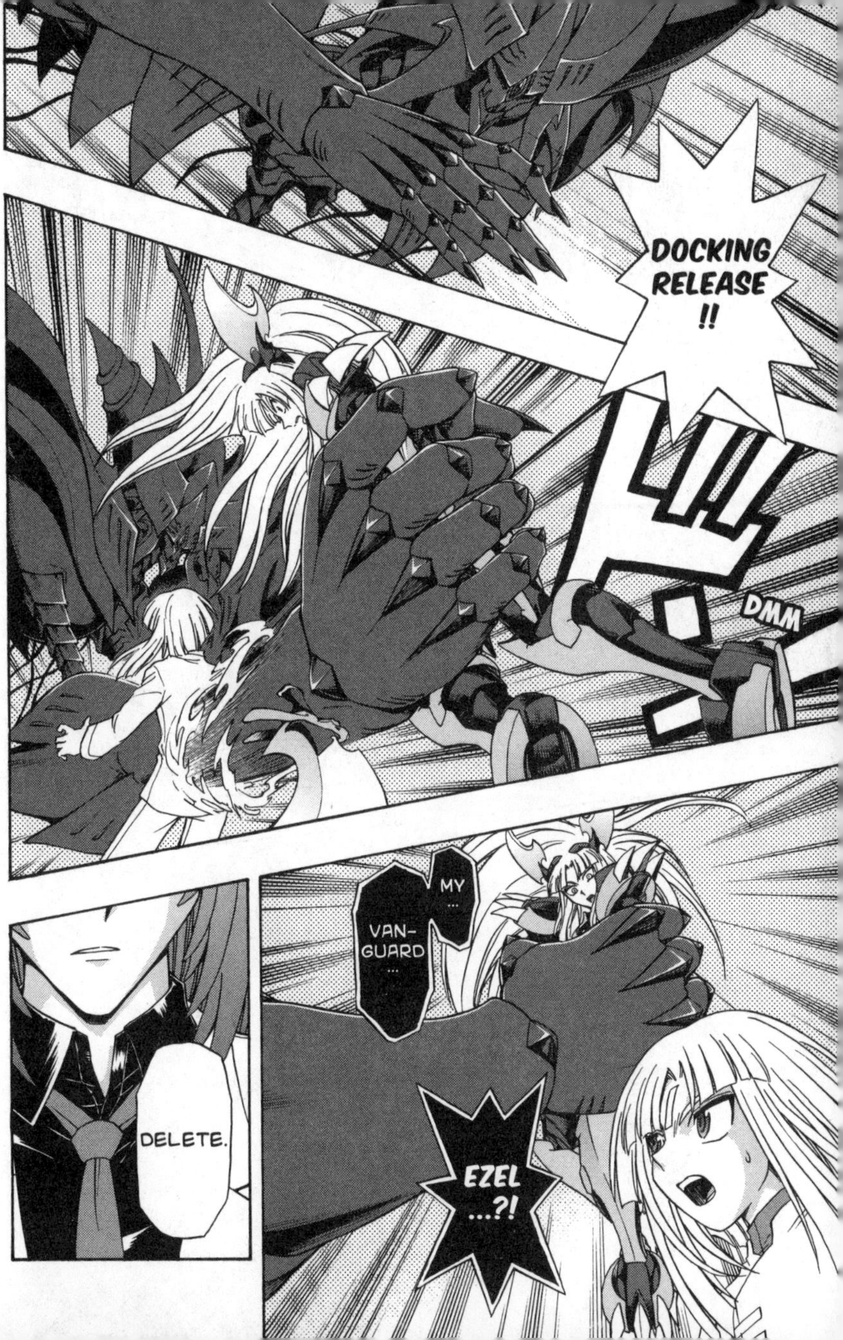
DOCKING RELEASE !!
DMM
MY ... VAN-GUARD ...
EZEL ...?!
DELETE.

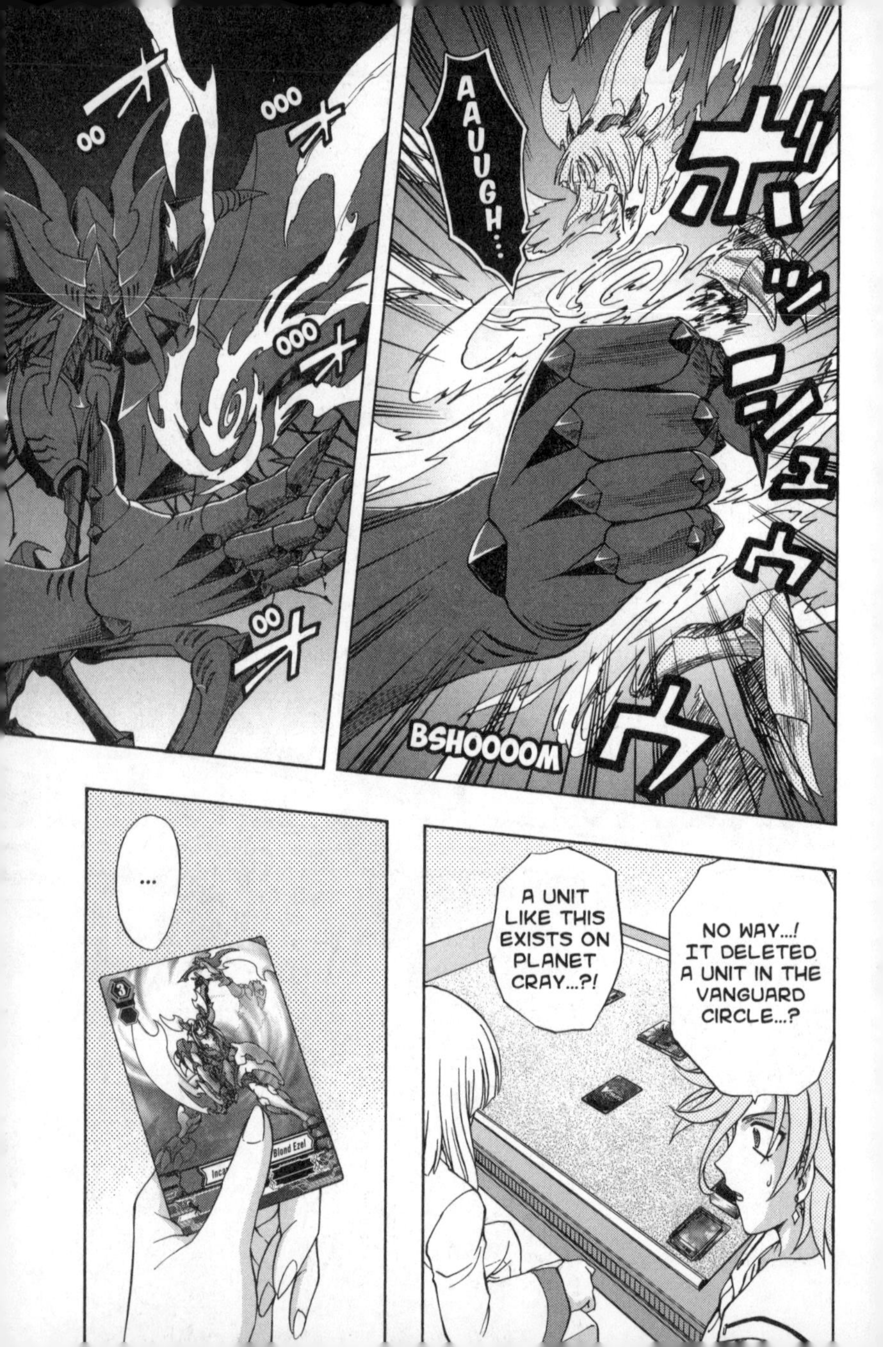
AAUUGH...
BSHOOOOM
OOO
OO
OOO
OO
NO WAY...! IT DELETED A UNIT IN THE VANGUARD CIRCLE...?
A UNIT LIKE THIS EXISTS ON PLANET CRAY...?!
...
Blond Ezel

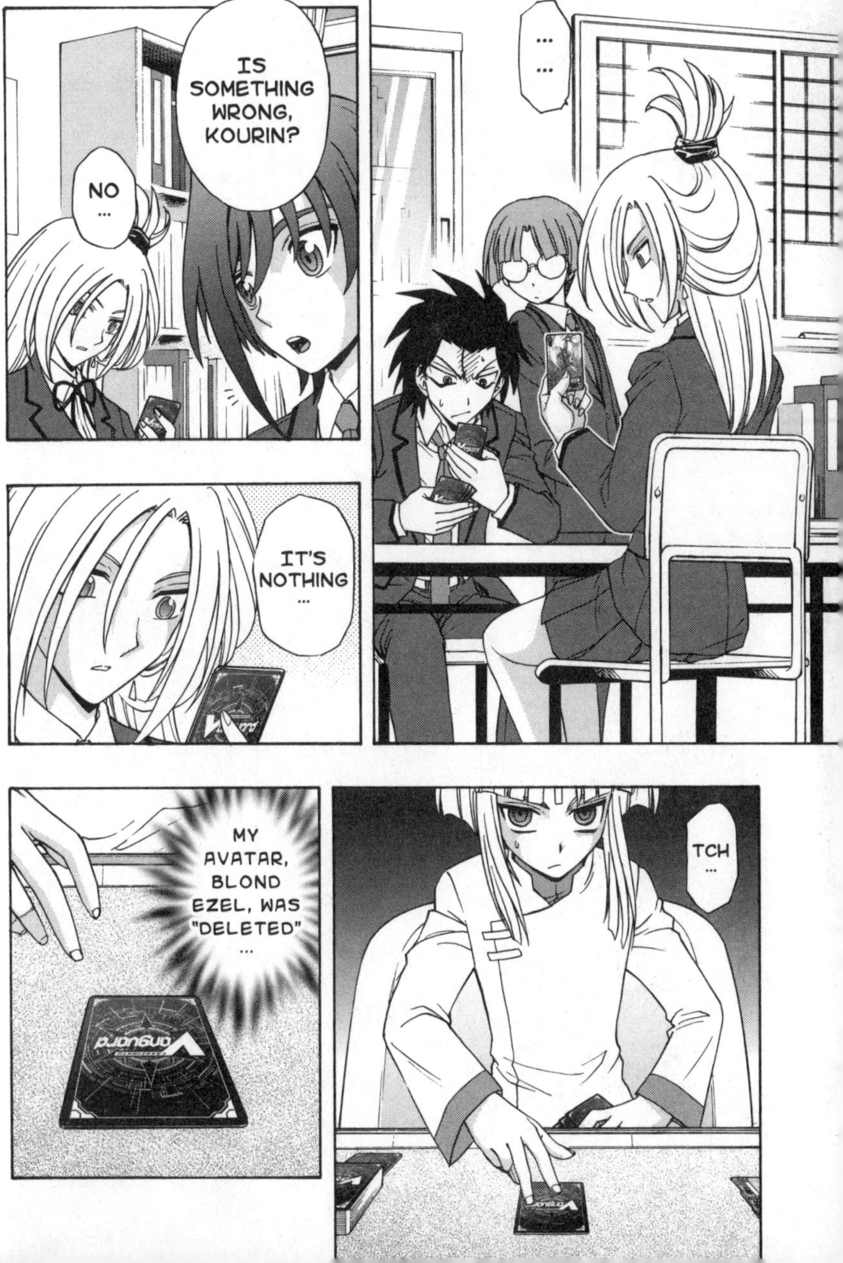
... ...
IS SOMETHING WRONG, KOURIN?
NO ...
IT'S NOTHING ...
TCH ...
MY AVATAR, BLOND EZEL, WAS "DELETED" ...

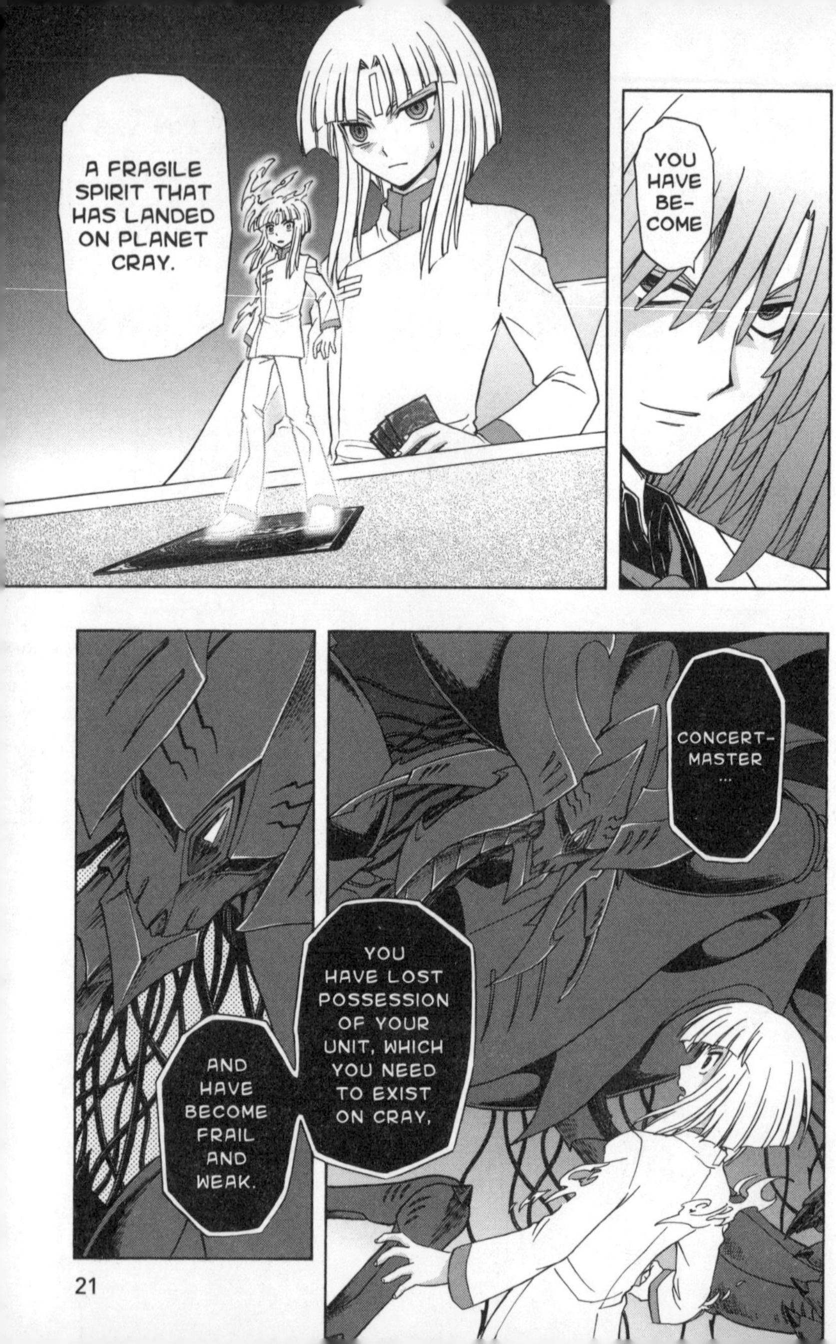
YOU HAVE BE- COME
A FRAGILE SPIRIT THAT HAS LANDED ON PLANET CRAY.
CONCERT- MASTER ...
YOU HAVE LOST POSSESSION OF YOUR UNIT, WHICH YOU NEED TO EXIST ON CRAY,
AND HAVE BECOME FRAIL AND WEAK.

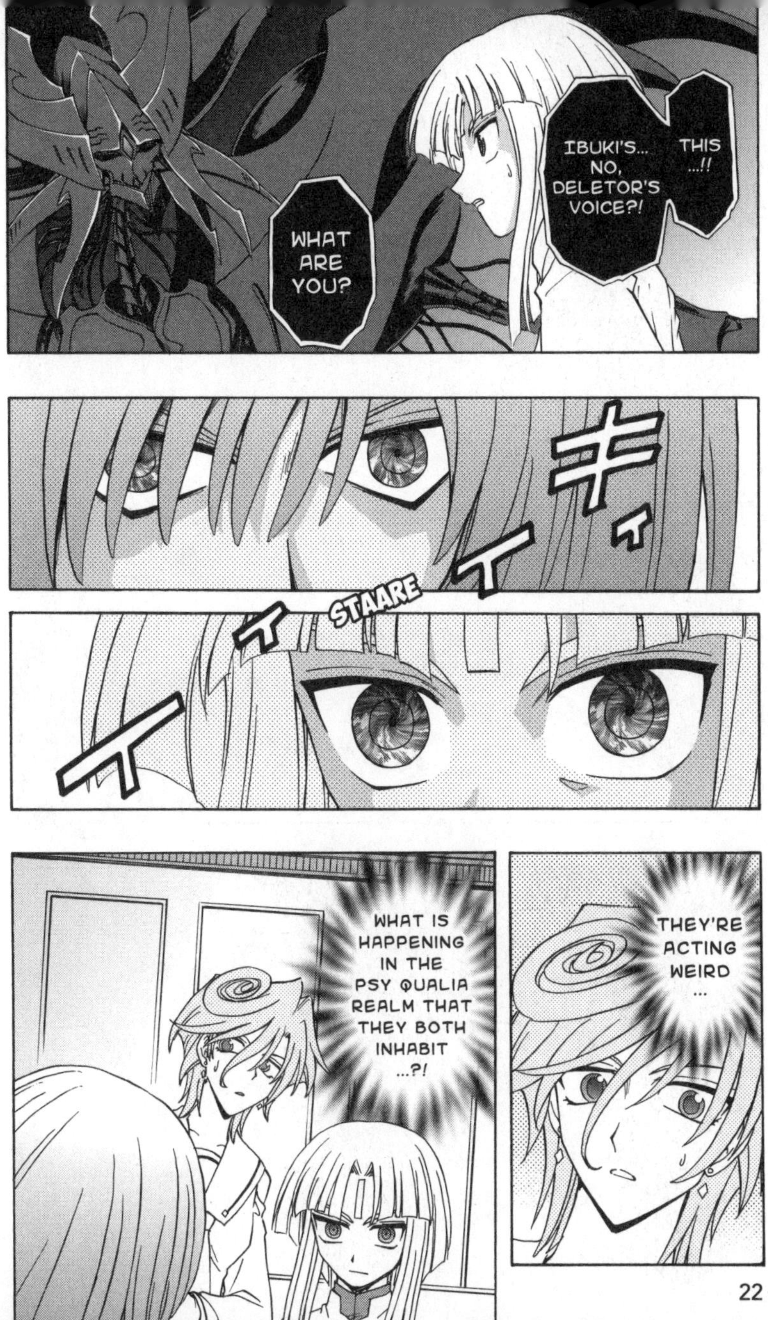
THIS ...!!
IBUKI'S... NO, DELETOR'S VOICE?!
WHAT ARE YOU?
キィイィイ
STAARE
THEY'RE ACTING WEIRD ...
WHAT IS HAPPENING IN THE PSY QUALIA REALM THAT THEY BOTH INHABIT ...?!

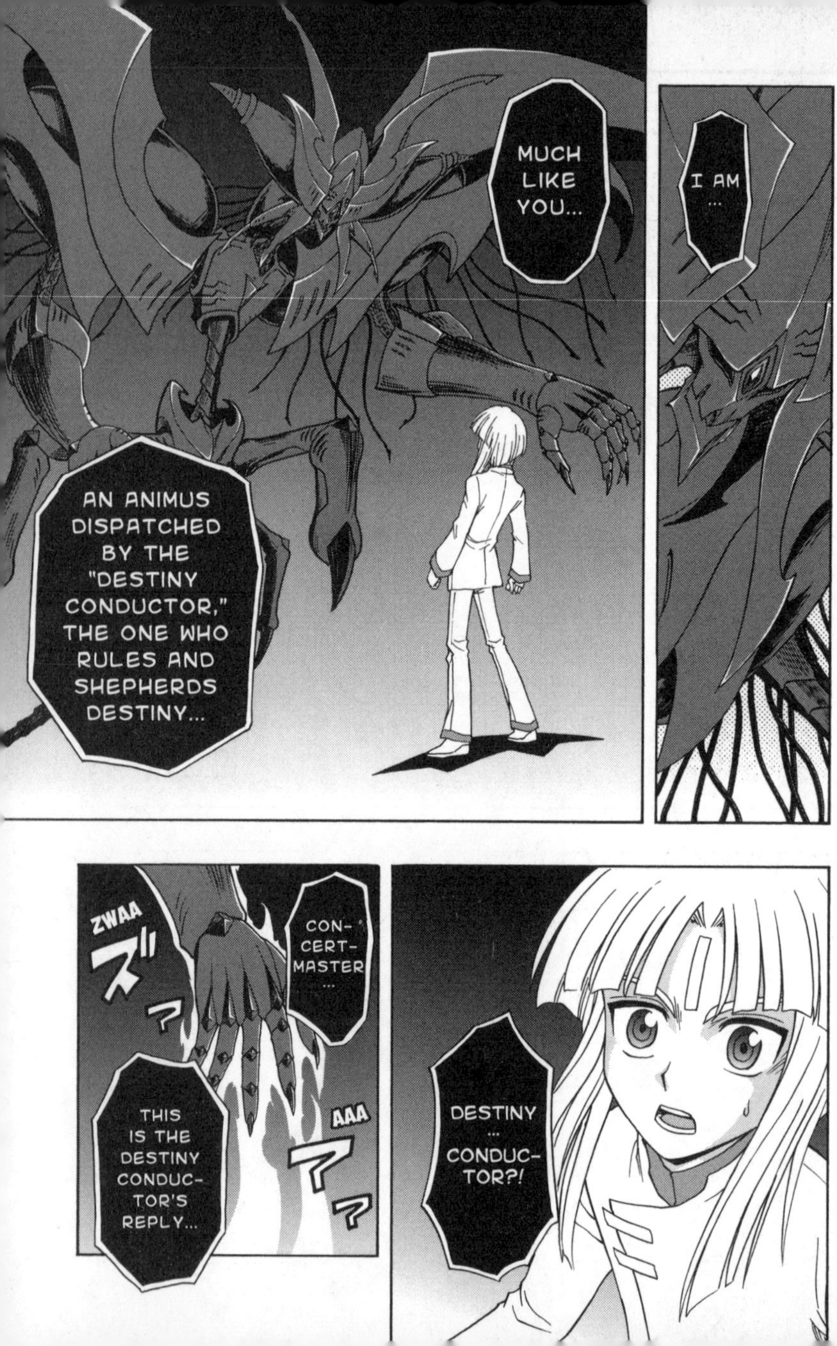
I AM ...
MUCH LIKE YOU...
AN ANIMUS DISPATCHED BY THE "DESTINY CONDUCTOR," THE ONE WHO RULES AND SHEPHERDS DESTINY...
DESTINY ... CONDUC-TOR?!
CON-CERT-MASTER ...
ZWAA
AAA
THIS IS THE DESTINY CONDUC-TOR'S REPLY...

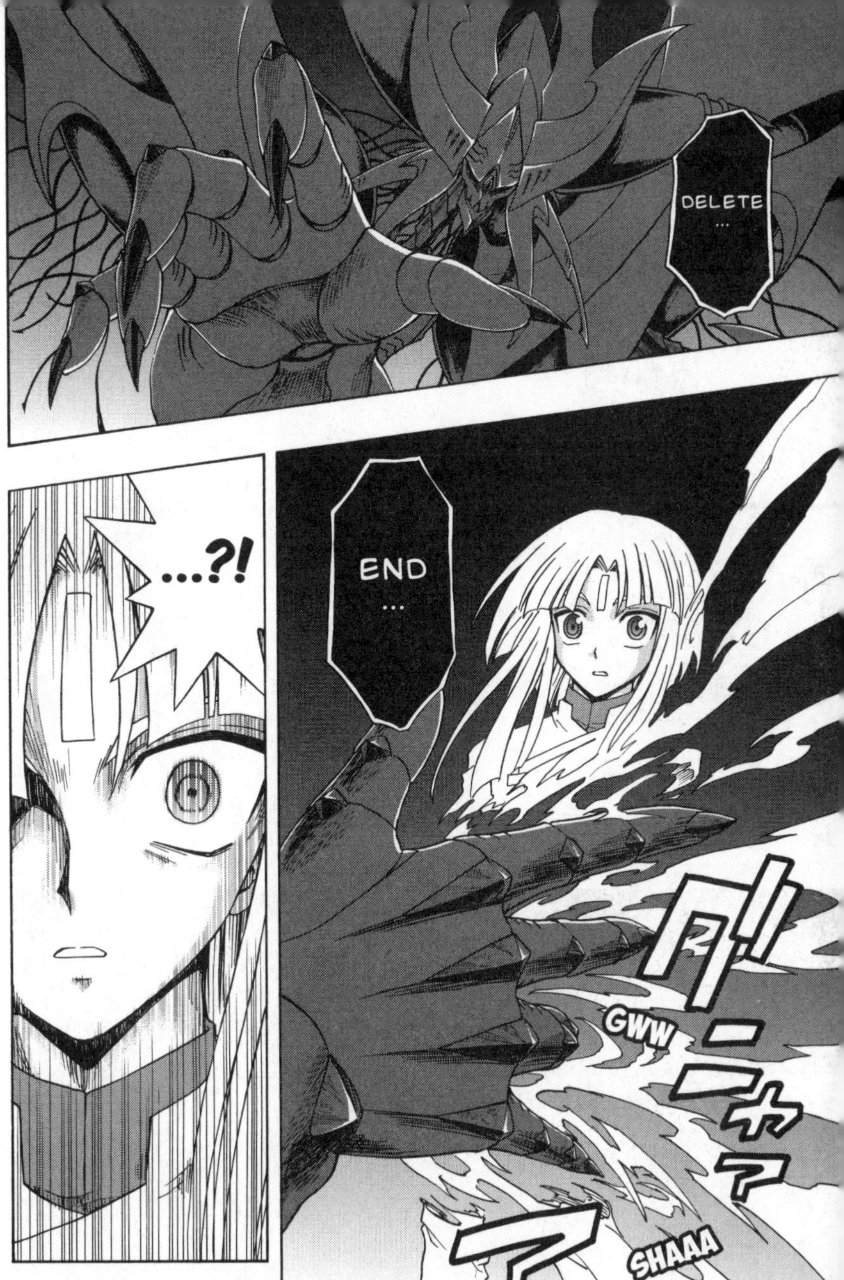
DELETE ...
END ...
GWW
SHAAA
...?!

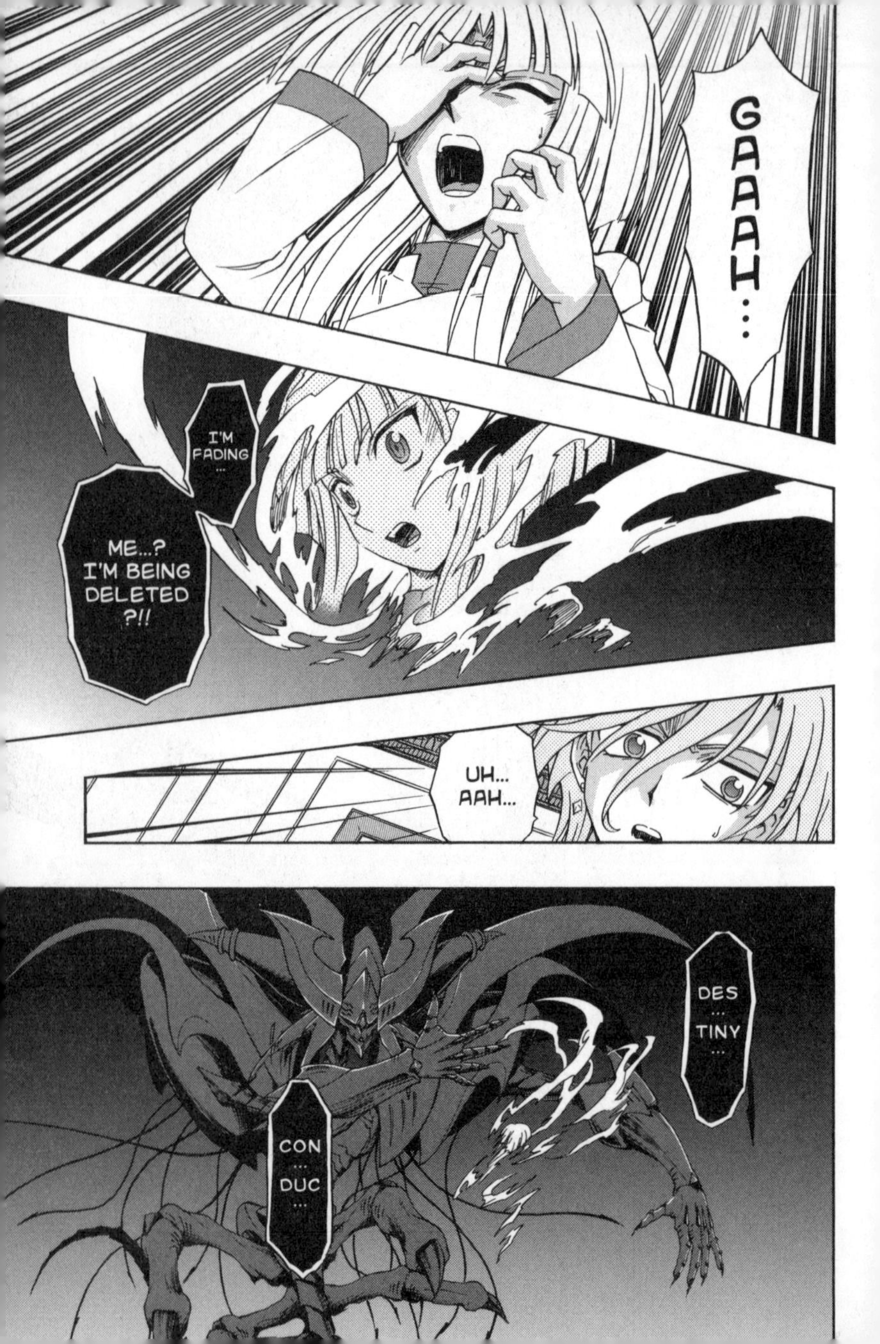
GAAAH...
I'M FADING ...
ME...? I'M BEING DELETED ?!!
UH... AAH...
DES ... TINY ...
CON ... DUC ...

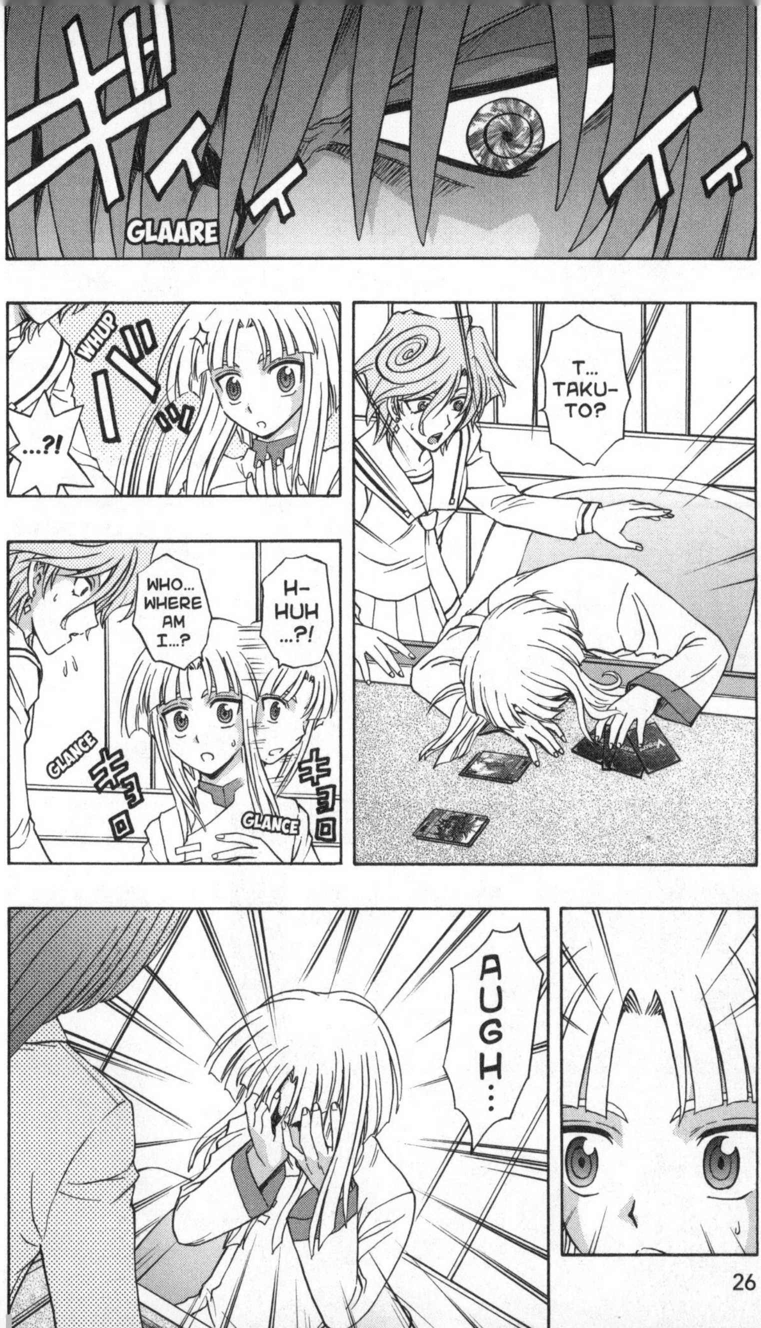
GLAARE
T... TAKU-TO?
WHUP
...?!
H-HUH ...?!
WHO... WHERE AM I...?
GLANCE
GLANCE
AUGH...

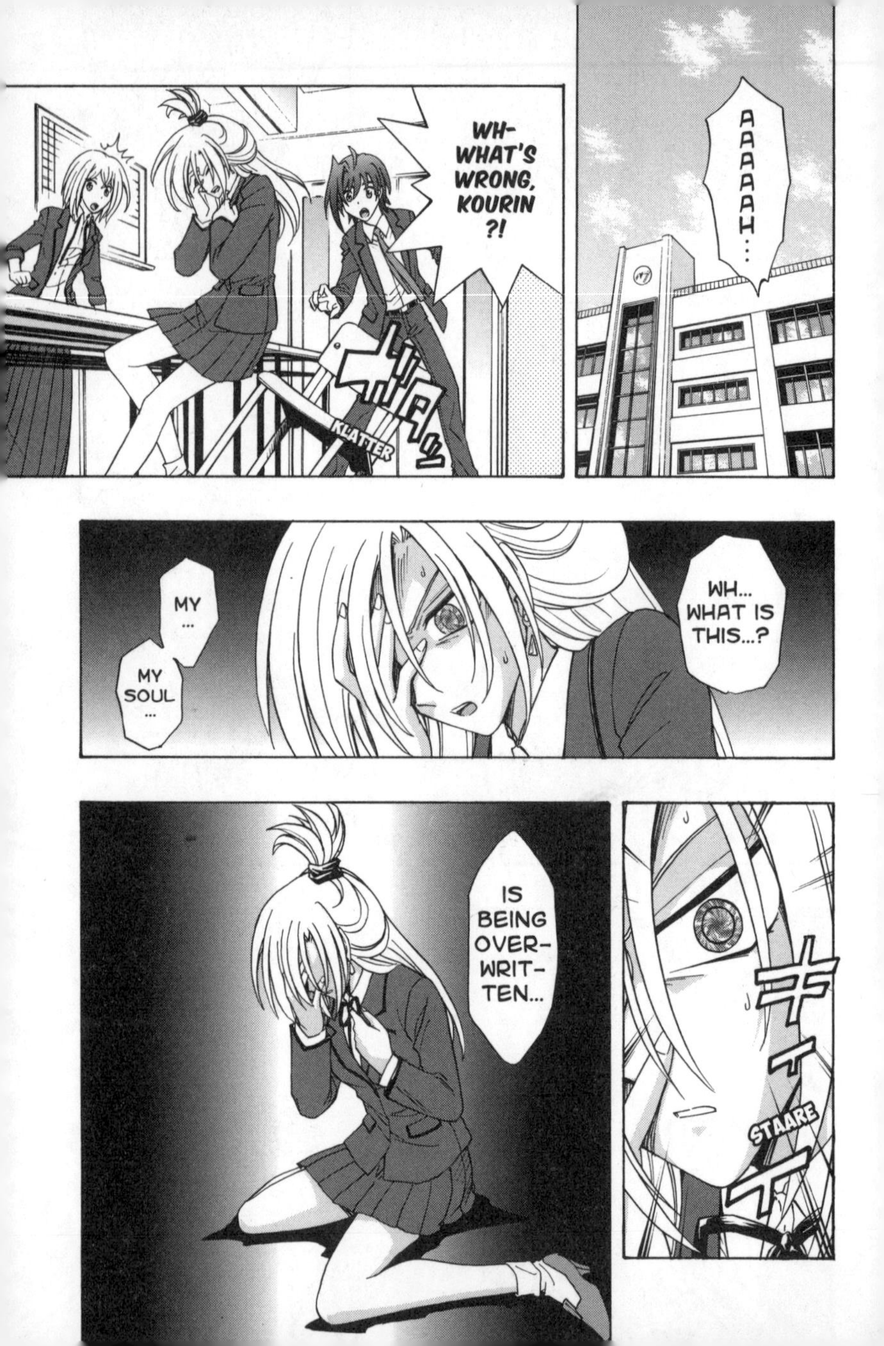
AAAAAAH...
WH- WHAT'S WRONG, KOURIN ?!
KLATTER
WH... WHAT IS THIS...?
MY ...
MY SOUL ...
STAARE
IS BEING OVER-WRIT-TEN...

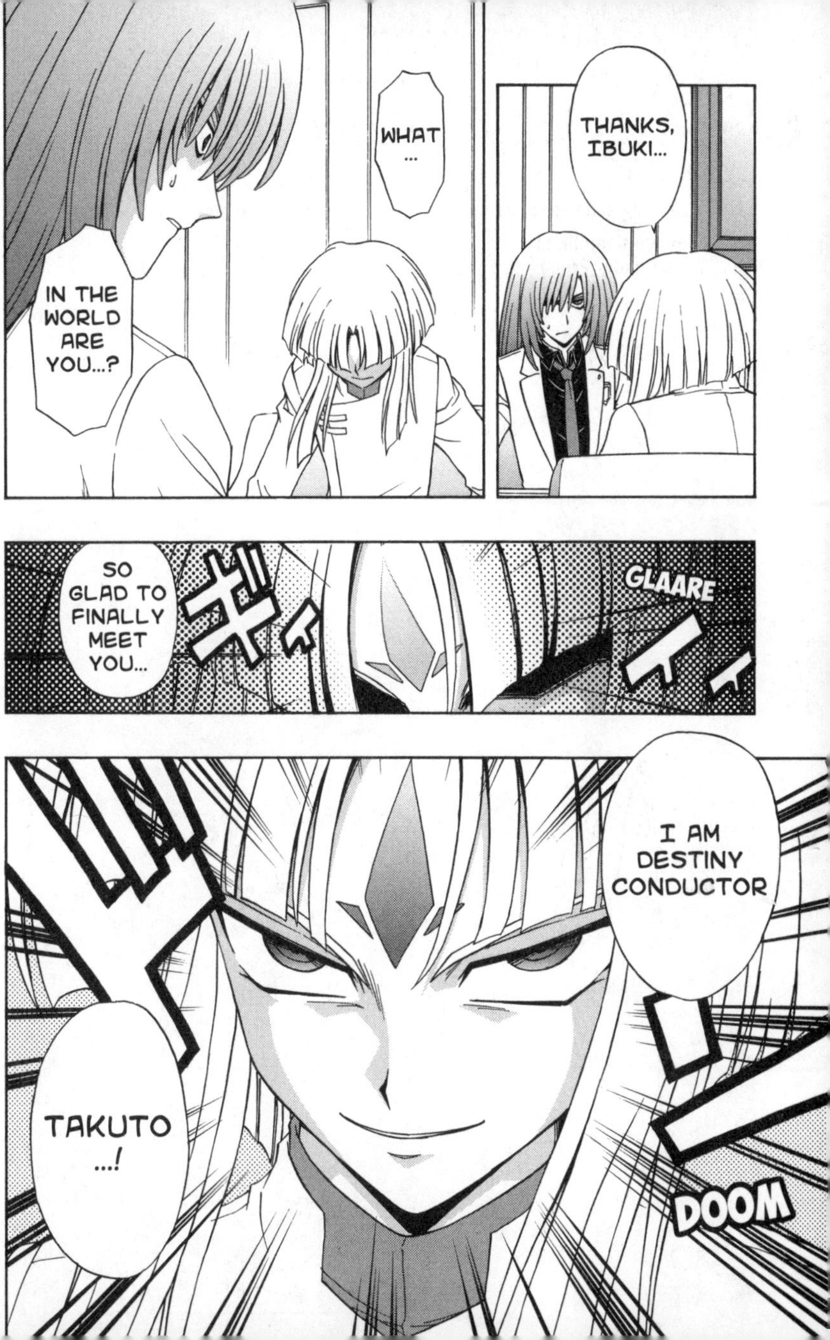
THANKS, IBUKI...
WHAT ...
IN THE WORLD ARE YOU...?
GLAARE
SO GLAD TO FINALLY MEET YOU...
I AM DESTINY CONDUCTOR
TAKUTO ...!
DOOM

BONUS!

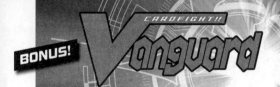

CARDFIGHT!! Vanguard

BONUS! VANGUARD NEVER-BEFORE-SEEN IMAGE BOARDS

We're releasing super-secret sketches used for the Vanguard Movie and TV Anime!

Movie Version Kouji Ibuki
High School Junior Preliminary Design

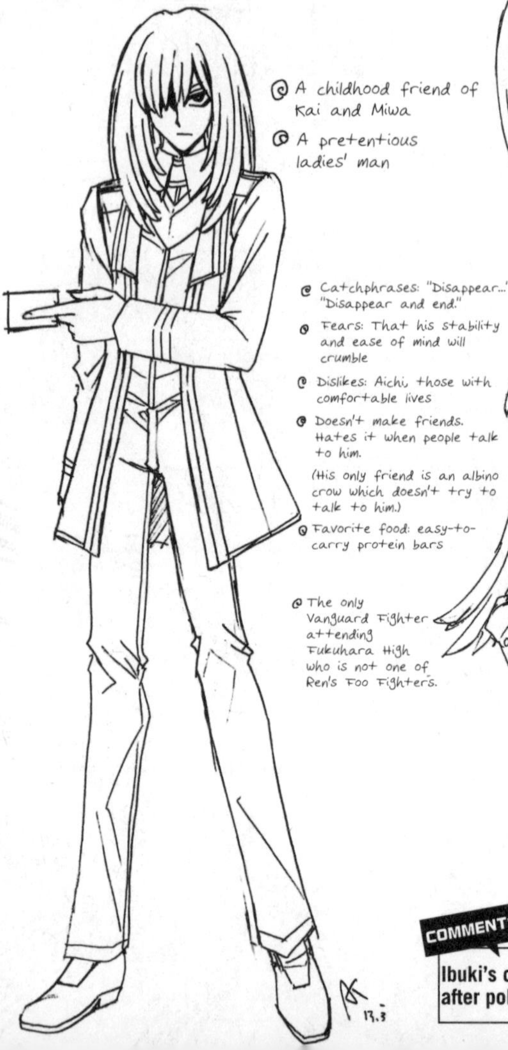

@ A childhood friend of Kai and Miwa
@ A pretentious ladies' man
@ Catchphrases: "Disappear..." "Disappear and end."
@ Fears: That his stability and ease of mind will crumble
@ Dislikes: Aichi, those with comfortable lives
@ Doesn't make friends. Hates it when people talk to him.
(His only friend is an albino crow which doesn't try to talk to him.)
@ Favorite food: easy-to-carry protein bars
@ The only Vanguard Fighter attending Fukuhara High who is not one of Ren's Foo Fighters.
13.3

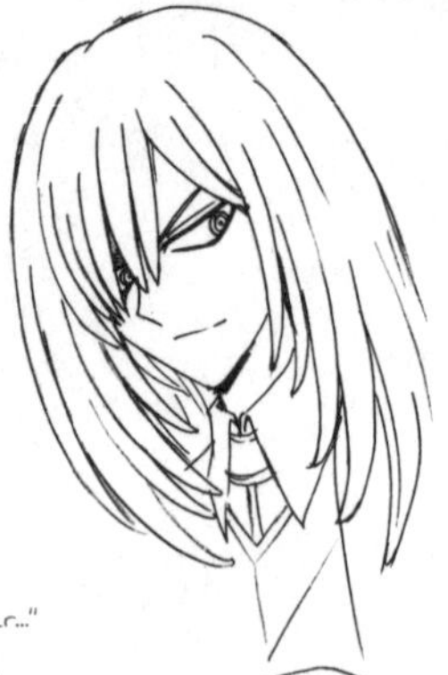

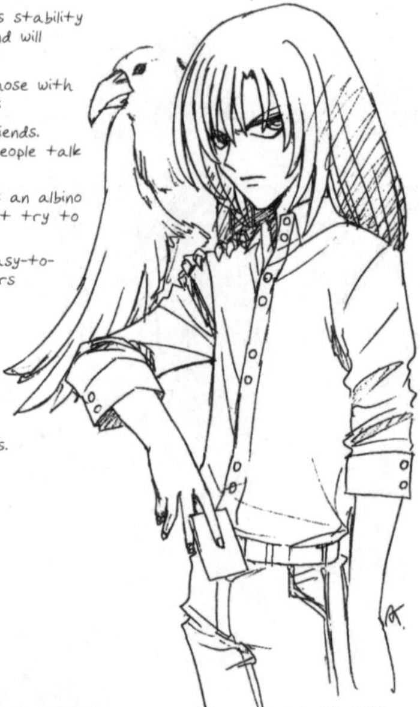

July 29, 2013

COMMENT:

Ibuki's character changed dramatically after polishing and refining him. —Itou

BONUS! CARDFIGHT!! Vanguard

BONUS! VANGUARD NEVER-BEFORE-SEEN IMAGE BOARDS

Miyaji Academy Boy's Summer Uniform—Movie Edition

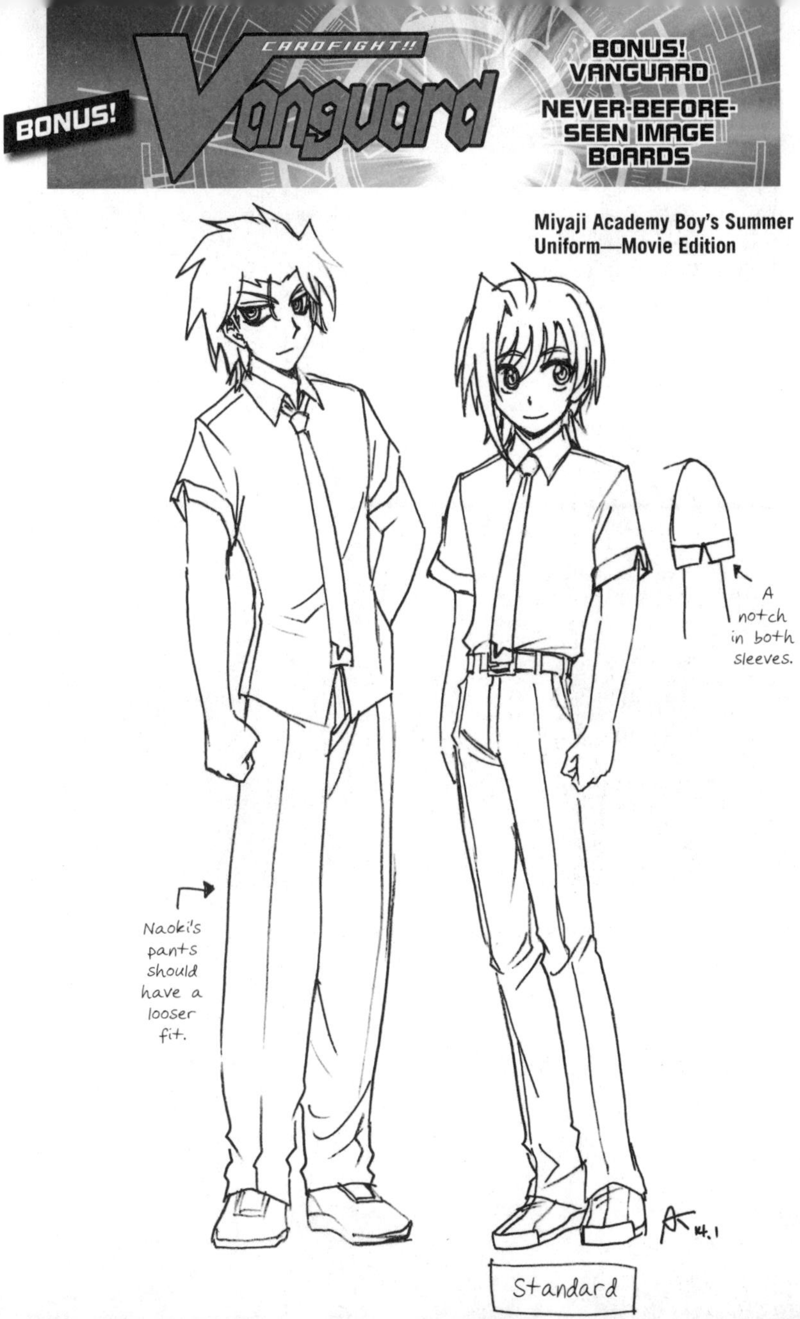
A notch in both sleeves.
Naoki's pants should have a looser fit.
14.1
Standard

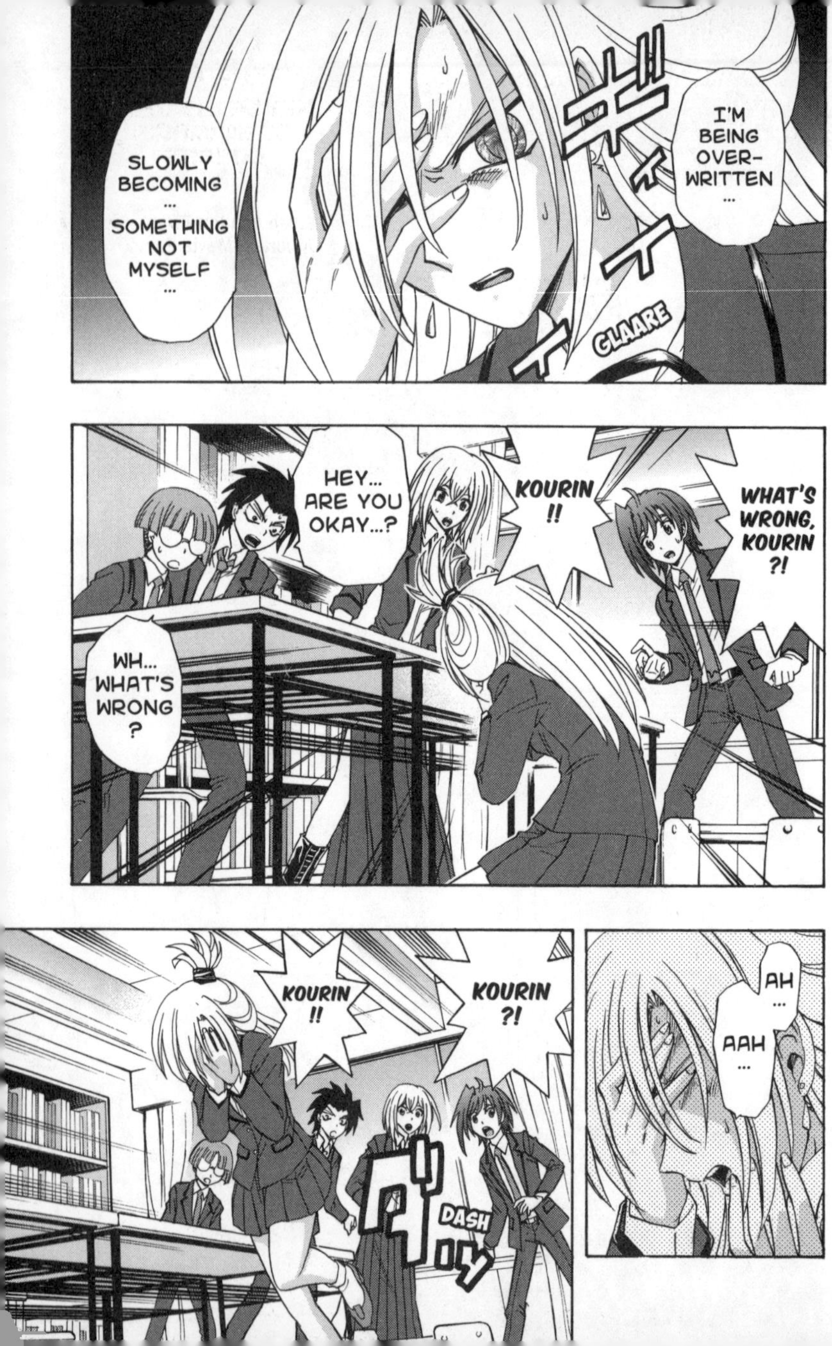
I'M BEING OVER-WRITTEN ...
GLAARE
SLOWLY BECOMING ... SOMETHING NOT MYSELF ...
WHAT'S WRONG, KOURIN ?!
KOURIN !!
HEY... ARE YOU OKAY...?
WH... WHAT'S WRONG ?
AH ... AAH ...
KOURIN ?!
KOURIN !!
DASH

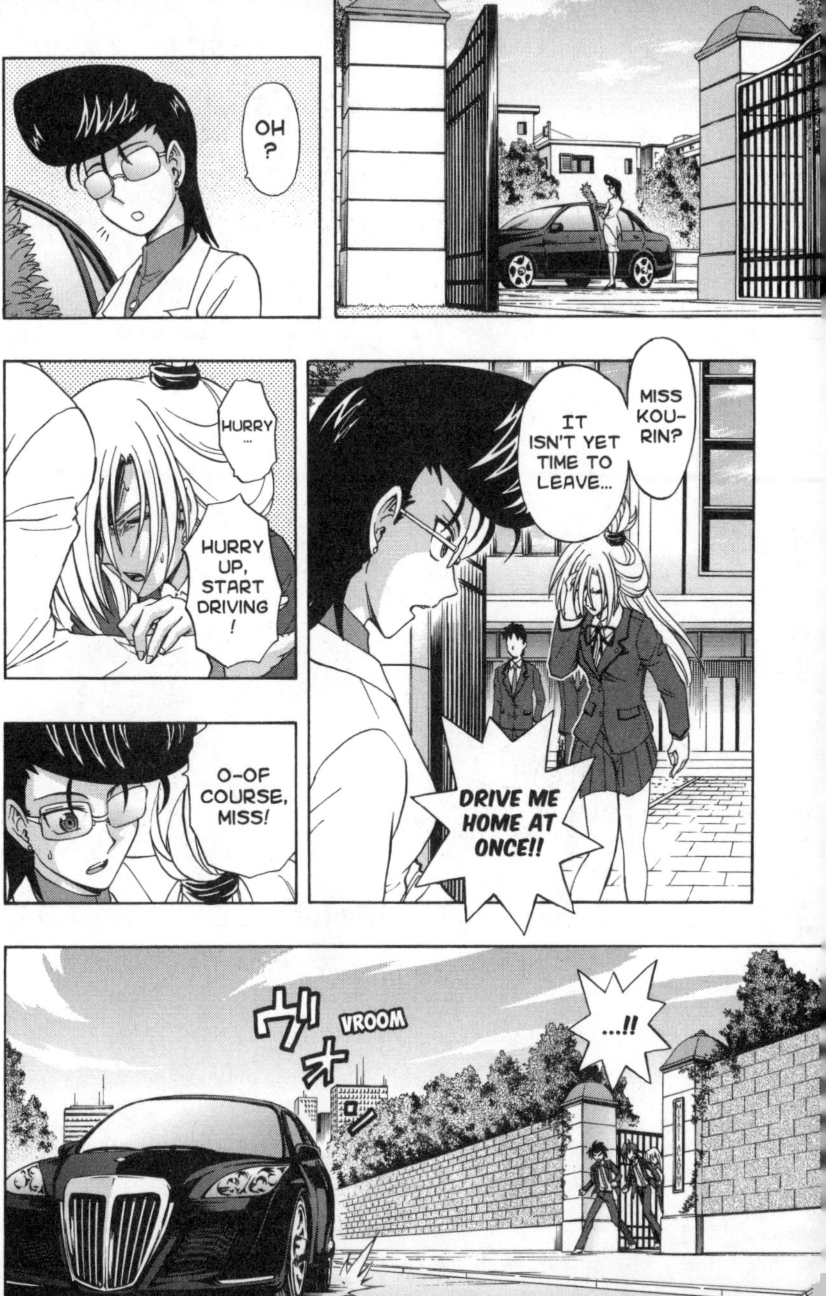

OH ?
MISS KOU-RIN?
IT ISN'T YET TIME TO LEAVE...
DRIVE ME HOME AT ONCE!!
HURRY ...
HURRY UP, START DRIVING !
O-OF COURSE, MISS!
...!!
VROOM

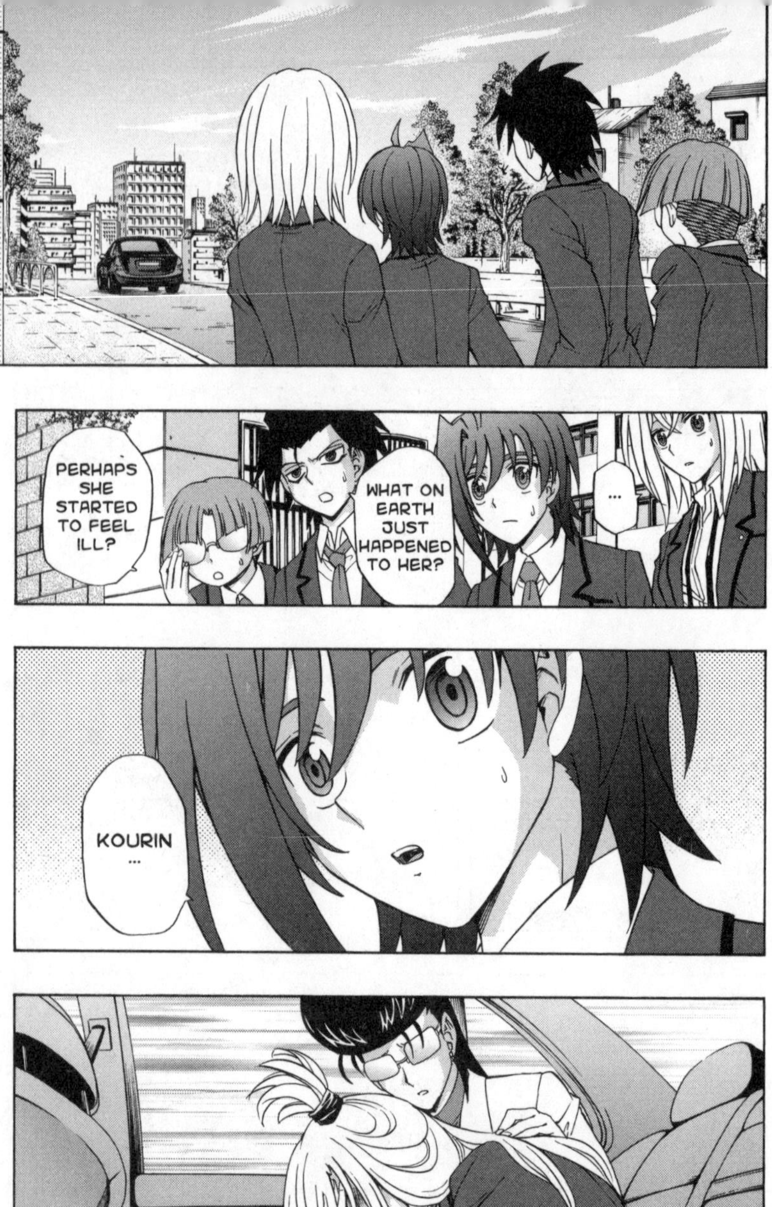
...
WHAT ON EARTH JUST HAPPENED TO HER?
PERHAPS SHE STARTED TO FEEL ILL?
KOURIN ...

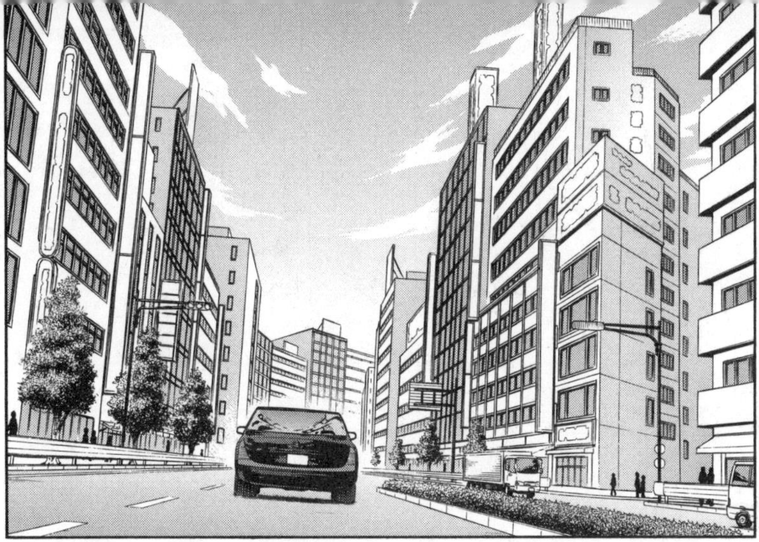

#38 PSY QUALIA ZOMBIE INVASION!

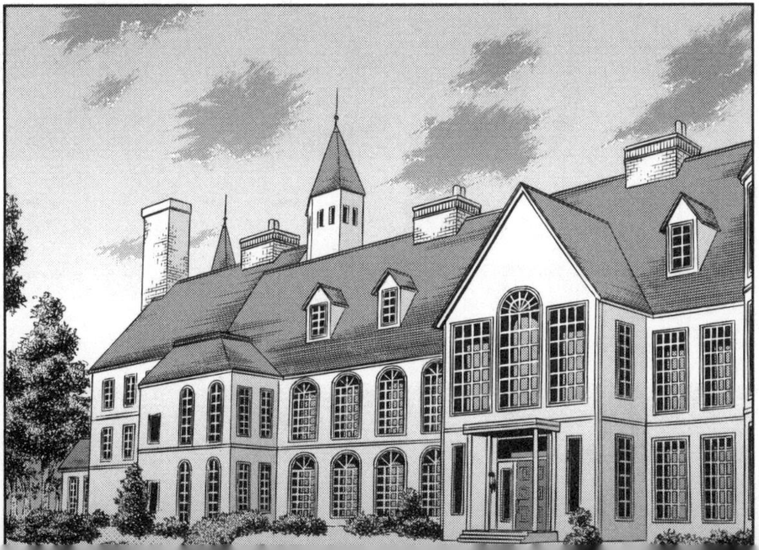

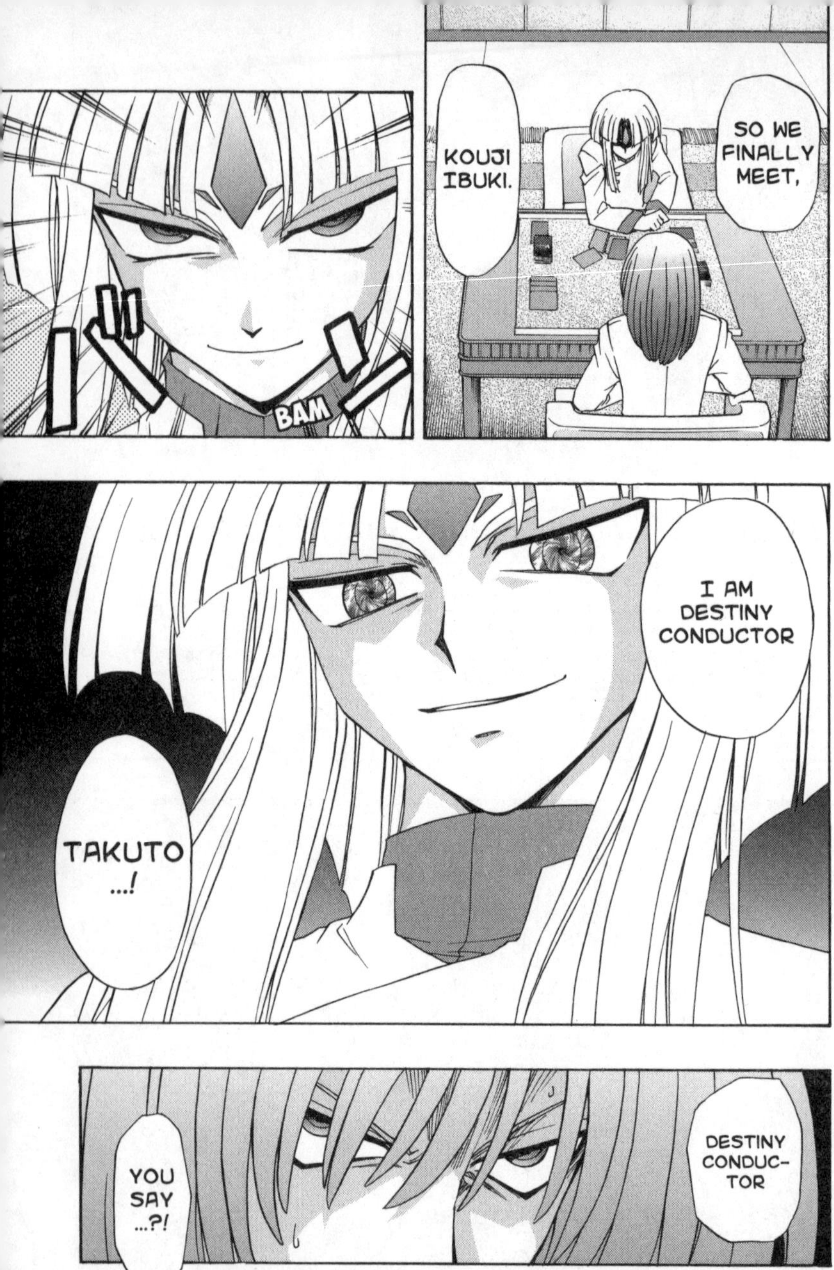
SO WE FINALLY MEET,
KOUJI IBUKI.
BAM
I AM DESTINY CONDUCTOR
TAKUTO ...!
DESTINY CONDUC-TOR
YOU SAY ...?!

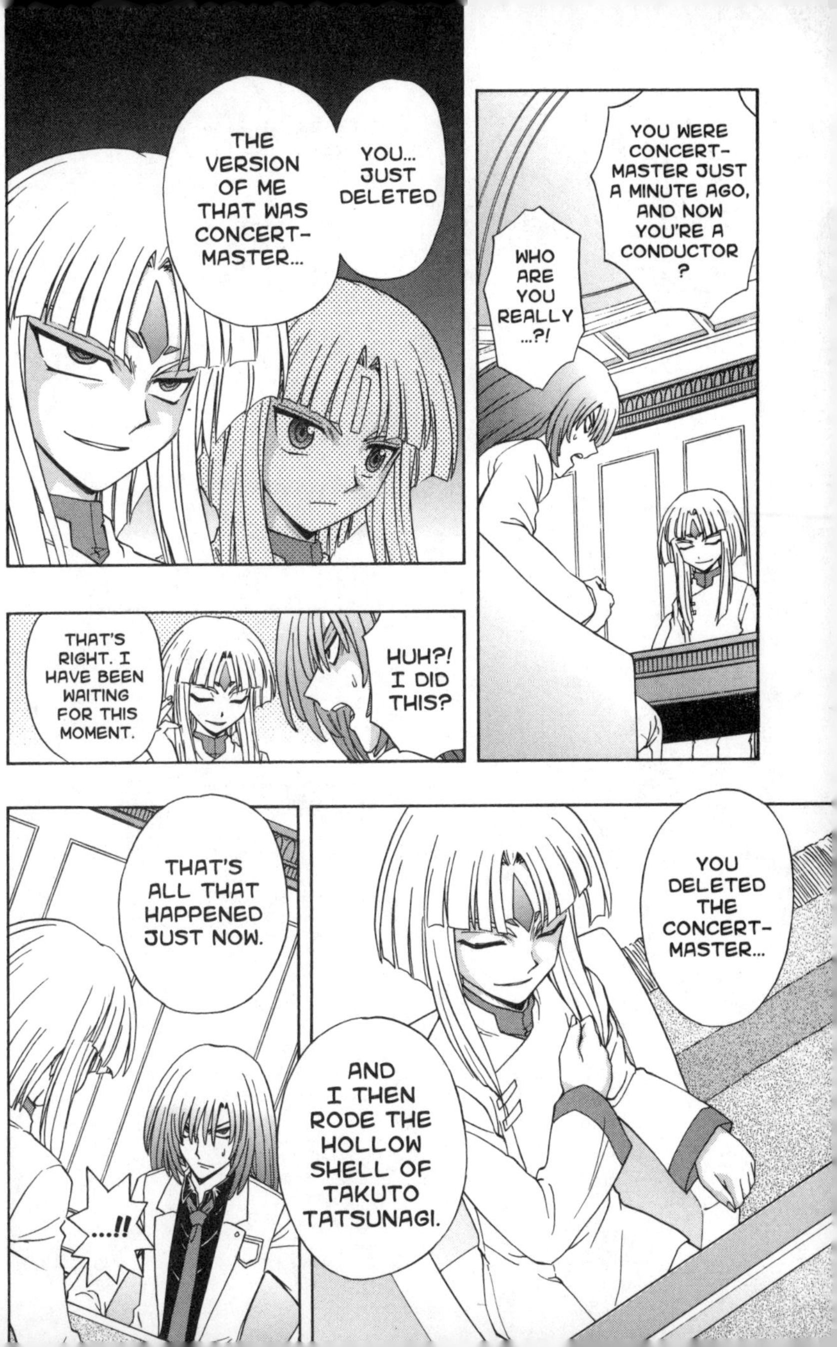
YOU WERE CONCERT-MASTER JUST A MINUTE AGO, AND NOW YOU'RE A CONDUCTOR ?
WHO ARE YOU REALLY ...?!
YOU... JUST DELETED
THE VERSION OF ME THAT WAS CONCERT-MASTER...
HUH?! I DID THIS?
THAT'S RIGHT. I HAVE BEEN WAITING FOR THIS MOMENT.
YOU DELETED THE CONCERT-MASTER...
AND I THEN RODE THE HOLLOW SHELL OF TAKUTO TATSUNAGI.
THAT'S ALL THAT HAPPENED JUST NOW.
...!!

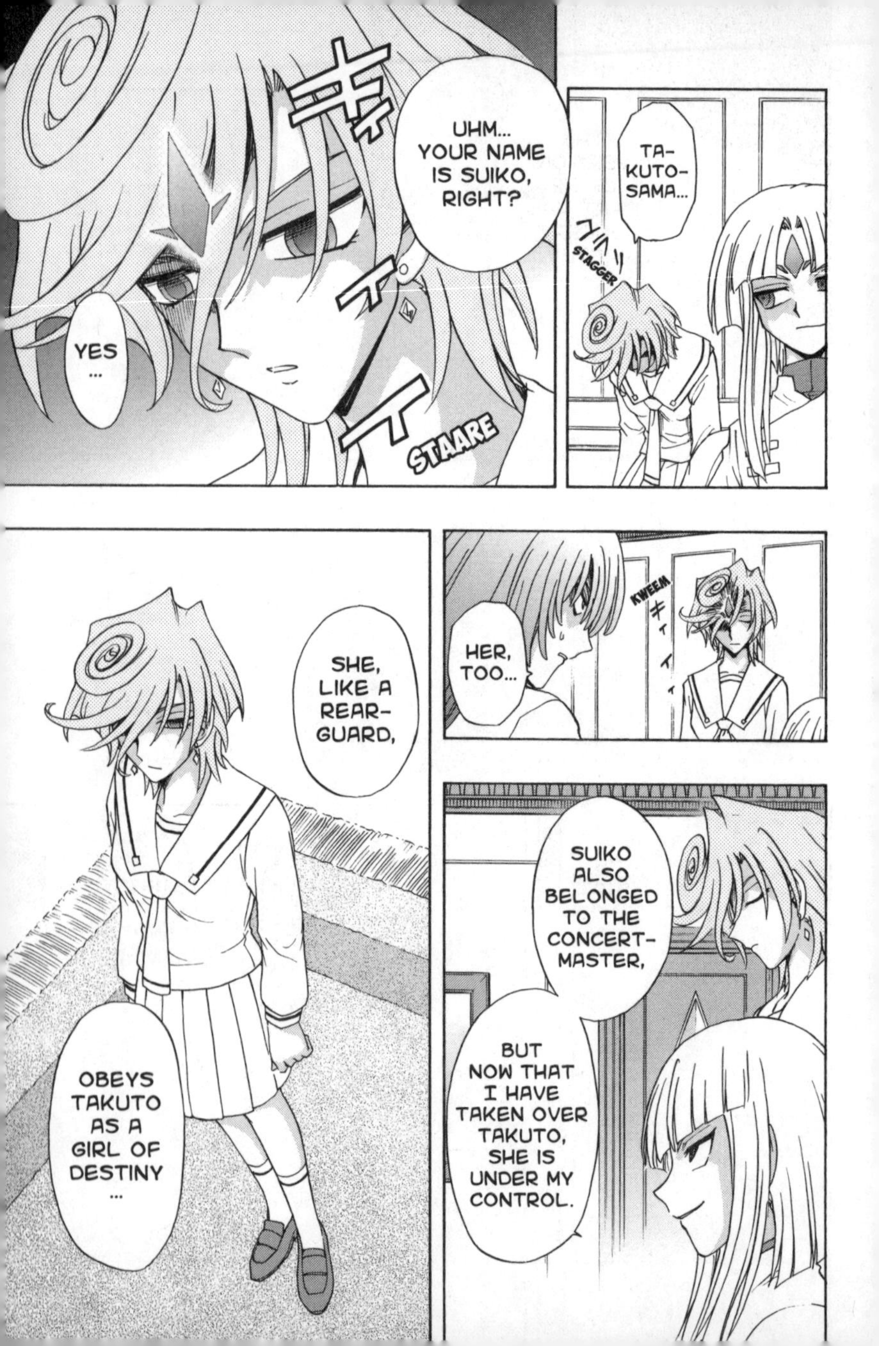
TA-KUTO-SAMA...
STAGGER
UHM... YOUR NAME IS SUIKO, RIGHT?
STAARE
YES ...
HER, TOO...
KWEEM
SUIKO ALSO BELONGED TO THE CONCERT-MASTER,
BUT NOW THAT I HAVE TAKEN OVER TAKUTO, SHE IS UNDER MY CONTROL.
SHE, LIKE A REAR-GUARD,
OBEYS TAKUTO AS A GIRL OF DESTINY ...

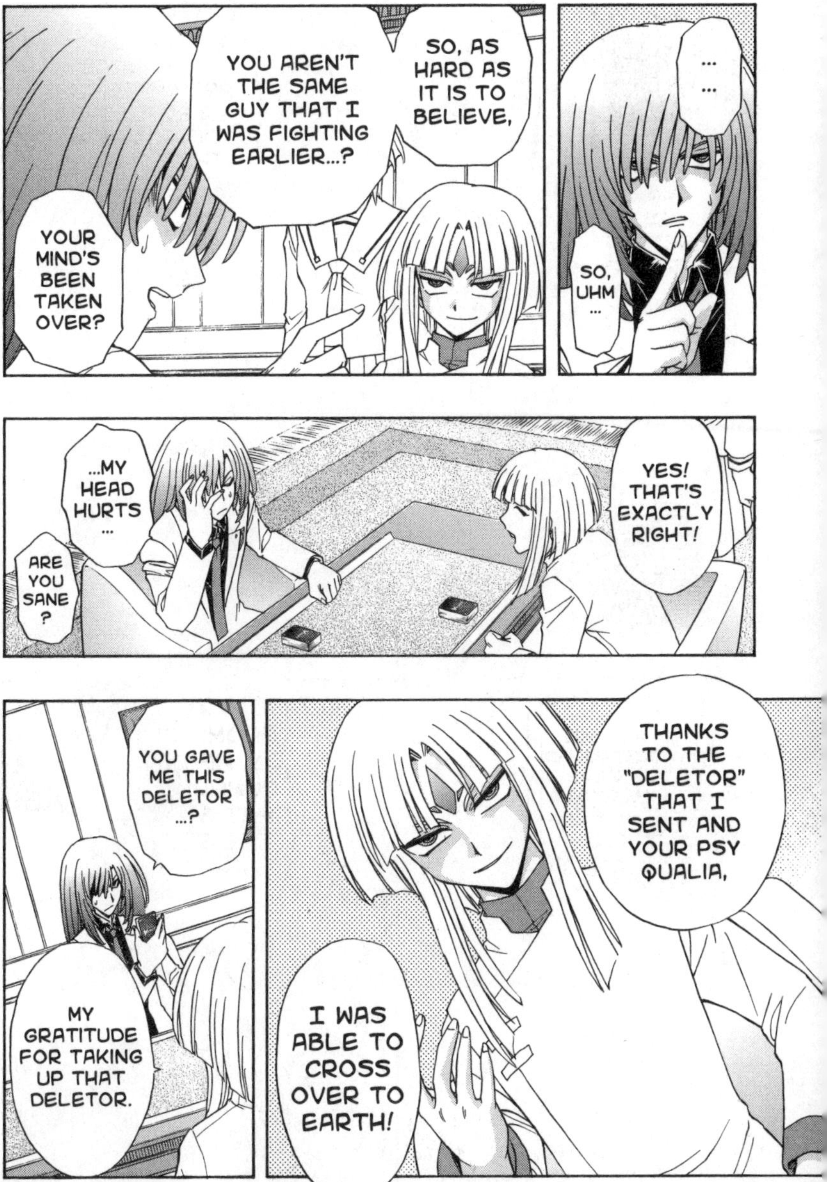

... ...
SO, UHM ...
SO, AS HARD AS IT IS TO BELIEVE,
YOU AREN'T THE SAME GUY THAT I WAS FIGHTING EARLIER...?
YOUR MIND'S BEEN TAKEN OVER?
YES! THAT'S EXACTLY RIGHT!
...MY HEAD HURTS ...
ARE YOU SANE ?
THANKS TO THE "DELETOR" THAT I SENT AND YOUR PSY QUALIA,
I WAS ABLE TO CROSS OVER TO EARTH!
YOU GAVE ME THIS DELETOR ...?
MY GRATITUDE FOR TAKING UP THAT DELETOR.

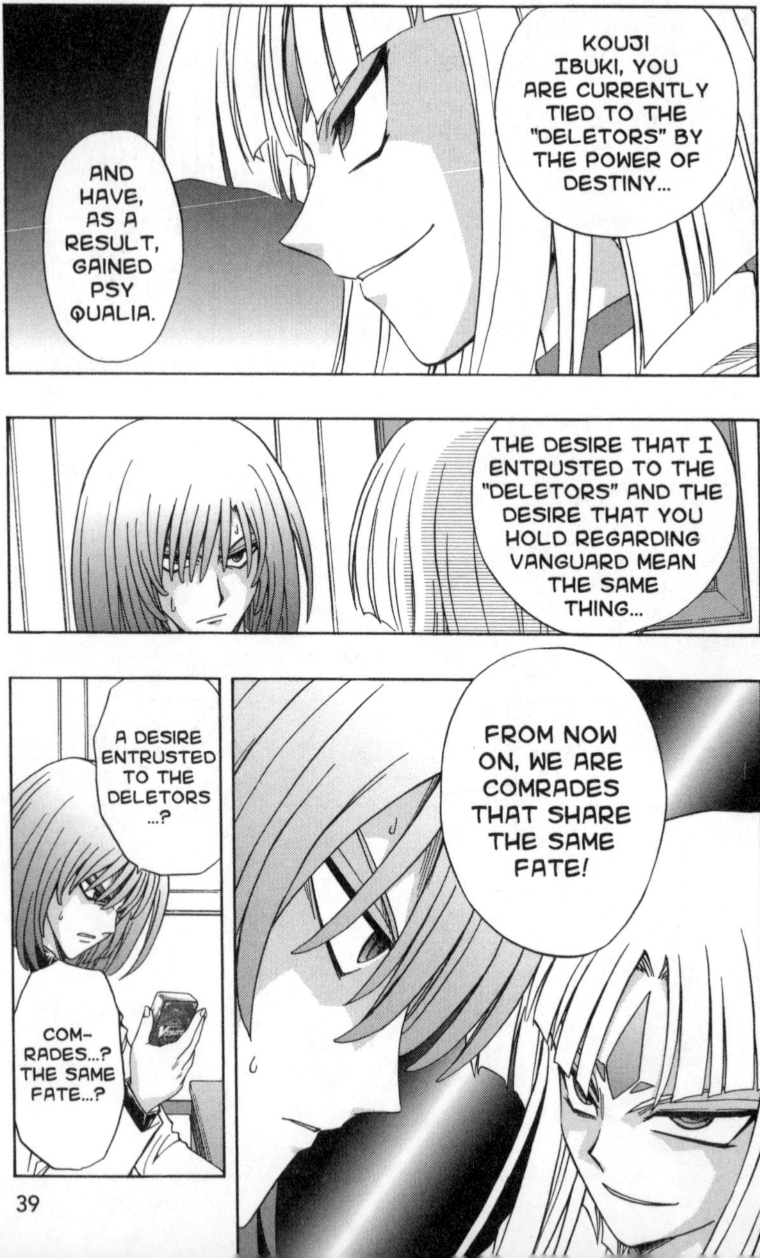
KOUJI IBUKI, YOU ARE CURRENTLY TIED TO THE "DELETORS" BY THE POWER OF DESTINY...
AND HAVE, AS A RESULT, GAINED PSY QUALIA.
THE DESIRE THAT I ENTRUSTED TO THE "DELETORS" AND THE DESIRE THAT YOU HOLD REGARDING VANGUARD MEAN THE SAME THING...
FROM NOW ON, WE ARE COMRADES THAT SHARE THE SAME FATE!
A DESIRE ENTRUSTED TO THE DELETORS ...?
COM-RADES...? THE SAME FATE...?

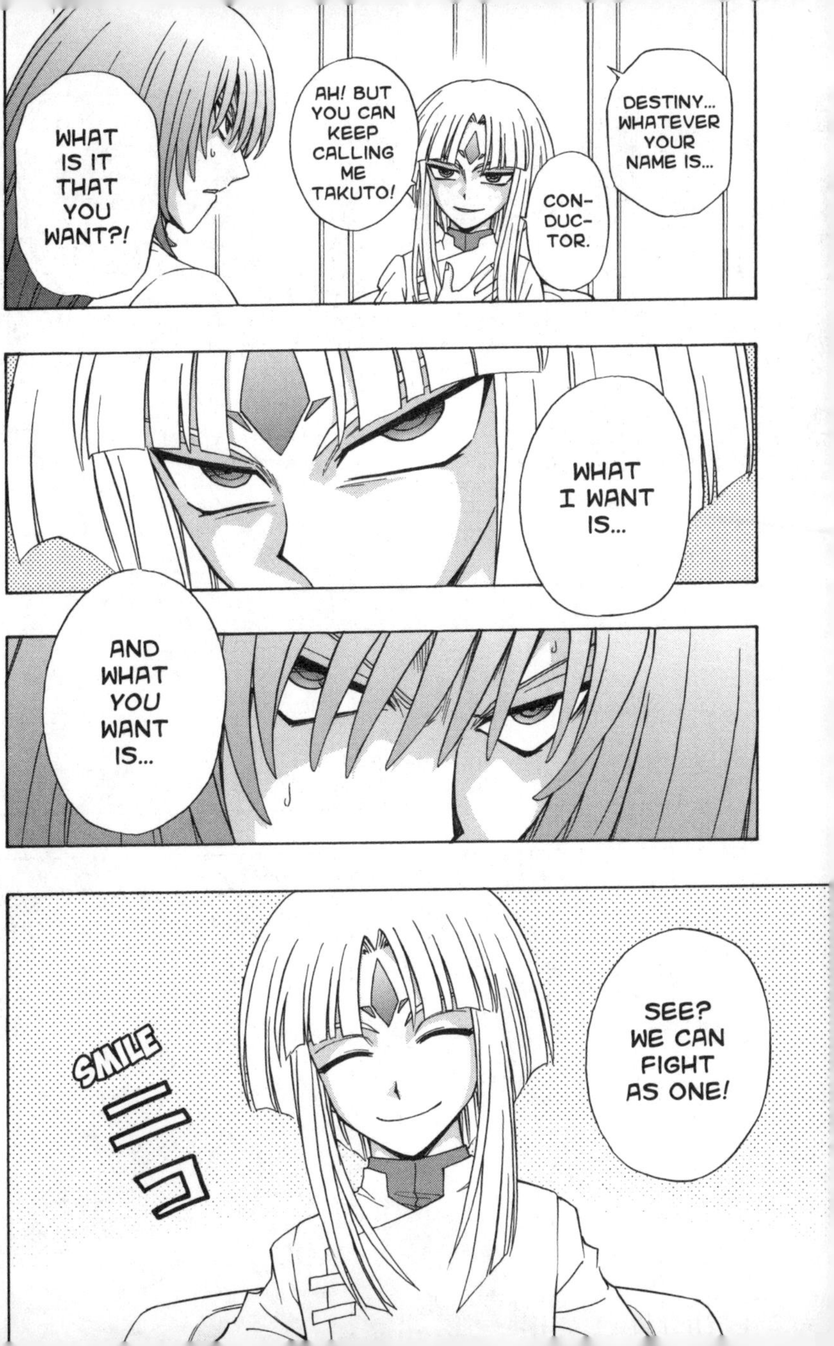
DESTINY... WHATEVER YOUR NAME IS...
CON-DUC-TOR.
AH! BUT YOU CAN KEEP CALLING ME TAKUTO!
WHAT IS IT THAT YOU WANT?!
WHAT I WANT IS...
AND WHAT YOU WANT IS...
SEE? WE CAN FIGHT AS ONE!
SMILE

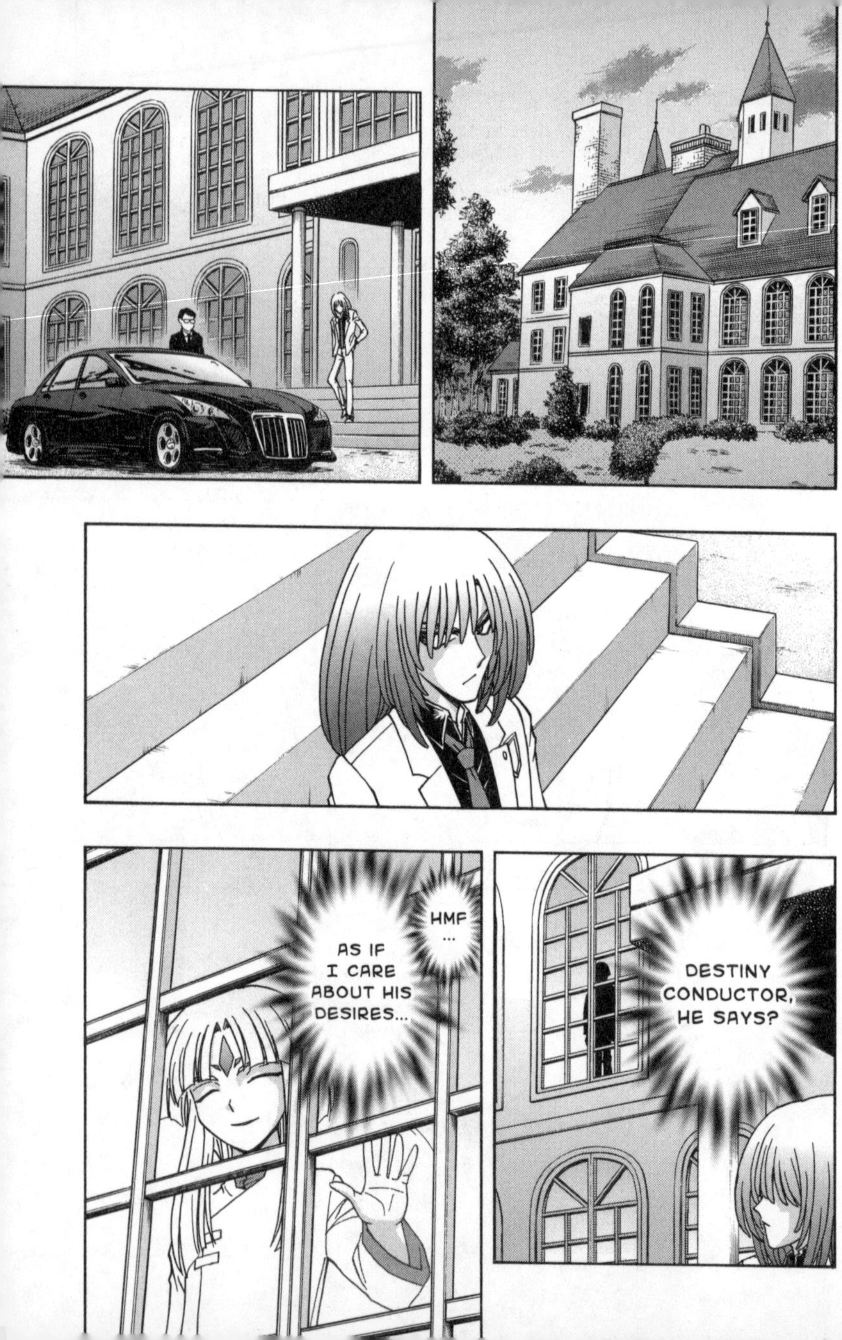
DESTINY CONDUCTOR, HE SAYS?
HMF ...
AS IF I CARE ABOUT HIS DESIRES...

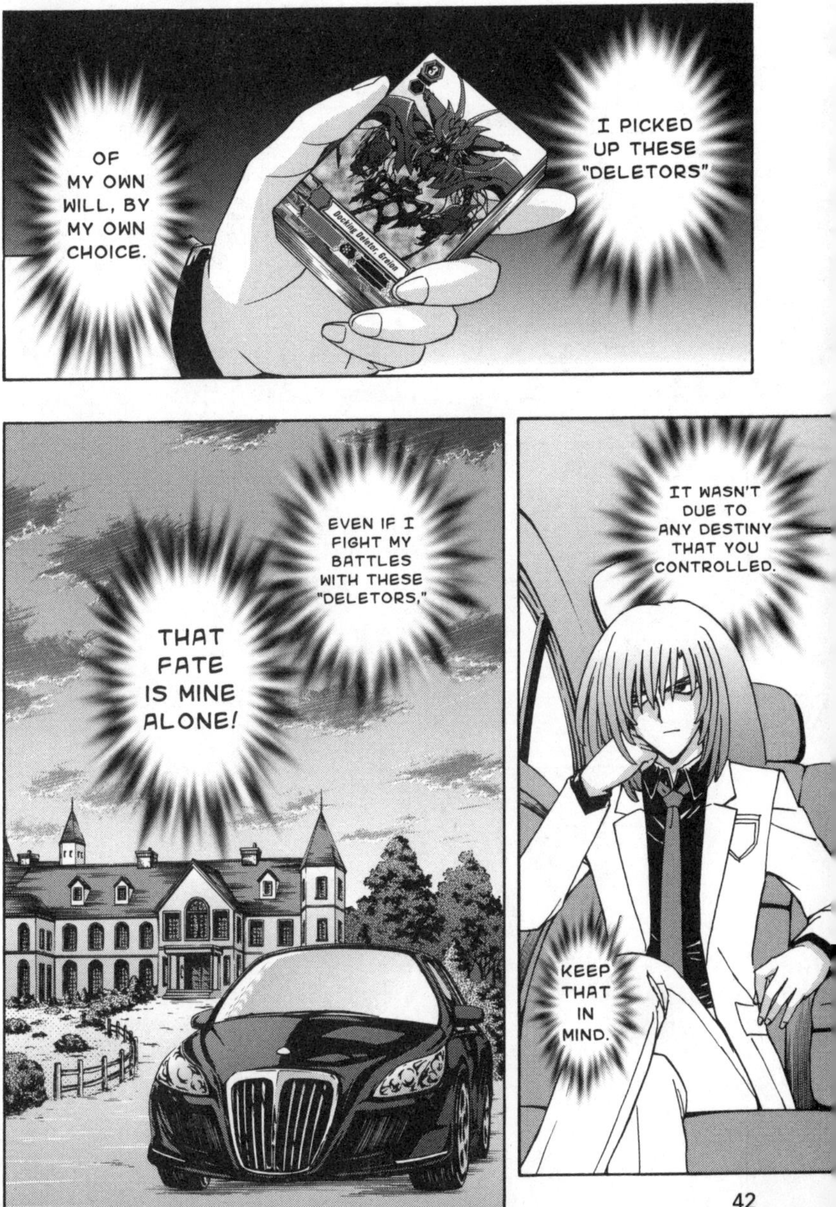
I PICKED UP THESE "DELETORS"
OF MY OWN WILL, BY MY OWN CHOICE.
Docking Deletor, Greion
IT WASN'T DUE TO ANY DESTINY THAT YOU CONTROLLED.
KEEP THAT IN MIND.
EVEN IF I FIGHT MY BATTLES WITH THESE "DELETORS,"
THAT FATE IS MINE ALONE!

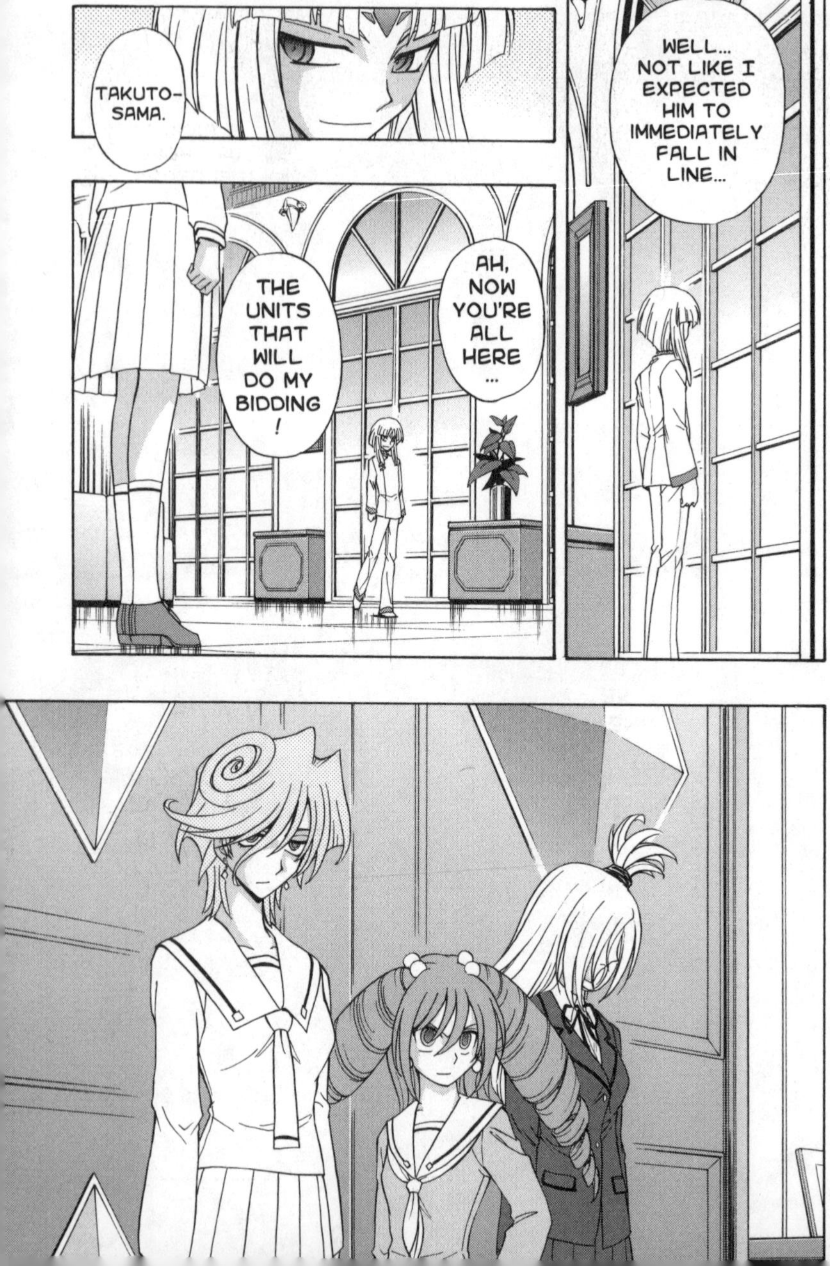
WELL... NOT LIKE I EXPECTED HIM TO IMMEDIATELY FALL IN LINE...
TAKUTO-SAMA.
AH, NOW YOU'RE ALL HERE ...
THE UNITS THAT WILL DO MY BIDDING !

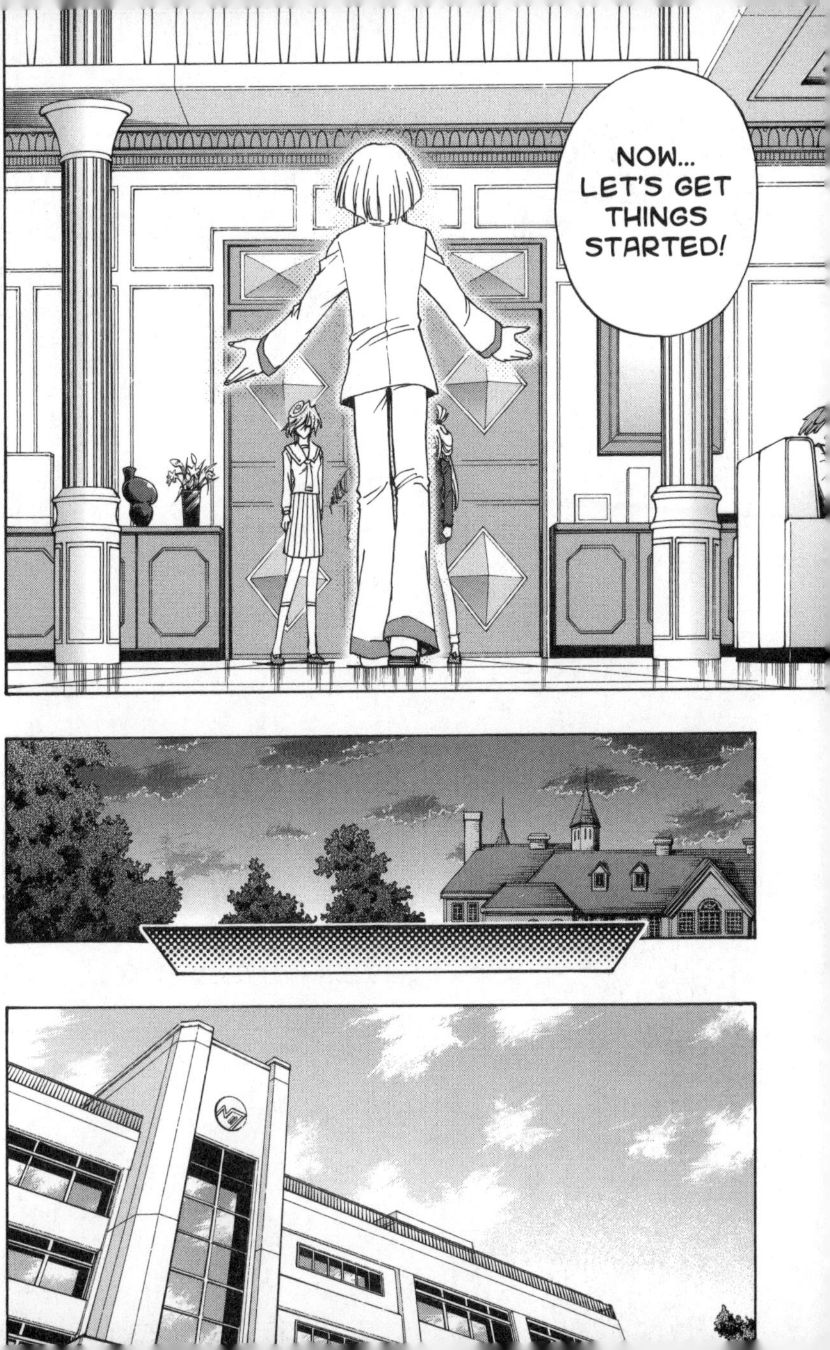
NOW... LET'S GET THINGS STARTED!

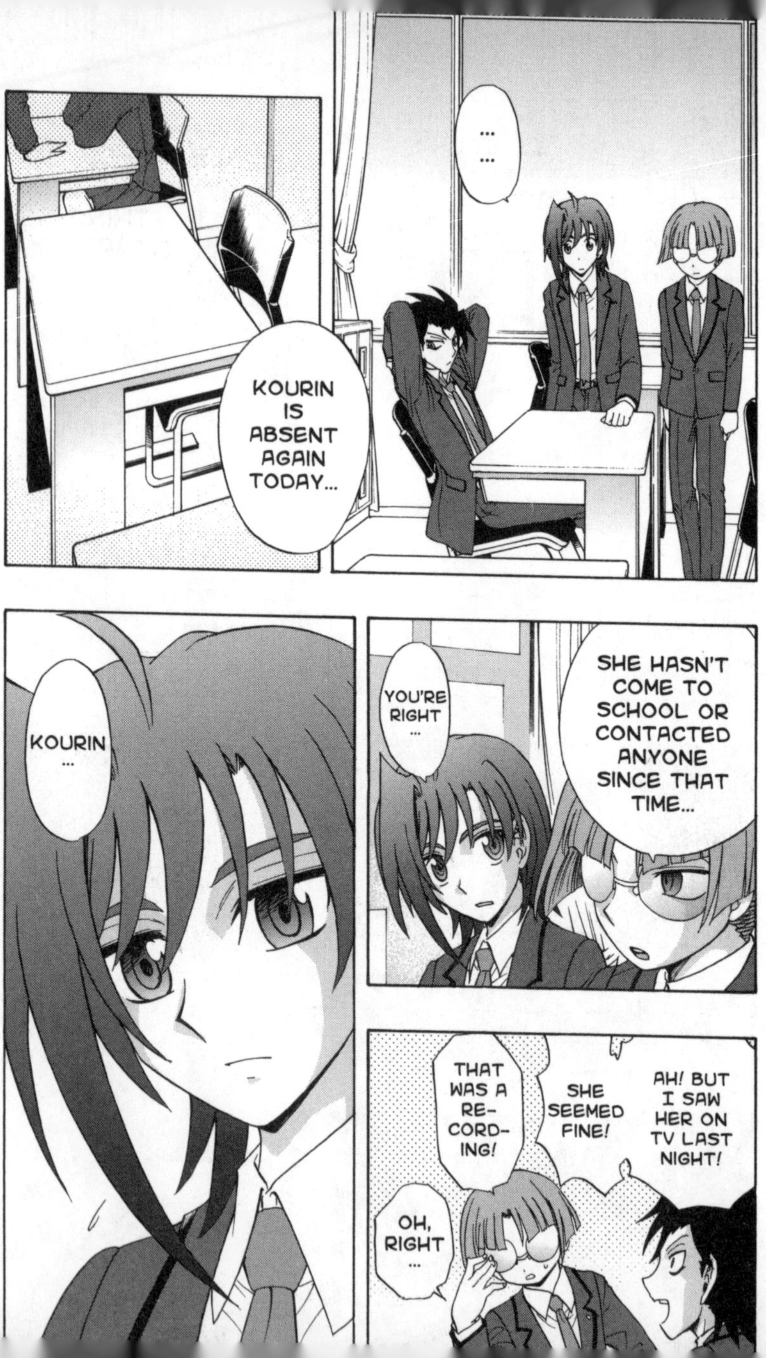
… …
KOURIN IS ABSENT AGAIN TODAY…
SHE HASN'T COME TO SCHOOL OR CONTACTED ANYONE SINCE THAT TIME…
YOU'RE RIGHT …
AH! BUT I SAW HER ON TV LAST NIGHT!
SHE SEEMED FINE!
THAT WAS A RE-CORD-ING!
OH, RIGHT …
KOURIN …

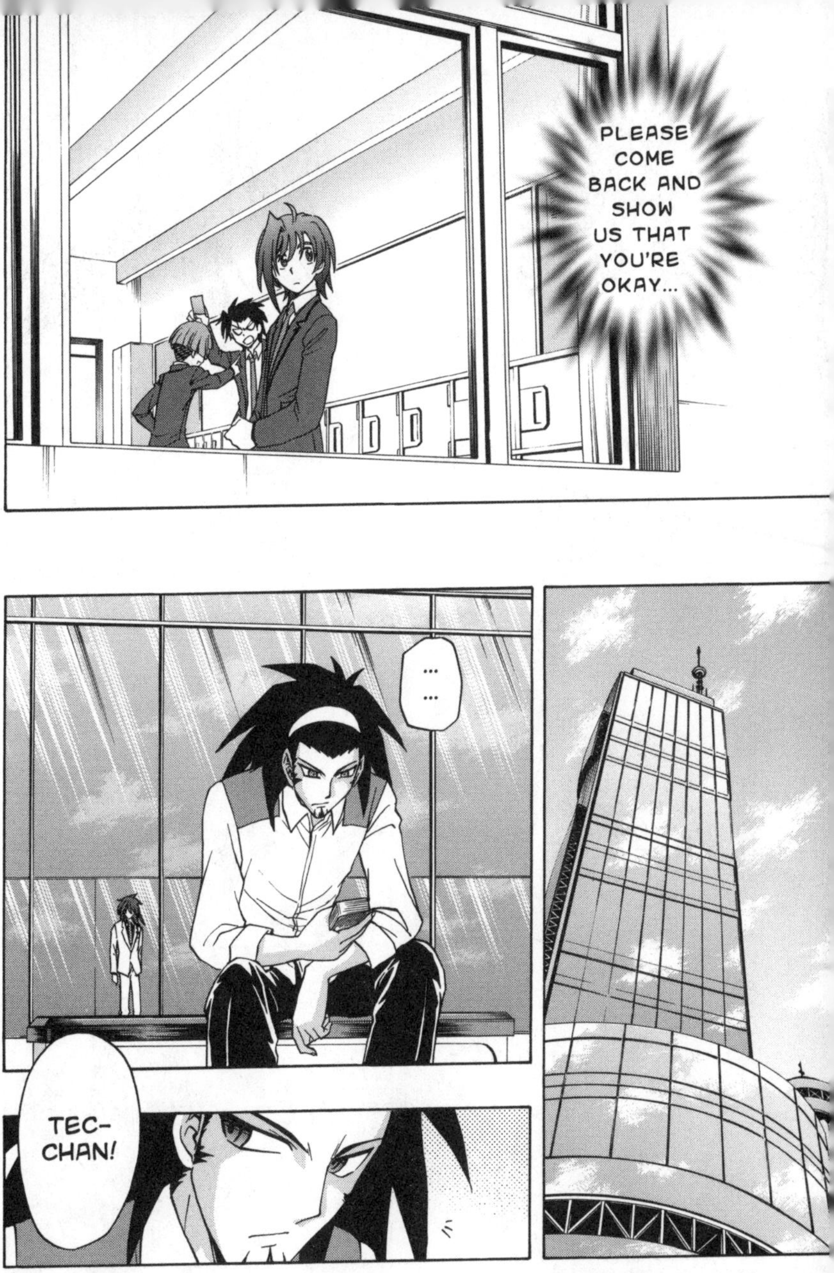
PLEASE COME BACK AND SHOW US THAT YOU'RE OKAY...
...
...
TEC-CHAN!

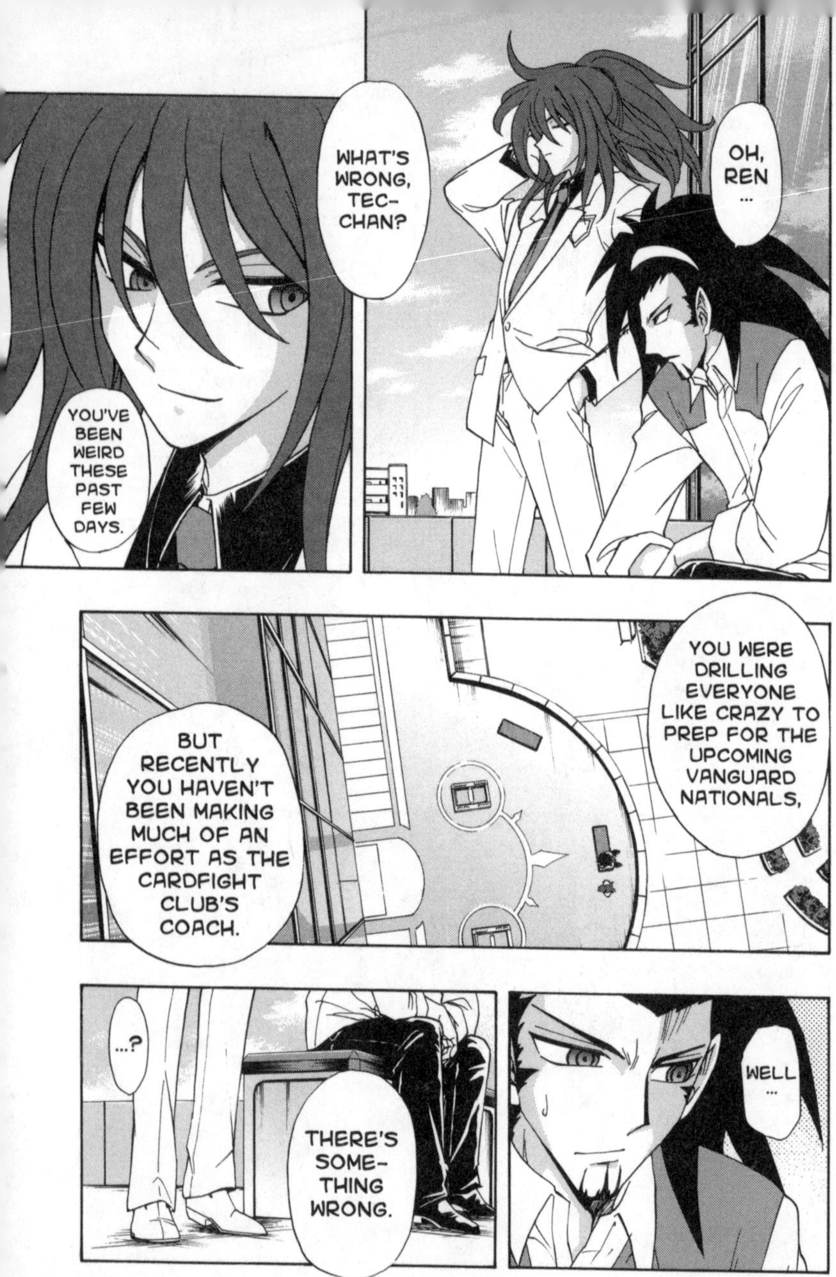
OH, REN ...
WHAT'S WRONG, TEC-CHAN?
YOU'VE BEEN WEIRD THESE PAST FEW DAYS.
YOU WERE DRILLING EVERYONE LIKE CRAZY TO PREP FOR THE UPCOMING VANGUARD NATIONALS,
BUT RECENTLY YOU HAVEN'T BEEN MAKING MUCH OF AN EFFORT AS THE CARDFIGHT CLUB'S COACH.
WELL ...
...?
THERE'S SOME-THING WRONG.

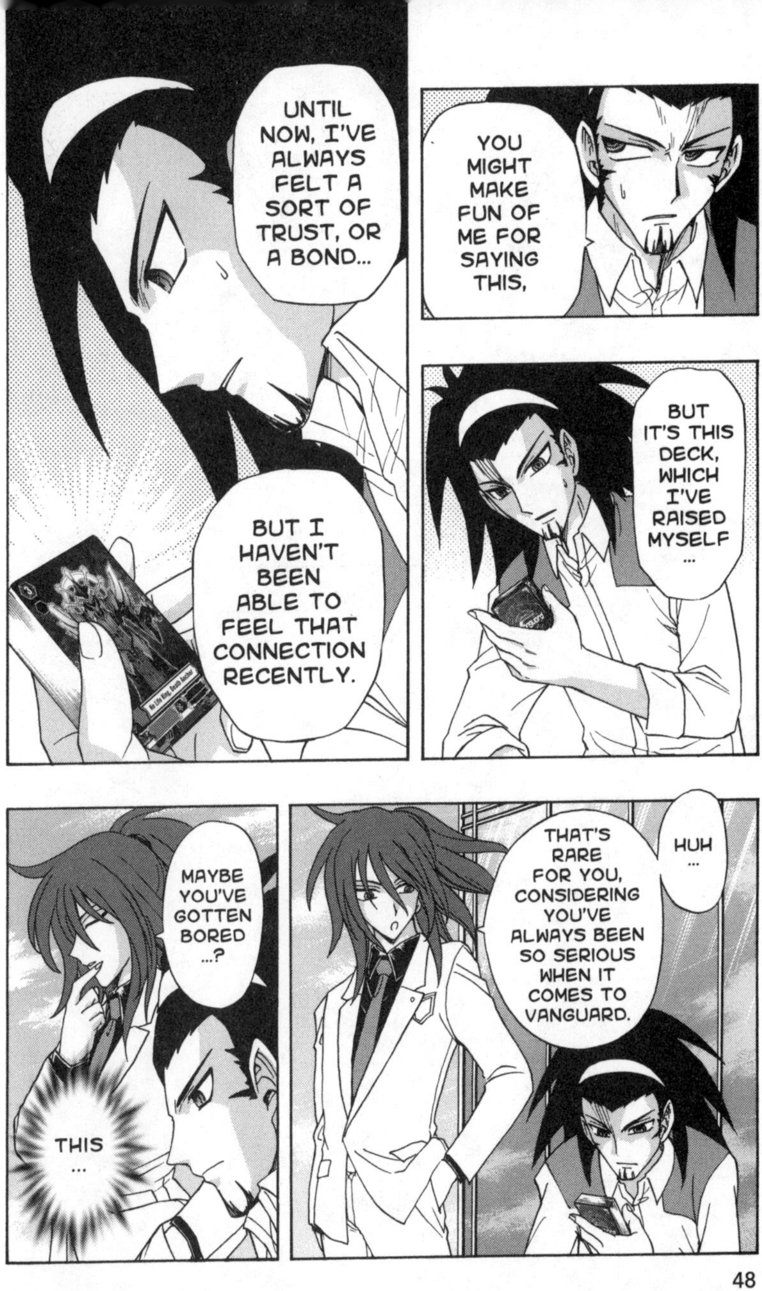
YOU MIGHT MAKE FUN OF ME FOR SAYING THIS,
BUT IT'S THIS DECK, WHICH I'VE RAISED MYSELF ...
UNTIL NOW, I'VE ALWAYS FELT A SORT OF TRUST, OR A BOND...
BUT I HAVEN'T BEEN ABLE TO FEEL THAT CONNECTION RECENTLY.
HUH ...
THAT'S RARE FOR YOU, CONSIDERING YOU'VE ALWAYS BEEN SO SERIOUS WHEN IT COMES TO VANGUARD.
MAYBE YOU'VE GOTTEN BORED ...?
THIS ...

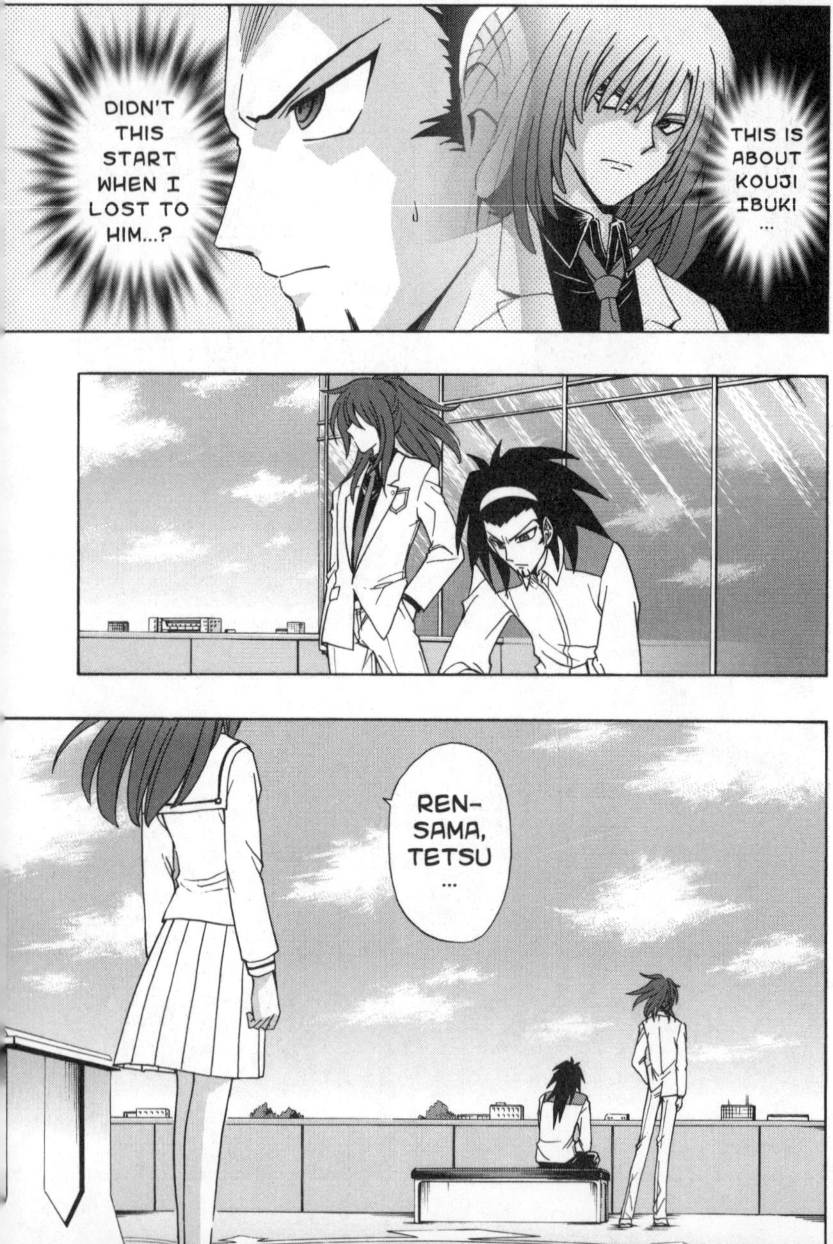
THIS IS ABOUT KOUJI IBUKI ...
DIDN'T THIS START WHEN I LOST TO HIM...?
REN-SAMA, TETSU ...

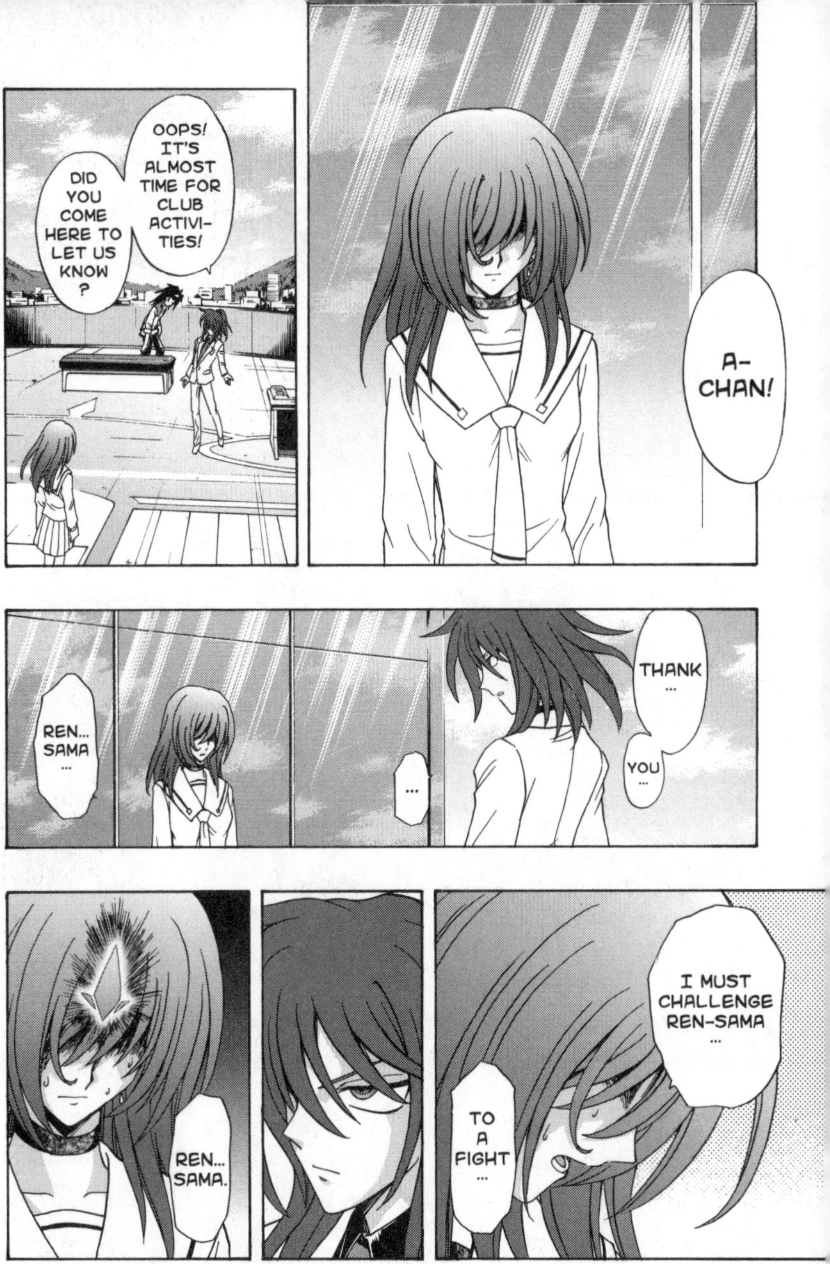
A-CHAN!
OOPS! IT'S ALMOST TIME FOR CLUB ACTIVI-TIES!
DID YOU COME HERE TO LET US KNOW ?
THANK ...
YOU ...
...
REN... SAMA ...
I MUST CHALLENGE REN-SAMA ...
TO A FIGHT ...
REN... SAMA.

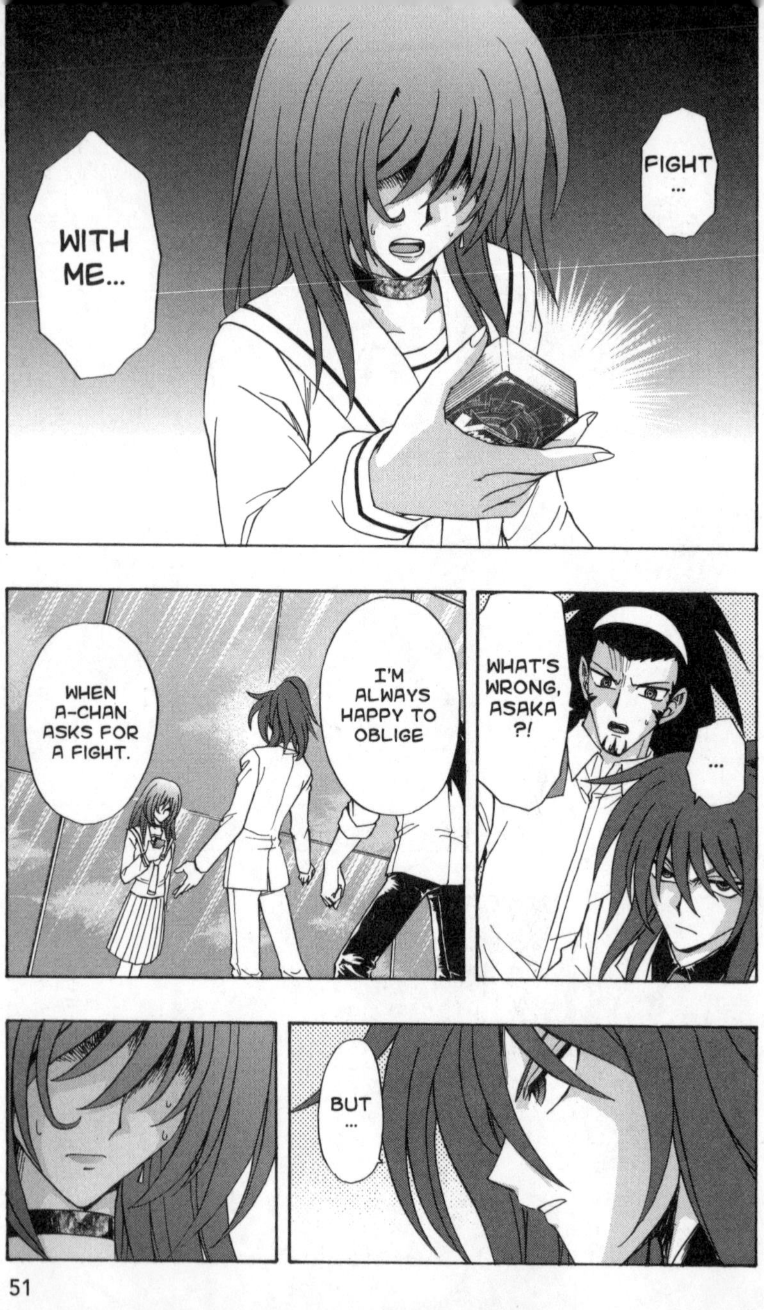
FIGHT ...
WITH ME...
WHAT'S WRONG, ASAKA ?!
...
I'M ALWAYS HAPPY TO OBLIGE
WHEN A-CHAN ASKS FOR A FIGHT.
BUT ...

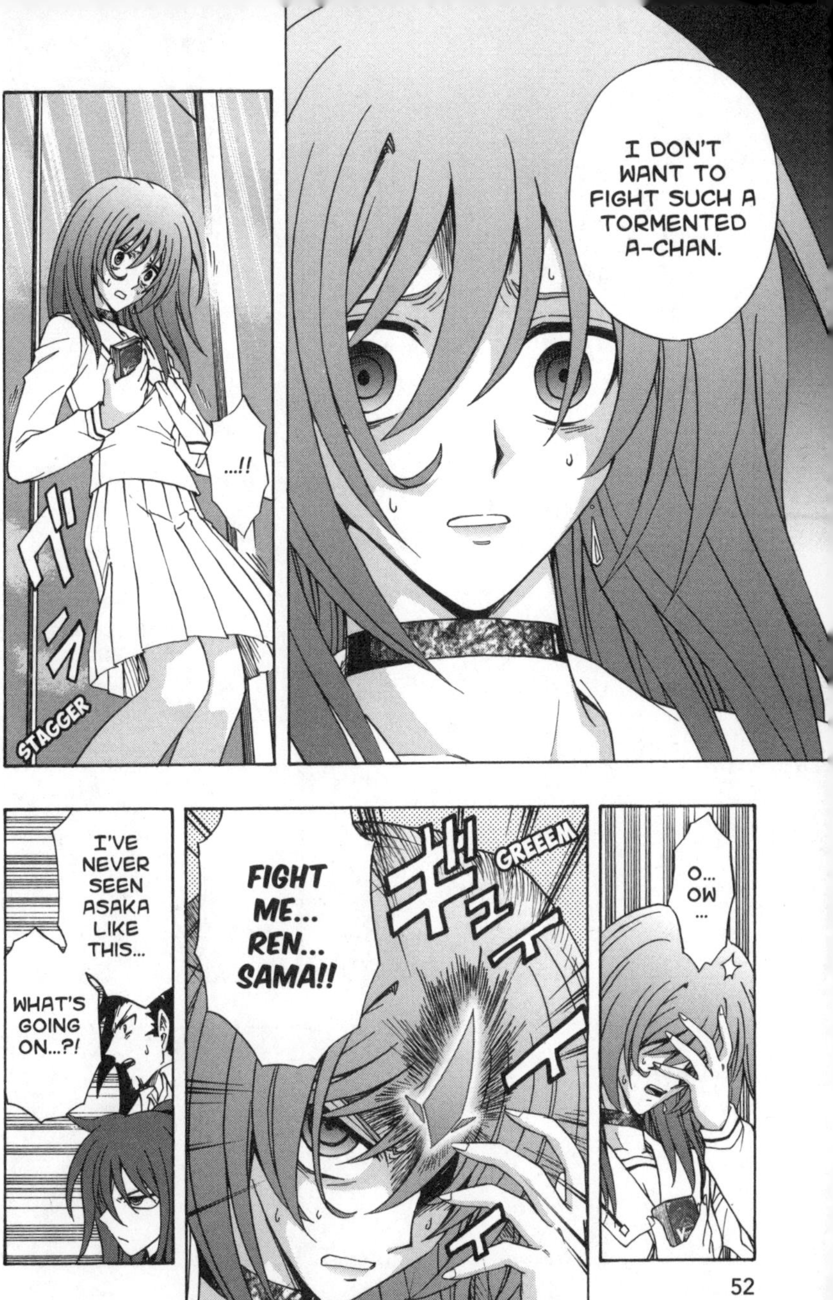
I DON'T WANT TO FIGHT SUCH A TORMENTED A-CHAN.
...!!
STAGGER
O... OW ...
GREEEM
FIGHT ME... REN... SAMA!!
I'VE NEVER SEEN ASAKA LIKE THIS...
WHAT'S GOING ON...?!

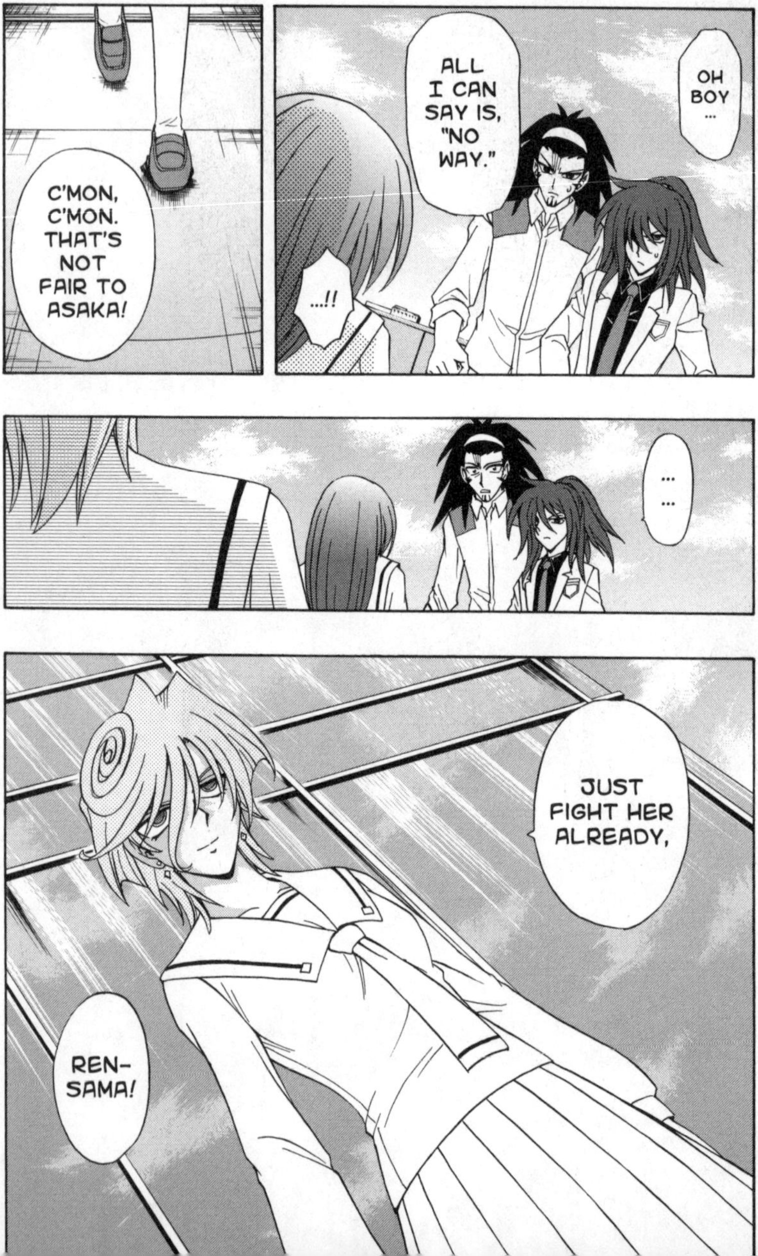
OH BOY ...
ALL I CAN SAY IS, "NO WAY."
...!!
C'MON, C'MON. THAT'S NOT FAIR TO ASAKA!
... ...
JUST FIGHT HER ALREADY,
REN-SAMA!

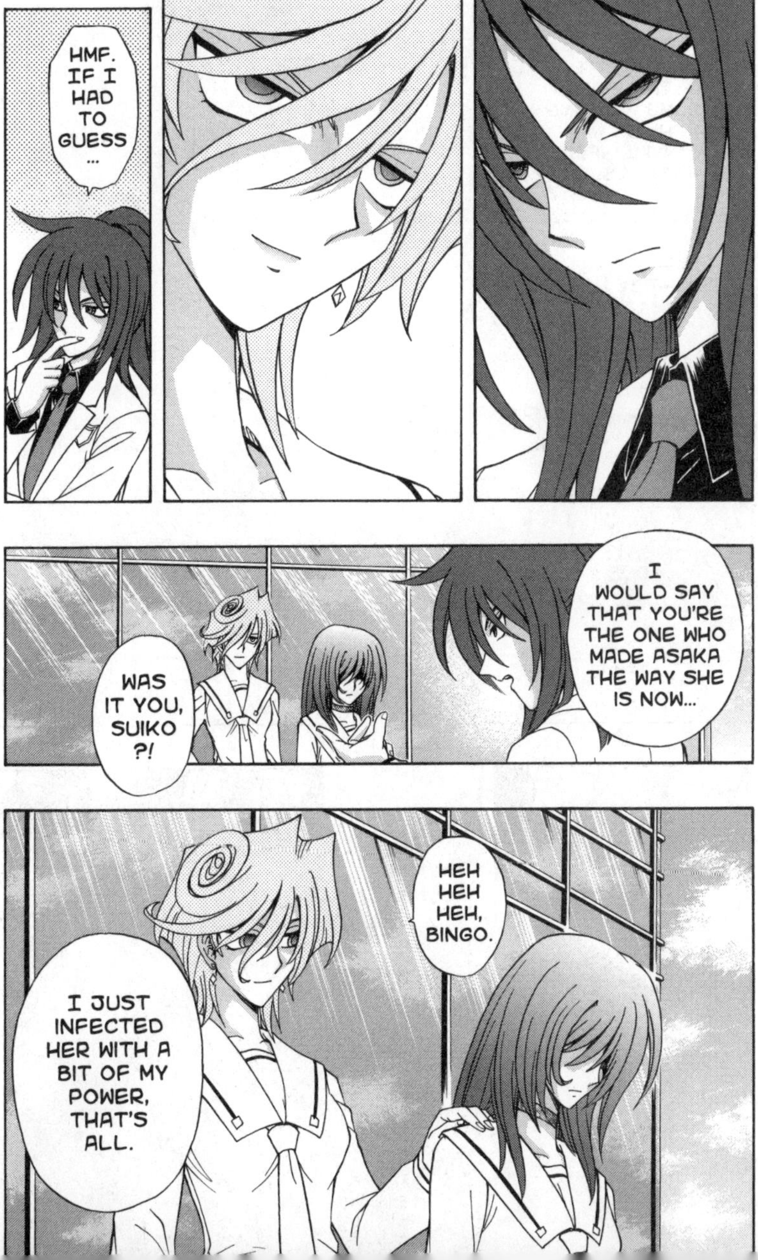
HMF. IF I HAD TO GUESS ...
I WOULD SAY THAT YOU'RE THE ONE WHO MADE ASAKA THE WAY SHE IS NOW...
WAS IT YOU, SUIKO ?!
HEH HEH HEH, BINGO.
I JUST INFECTED HER WITH A BIT OF MY POWER, THAT'S ALL.

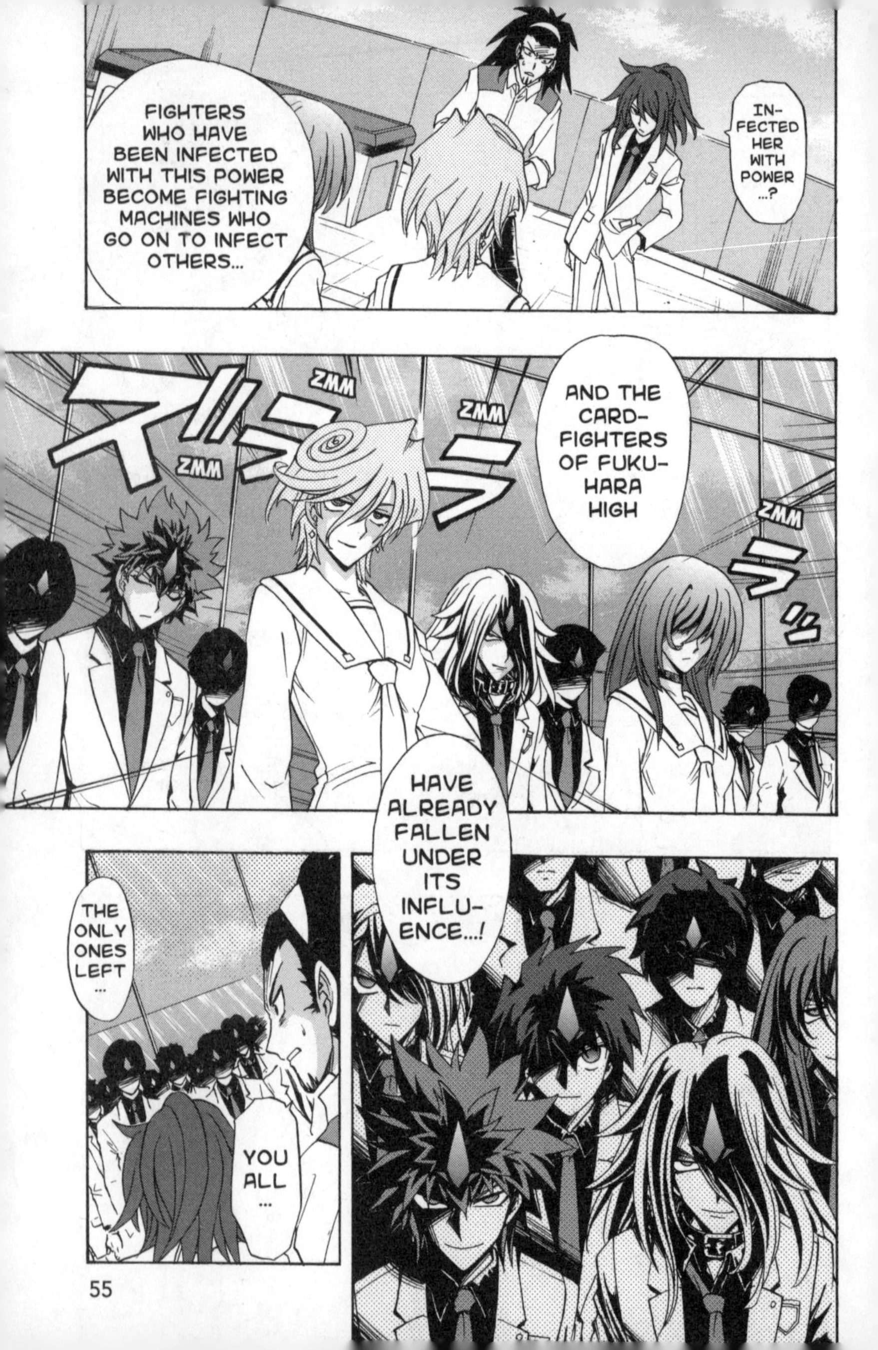
INFECTED HER WITH POWER...?
FIGHTERS WHO HAVE BEEN INFECTED WITH THIS POWER BECOME FIGHTING MACHINES WHO GO ON TO INFECT OTHERS...
ZMM
ZMM
AND THE CARDFIGHTERS OF FUKUHARA HIGH
ZMM
ZMM
HAVE ALREADY FALLEN UNDER ITS INFLUENCE...!
THE ONLY ONES LEFT...
YOU ALL...

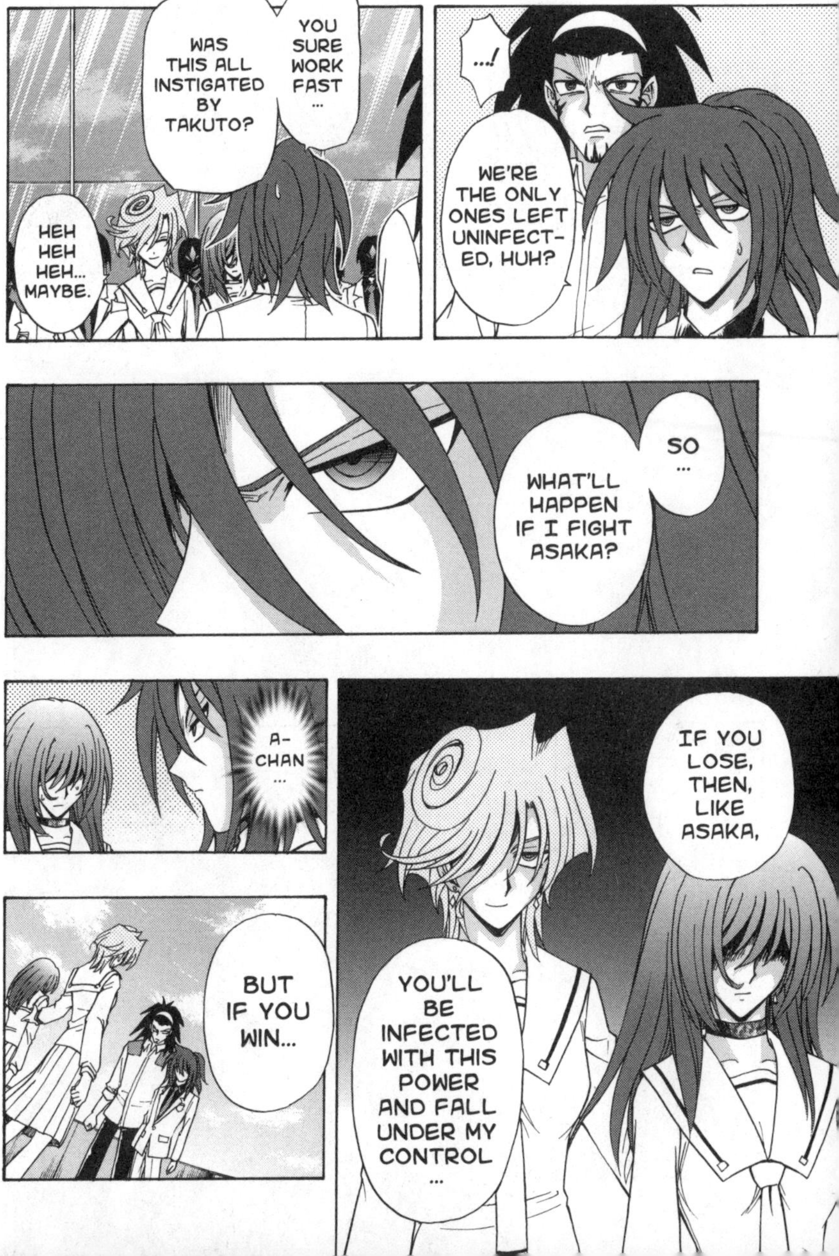
...!
WE'RE THE ONLY ONES LEFT UNINFECTED, HUH?
YOU SURE WORK FAST ...
WAS THIS ALL INSTIGATED BY TAKUTO?
HEH HEH HEH... MAYBE.
SO ...
WHAT'LL HAPPEN IF I FIGHT ASAKA?
IF YOU LOSE, THEN, LIKE ASAKA,
YOU'LL BE INFECTED WITH THIS POWER AND FALL UNDER MY CONTROL ...
A-CHAN ...
BUT IF YOU WIN...

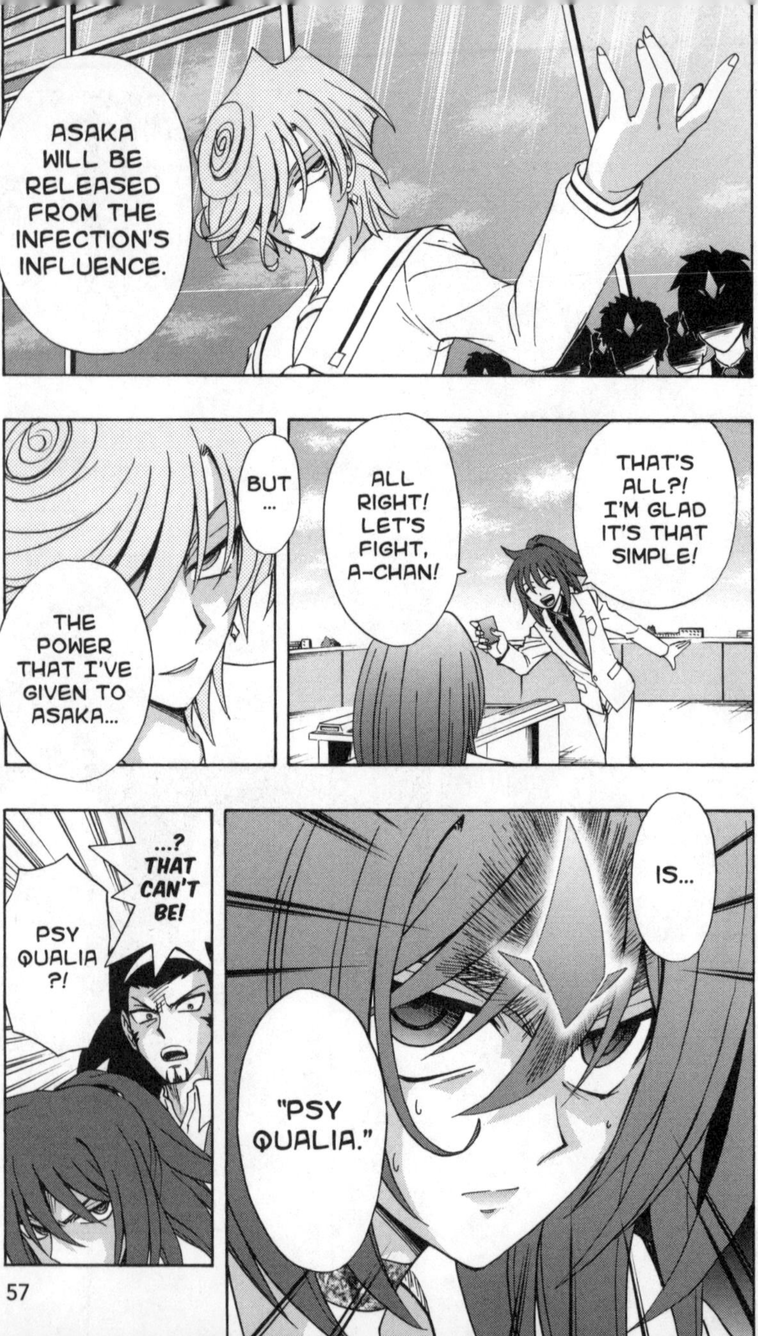
ASAKA WILL BE RELEASED FROM THE INFECTION'S INFLUENCE.
THAT'S ALL?! I'M GLAD IT'S THAT SIMPLE!
ALL RIGHT! LET'S FIGHT, A-CHAN!
BUT ...
THE POWER THAT I'VE GIVEN TO ASAKA...
IS...
"PSY QUALIA."
...? THAT CAN'T BE!
PSY QUALIA ?!

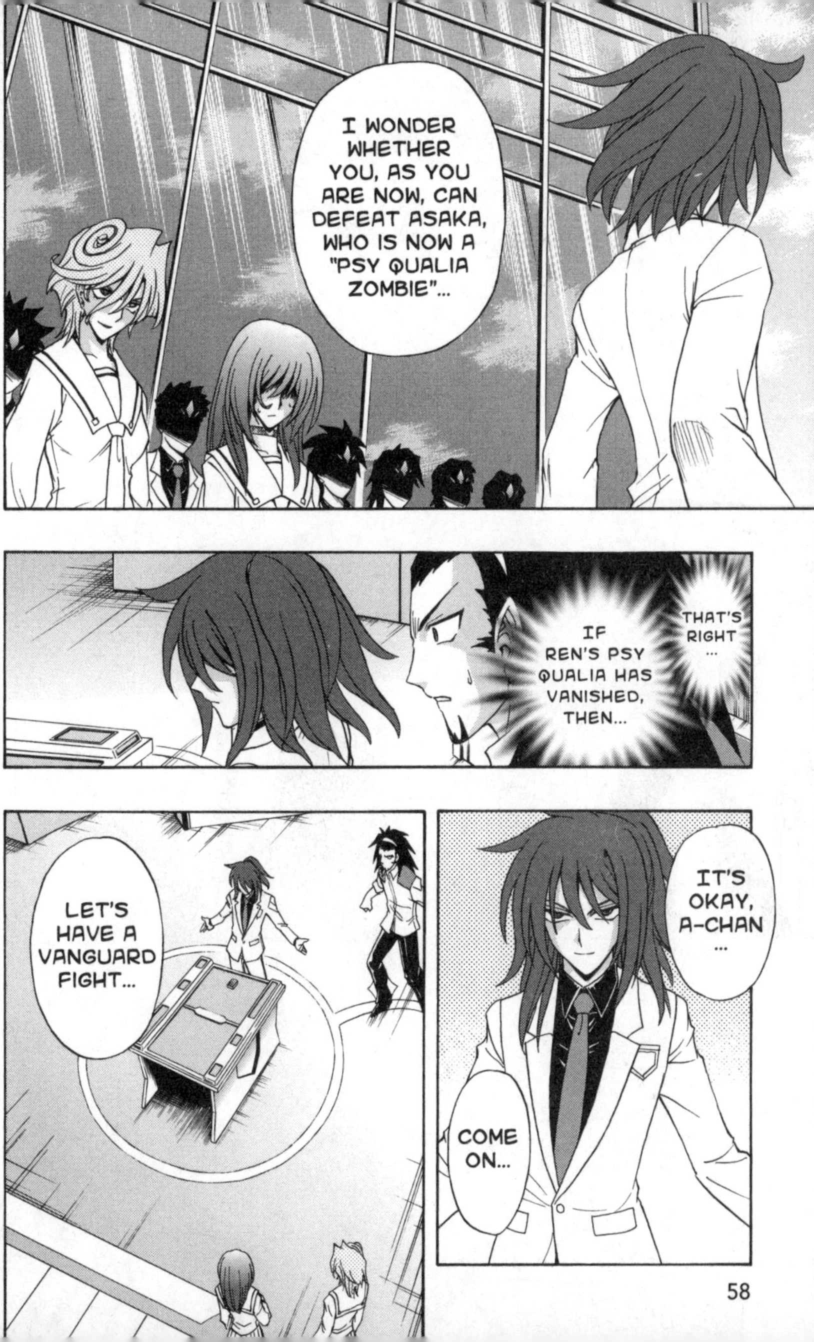
I WONDER WHETHER YOU, AS YOU ARE NOW, CAN DEFEAT ASAKA, WHO IS NOW A "PSY QUALIA ZOMBIE"...
THAT'S RIGHT ...
IF REN'S PSY QUALIA HAS VANISHED, THEN...
IT'S OKAY, A-CHAN ...
COME ON...
LET'S HAVE A VANGUARD FIGHT...

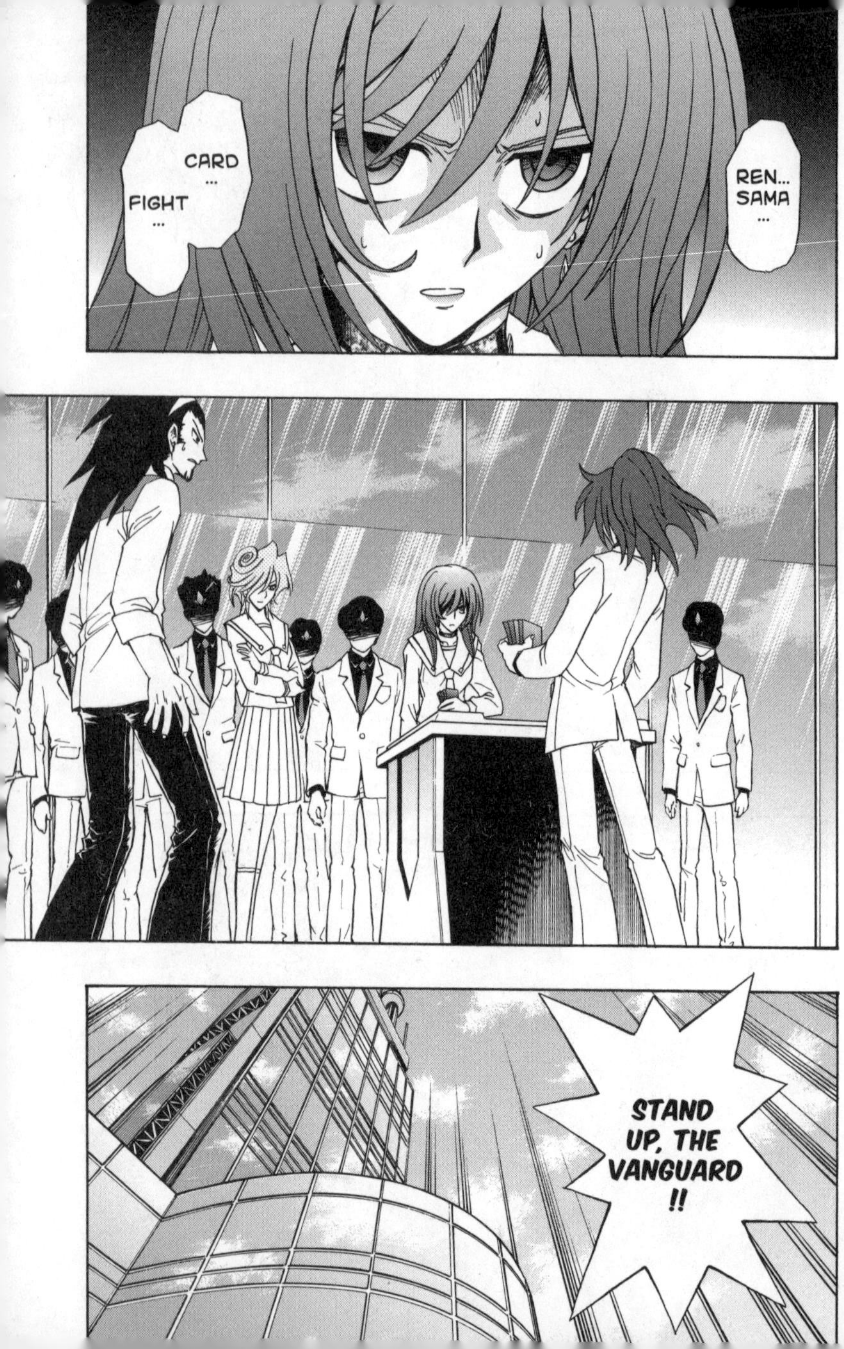
REN... SAMA ...
CARD ... FIGHT ...
STAND UP, THE VANGUARD !!

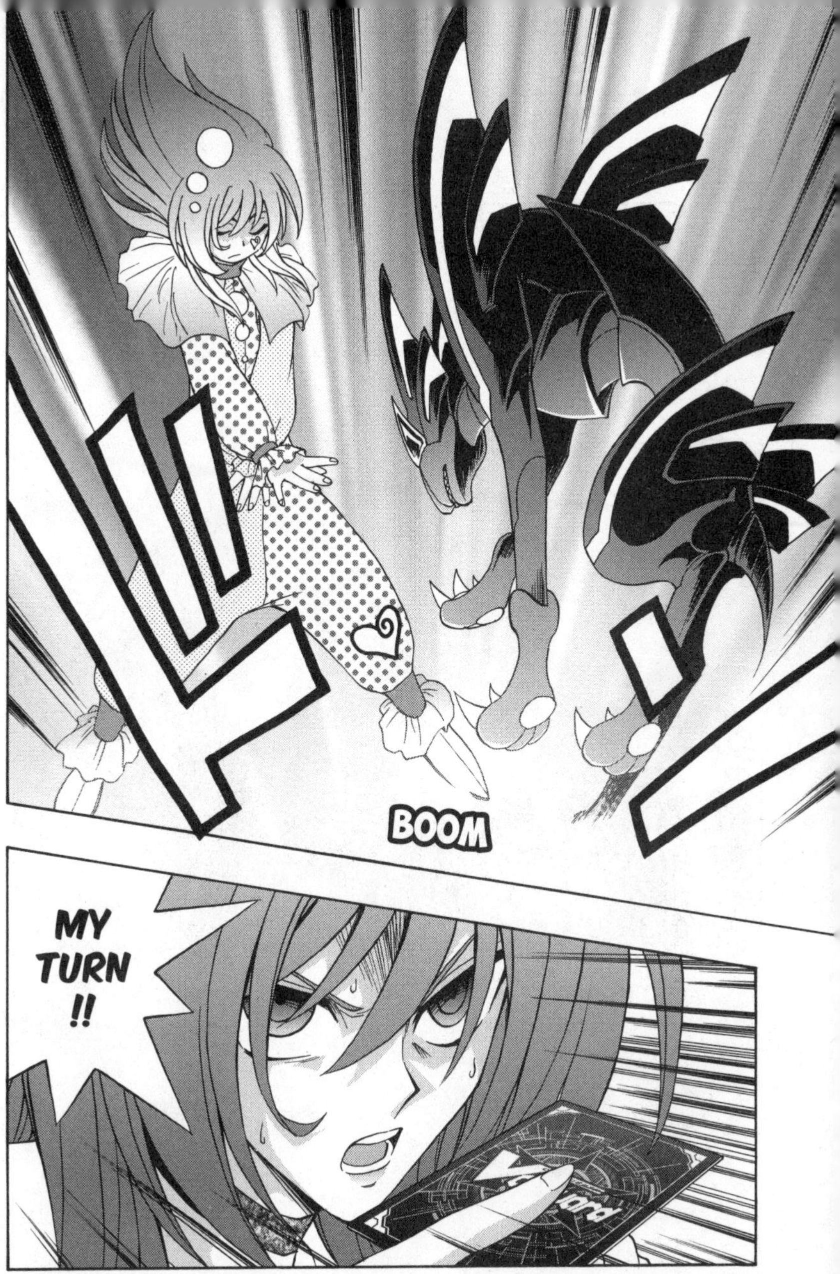
BOOM
MY TURN !!

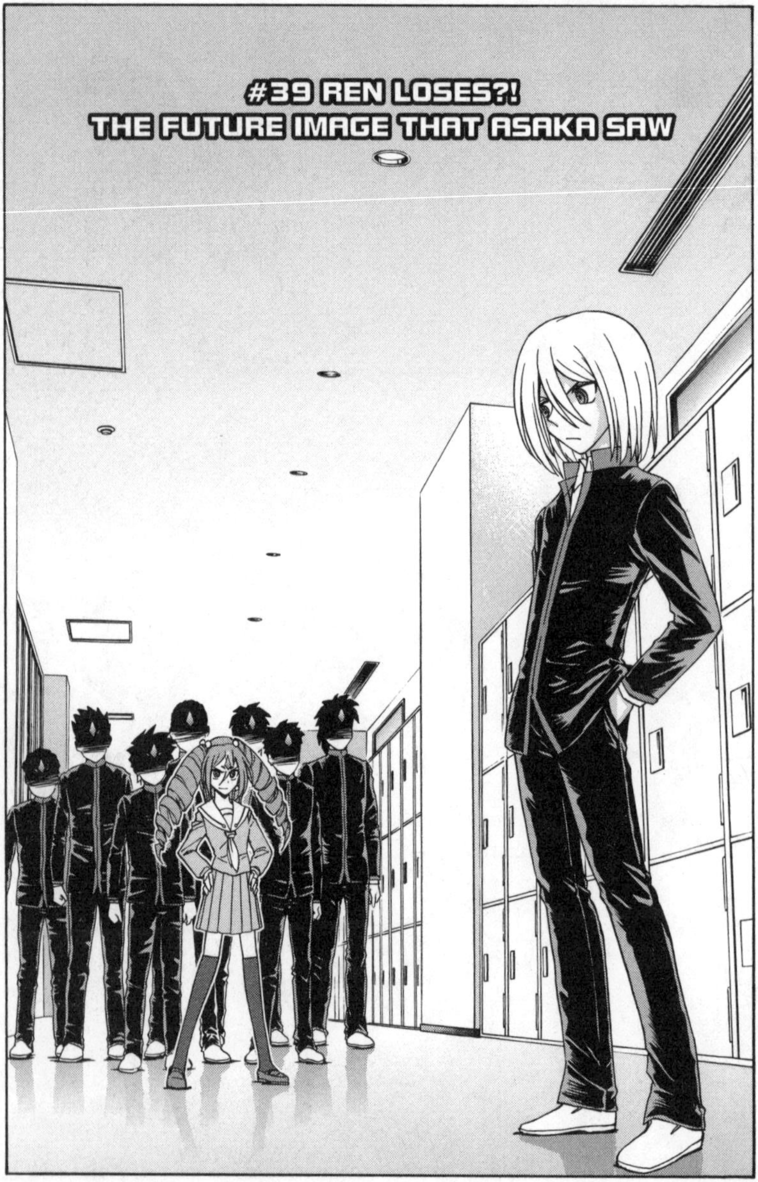
#39 REN LOSES?!
THE FUTURE IMAGE THAT ASAKA SAW

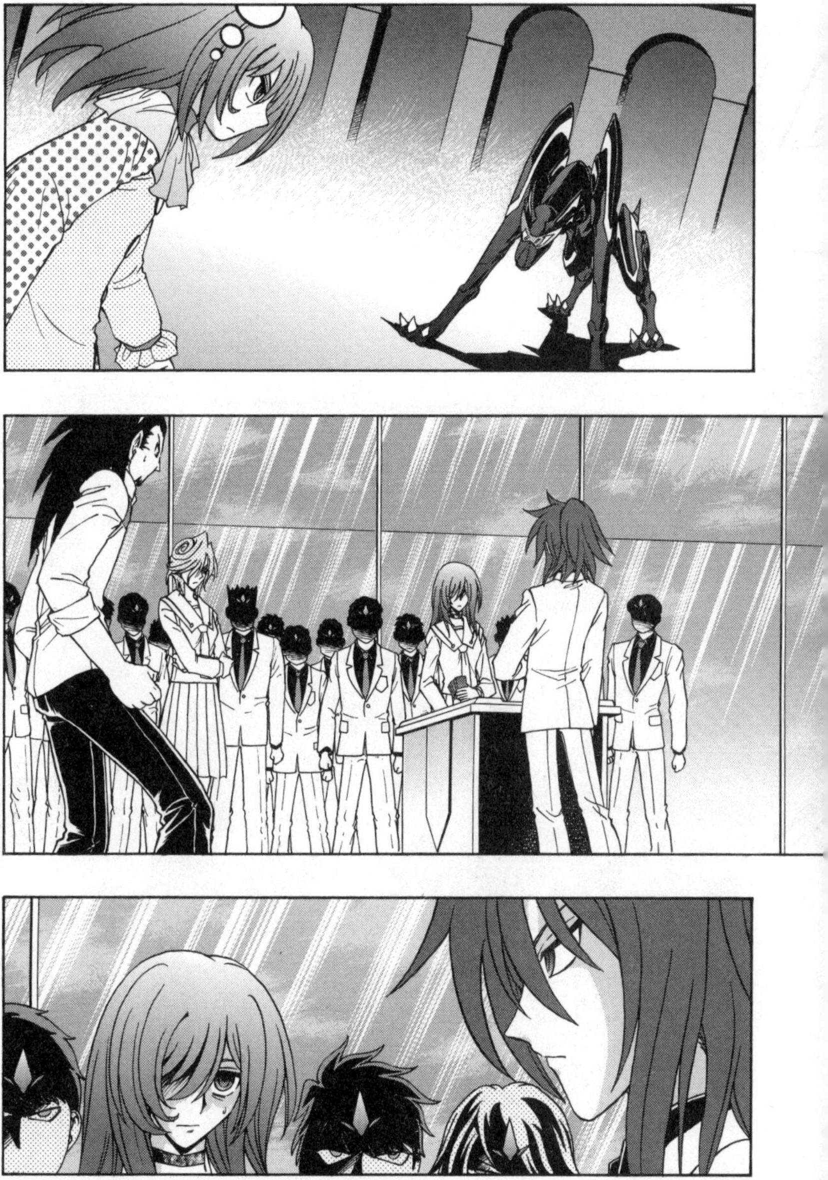

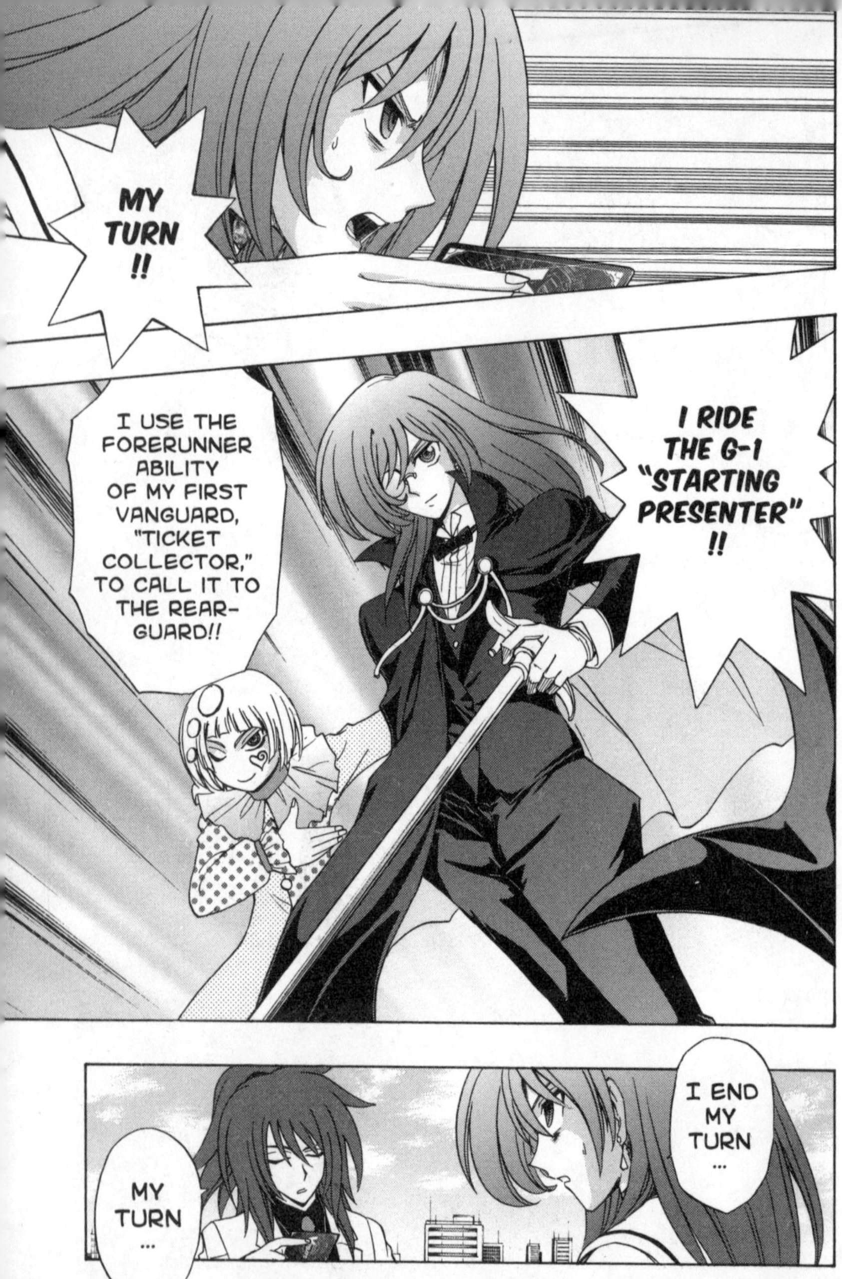
MY TURN !!
I RIDE THE G-1 "STARTING PRESENTER" !!
I USE THE FORERUNNER ABILITY OF MY FIRST VANGUARD, "TICKET COLLECTOR," TO CALL IT TO THE REAR-GUARD!!
I END MY TURN ...
MY TURN ...

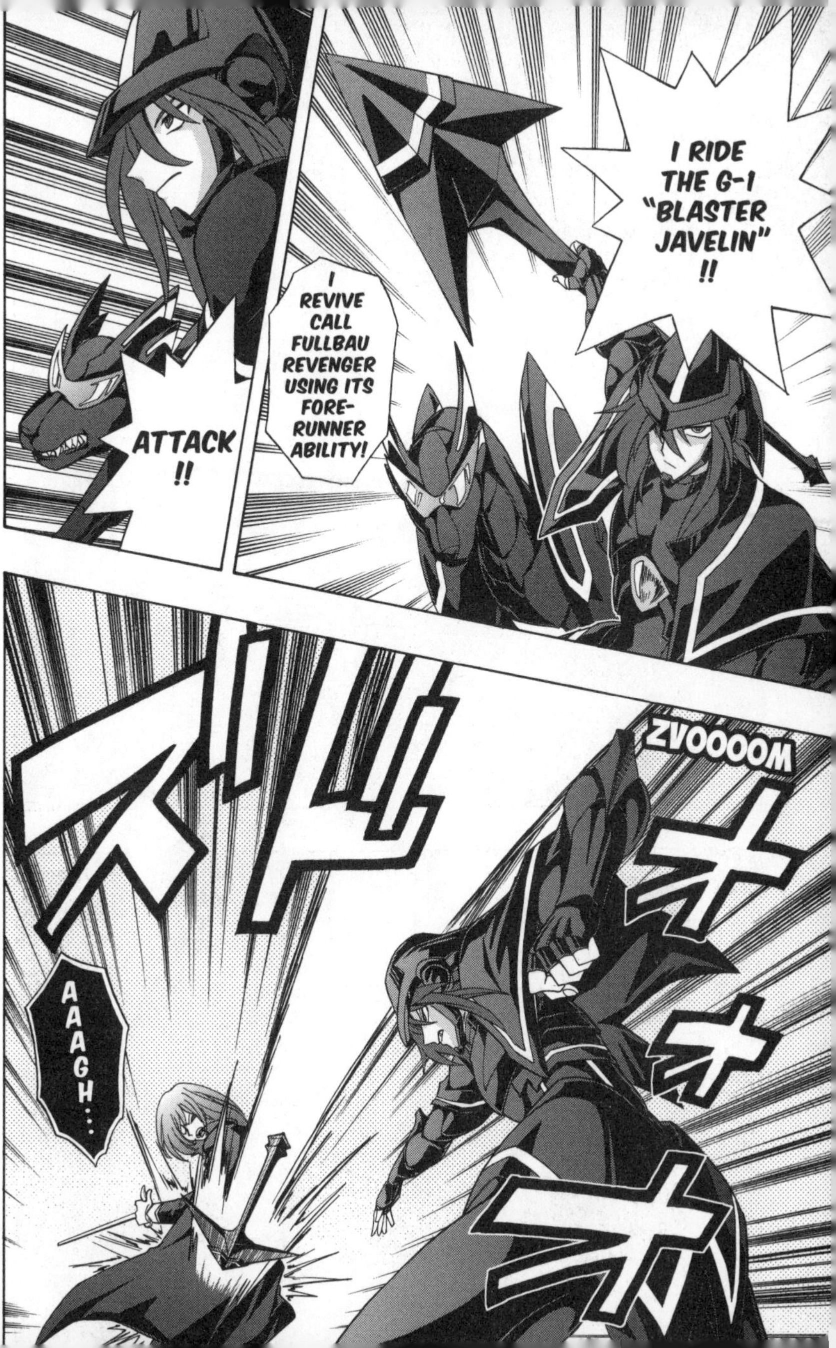
I RIDE THE G-1 "BLASTER JAVELIN" !!
I REVIVE CALL FULLBAU REVENGER USING ITS FORE-RUNNER ABILITY!
ATTACK !!
ZVOOOOM
AAAGH...

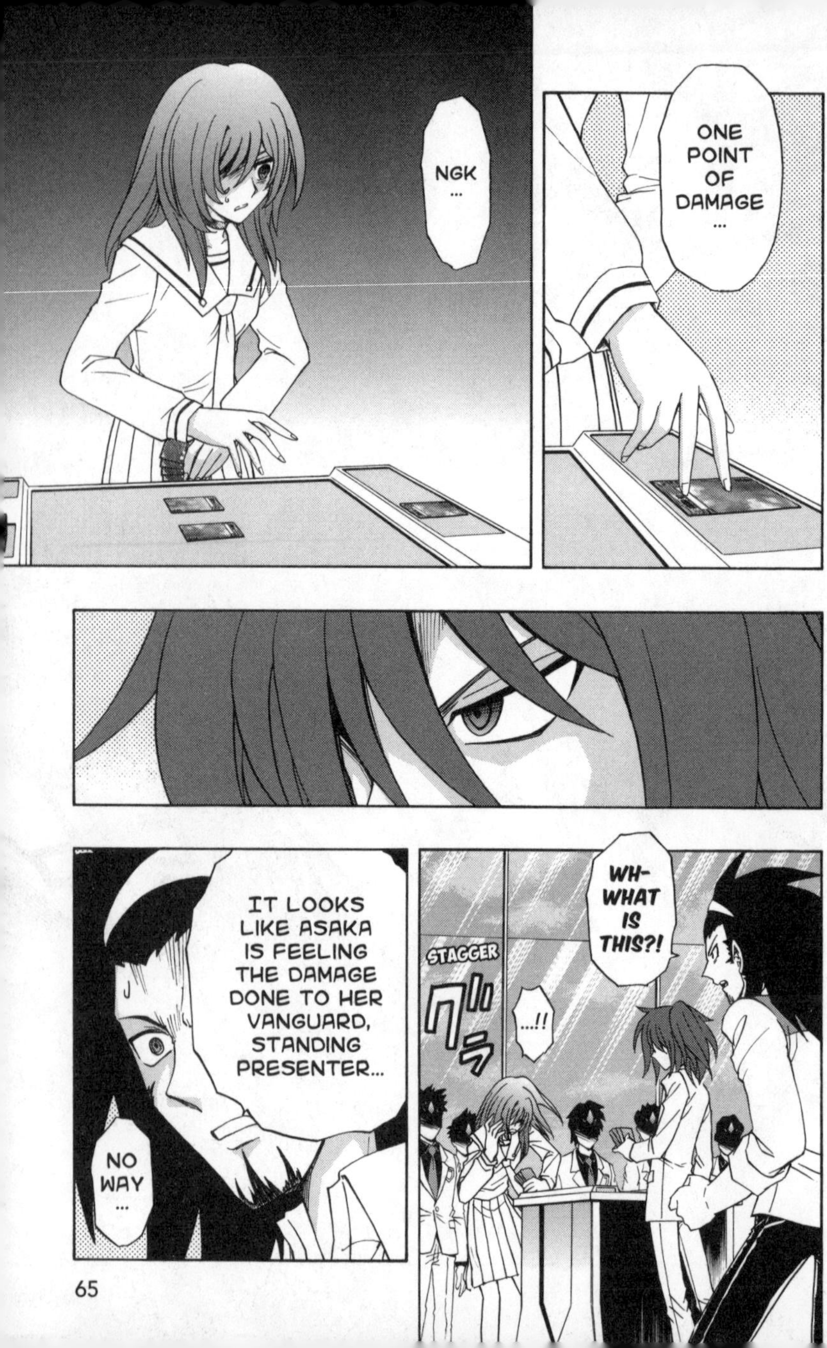
ONE POINT OF DAMAGE ...
NGK ...
WH- WHAT IS THIS?!
STAGGER
...!!
IT LOOKS LIKE ASAKA IS FEELING THE DAMAGE DONE TO HER VANGUARD, STANDING PRESENTER...
NO WAY ...

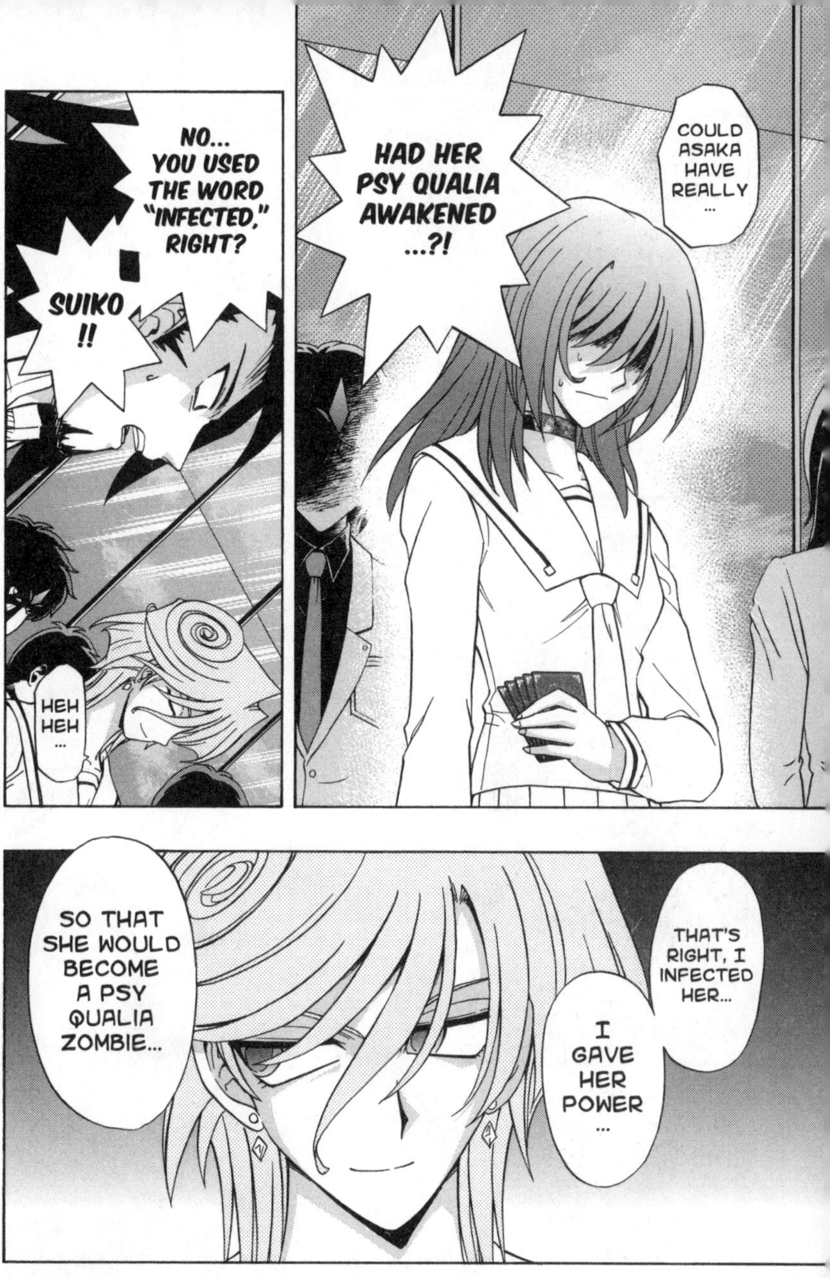
COULD ASAKA HAVE REALLY ...
HAD HER PSY QUALIA AWAKENED ...?!
NO... YOU USED THE WORD "INFECTED," RIGHT?
SUIKO !!
HEH HEH ...
THAT'S RIGHT, I INFECTED HER...
I GAVE HER POWER ...
SO THAT SHE WOULD BECOME A PSY QUALIA ZOMBIE...

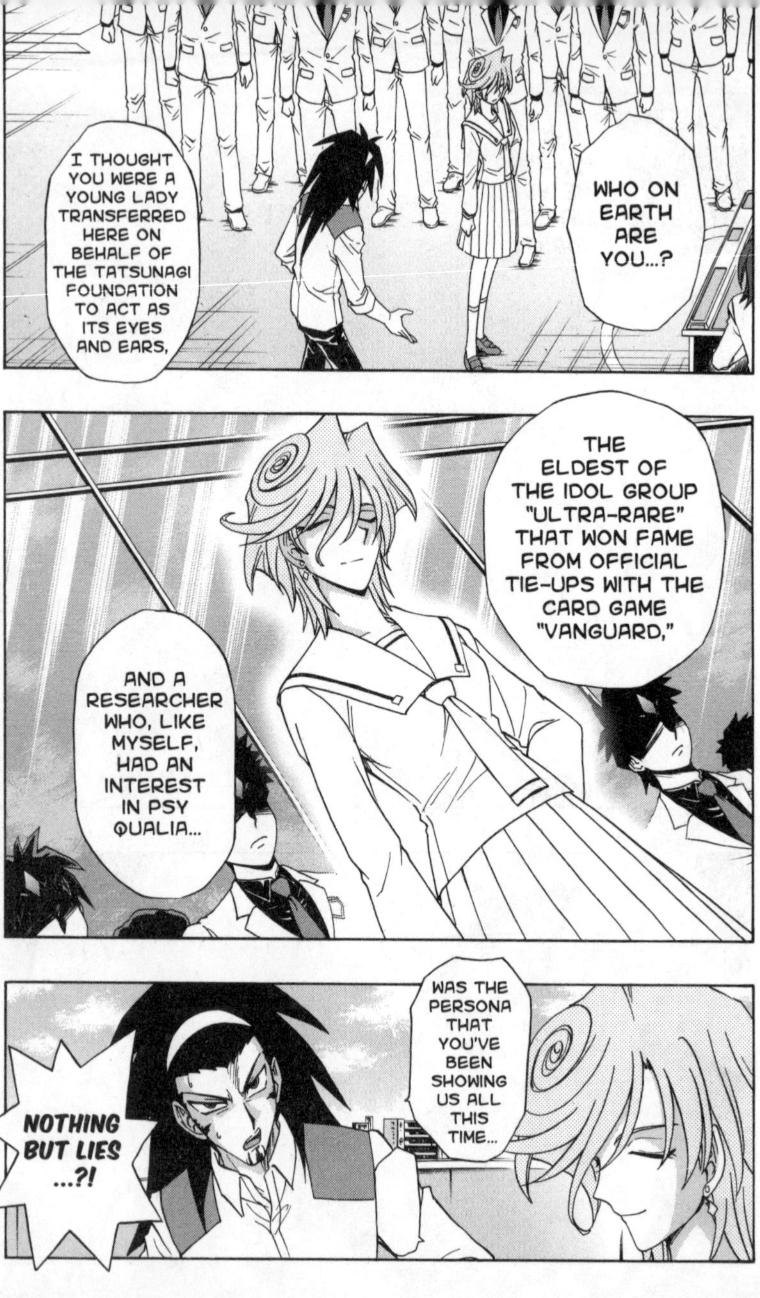
WHO ON EARTH ARE YOU...?
I THOUGHT YOU WERE A YOUNG LADY TRANSFERRED HERE ON BEHALF OF THE TATSUNAGI FOUNDATION TO ACT AS ITS EYES AND EARS,
THE ELDEST OF THE IDOL GROUP "ULTRA-RARE" THAT WON FAME FROM OFFICIAL TIE-UPS WITH THE CARD GAME "VANGUARD,"
AND A RESEARCHER WHO, LIKE MYSELF, HAD AN INTEREST IN PSY QUALIA...
WAS THE PERSONA THAT YOU'VE BEEN SHOWING US ALL THIS TIME...
NOTHING BUT LIES ...?!

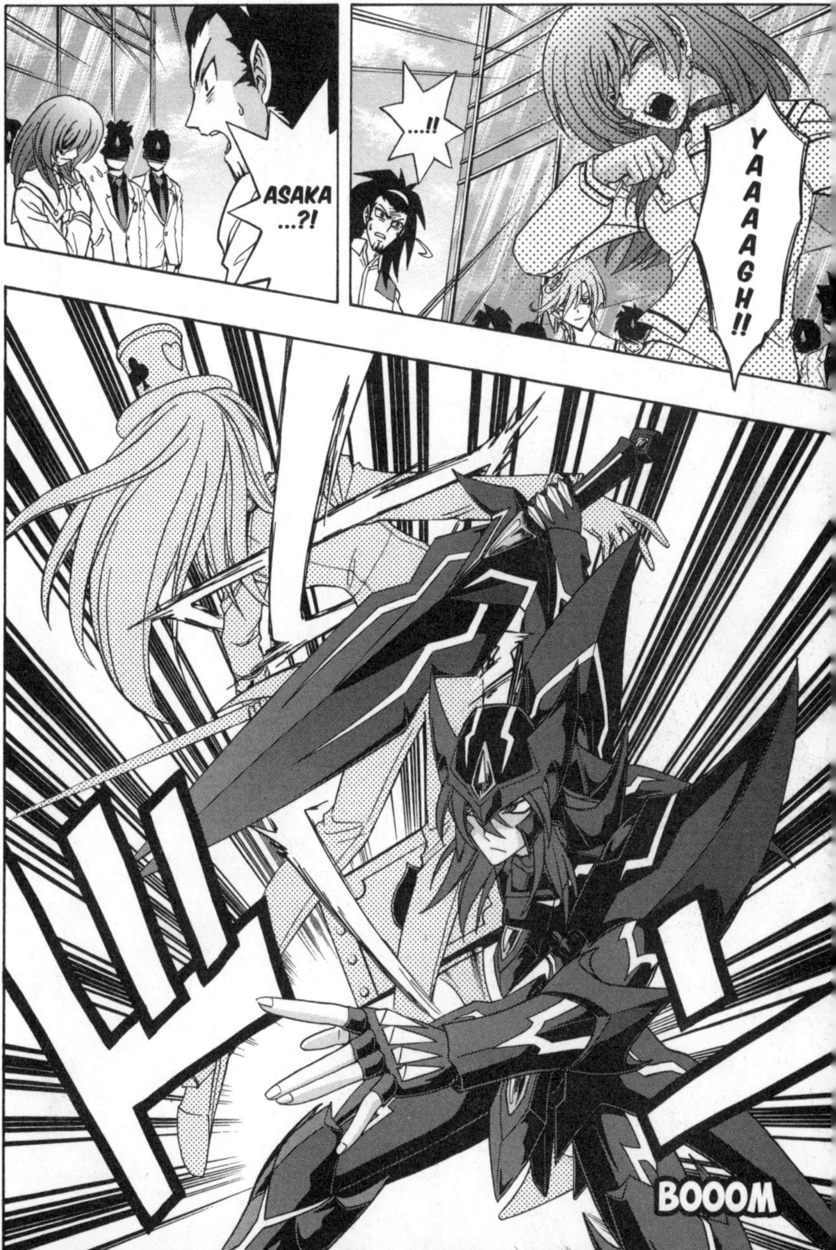
YAAAAAGH!!
...!!
ASAKA ...?!
BOOOM

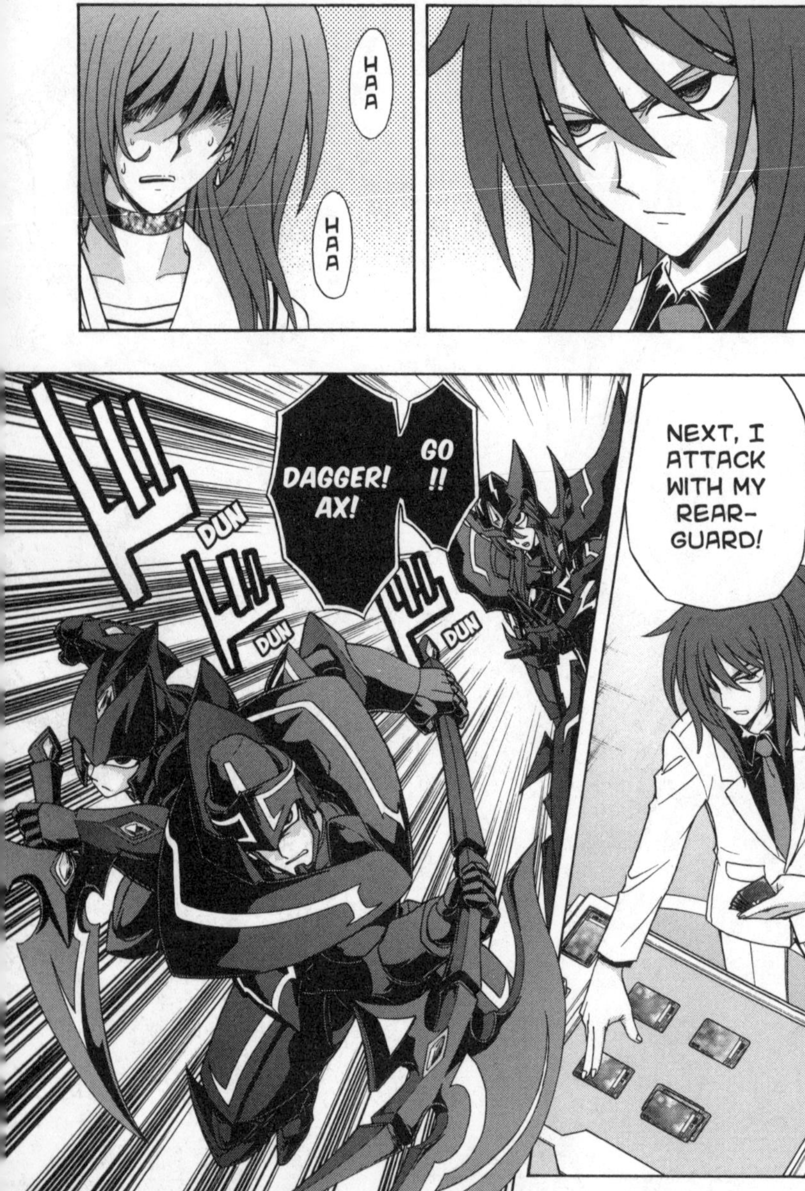
HAA
HAA
NEXT, I ATTACK WITH MY REAR-GUARD!
GO !!
DAGGER! AX!
DUN
DUN
DUN

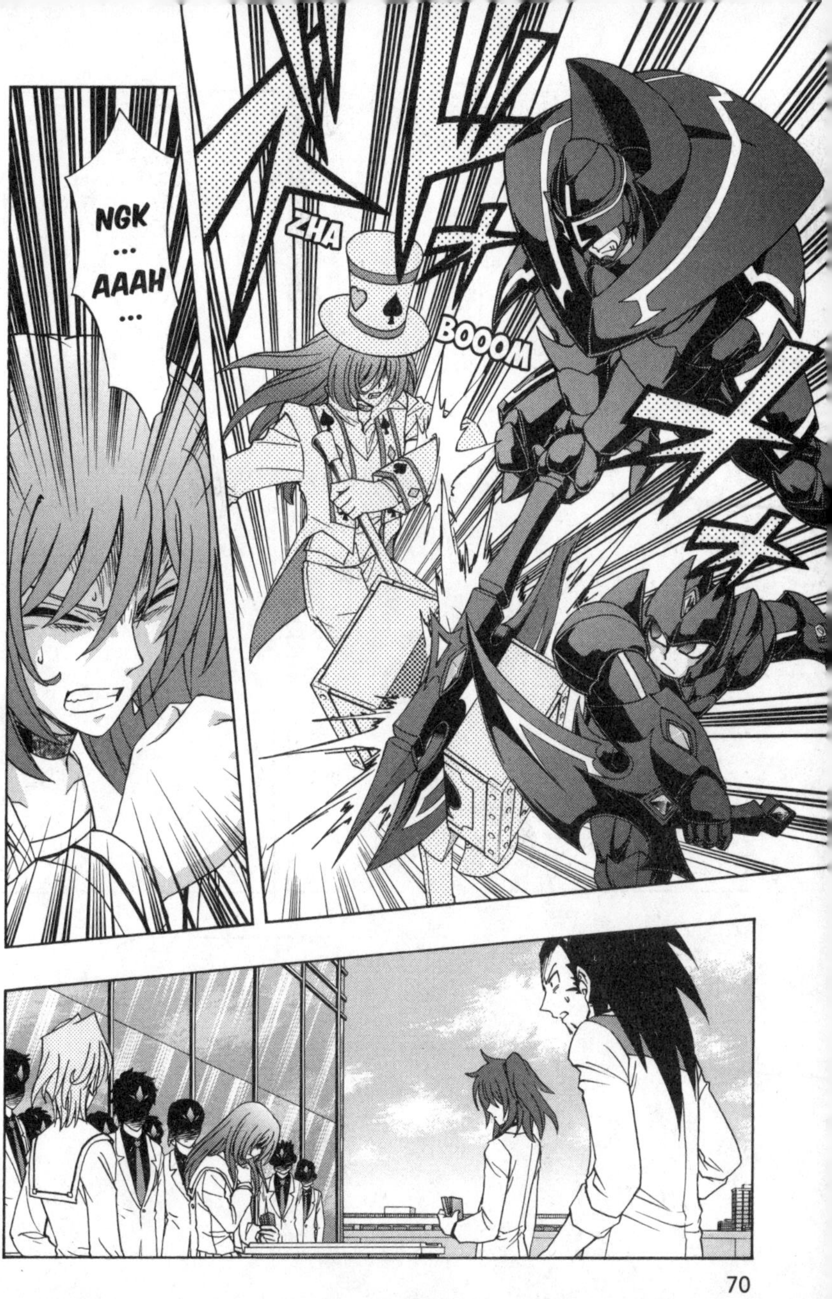
ZHA
BOOOM
NGK ... AAAH ...

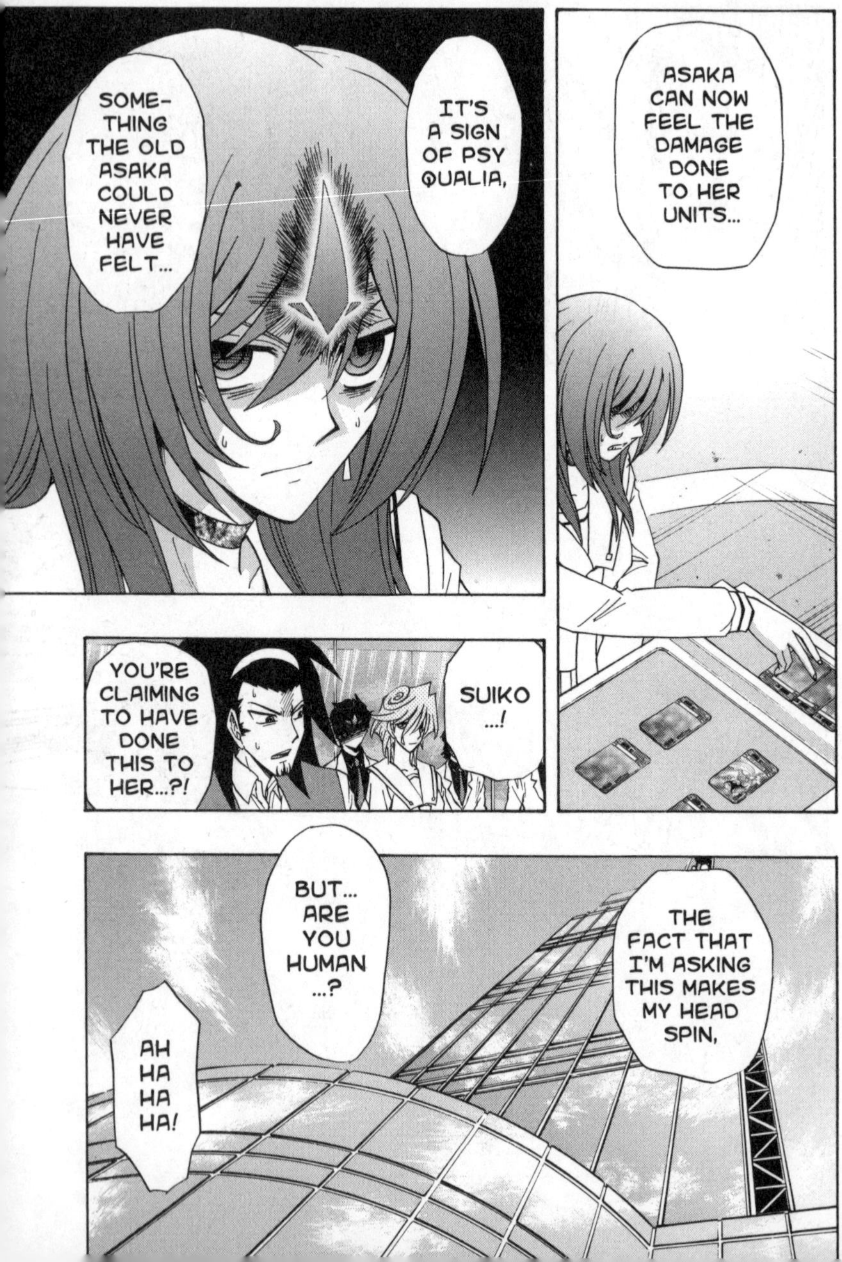
ASAKA CAN NOW FEEL THE DAMAGE DONE TO HER UNITS...
IT'S A SIGN OF PSY QUALIA,
SOME-THING THE OLD ASAKA COULD NEVER HAVE FELT...
SUIKO ...!
YOU'RE CLAIMING TO HAVE DONE THIS TO HER...?!
THE FACT THAT I'M ASKING THIS MAKES MY HEAD SPIN,
BUT... ARE YOU HUMAN ...?
AH HA HA HA!

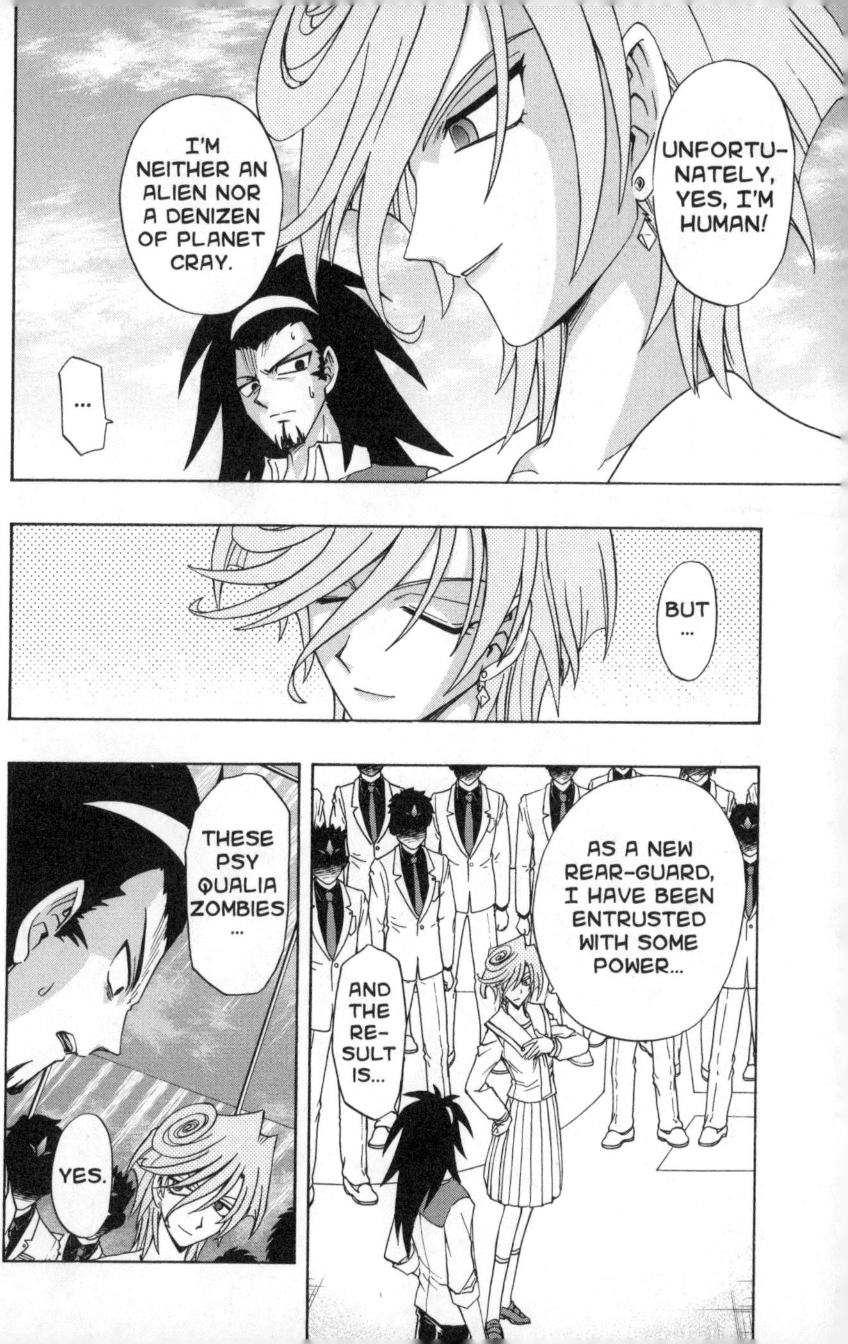
UNFORTUNATELY, YES, I'M HUMAN!
I'M NEITHER AN ALIEN NOR A DENIZEN OF PLANET CRAY.
...
BUT ...
AS A NEW REAR-GUARD, I HAVE BEEN ENTRUSTED WITH SOME POWER...
AND THE RESULT IS...
THESE PSY QUALIA ZOMBIES ...
YES.

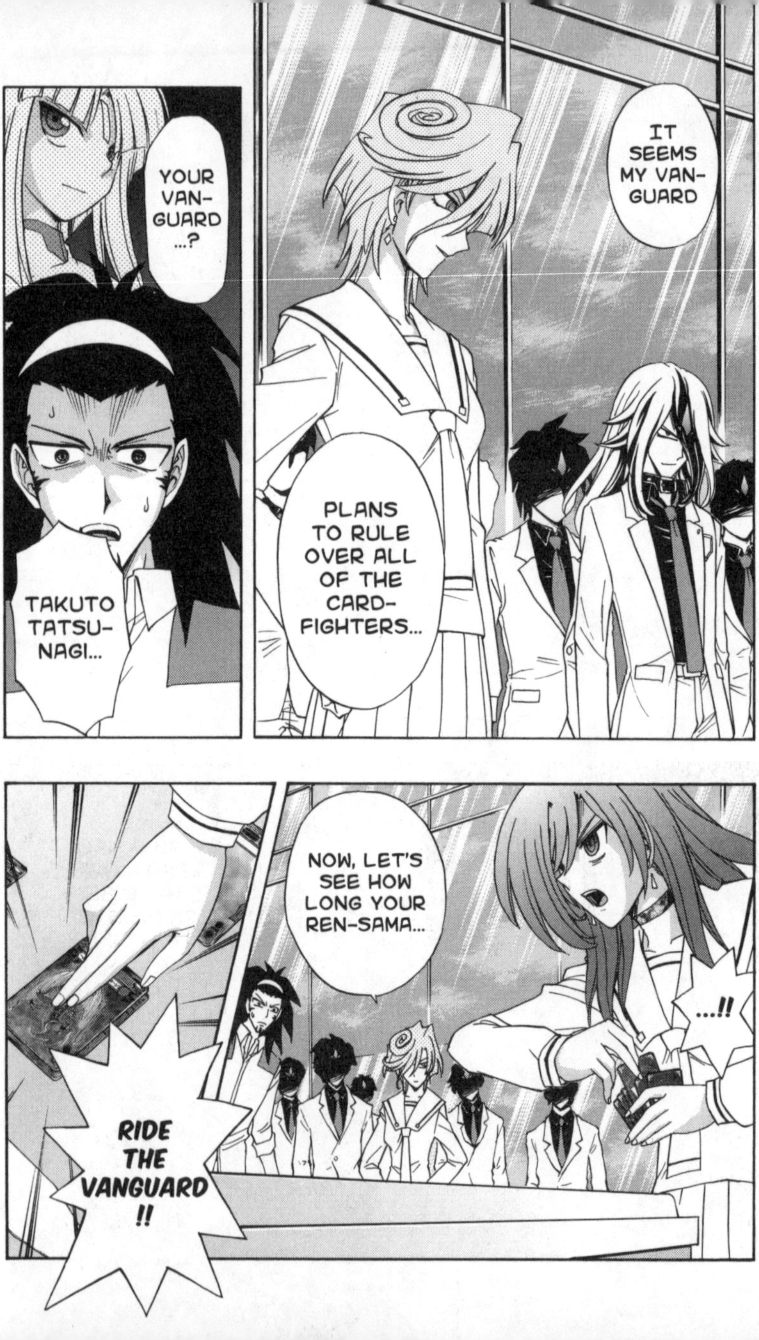
IT SEEMS MY VAN-GUARD
PLANS TO RULE OVER ALL OF THE CARD-FIGHTERS...
YOUR VAN-GUARD ...?
TAKUTO TATSU-NAGI...
NOW, LET'S SEE HOW LONG YOUR REN-SAMA...
...!!
RIDE THE VANGUARD !!

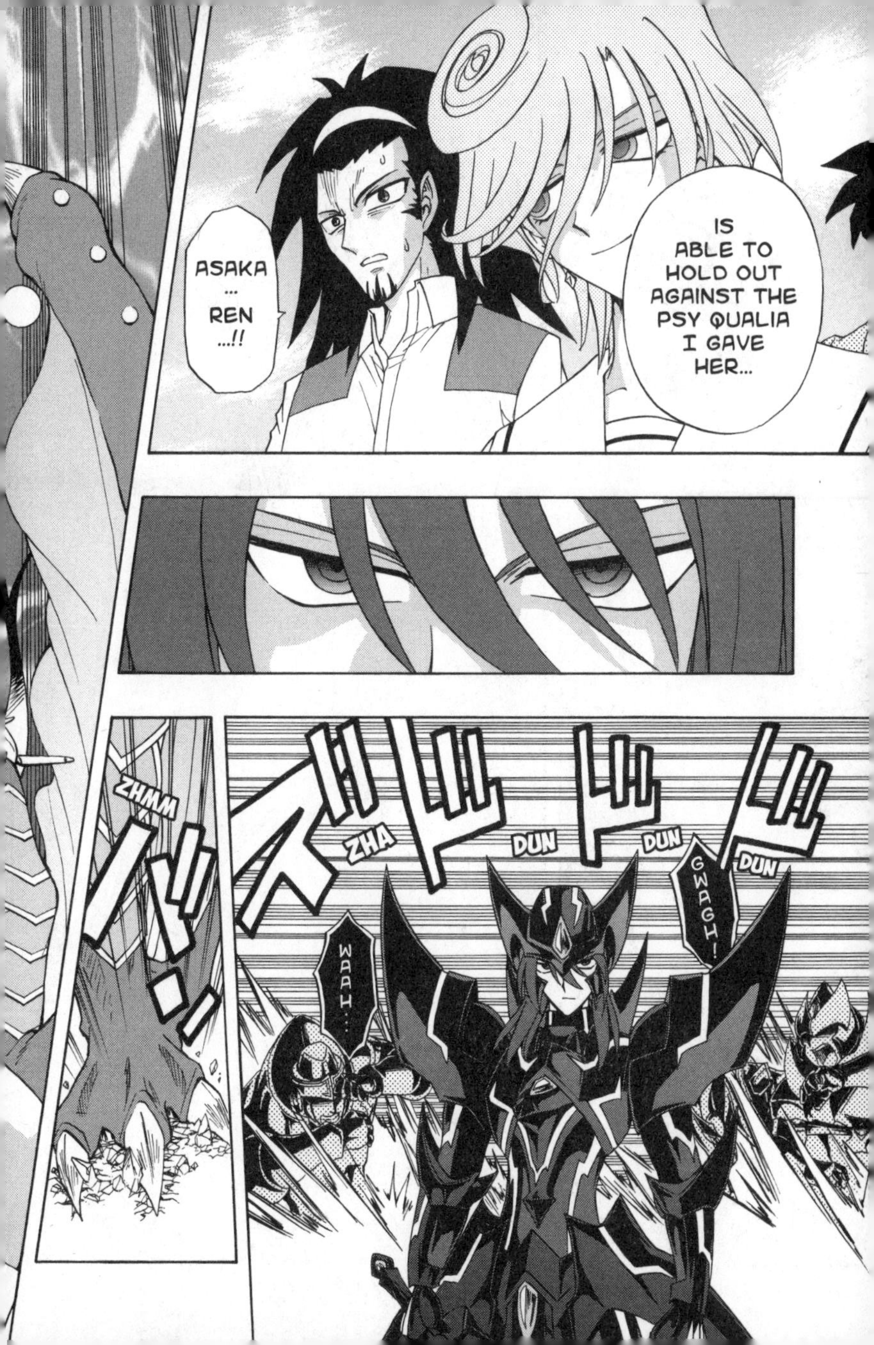
IS ABLE TO HOLD OUT AGAINST THE PSY QUALIA I GAVE HER...
ASAKA ... REN ...!!
DUN
GWAGH!
DUN
DUN
ZHA
WAAAH...
ZHMM

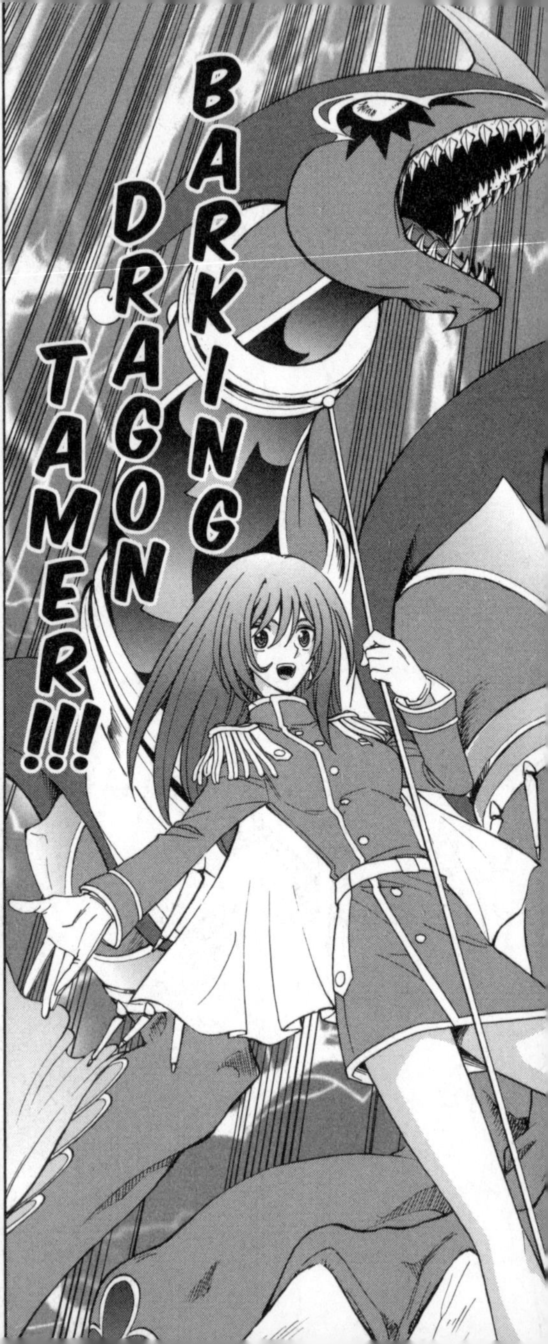
BARKING DRAGON TAMER!!!

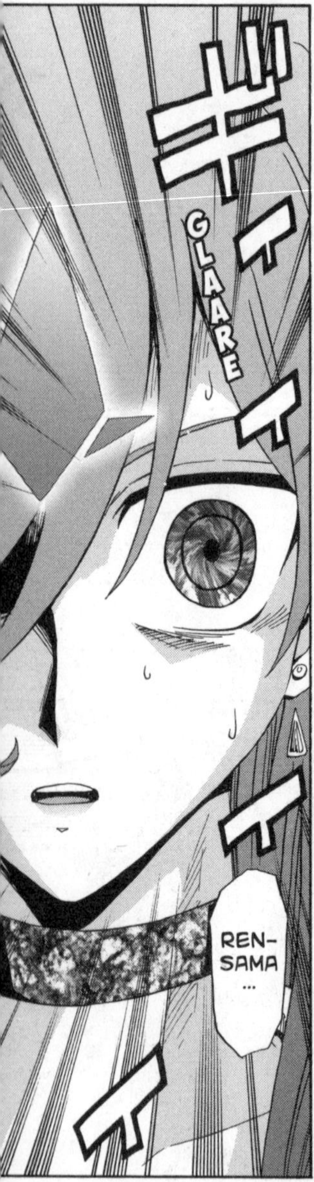
GLAARE
REN-SAMA ...

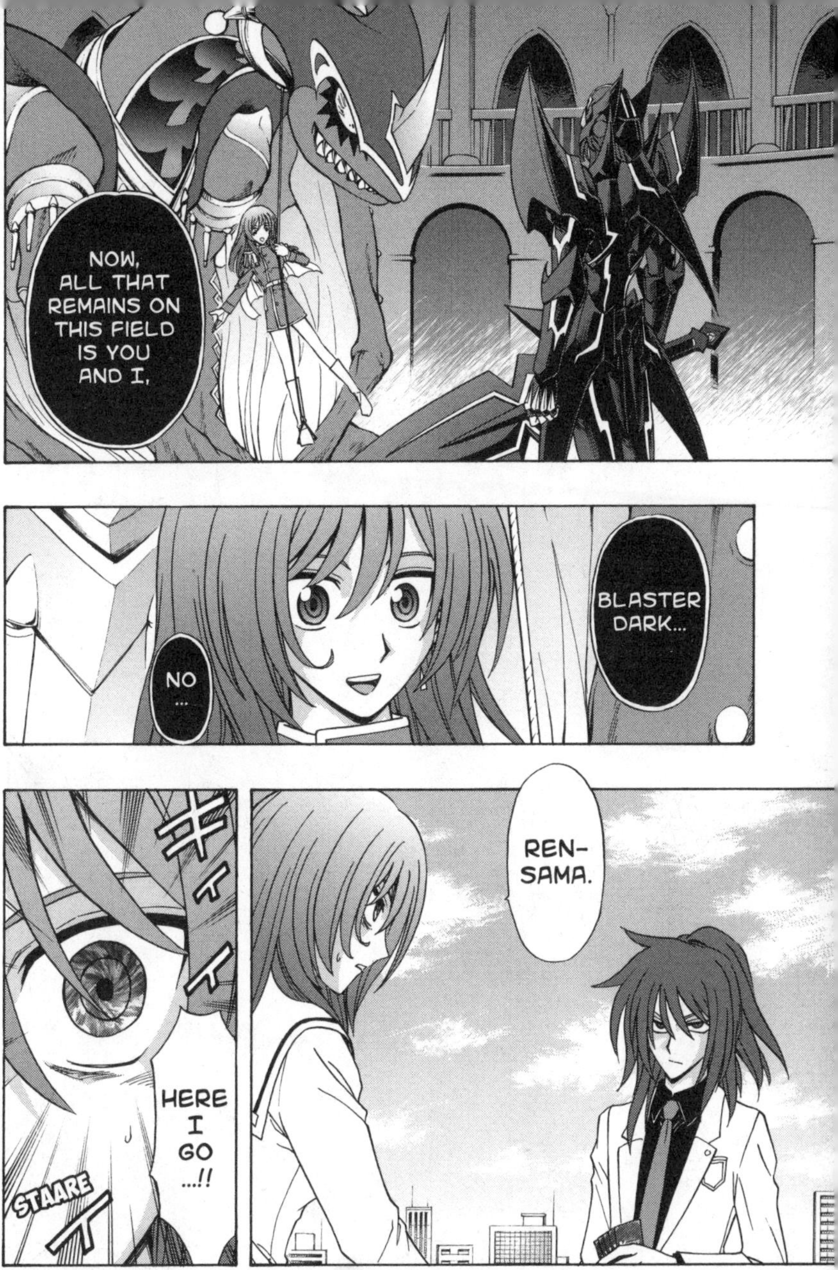
NOW, ALL THAT REMAINS ON THIS FIELD IS YOU AND I,
BLASTER DARK...
NO ...
REN-SAMA.
HERE I GO ...!!
STAARE

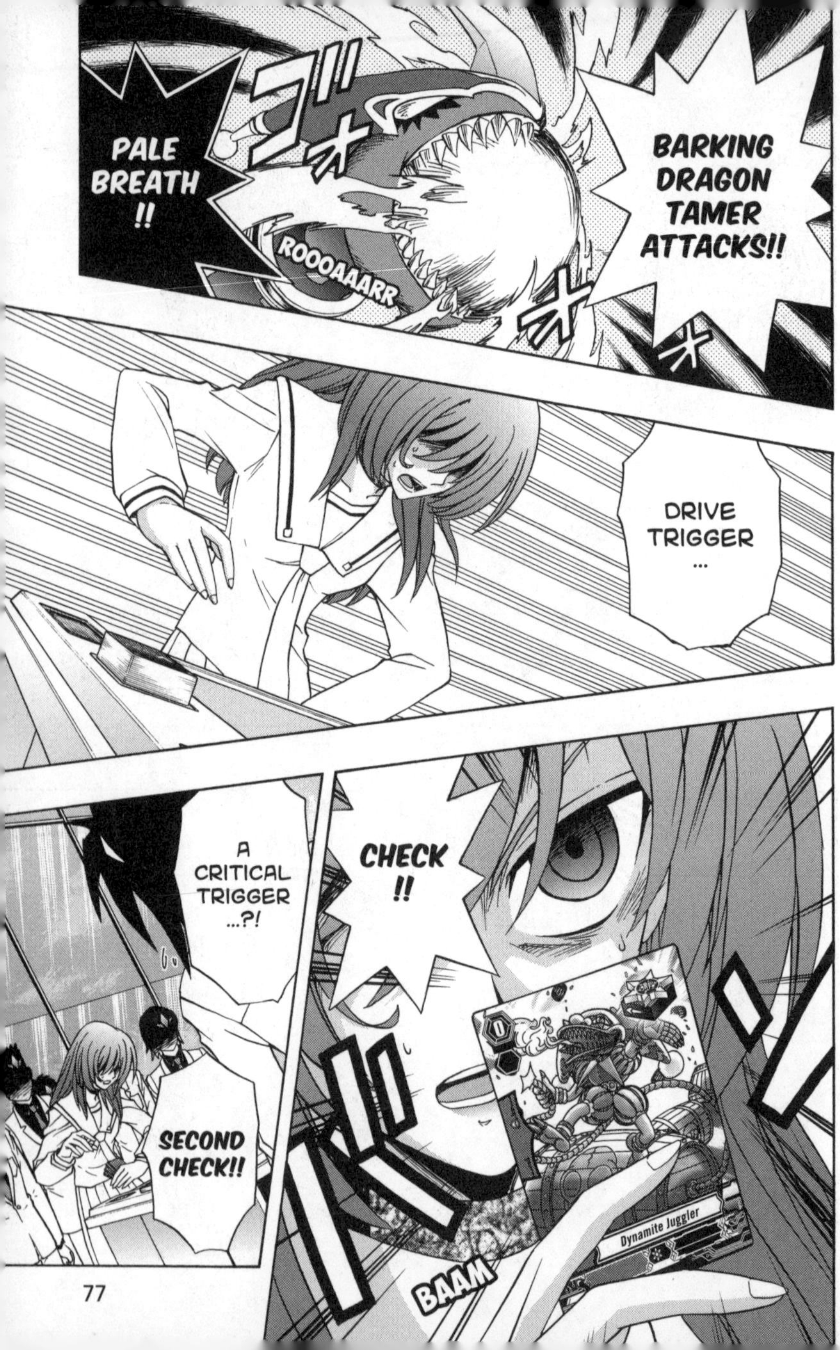

BARKING DRAGON TAMER ATTACKS!!
ROOOAAARR
PALE BREATH!!
DRIVE TRIGGER...
CHECK!!
Dynamite Juggler
BAAM
A CRITICAL TRIGGER...?!
SECOND CHECK!!

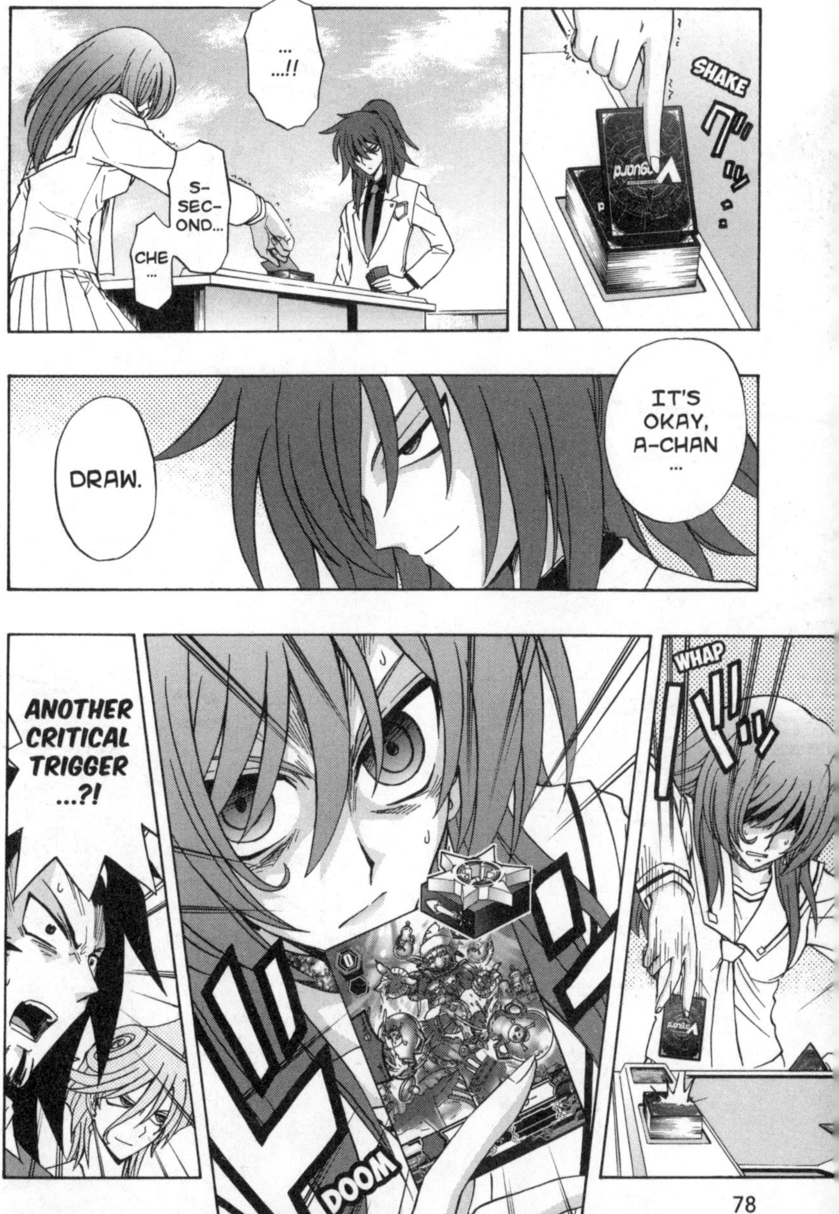
SHAKE
...
...!!
S-SECOND...
CHE ...
IT'S OKAY, A-CHAN ...
DRAW.
WHAP
DOOM
ANOTHER CRITICAL TRIGGER ...?!

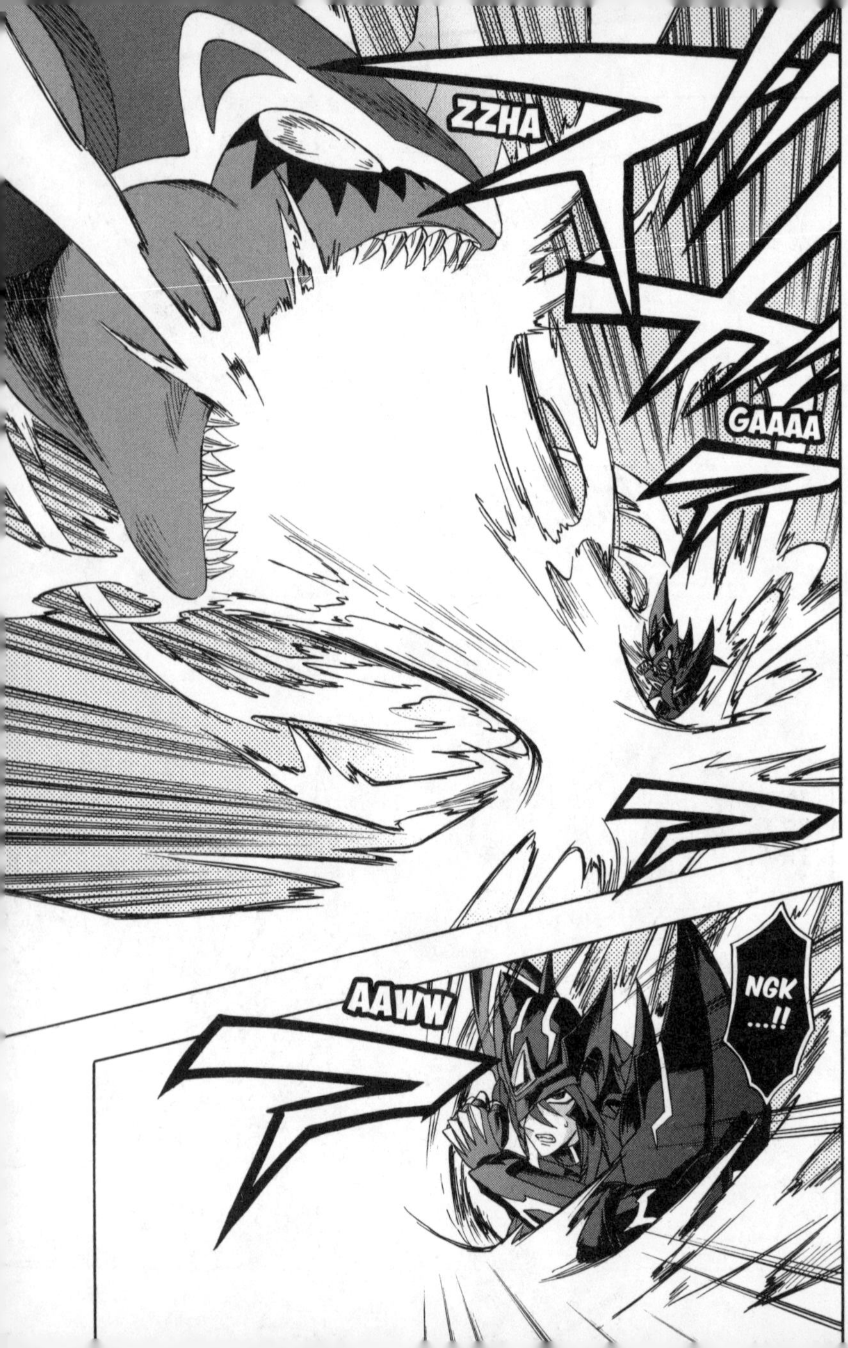
ZZHA
GAAAA
NGK ...!!
AAWW

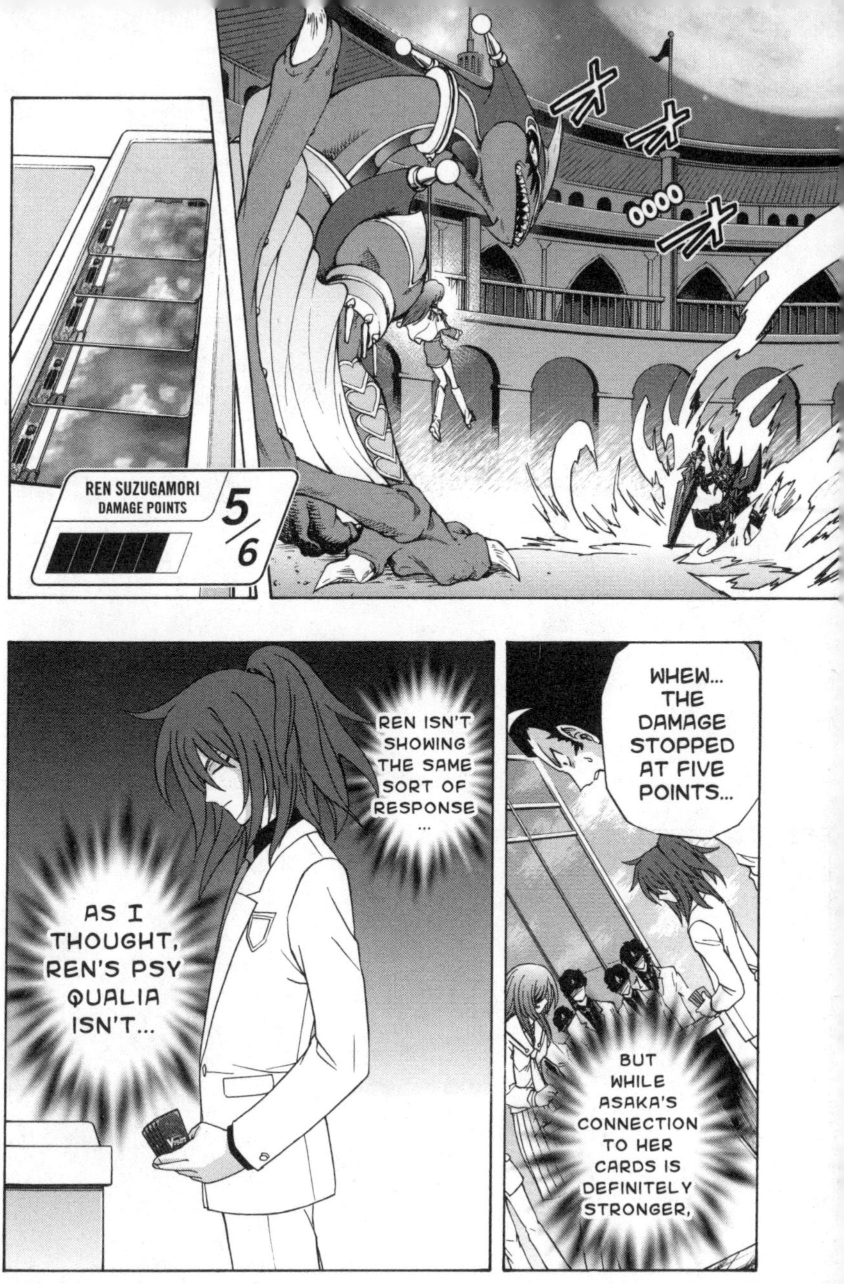

オオオ
OOOO
REN SUZUGAMORI
DAMAGE POINTS
5/6
WHEW... THE DAMAGE STOPPED AT FIVE POINTS...
BUT WHILE ASAKA'S CONNECTION TO HER CARDS IS DEFINITELY STRONGER,
REN ISN'T SHOWING THE SAME SORT OF RESPONSE ...
AS I THOUGHT, REN'S PSY QUALIA ISN'T...

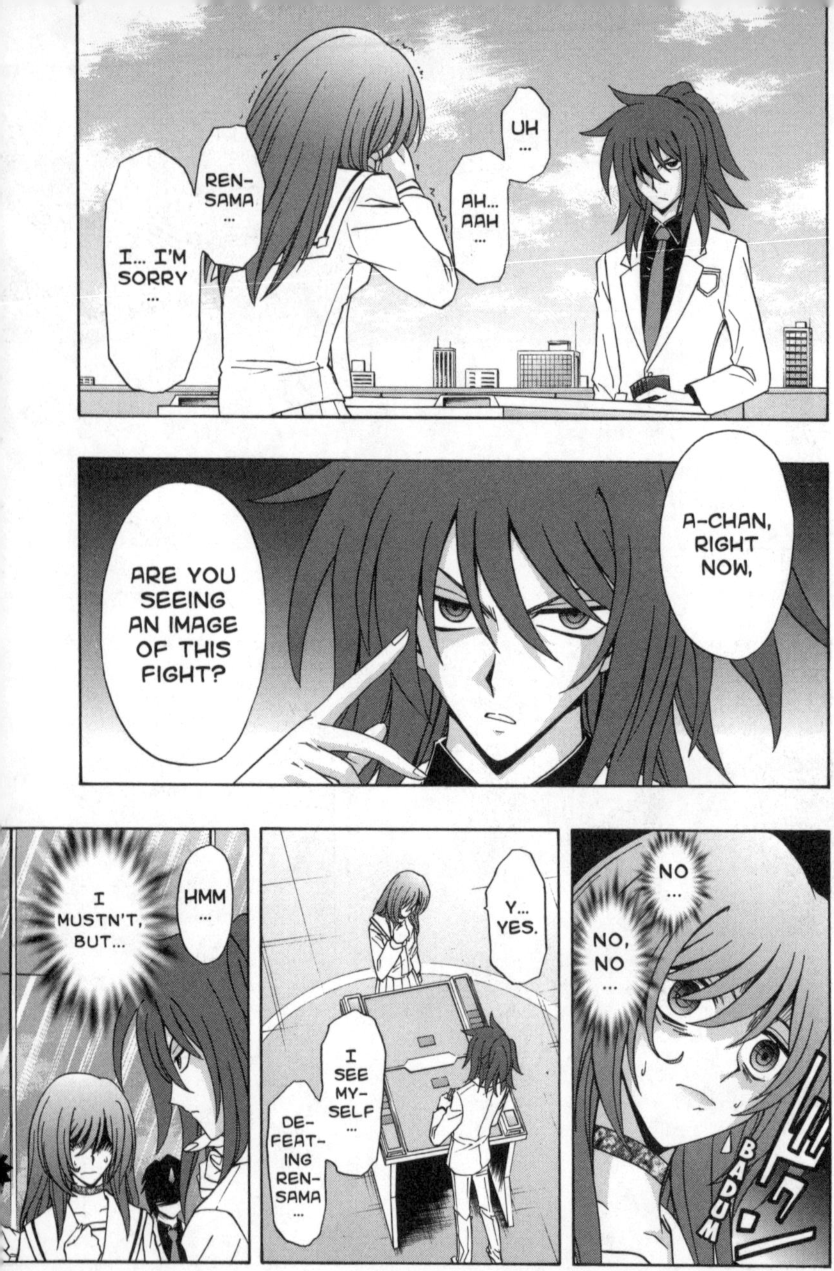
UH ...
AH... AAH ...
REN-SAMA ...
I... I'M SORRY ...
A-CHAN, RIGHT NOW,
ARE YOU SEEING AN IMAGE OF THIS FIGHT?
NO ...
NO, NO ...
BADUM
Y... YES.
I SEE MYSELF ...
DEFEATING REN-SAMA ...
HMM ...
I MUSTN'T, BUT...

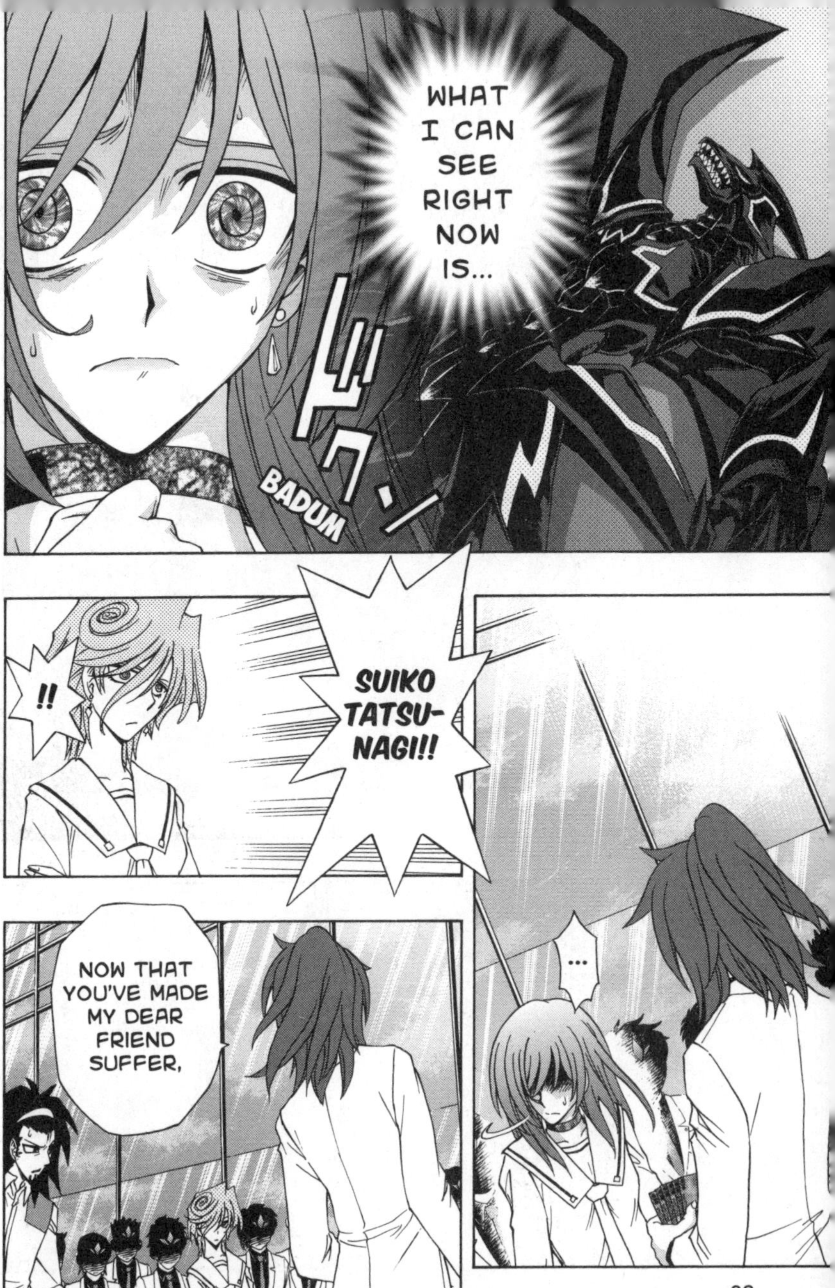
WHAT I CAN SEE RIGHT NOW IS...
BADUM
...
SUIKO TATSUNAGI!!
!!
NOW THAT YOU'VE MADE MY DEAR FRIEND SUFFER,

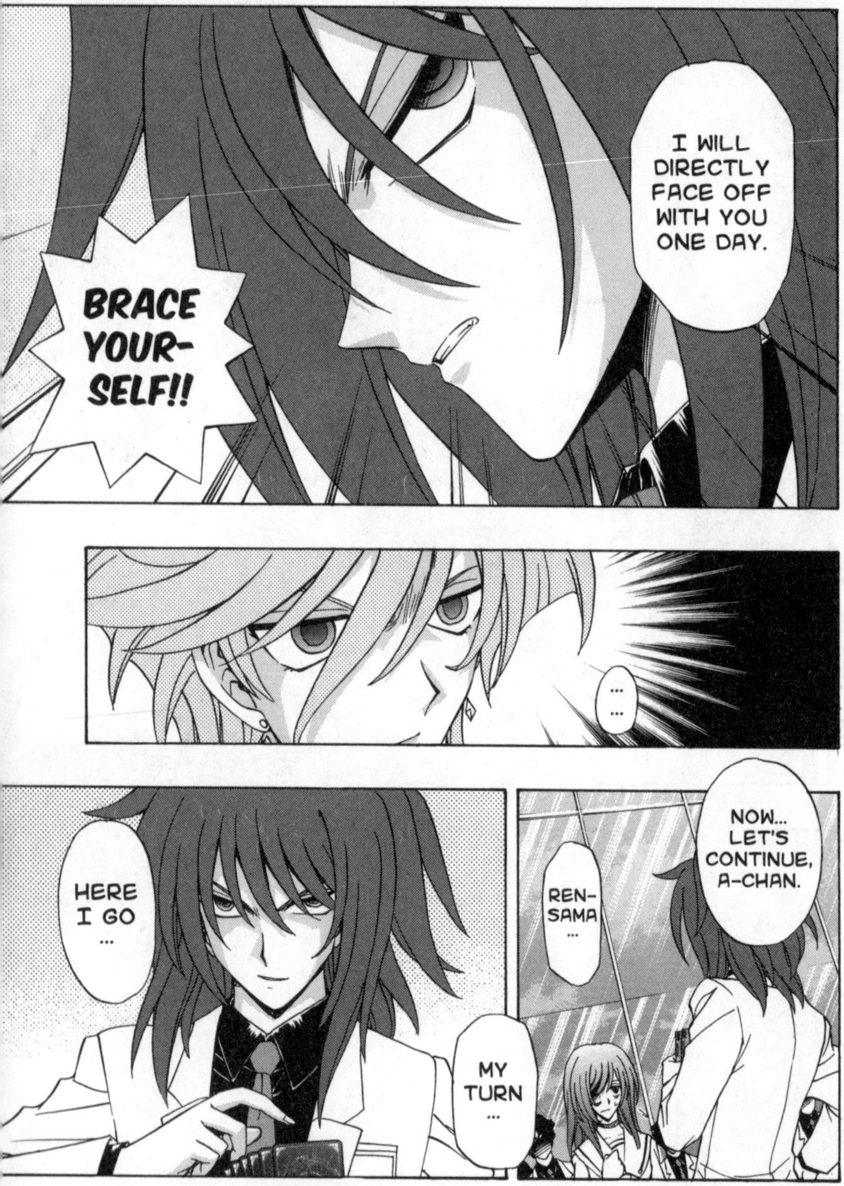
I WILL DIRECTLY FACE OFF WITH YOU ONE DAY.
BRACE YOUR-SELF!!
... ...
NOW... LET'S CONTINUE, A-CHAN.
REN-SAMA ...
HERE I GO ...
MY TURN ...

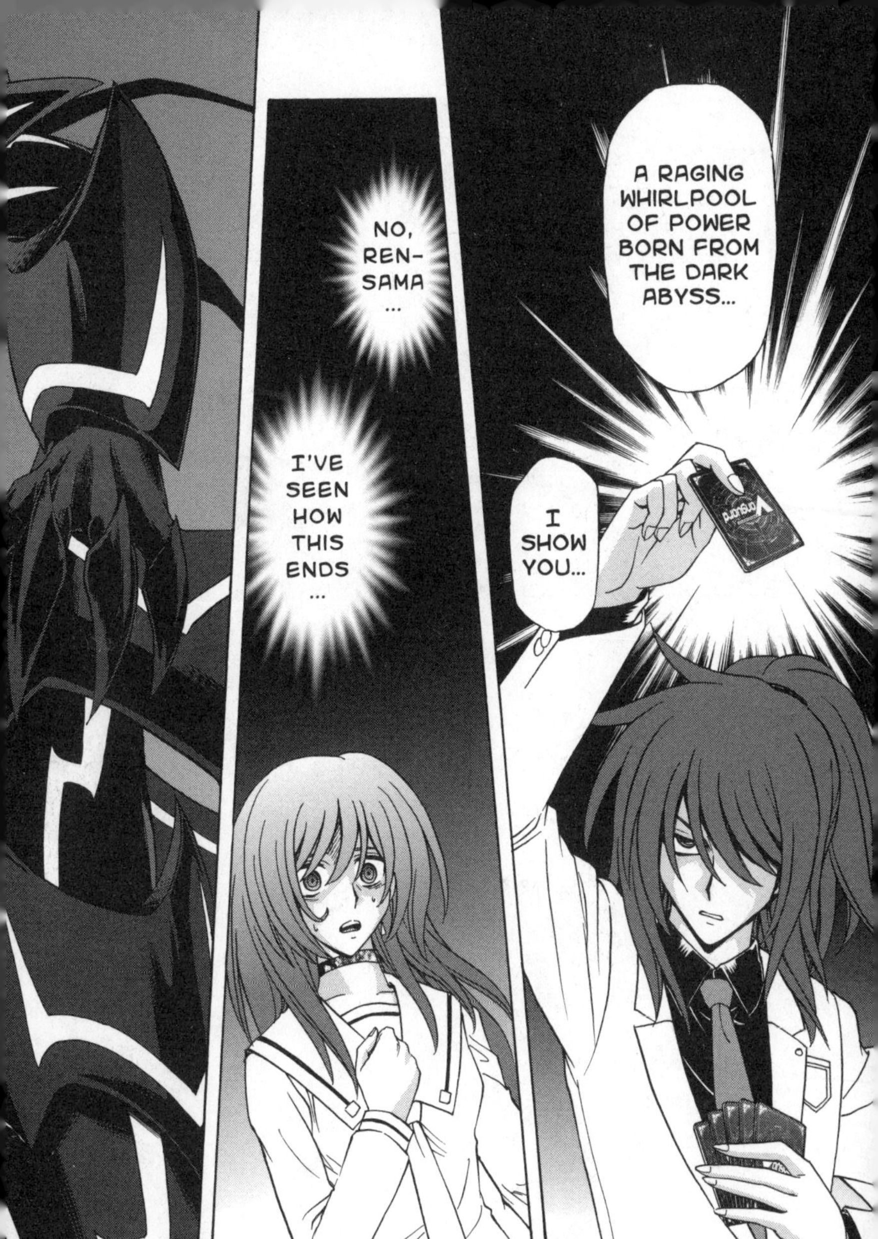
I SHOW YOU...
A RAGING WHIRLPOOL OF POWER BORN FROM THE DARK ABYSS...
NO, REN-SAMA...
I'VE SEEN HOW THIS ENDS...

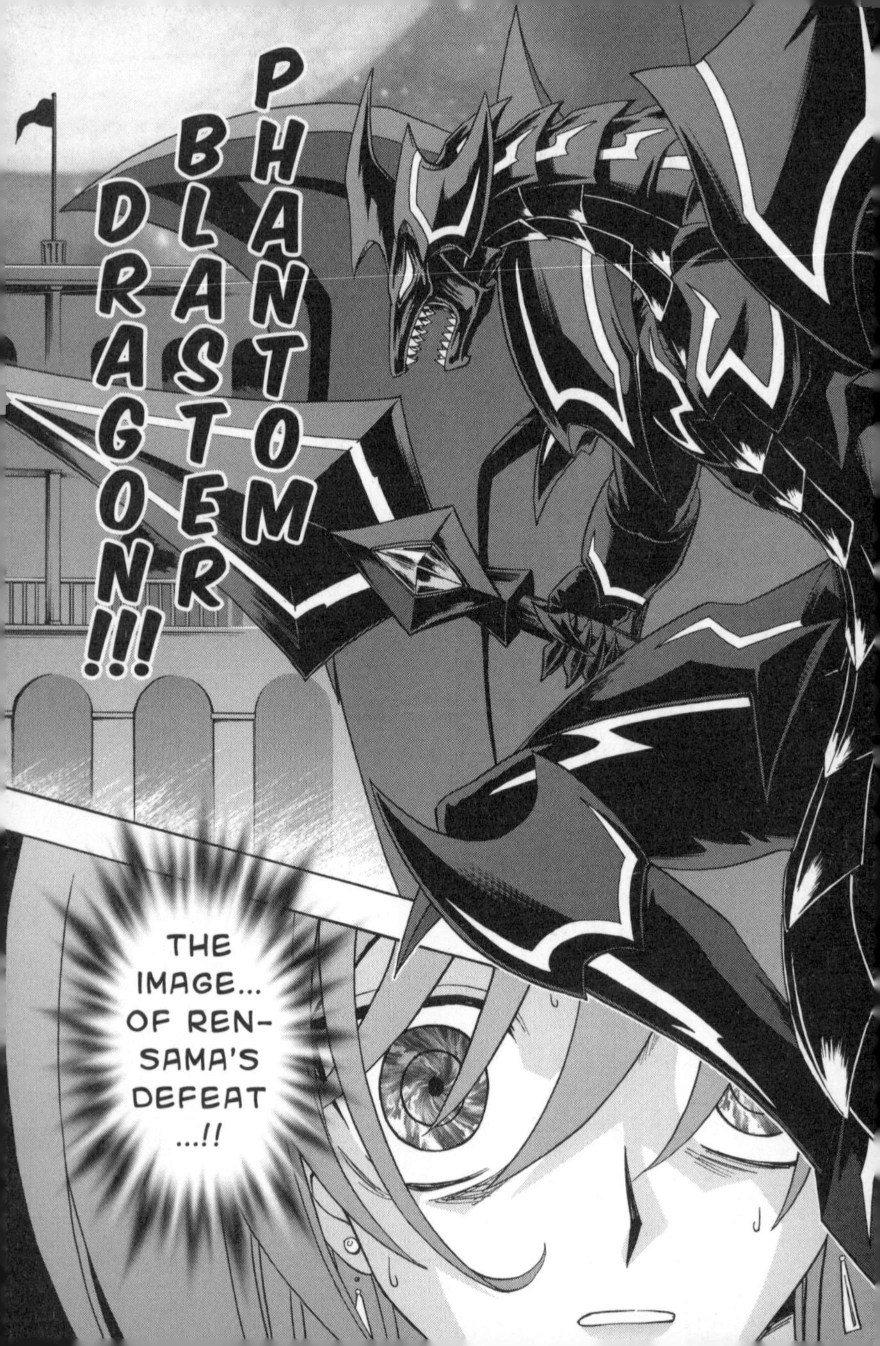
PHANTOM BLASTER DRAGON!!!
THE IMAGE... OF REN-SAMA'S DEFEAT ...!!

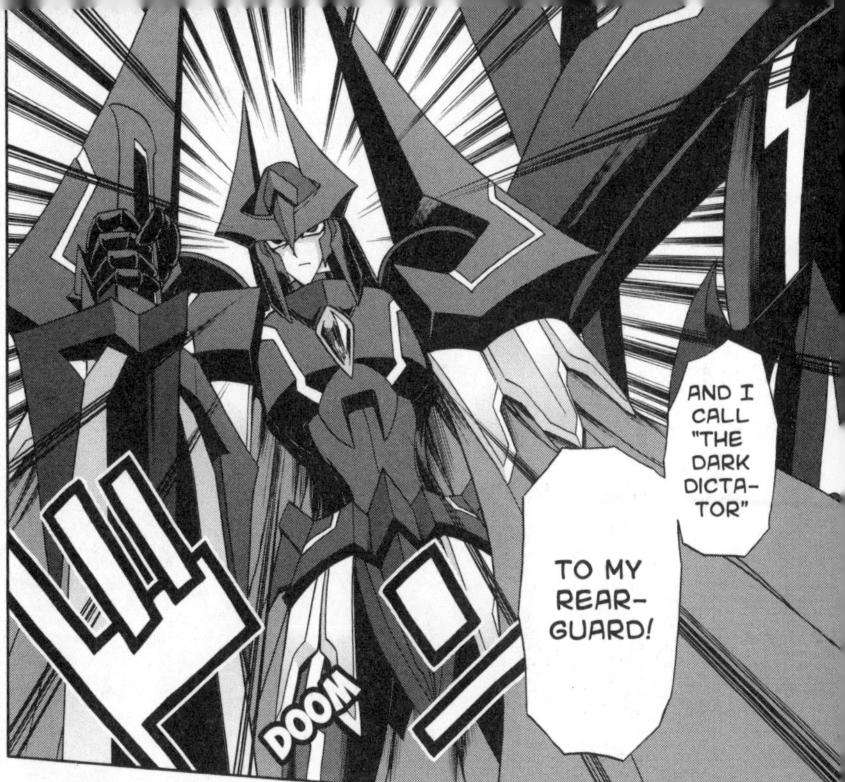
AND I CALL "THE DARK DICTATOR"
TO MY REAR-GUARD!
DOOM

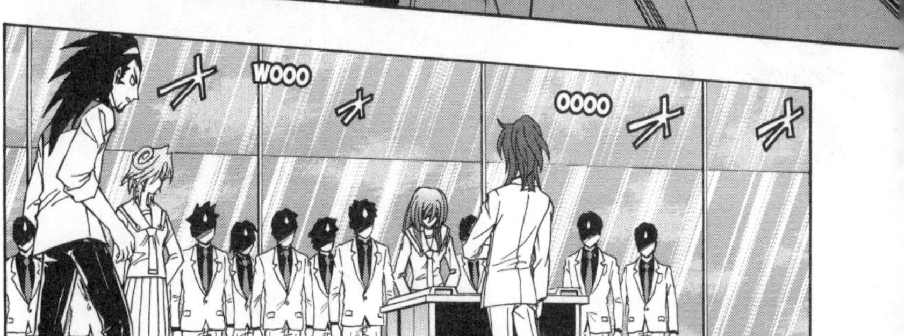
OOOO
WOOO

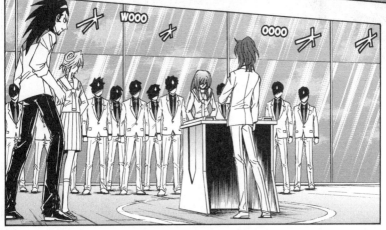

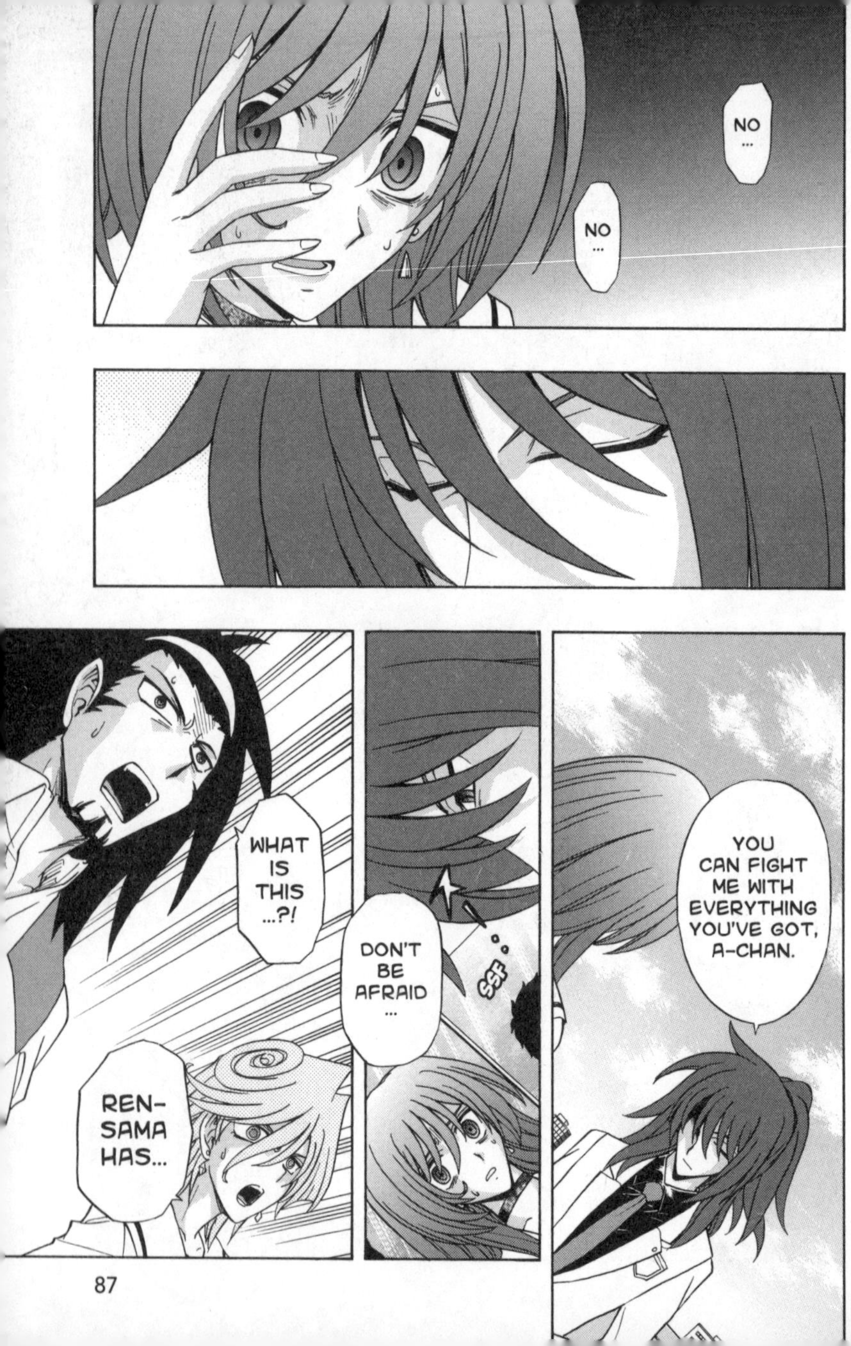
NO ...
NO ...
YOU CAN FIGHT ME WITH EVERYTHING YOU'VE GOT, A-CHAN.
SSF
DON'T BE AFRAID ...
WHAT IS THIS ...?!
REN-SAMA HAS...

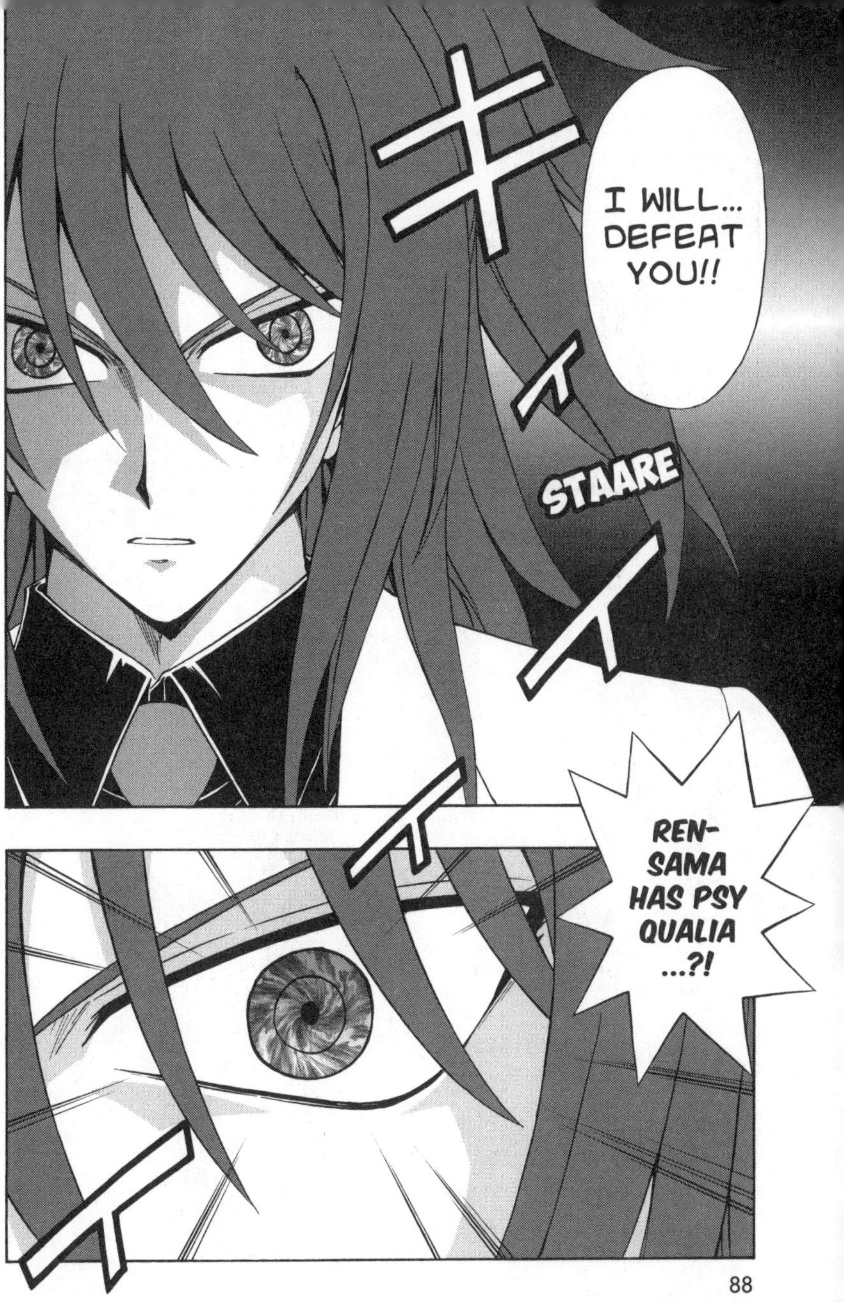
I WILL... DEFEAT YOU!!
STAARE
REN-SAMA HAS PSY QUALIA ...?!

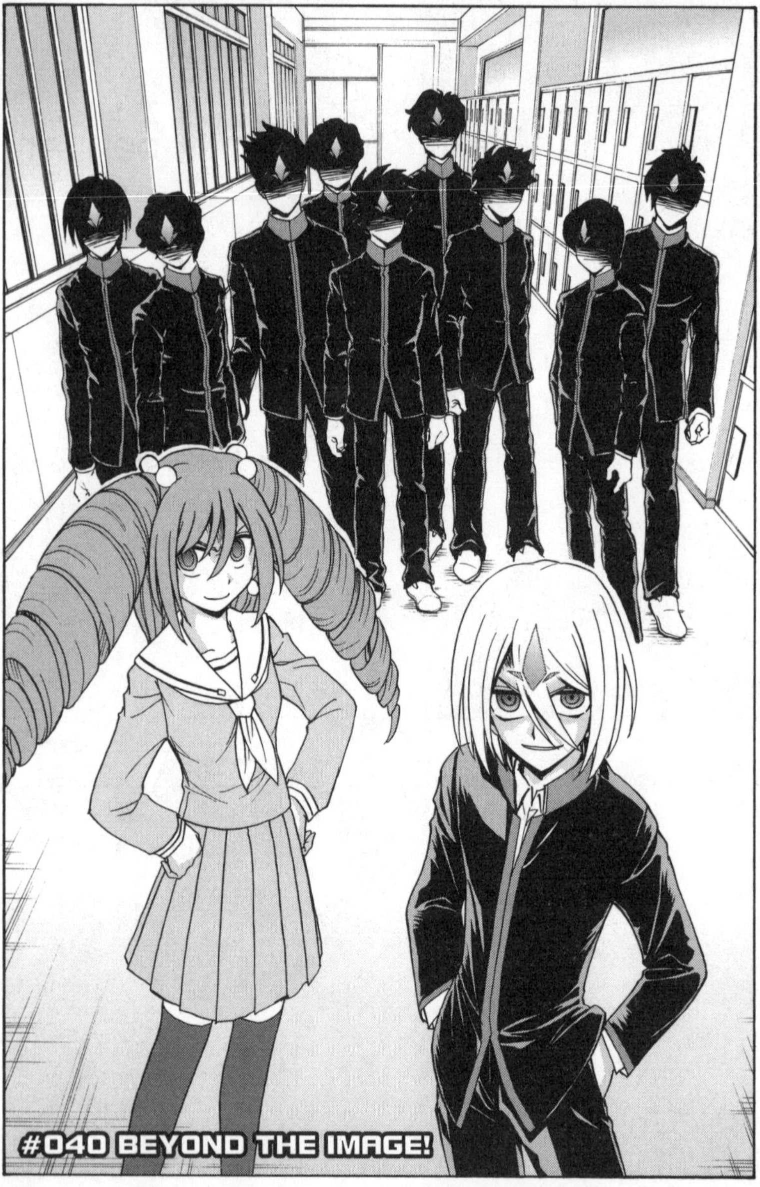
#040 BEYOND THE IMAGE!

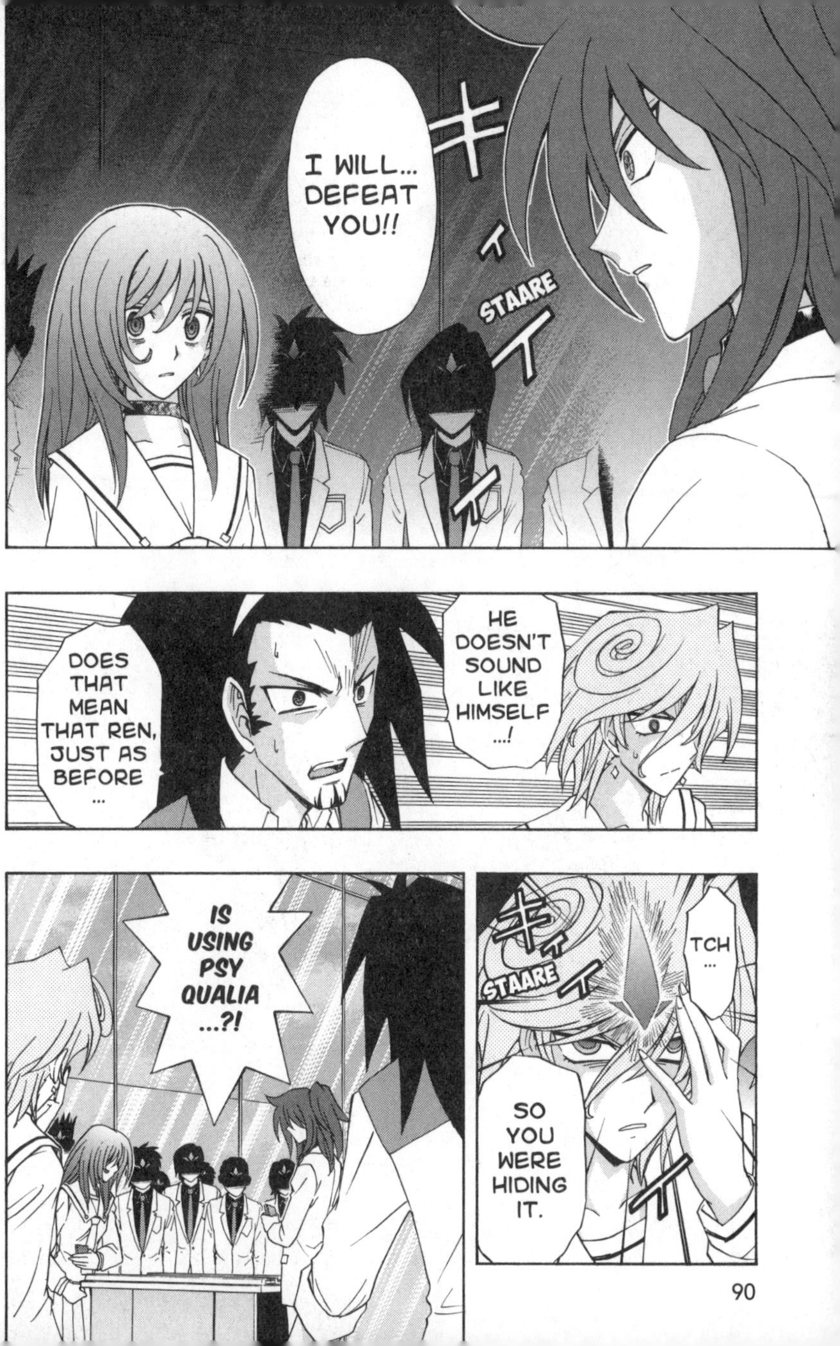
I WILL... DEFEAT YOU!!
STAARE
HE DOESN'T SOUND LIKE HIMSELF ...!
DOES THAT MEAN THAT REN, JUST AS BEFORE ...
TCH ...
STAARE
SO YOU WERE HIDING IT.
IS USING PSY QUALIA ...?!

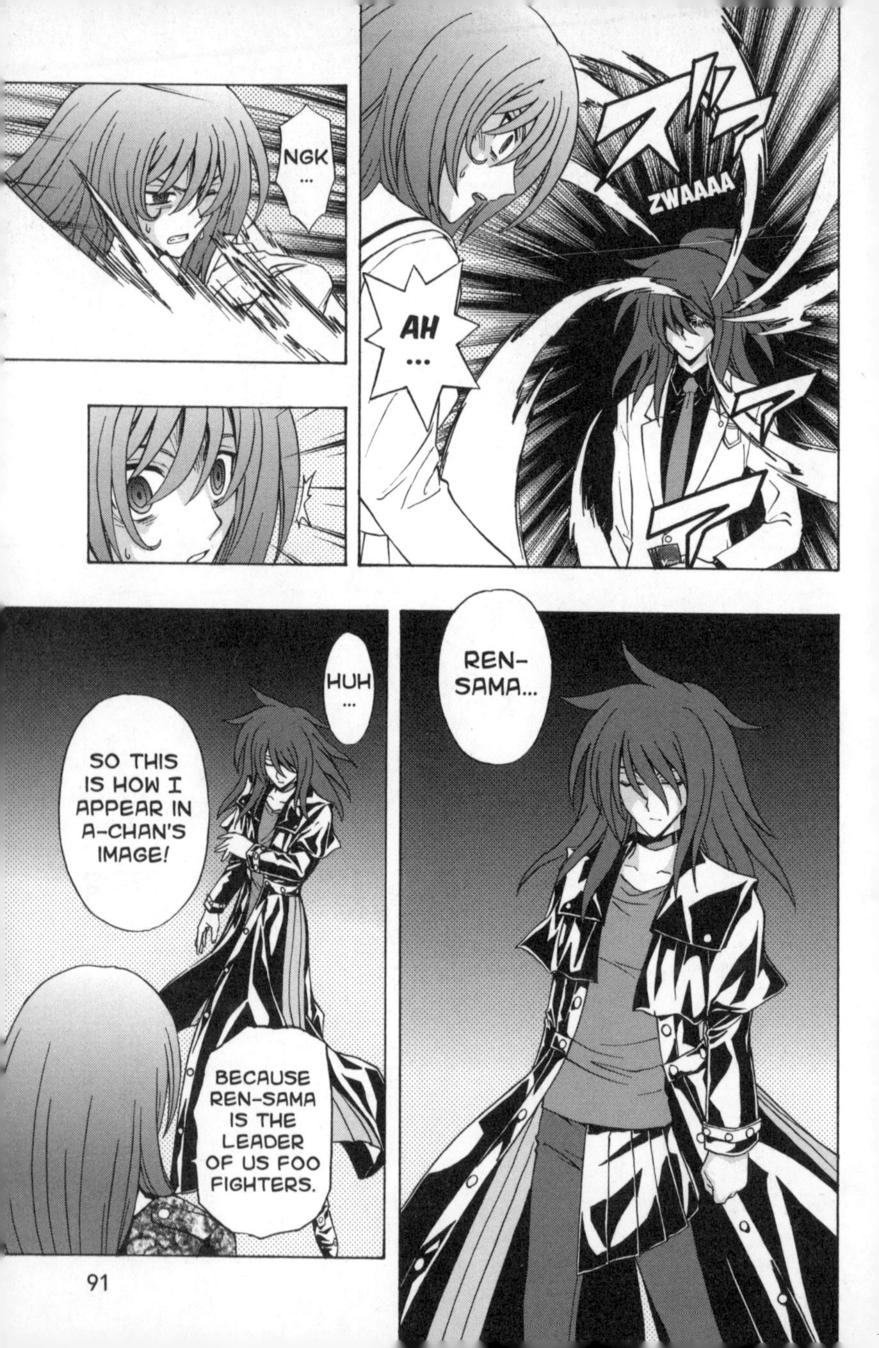
ZWAAAA
AH ...
NGK ...
REN-SAMA...
HUH ...
SO THIS IS HOW I APPEAR IN A-CHAN'S IMAGE!
BECAUSE REN-SAMA IS THE LEADER OF US FOO FIGHTERS.

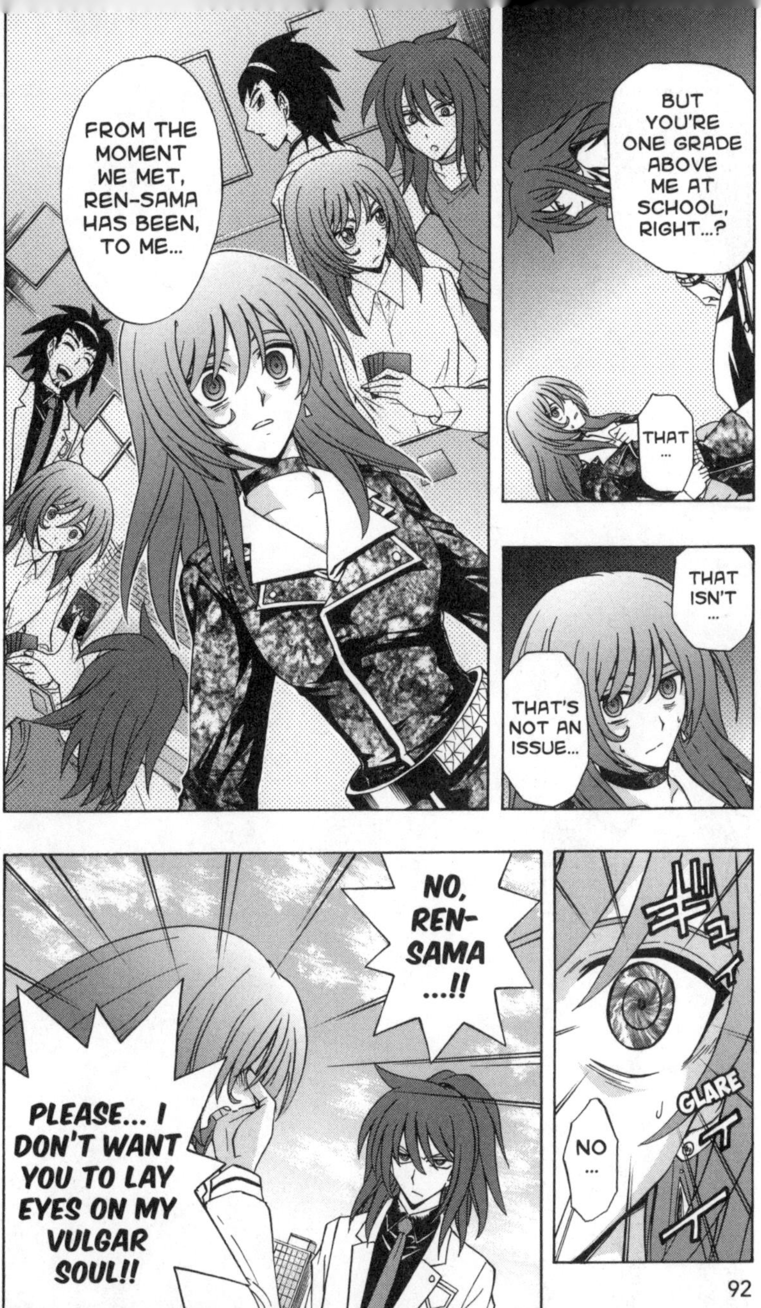
BUT YOU'RE ONE GRADE ABOVE ME AT SCHOOL, RIGHT...?
THAT ...
THAT ISN'T ...
THAT'S NOT AN ISSUE...
FROM THE MOMENT WE MET, REN-SAMA HAS BEEN, TO ME...
GLARE
NO ...
NO, REN-SAMA ...!!
PLEASE... I DON'T WANT YOU TO LAY EYES ON MY VULGAR SOUL!!

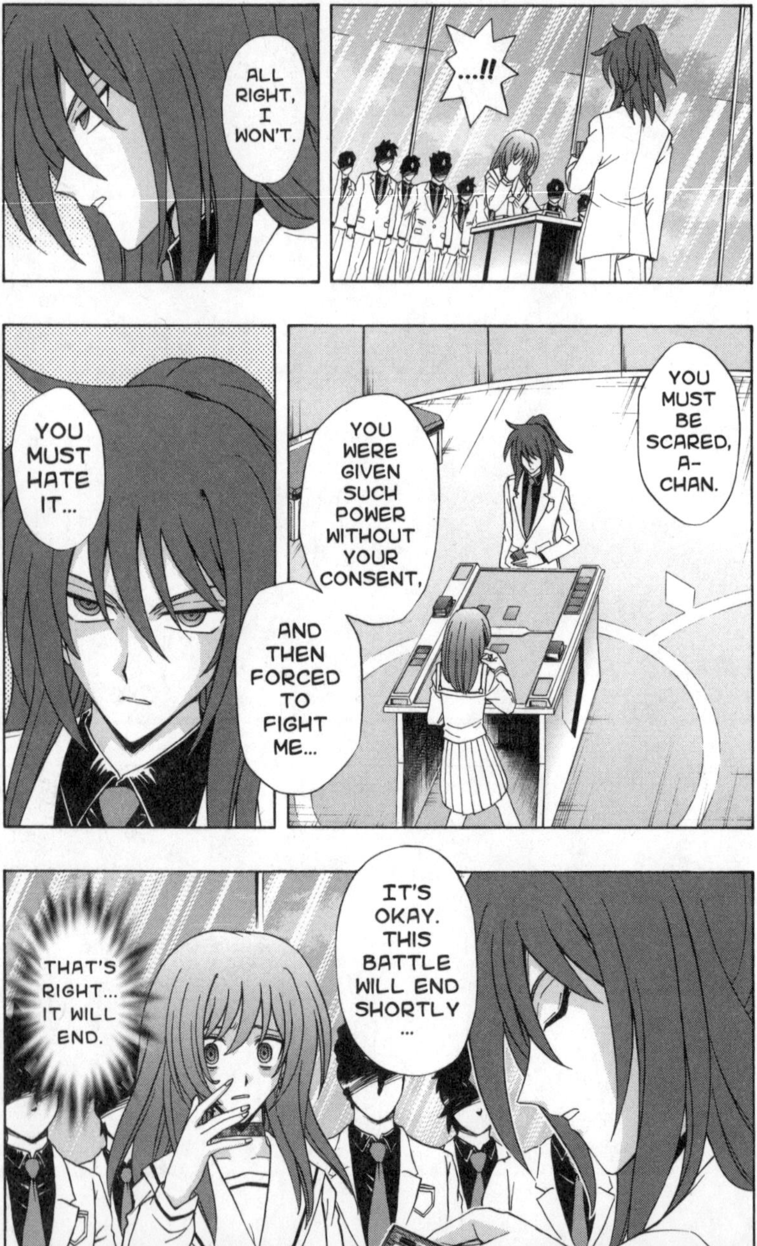
...!!
ALL RIGHT, I WON'T.
YOU MUST BE SCARED, A-CHAN.
YOU WERE GIVEN SUCH POWER WITHOUT YOUR CONSENT,
AND THEN FORCED TO FIGHT ME...
YOU MUST HATE IT...
IT'S OKAY. THIS BATTLE WILL END SHORTLY...
THAT'S RIGHT... IT WILL END.

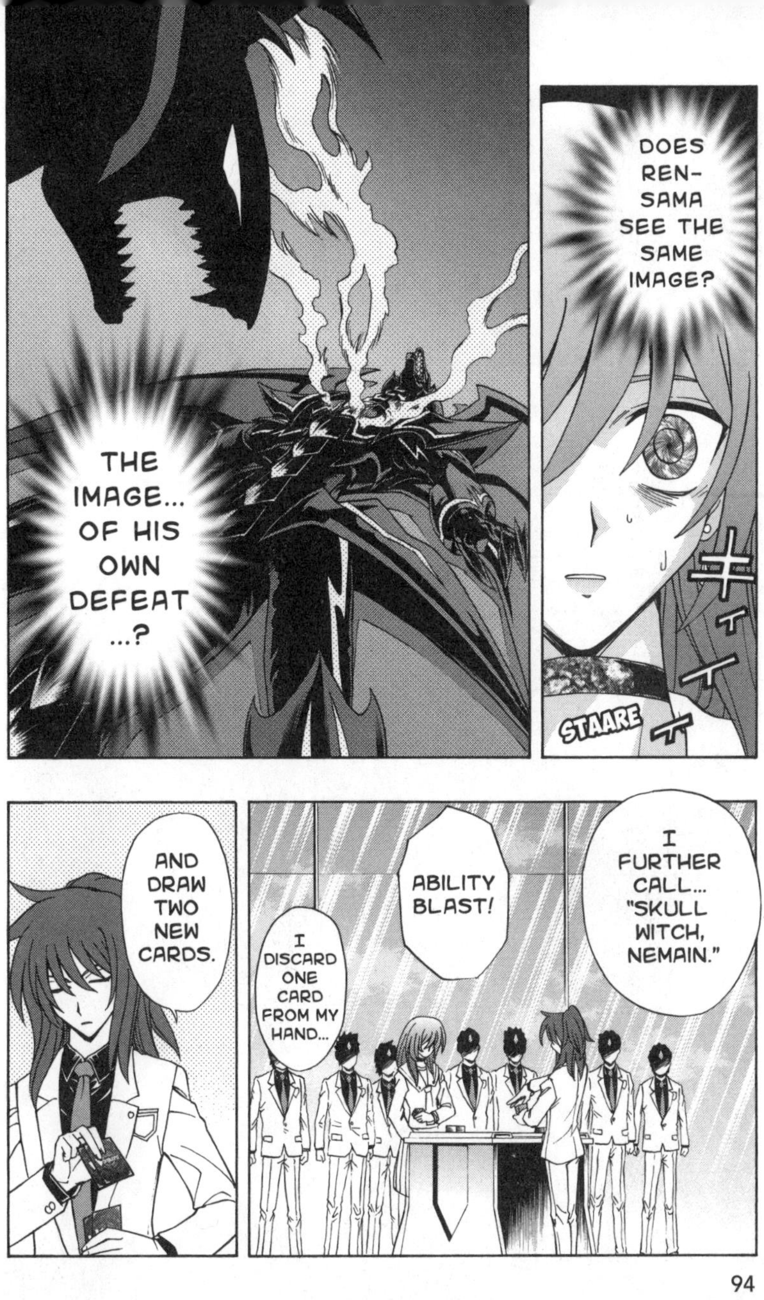
DOES REN-SAMA SEE THE SAME IMAGE?
STAARE
THE IMAGE... OF HIS OWN DEFEAT ...?
I FURTHER CALL... "SKULL WITCH, NEMAIN."
ABILITY BLAST!
I DISCARD ONE CARD FROM MY HAND...
AND DRAW TWO NEW CARDS.

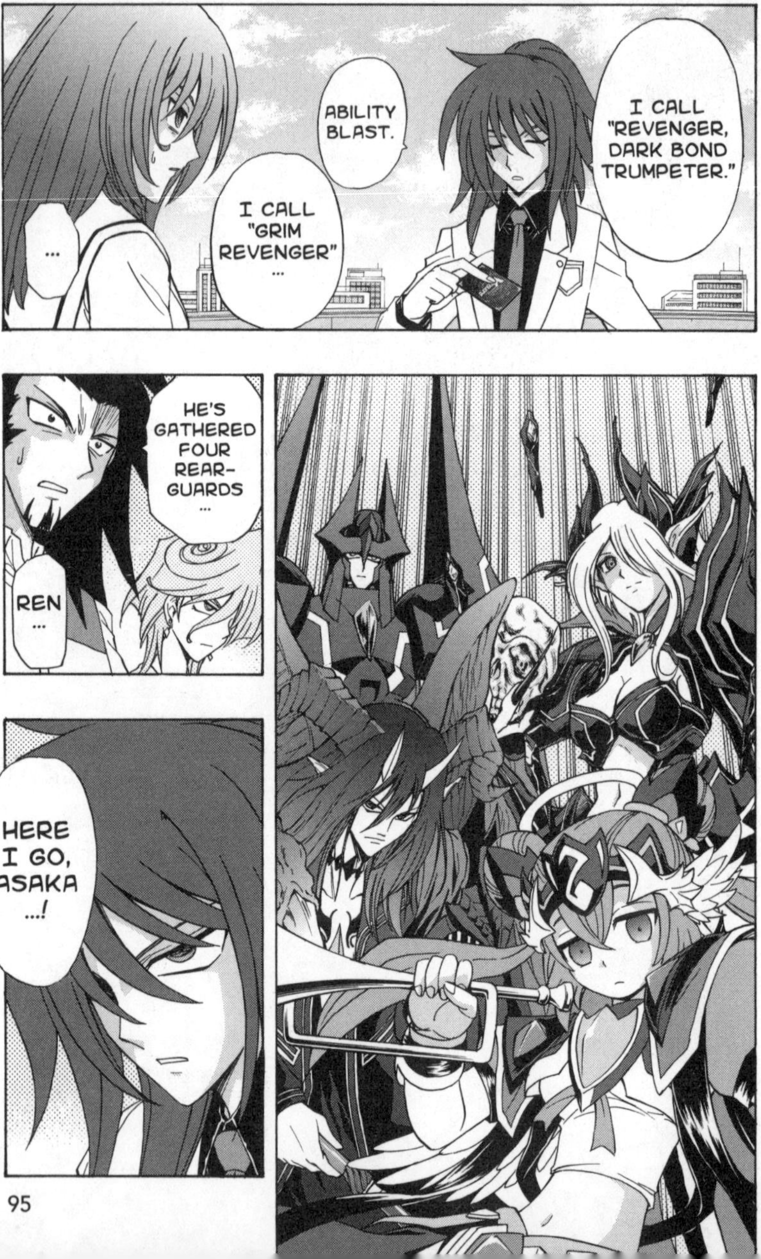
I CALL "REVENGER, DARK BOND TRUMPETER."
ABILITY BLAST.
I CALL "GRIM REVENGER" ...
...
HE'S GATHERED FOUR REAR-GUARDS ...
REN ...
HERE I GO, ASAKA ...!

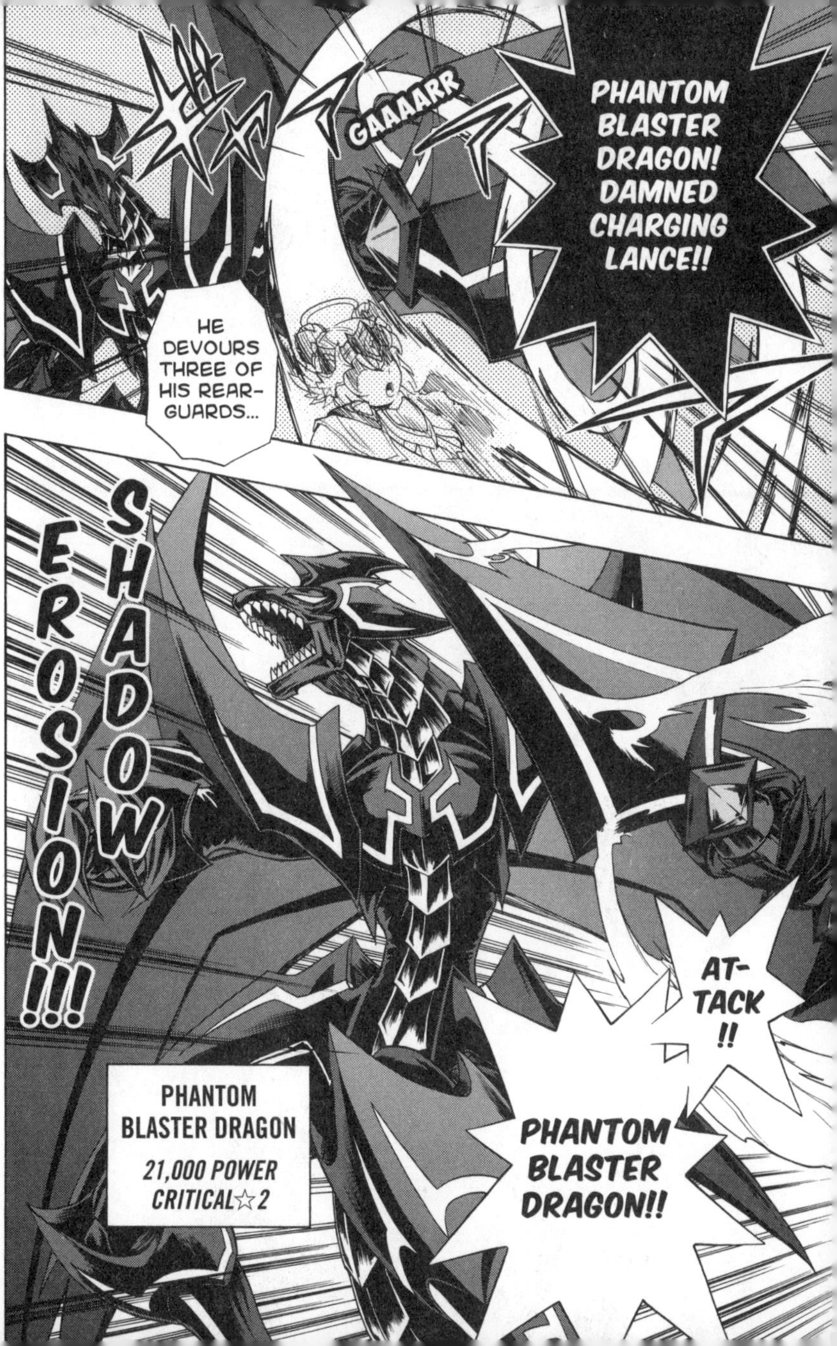
PHANTOM BLASTER DRAGON! DAMNED CHARGING LANCE!!
GAAAARR
HE DEVOURS THREE OF HIS REAR-GUARDS...
AT-TACK!!
PHANTOM BLASTER DRAGON!!
SHADOW EROSION!!!
PHANTOM BLASTER DRAGON
21,000 POWER CRITICAL☆2

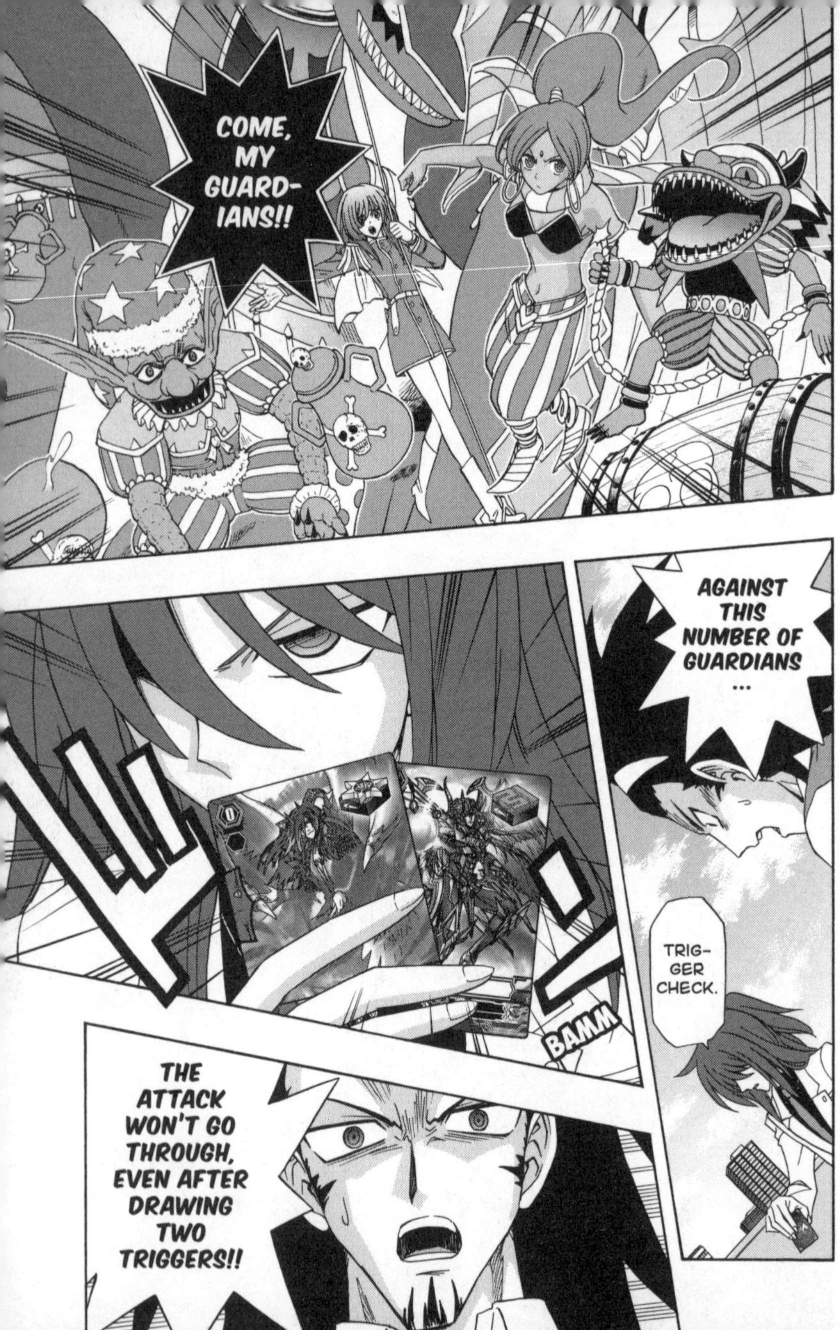
COME, MY GUARD-IANS!!
AGAINST THIS NUMBER OF GUARDIANS ...
TRIG-GER CHECK.
BAMM
THE ATTACK WON'T GO THROUGH, EVEN AFTER DRAWING TWO TRIGGERS!!

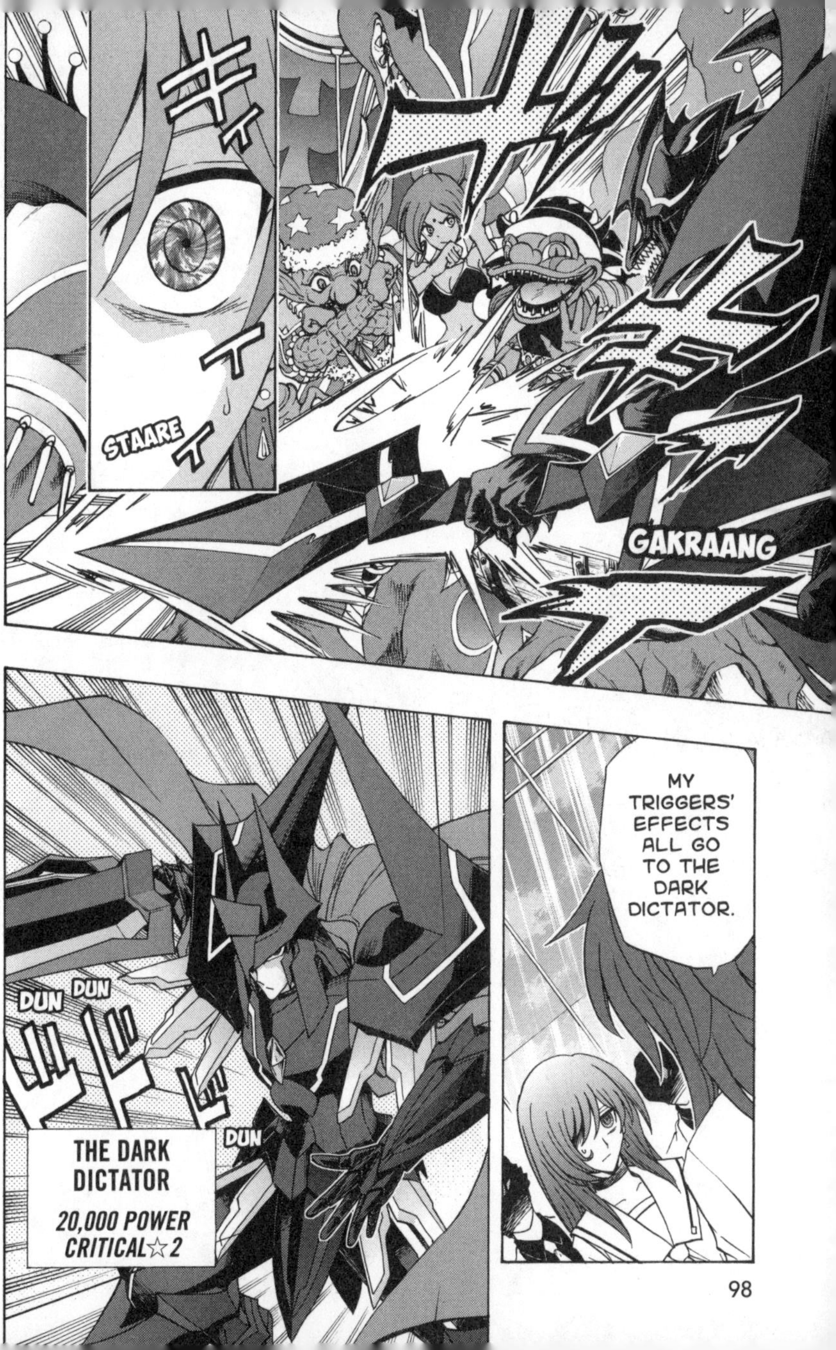
STAARE
GAKRAANG
MY TRIGGERS' EFFECTS ALL GO TO THE DARK DICTATOR.
DUN
DUN
DUN
THE DARK DICTATOR
20,000 POWER CRITICAL☆2

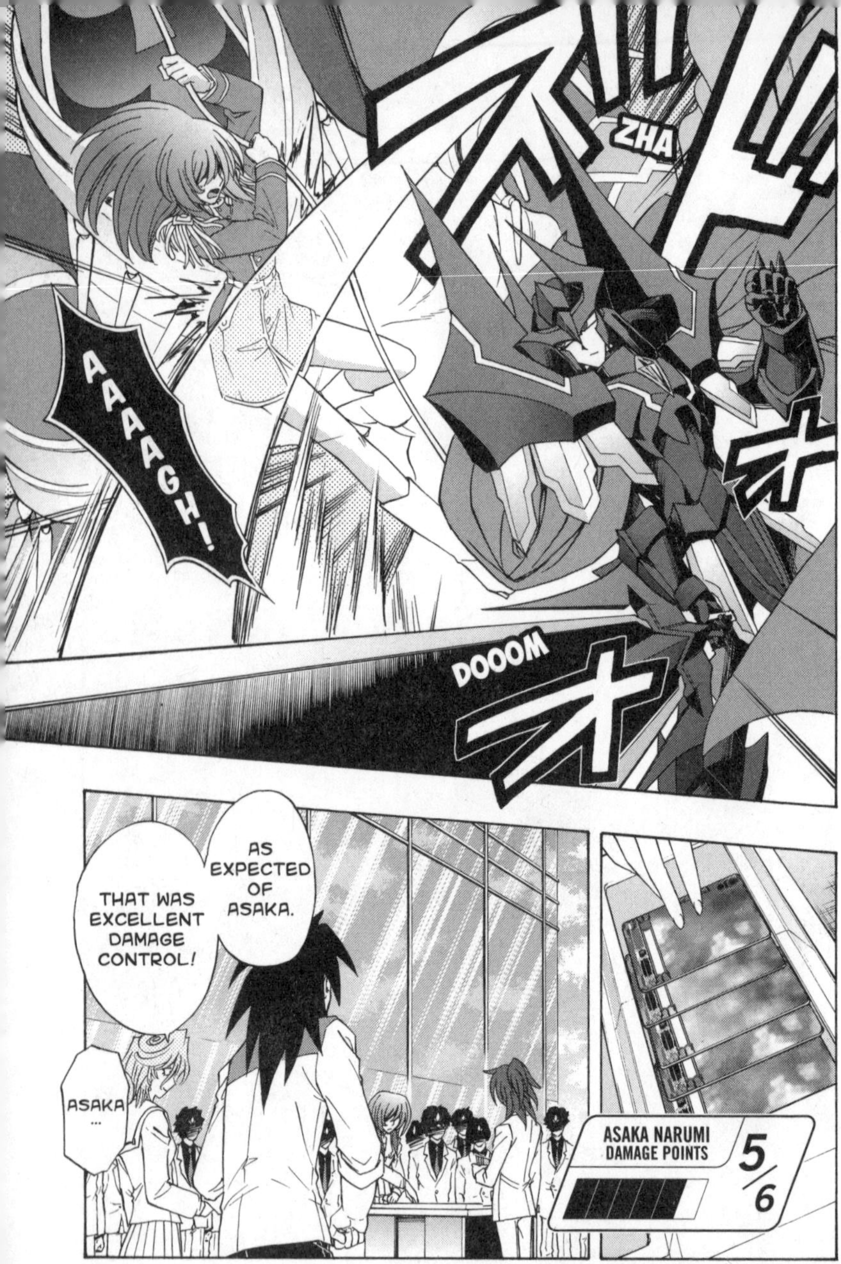
ZHA
AAAAGH!
DOOOM
ASAKA NARUMI DAMAGE POINTS
5/6
AS EXPECTED OF ASAKA.
THAT WAS EXCELLENT DAMAGE CONTROL!
ASAKA ...

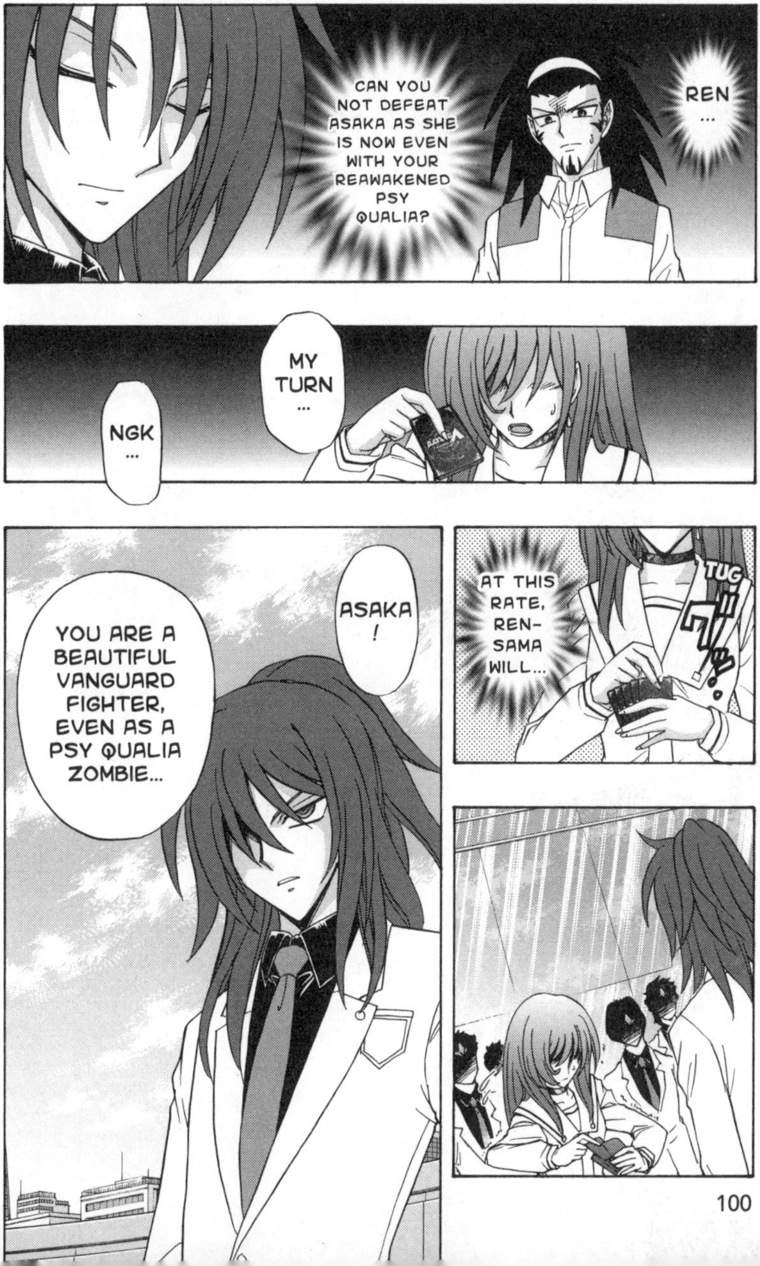
REN ...
CAN YOU NOT DEFEAT ASAKA AS SHE IS NOW EVEN WITH YOUR REAWAKENED PSY QUALIA?
MY TURN ...
NGK ...
TUG
AT THIS RATE, REN-SAMA WILL...
ASAKA !
YOU ARE A BEAUTIFUL VANGUARD FIGHTER, EVEN AS A PSY QUALIA ZOMBIE...

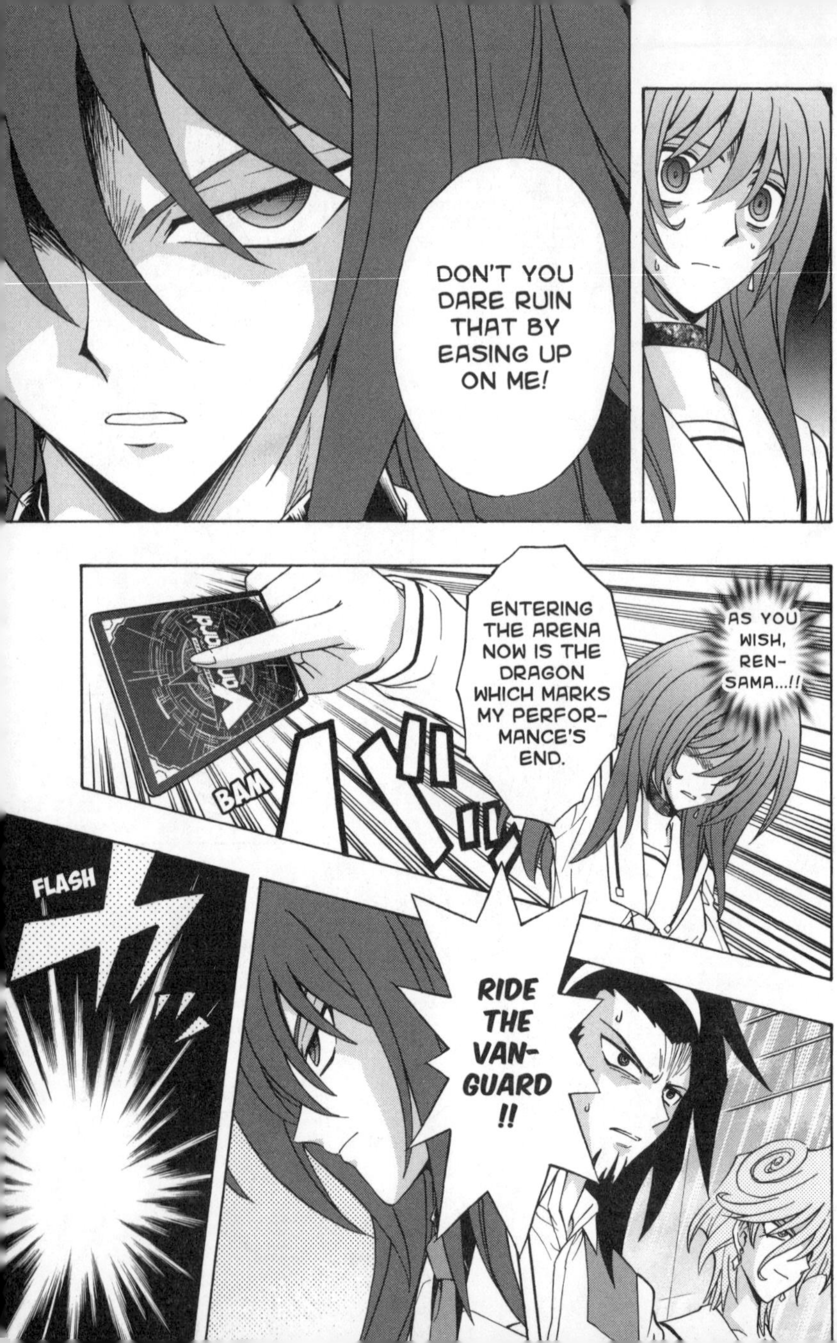
DON'T YOU DARE RUIN THAT BY EASING UP ON ME!
AS YOU WISH, REN-SAMA...!!
ENTERING THE ARENA NOW IS THE DRAGON WHICH MARKS MY PERFORMANCE'S END.
BAM
RIDE THE VANGUARD!!
FLASH

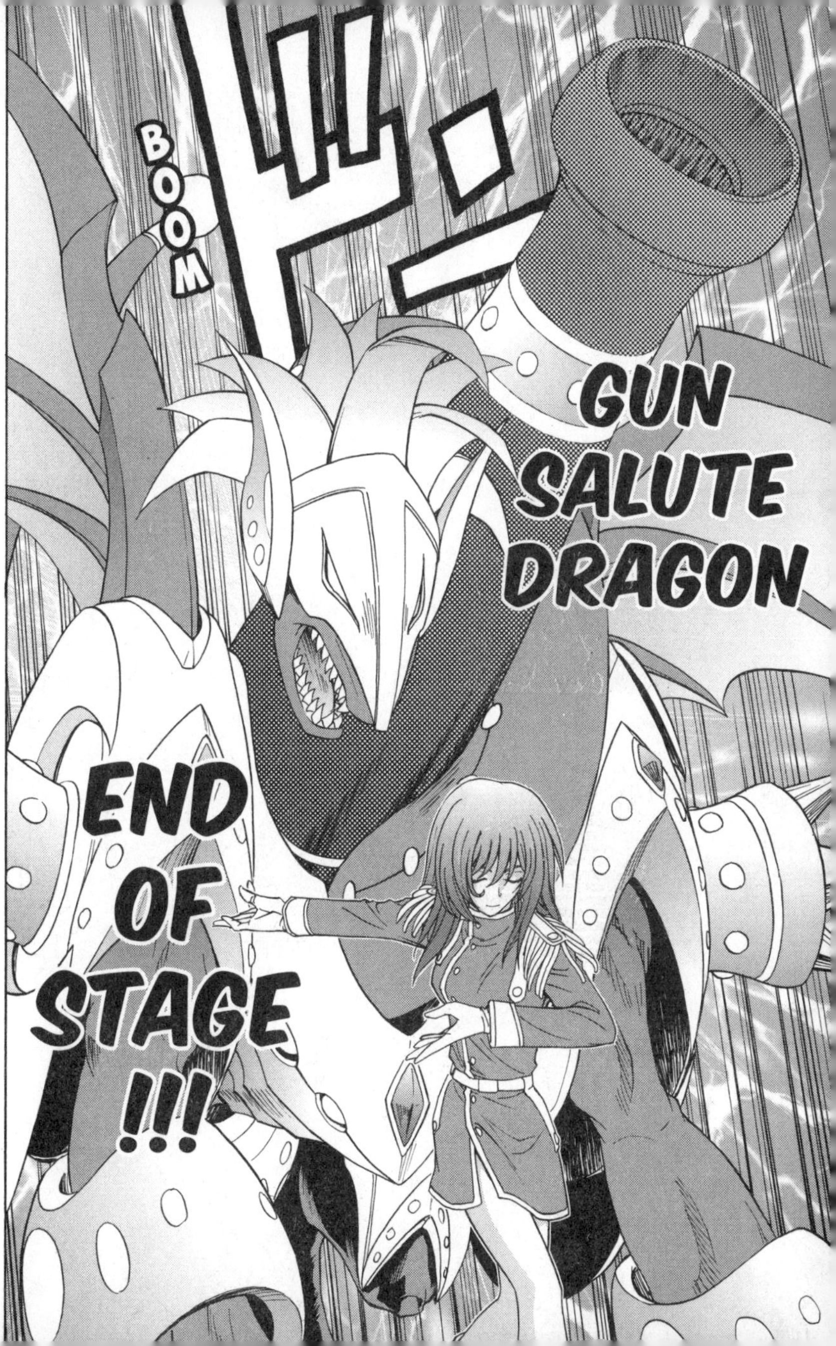
BOOM
GUN SALUTE DRAGON
END OF STAGE !!!

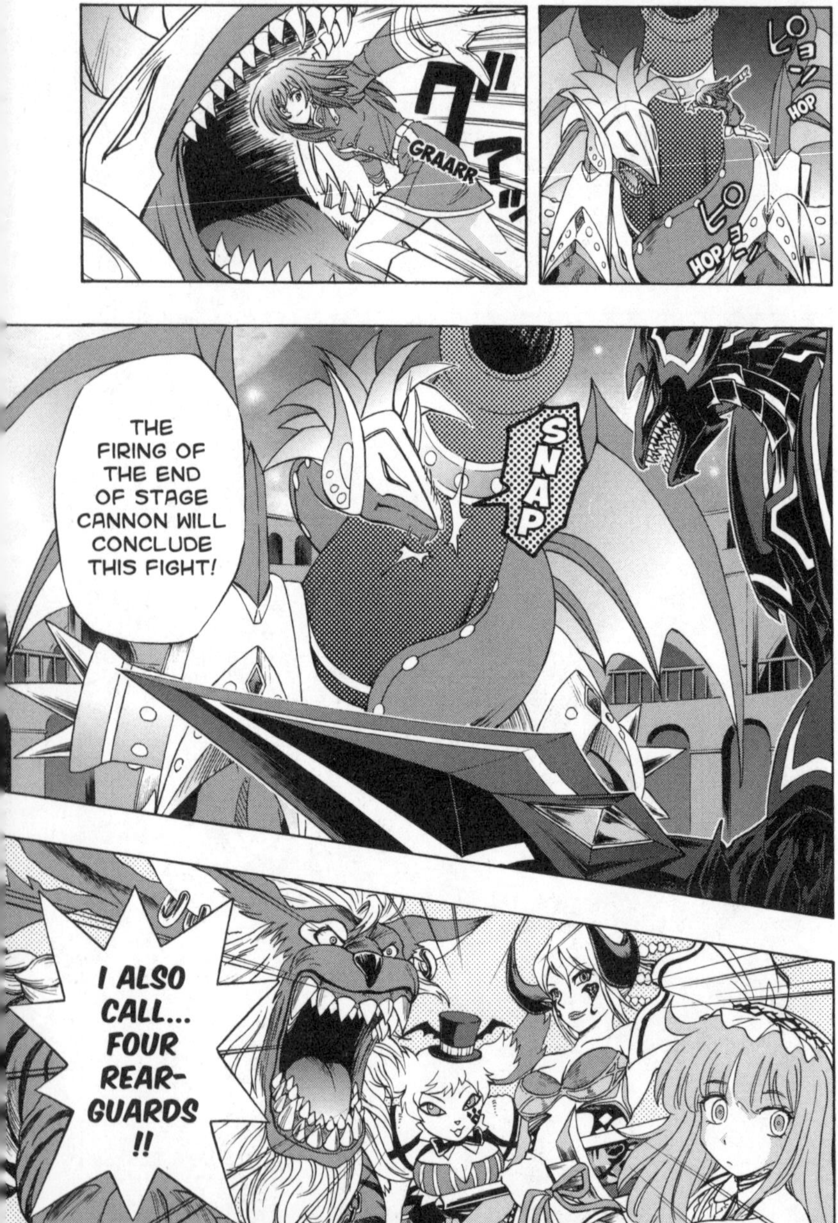
HOP
HOP
GRAARR
THE FIRING OF THE END OF STAGE CANNON WILL CONCLUDE THIS FIGHT!
SNAP
I ALSO CALL... FOUR REAR-GUARDS !!

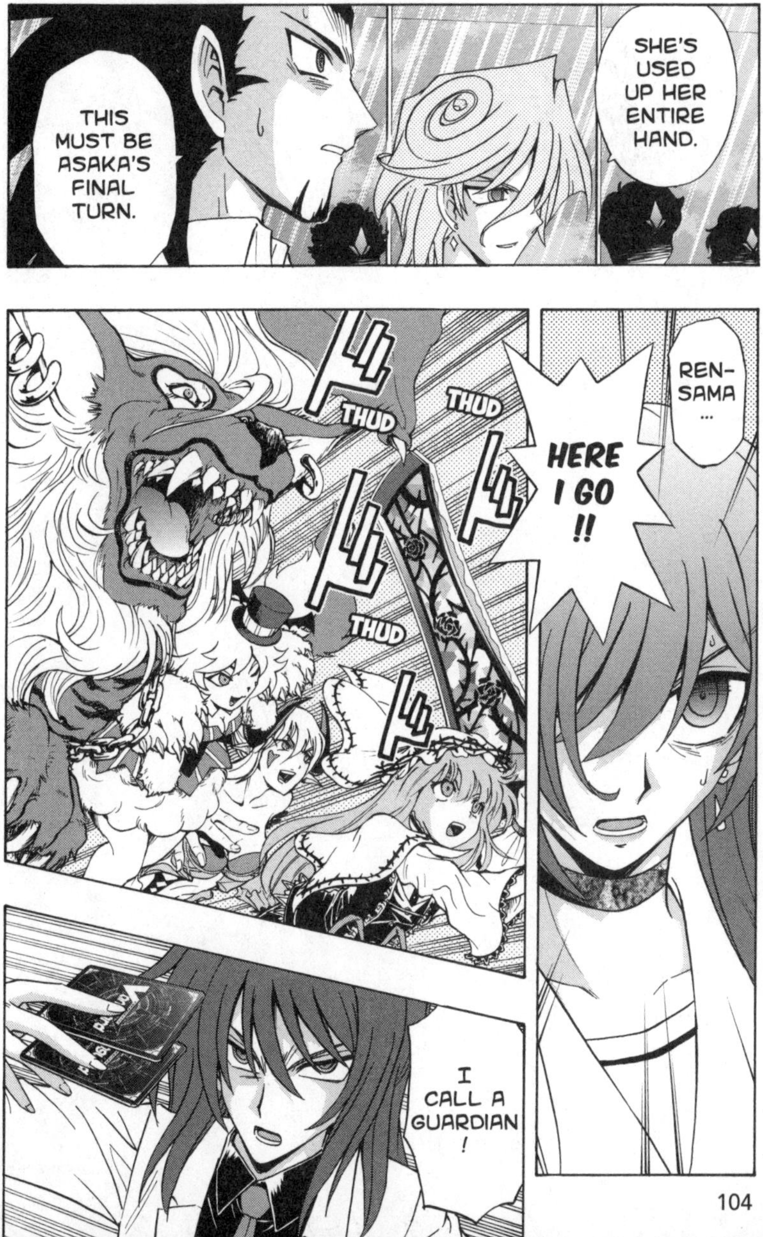
SHE'S USED UP HER ENTIRE HAND.
THIS MUST BE ASAKA'S FINAL TURN.
REN-SAMA ...
HERE I GO !!
THUD
THUD
THUD
I CALL A GUARDIAN !

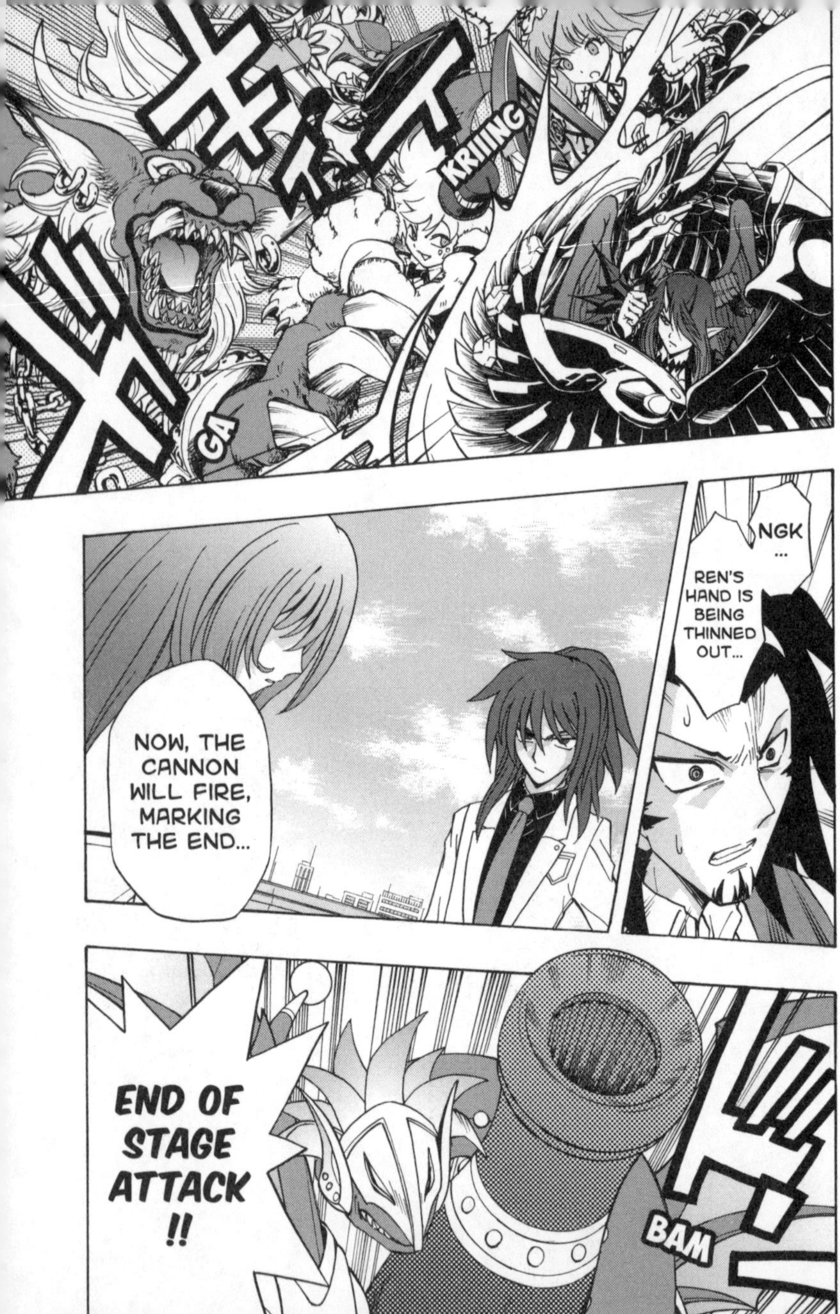
KRIIING
GA
NGK ...
REN'S HAND IS BEING THINNED OUT...
NOW, THE CANNON WILL FIRE, MARKING THE END...
END OF STAGE ATTACK !!
BAM

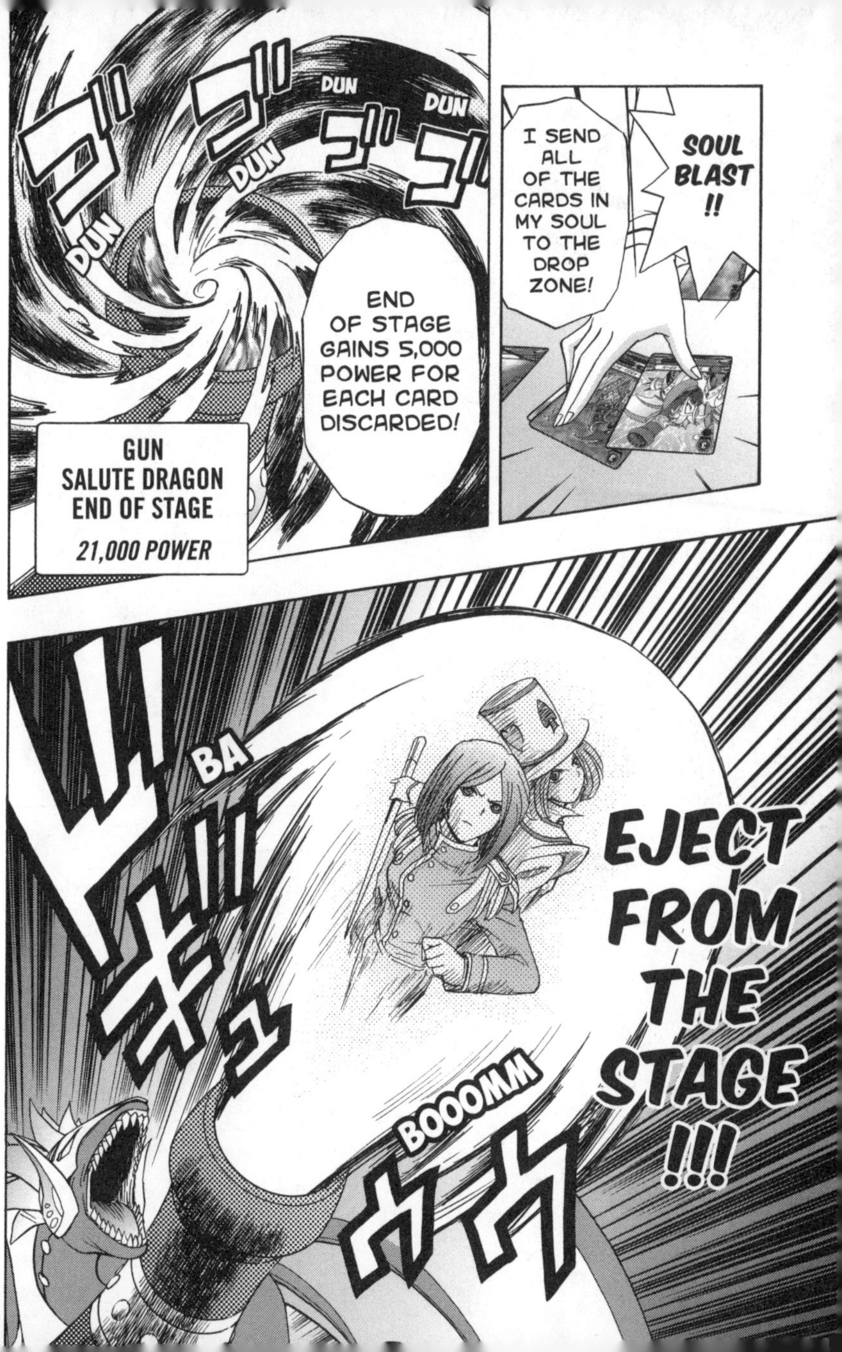
SOUL BLAST !!
I SEND ALL OF THE CARDS IN MY SOUL TO THE DROP ZONE!
DUN
DUN
DUN
DUN
END OF STAGE GAINS 5,000 POWER FOR EACH CARD DISCARDED!
GUN SALUTE DRAGON END OF STAGE
21,000 POWER
EJECT FROM THE STAGE !!!
BOOOMM
BA

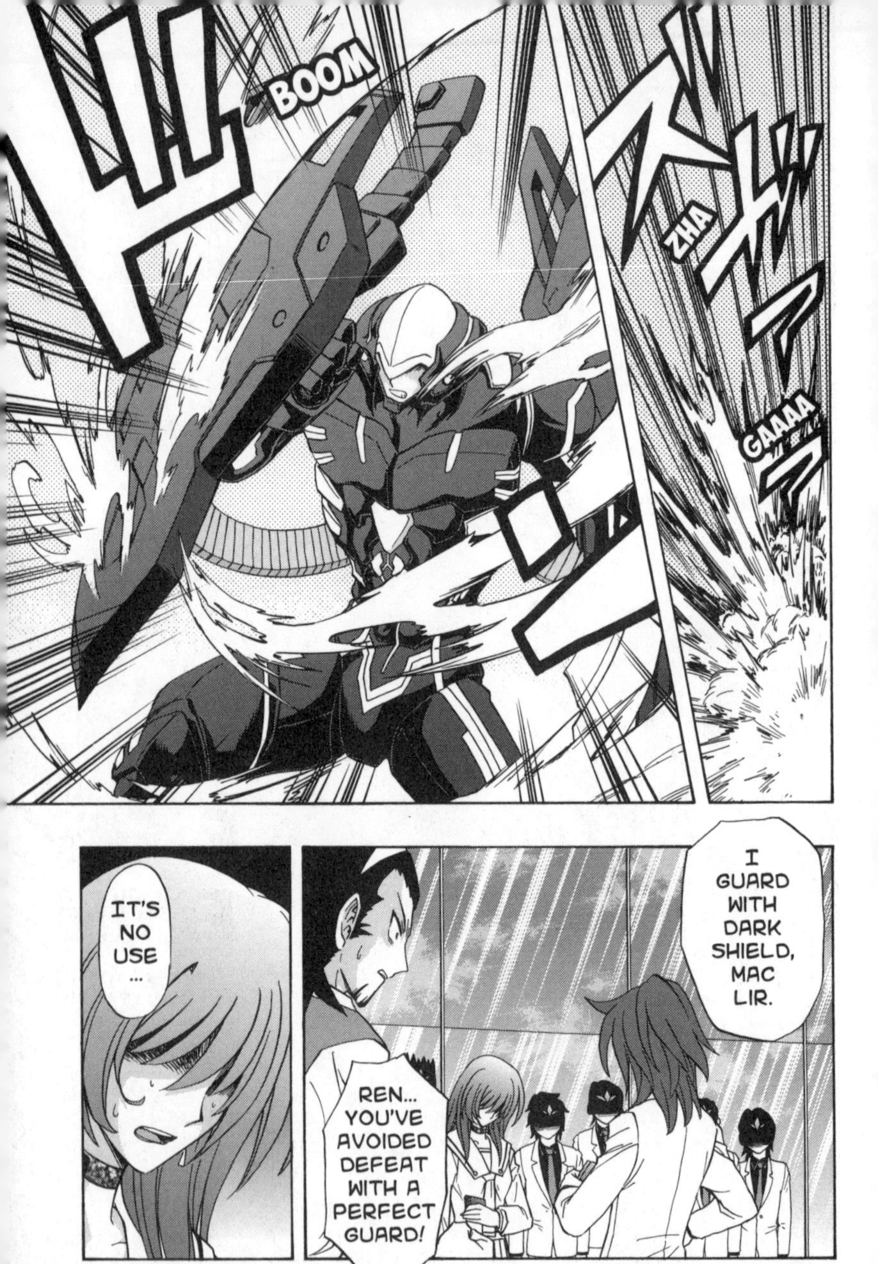
ZHA
GAAAA
BOOM
I GUARD WITH DARK SHIELD, MAC LIR.
REN... YOU'VE AVOIDED DEFEAT WITH A PERFECT GUARD!
IT'S NO USE ...

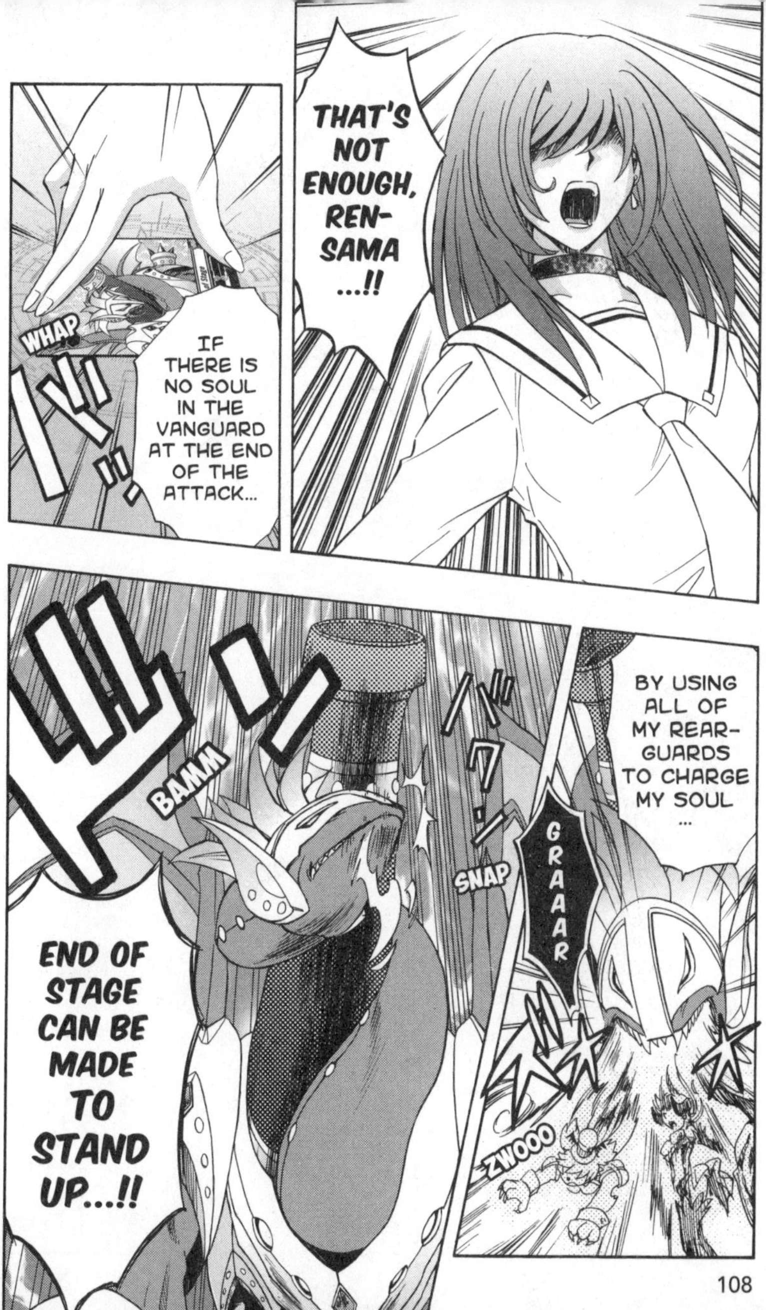
THAT'S NOT ENOUGH, REN-SAMA ...!!
WHAP
IF THERE IS NO SOUL IN THE VANGUARD AT THE END OF THE ATTACK...
BY USING ALL OF MY REAR-GUARDS TO CHARGE MY SOUL ...
GRAAAR
ZWOOO
SNAP
BAMM
END OF STAGE CAN BE MADE TO STAND UP...!!

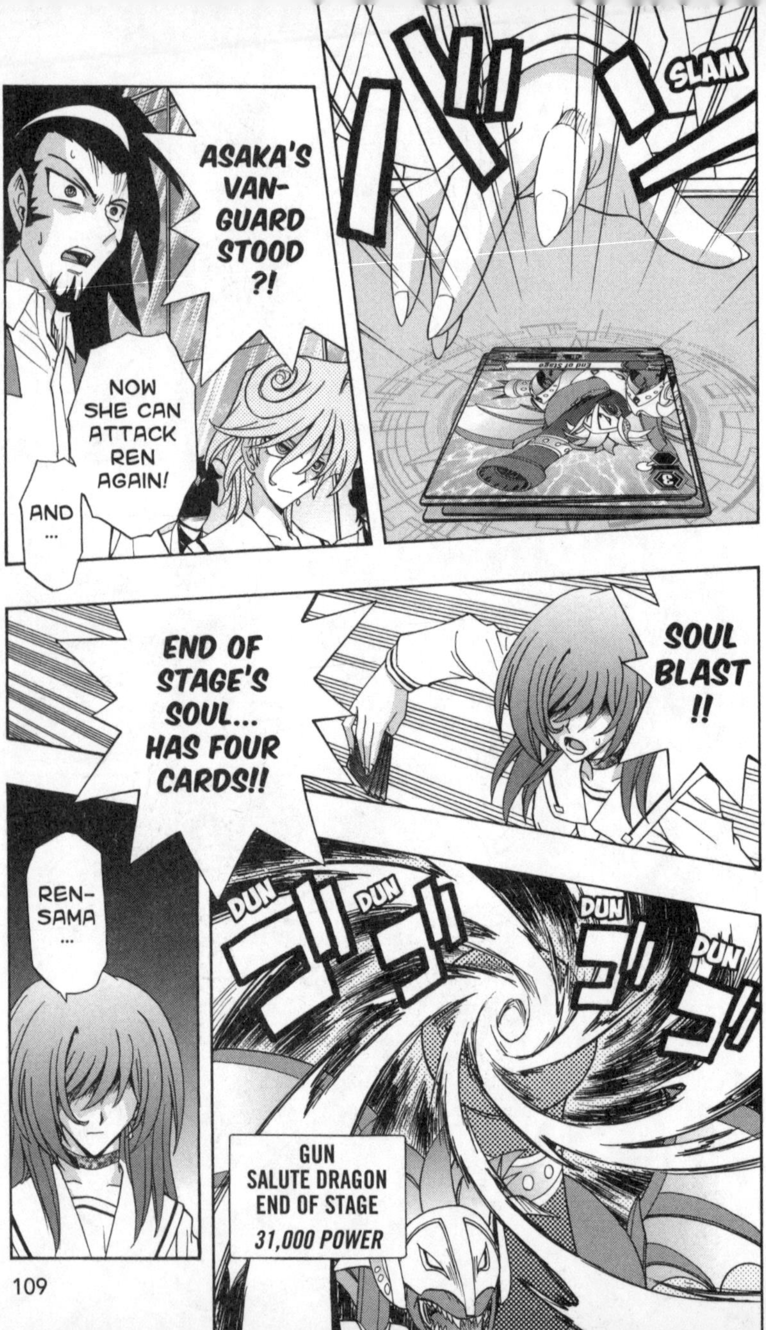
SLAM
ASAKA'S VAN-GUARD STOOD ?!
NOW SHE CAN ATTACK REN AGAIN!
AND ...
SOUL BLAST !!
END OF STAGE'S SOUL... HAS FOUR CARDS!!
DUN DUN DUN DUN
GUN SALUTE DRAGON END OF STAGE
31,000 POWER
REN-SAMA ...

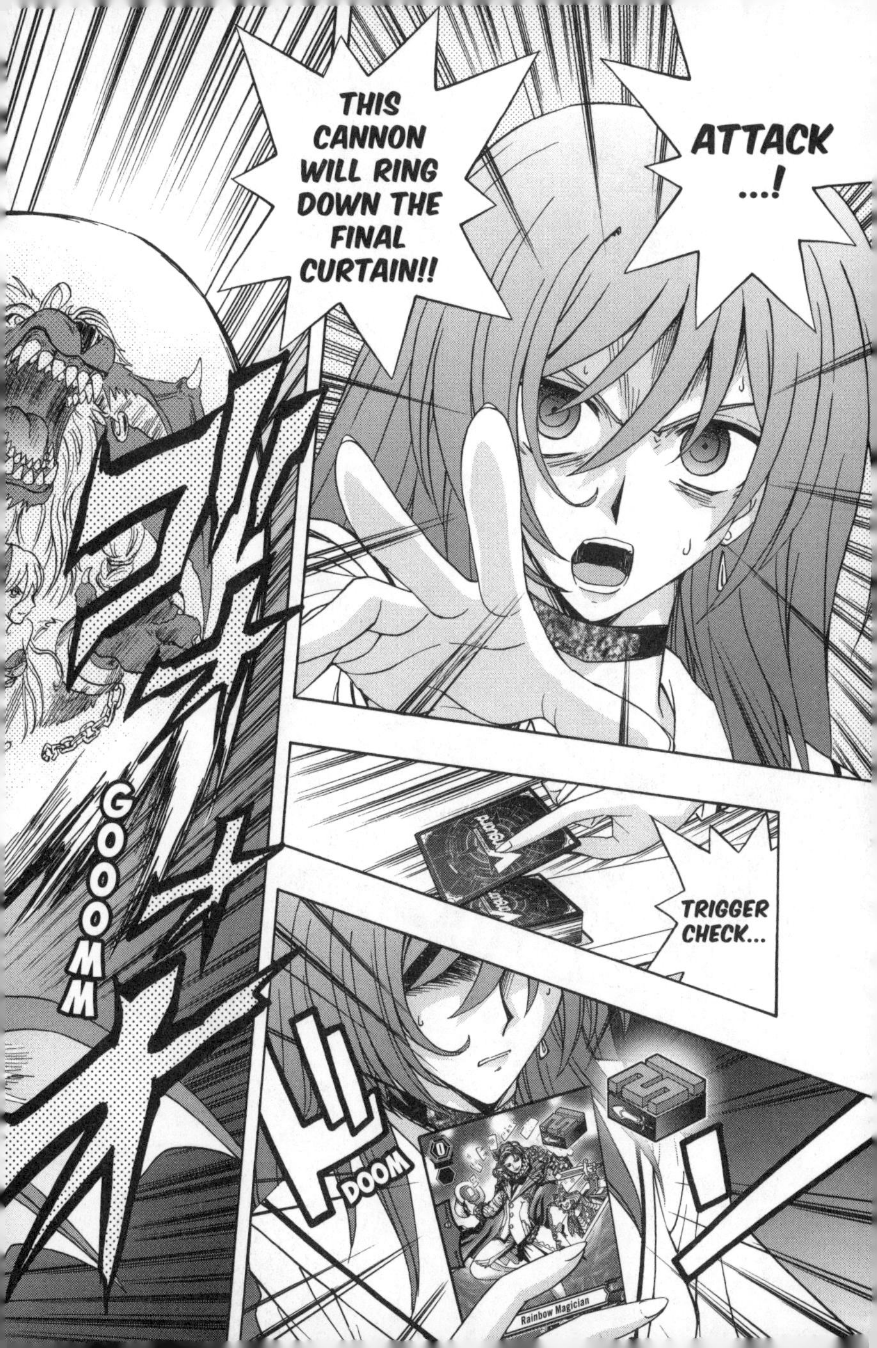

THIS CANNON WILL RING DOWN THE FINAL CURTAIN!!
ATTACK ...!
TRIGGER CHECK...
DOOM
Rainbow Magician
GOOOMM

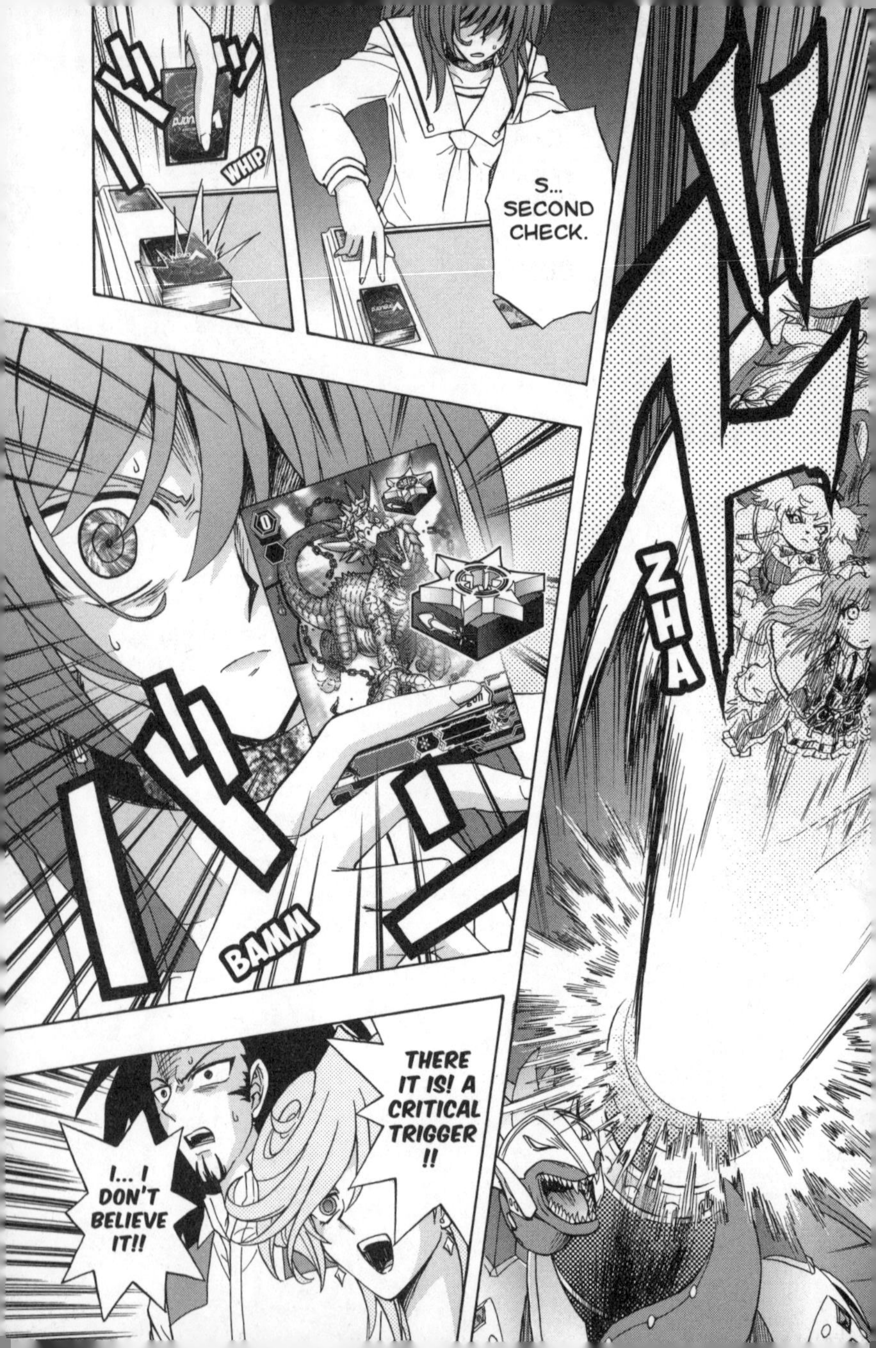
ZHA
S... SECOND CHECK.
WHIP
BAMM
THERE IT IS! A CRITICAL TRIGGER !!
I... I DON'T BELIEVE IT!!

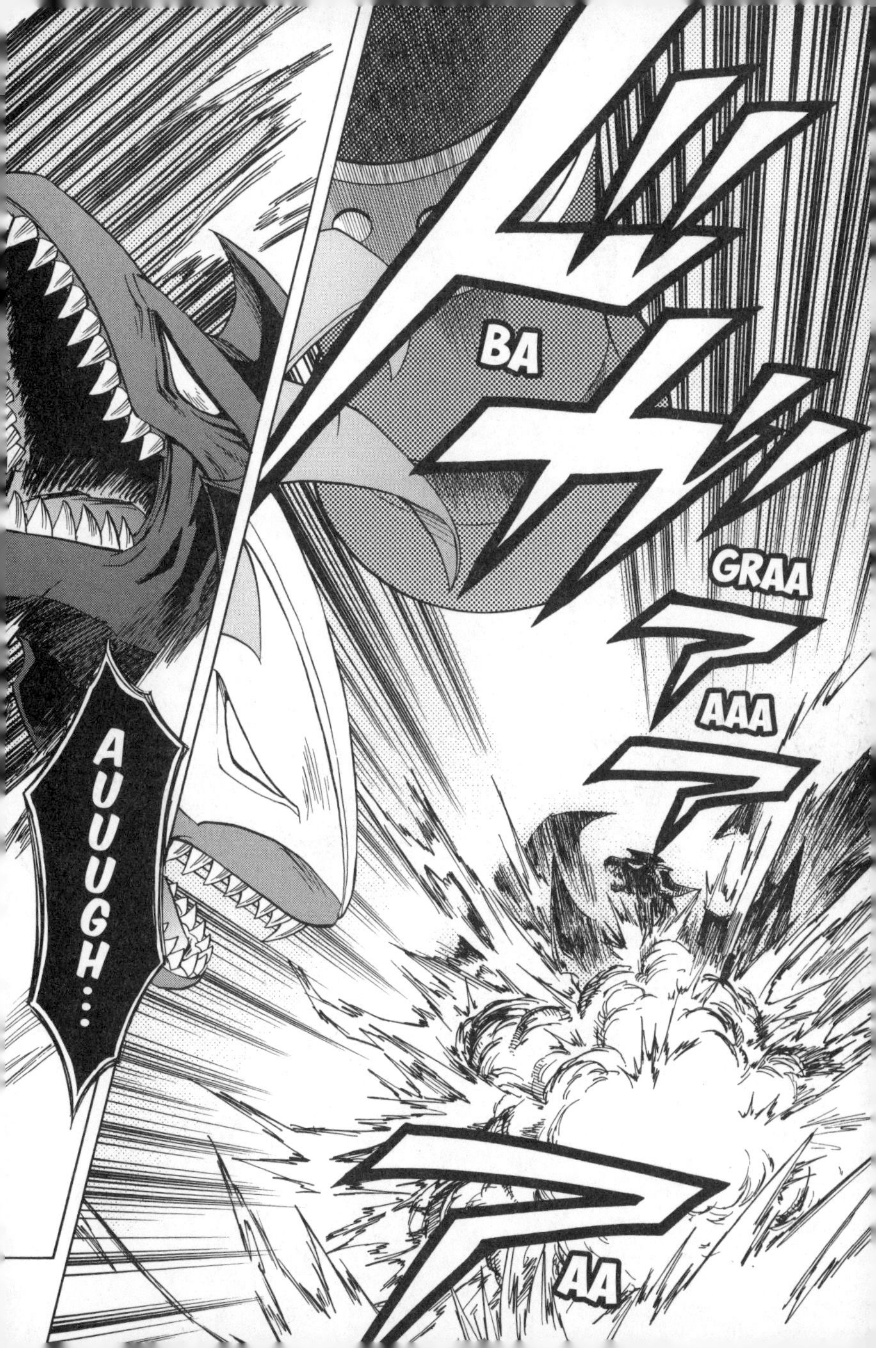
BA
GRAA
AAA
AA
AUUUGH...

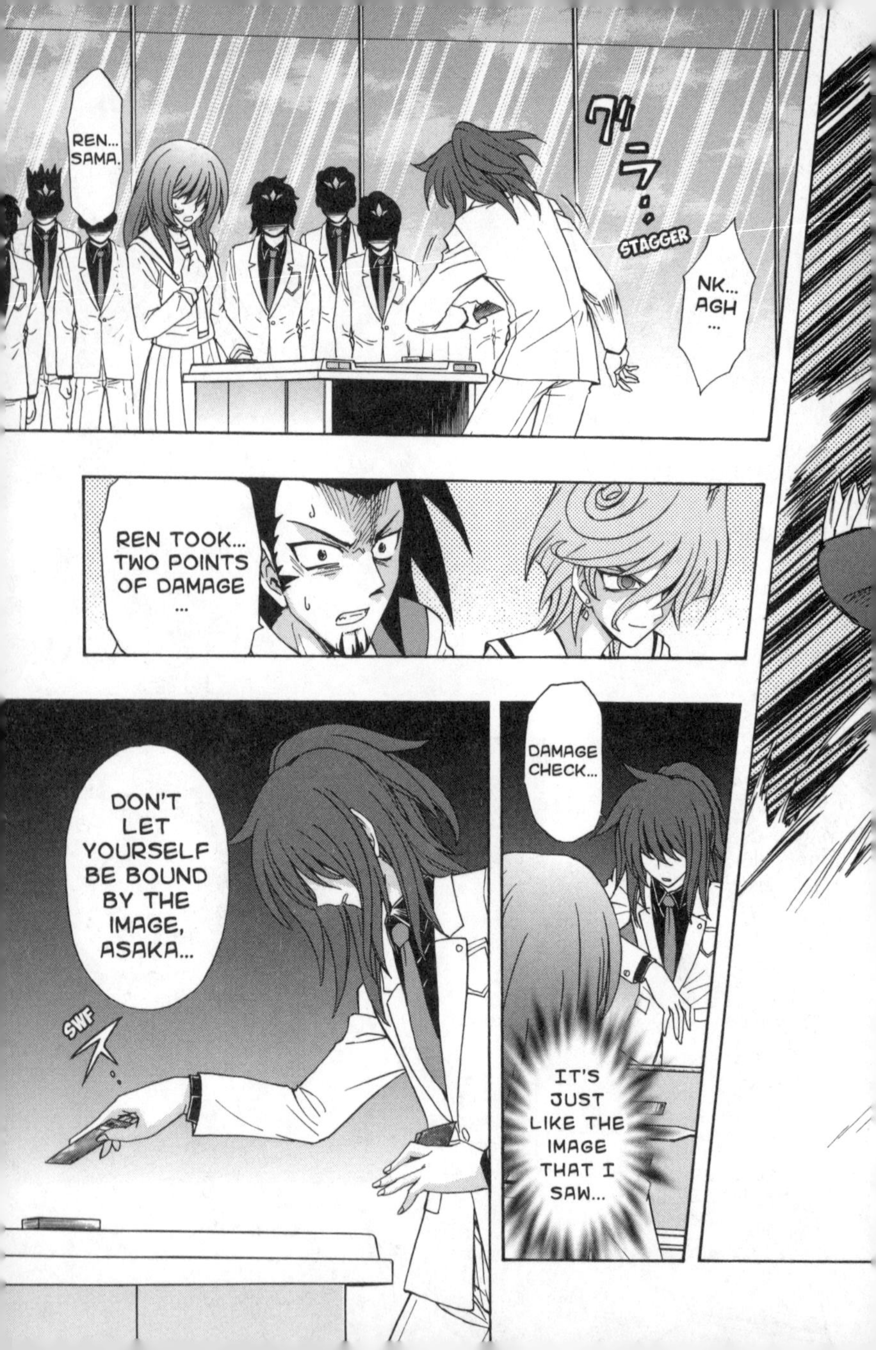
NK... AGH...
STAGGER
REN... SAMA.
REN TOOK... TWO POINTS OF DAMAGE...
DAMAGE CHECK...
IT'S JUST LIKE THE IMAGE THAT I SAW...
DON'T LET YOURSELF BE BOUND BY THE IMAGE, ASAKA...
SWF

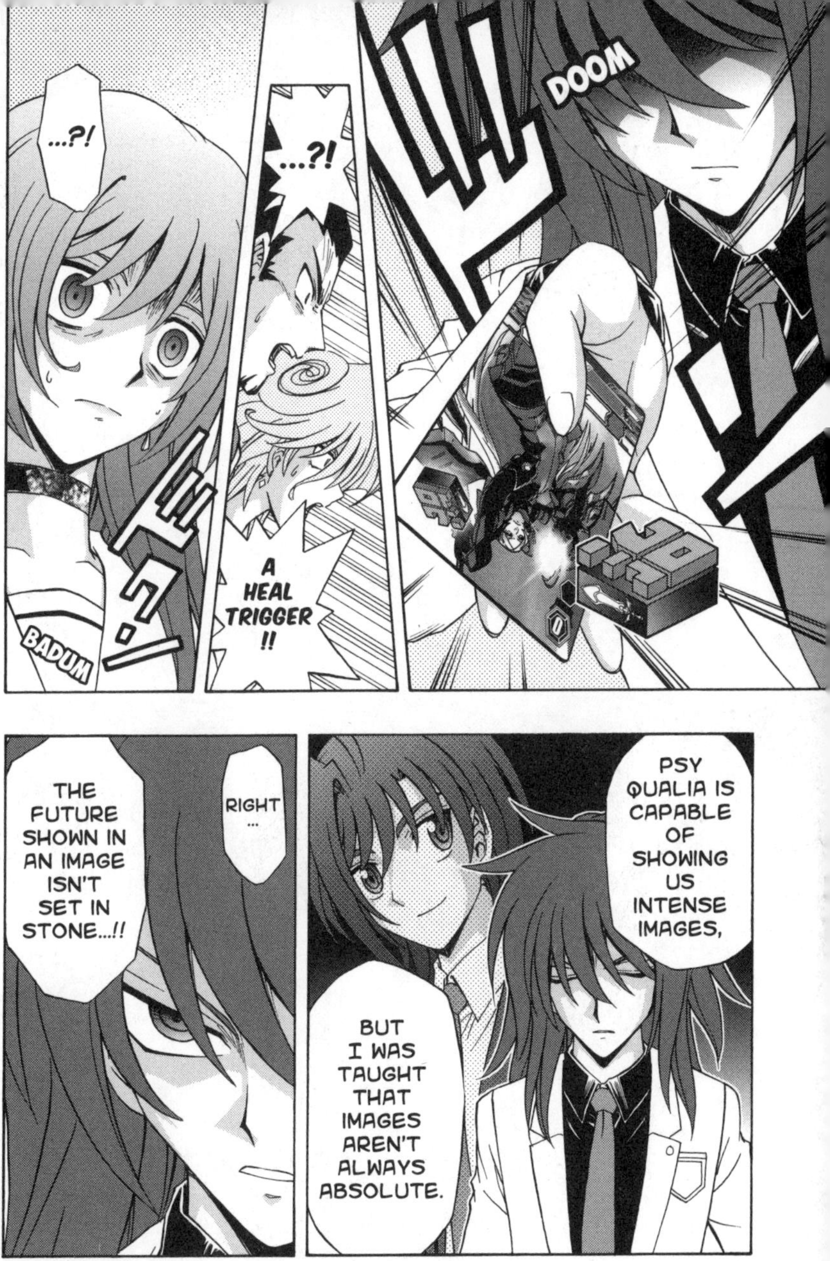
DOOM
...?!
A HEAL TRIGGER !!
...?!
BADUM
PSY QUALIA IS CAPABLE OF SHOWING US INTENSE IMAGES,
BUT I WAS TAUGHT THAT IMAGES AREN'T ALWAYS ABSOLUTE.
RIGHT ...
THE FUTURE SHOWN IN AN IMAGE ISN'T SET IN STONE...!!

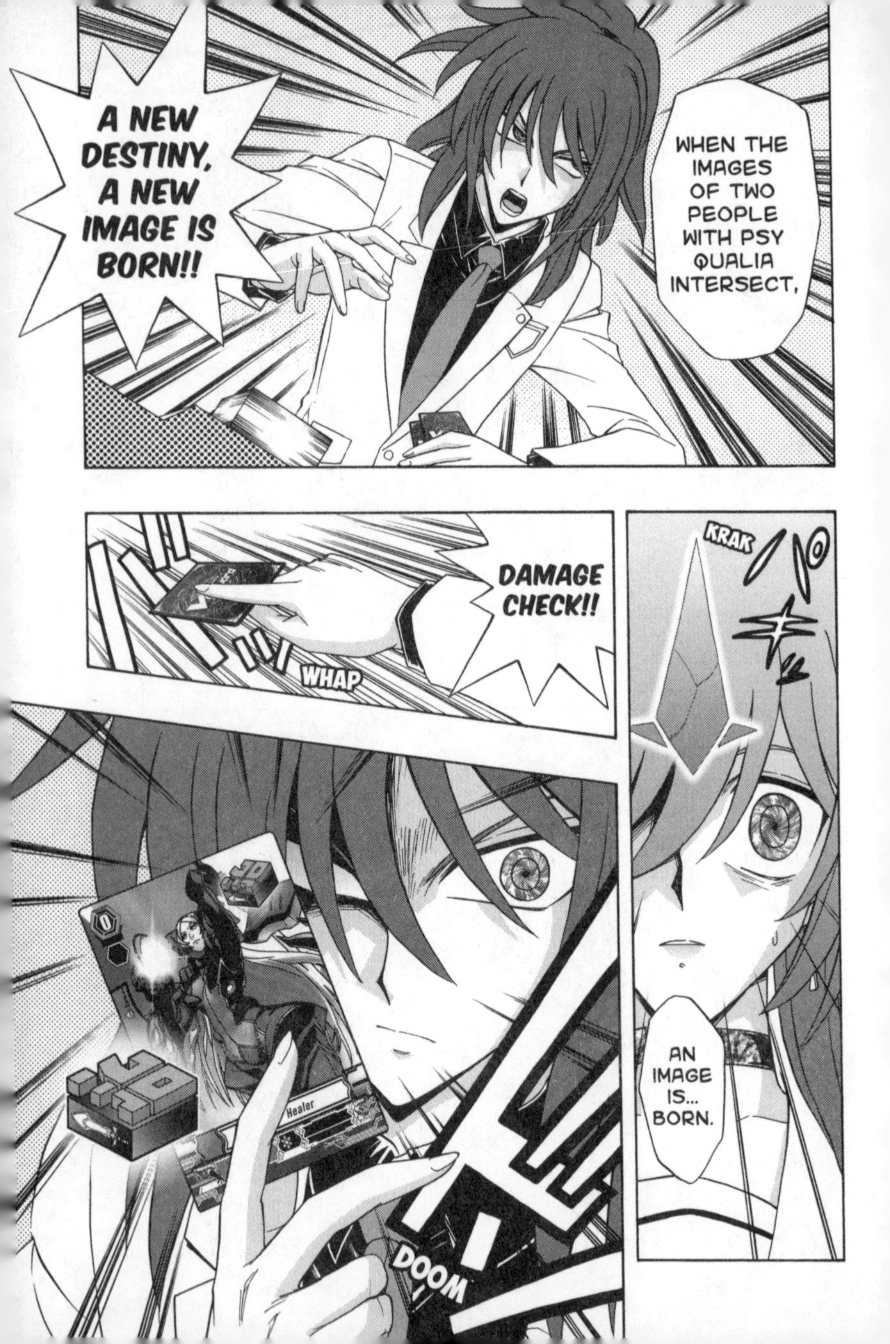
WHEN THE IMAGES OF TWO PEOPLE WITH PSY QUALIA INTERSECT,
A NEW DESTINY, A NEW IMAGE IS BORN!!
KRAK
AN IMAGE IS... BORN.
DAMAGE CHECK!!
WHAP
Healer
DOOM

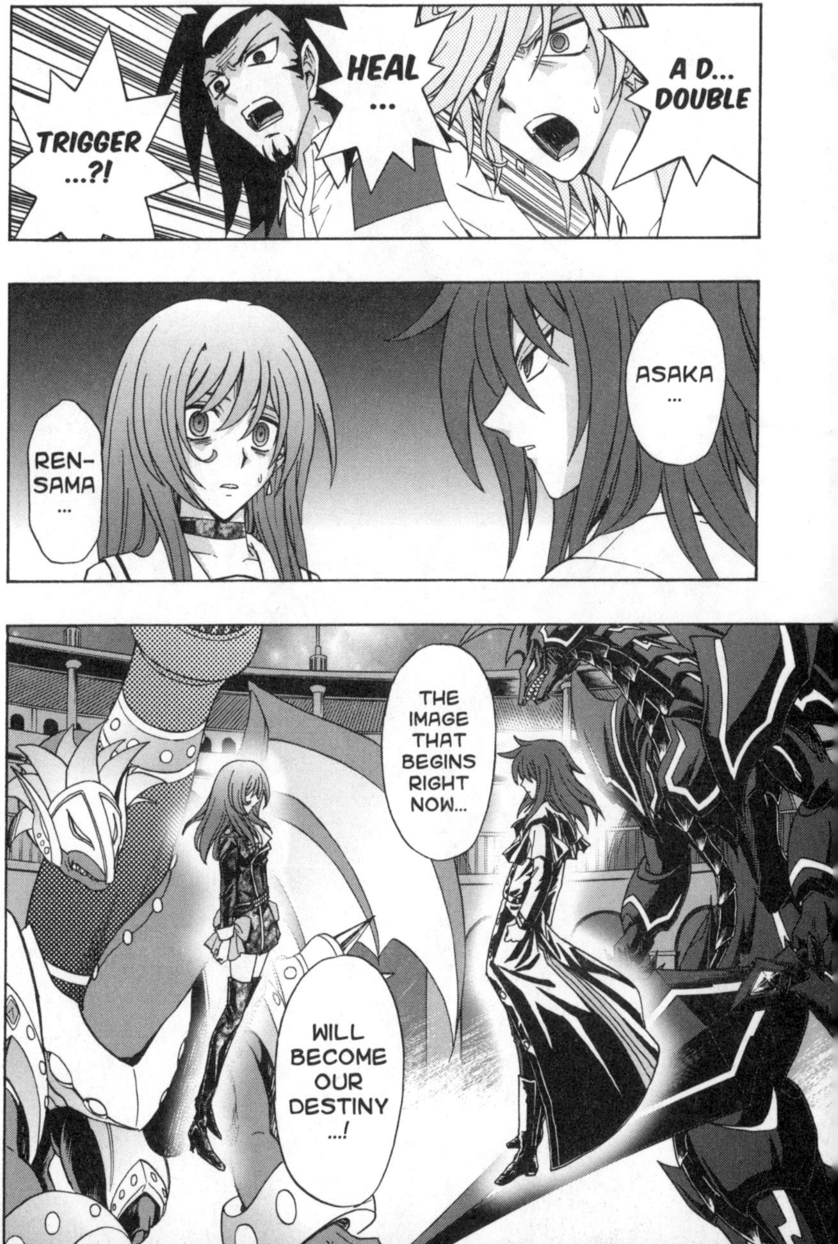
A D... DOUBLE
HEAL ...
TRIGGER ...?!
ASAKA ...
REN-SAMA ...
THE IMAGE THAT BEGINS RIGHT NOW...
WILL BECOME OUR DESTINY ...!

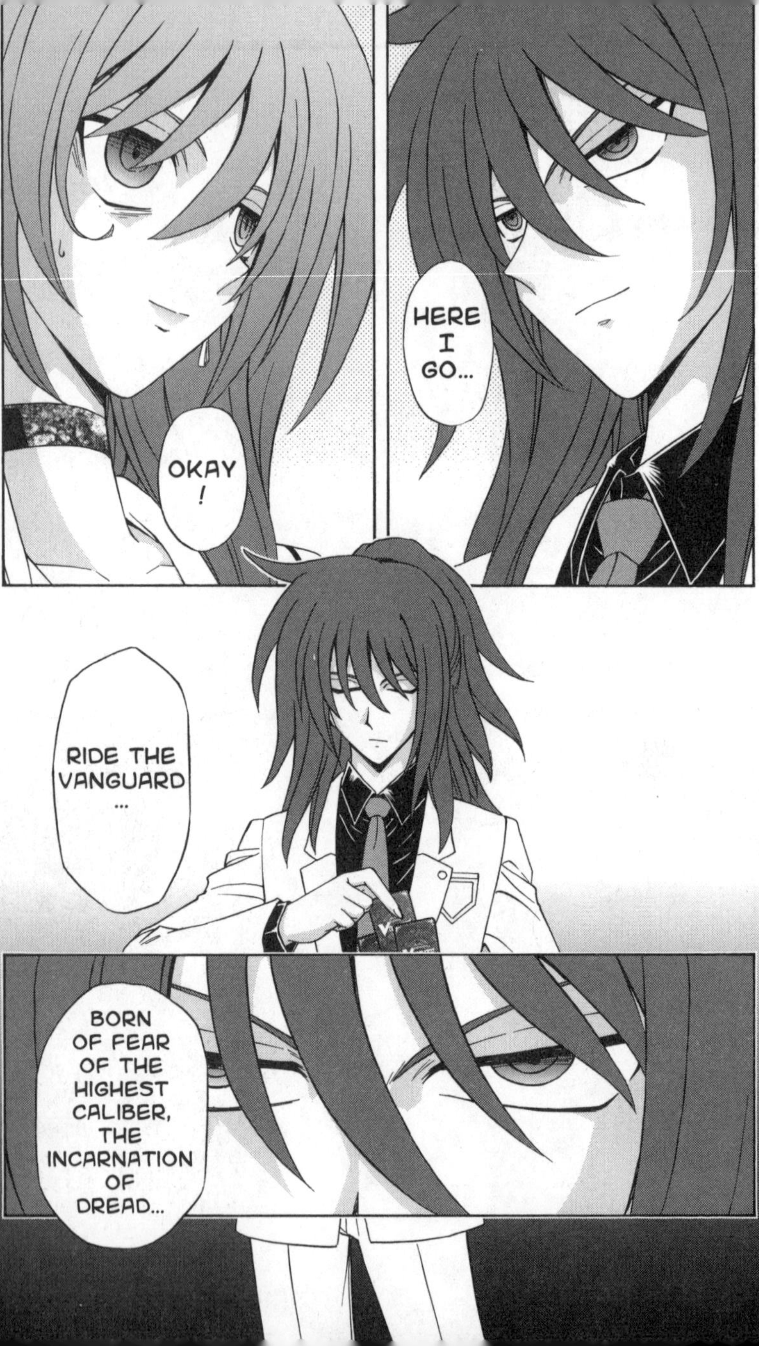
HERE I GO...
OKAY!
RIDE THE VANGUARD...
BORN OF FEAR OF THE HIGHEST CALIBER, THE INCARNATION OF DREAD...

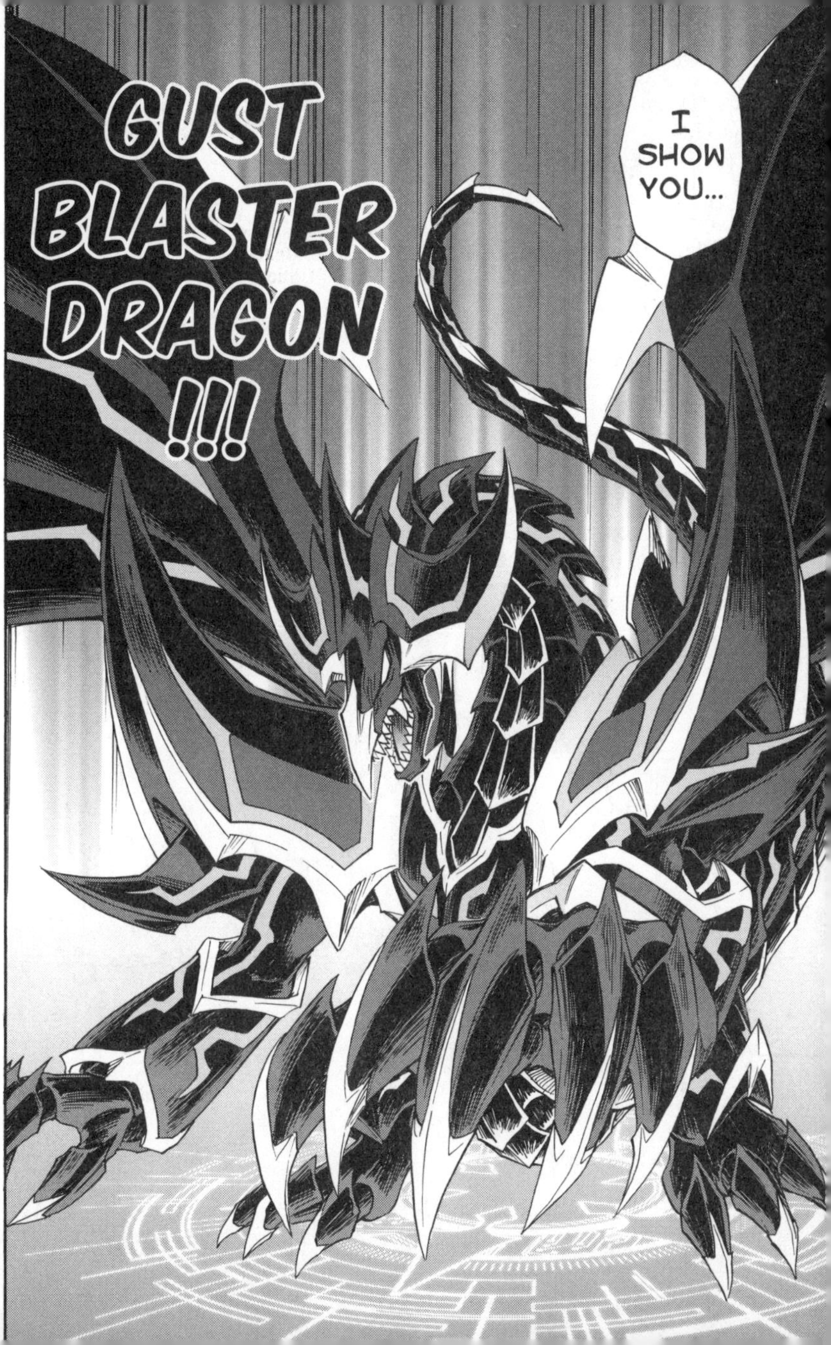
I SHOW YOU...
GUST BLASTER DRAGON !!!

BONUS! CARDFIGHT!! Vanguard

BONUS! VANGUARD NEVER-BEFORE-SEEN IMAGE BOARDS

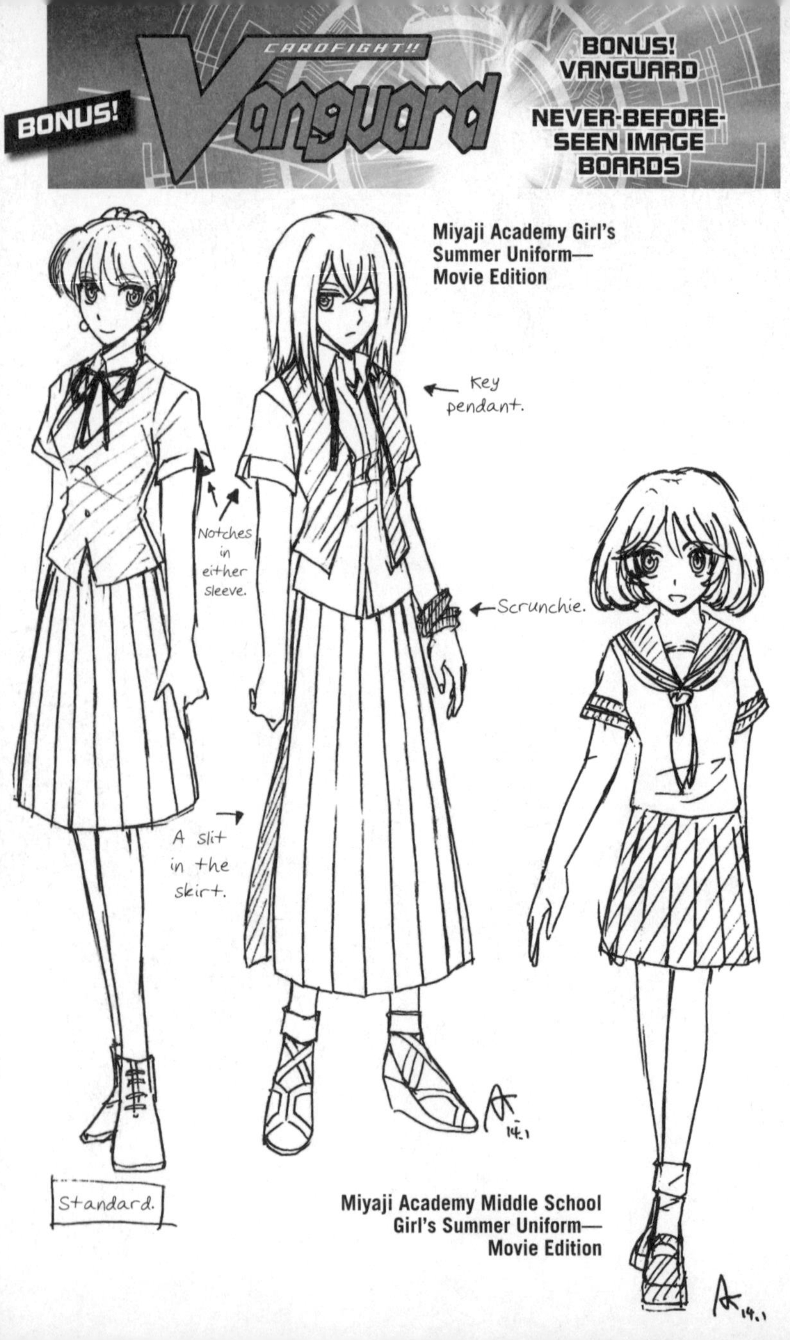
Key pendant.
Notches in either sleeve.
Scrunchie.
A slit in the skirt.
Standard.
14.1
14.1

Miyaji Academy Girl's Summer Uniform—Movie Edition

Miyaji Academy Middle School Girl's Summer Uniform—Movie Edition

BONUS! CARDFIGHT!! Vanguard

BONUS! VANGUARD NEVER-BEFORE-SEEN IMAGE BOARDS

Hitsue High School Boy's Summer Uniform—Movie Edition

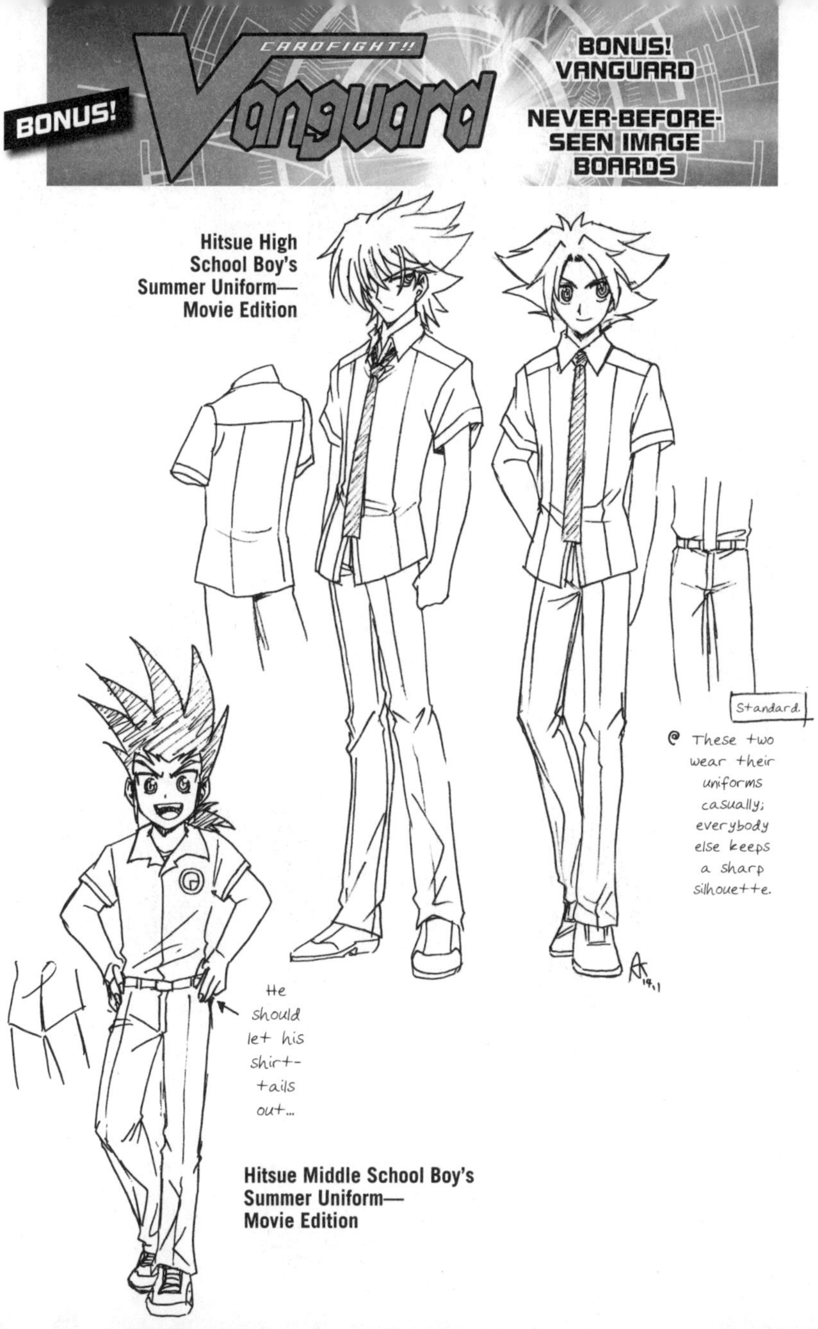
Standard.
These two wear their uniforms casually; everybody else keeps a sharp silhouette.
He should let his shirt-tails out...

Hitsue Middle School Boy's Summer Uniform—Movie Edition

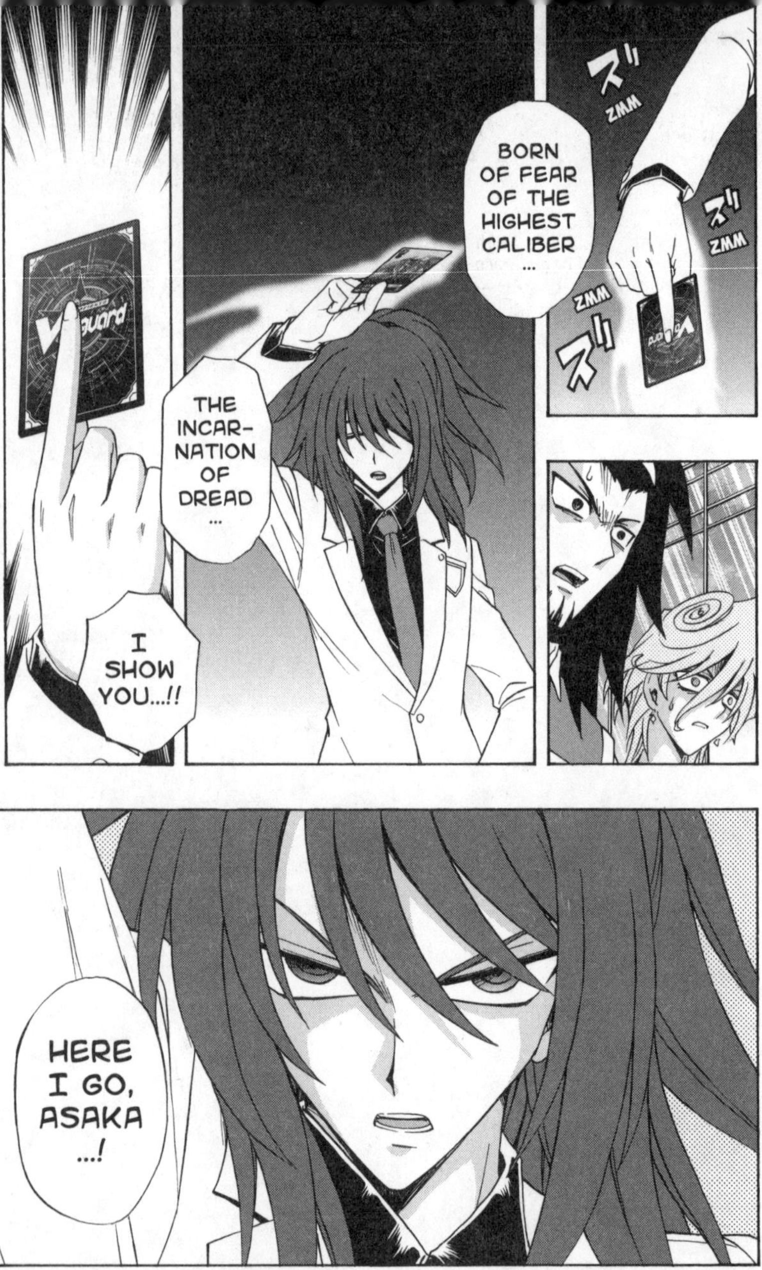
ズリ
ZMM
BORN OF FEAR OF THE HIGHEST CALIBER ...
ズリ
ZMM
ズリ
ZMM
THE INCARNATION OF DREAD ...
I SHOW YOU...!!
HERE I GO, ASAKA ...!

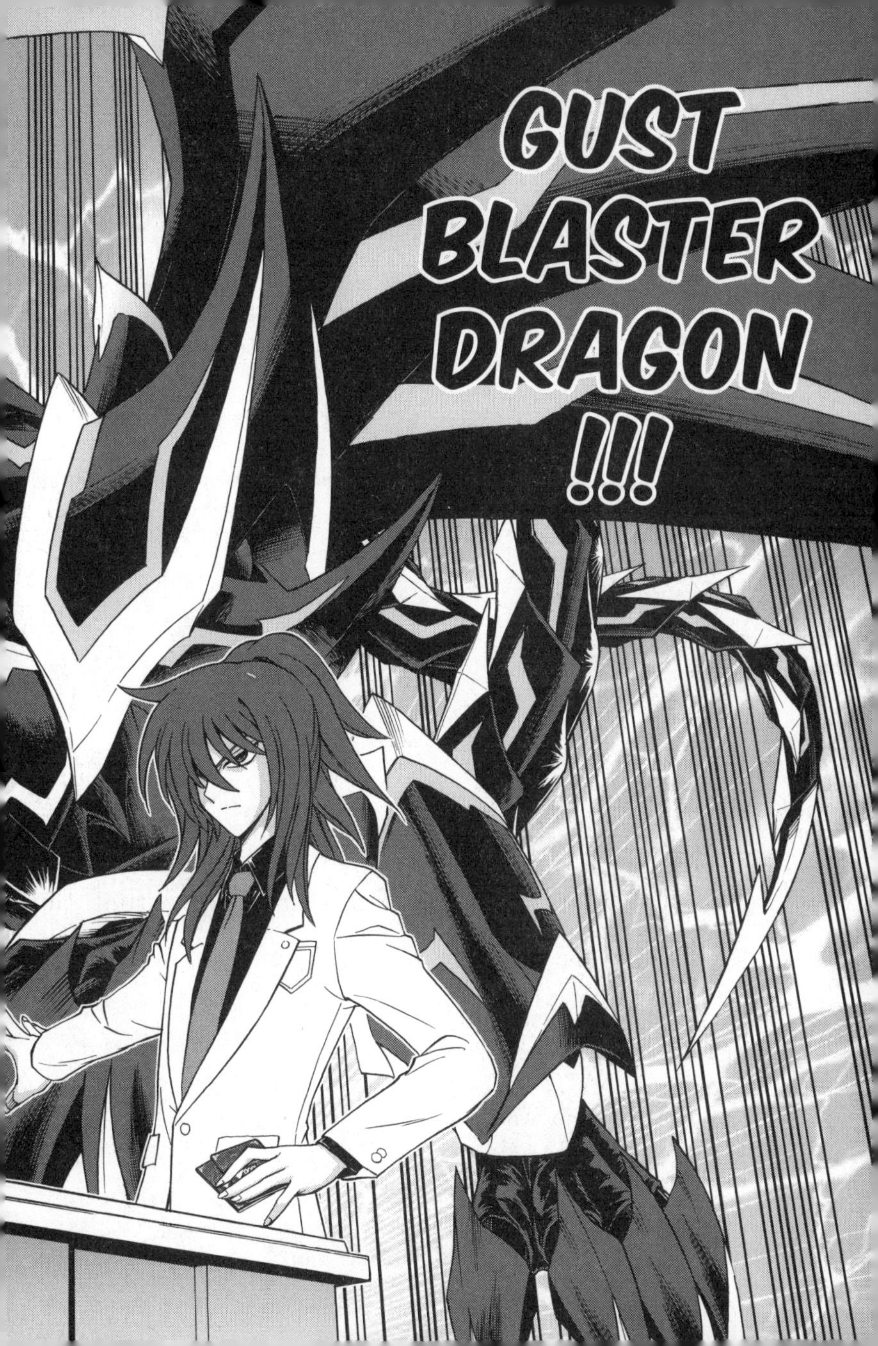
GUST BLASTER DRAGON !!!

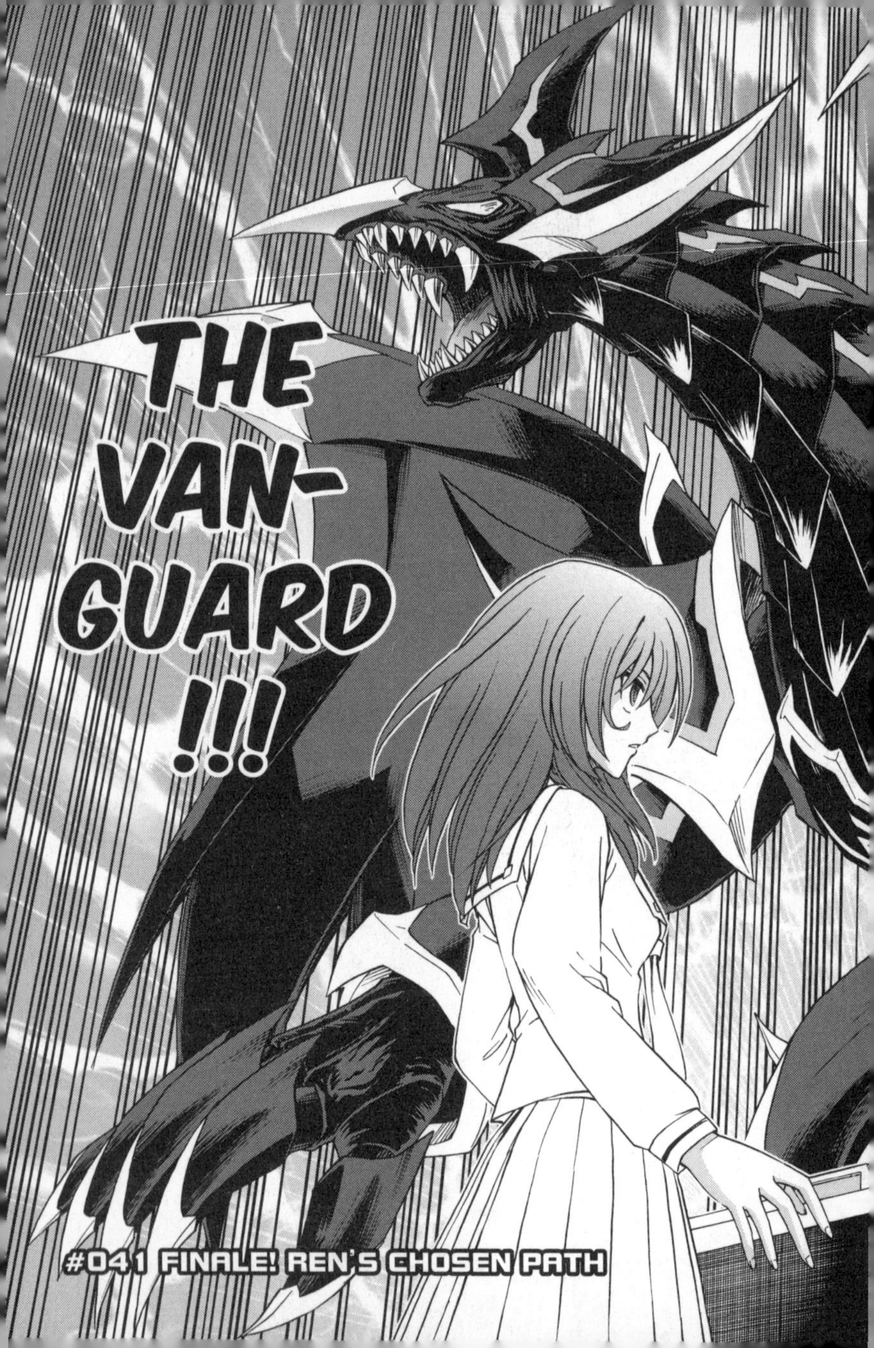
THE VAN-GUARD !!!
#041 FINALE! REN'S CHOSEN PATH

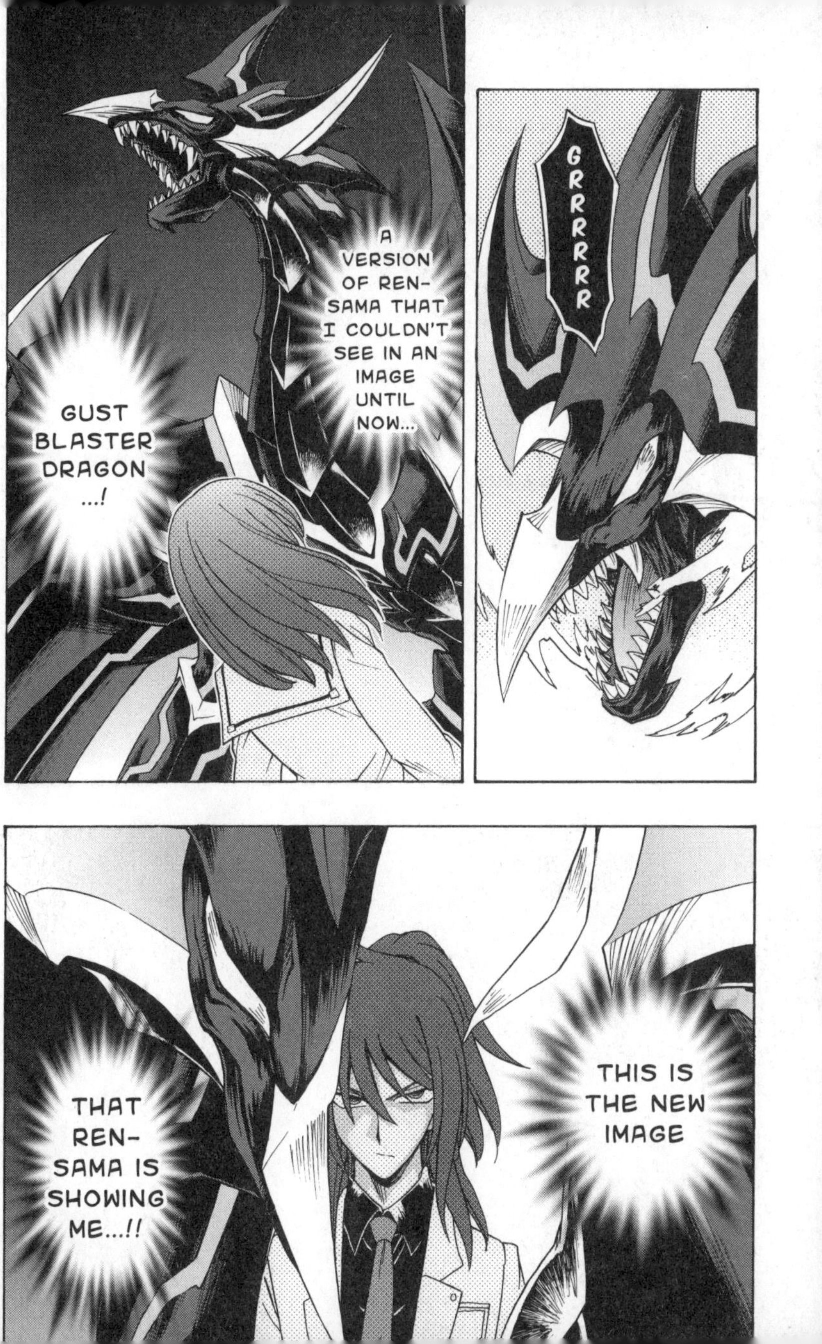
GRRRRR
A VERSION OF REN-SAMA THAT I COULDN'T SEE IN AN IMAGE UNTIL NOW...
GUST BLASTER DRAGON ...!
THIS IS THE NEW IMAGE
THAT REN-SAMA IS SHOWING ME...!!

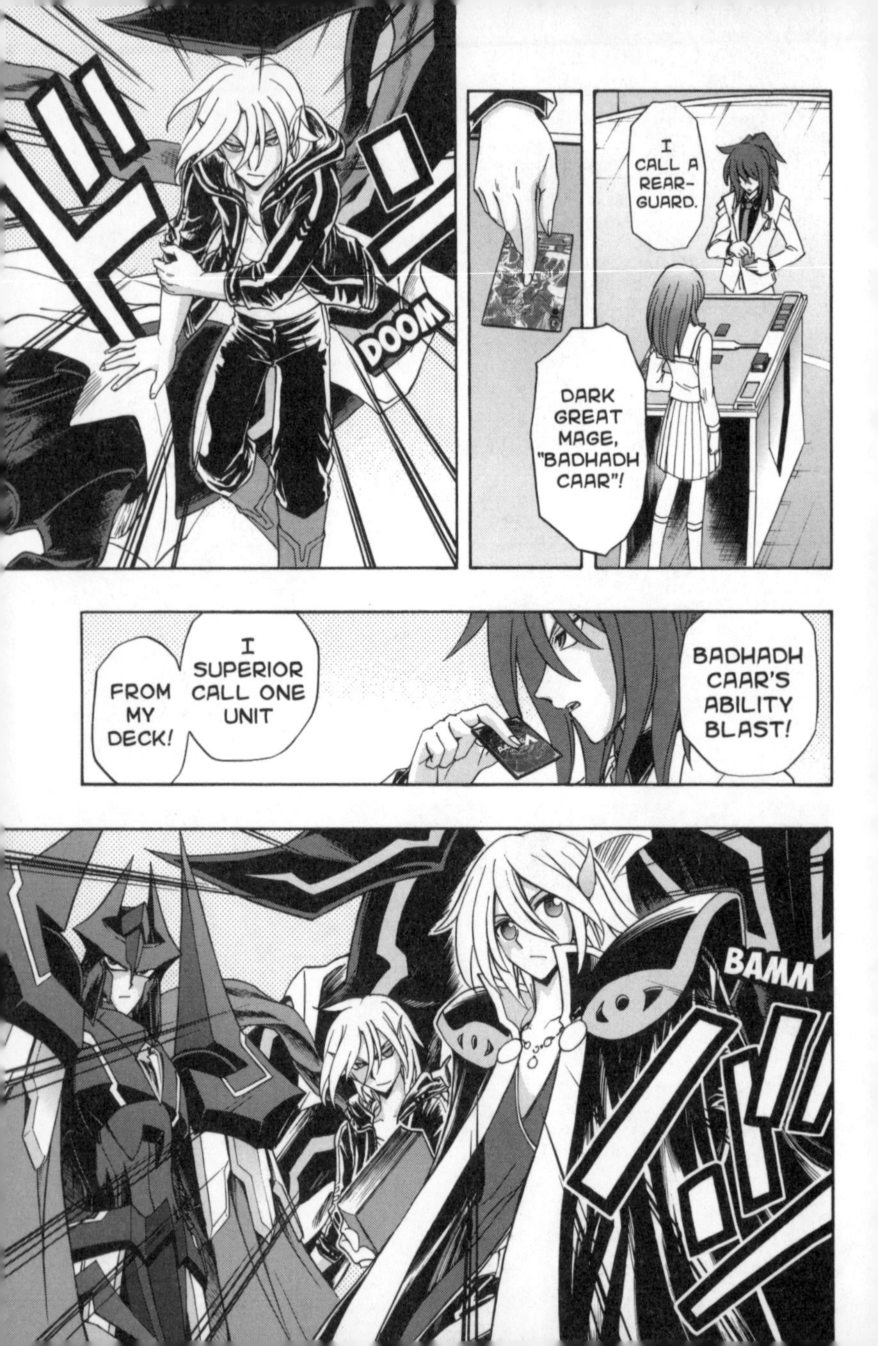
I CALL A REAR-GUARD.
DARK GREAT MAGE, "BADHADH CAAR"!
DOOM
BADHADH CAAR'S ABILITY BLAST!
I SUPERIOR CALL ONE UNIT
FROM MY DECK!
BAMM

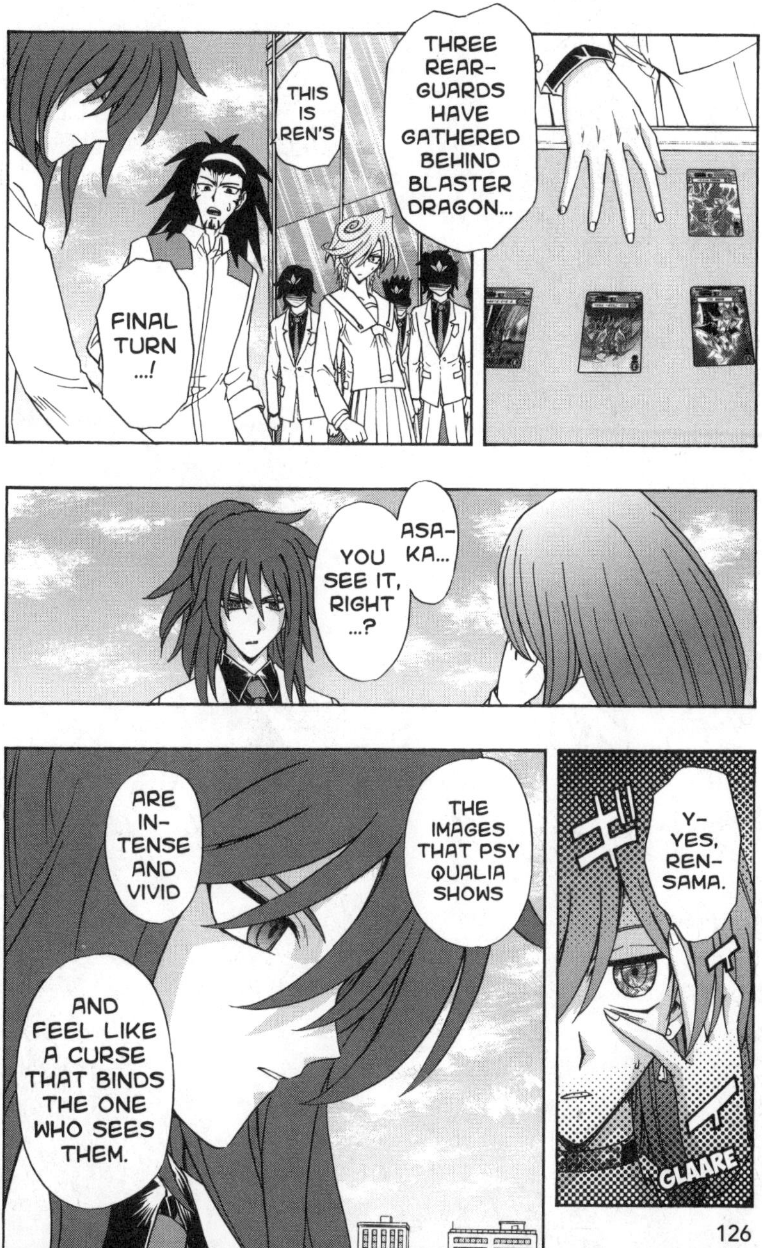
THREE REAR-GUARDS HAVE GATHERED BEHIND BLASTER DRAGON...
THIS IS REN'S
FINAL TURN ...!
ASA-KA...
YOU SEE IT, RIGHT ...?
Y-YES, REN-SAMA.
GLAARE
THE IMAGES THAT PSY QUALIA SHOWS
ARE IN-TENSE AND VIVID
AND FEEL LIKE A CURSE THAT BINDS THE ONE WHO SEES THEM.

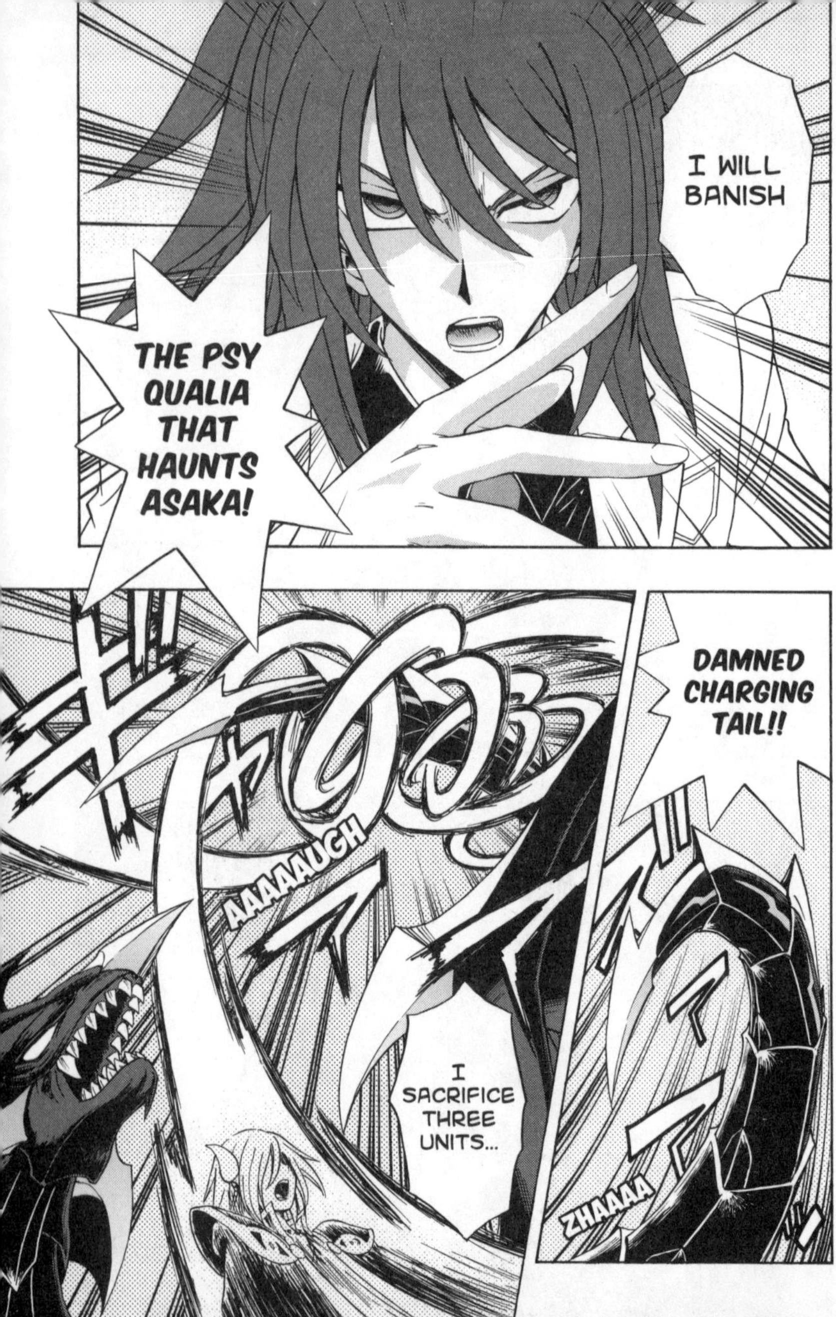
I WILL BANISH
THE PSY QUALIA THAT HAUNTS ASAKA!
DAMNED CHARGING TAIL!!
ZHAAAA
AAAAAUGH
I SACRIFICE THREE UNITS...

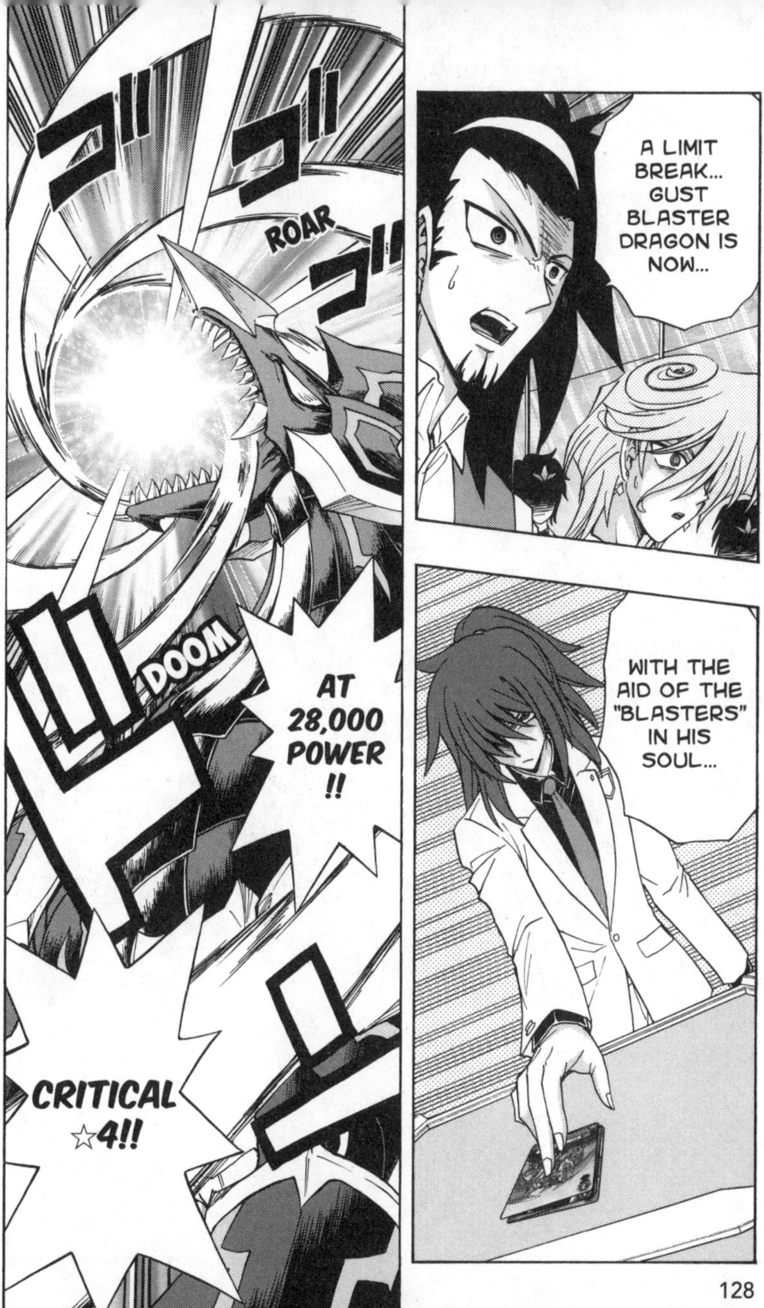
A LIMIT BREAK... GUST BLASTER DRAGON IS NOW...
WITH THE AID OF THE "BLASTERS" IN HIS SOUL...
ROAR
DOOM
AT 28,000 POWER !!
CRITICAL ☆4!!

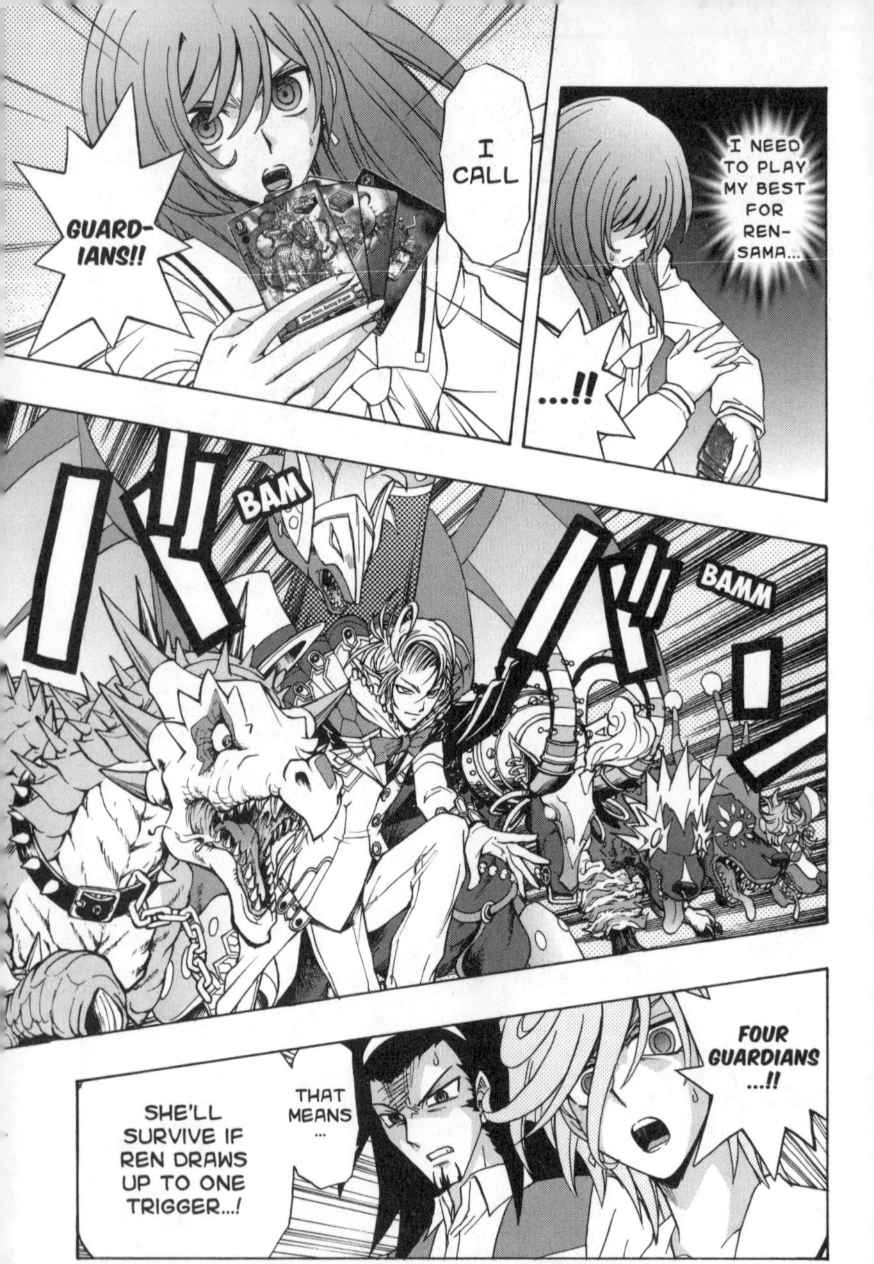
I NEED TO PLAY MY BEST FOR REN-SAMA...
...!!
I CALL
GUARDIANS!!
BAMM
BAM
FOUR GUARDIANS ...!!
THAT MEANS ...
SHE'LL SURVIVE IF REN DRAWS UP TO ONE TRIGGER...!

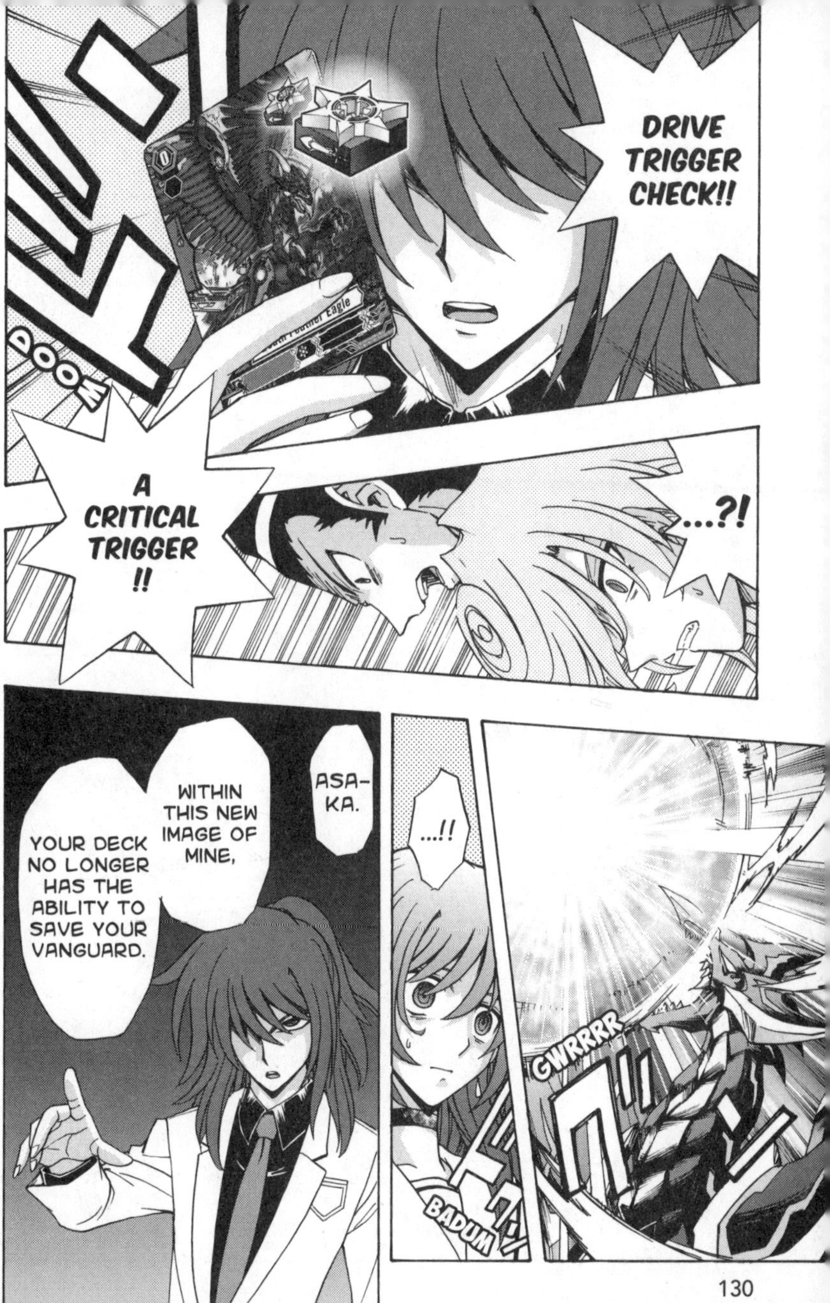
DRIVE TRIGGER CHECK!!
DOOM
...?!
A CRITICAL TRIGGER !!
GWRRRR
BADUM
...!!
ASA-KA.
WITHIN THIS NEW IMAGE OF MINE,
YOUR DECK NO LONGER HAS THE ABILITY TO SAVE YOUR VANGUARD.

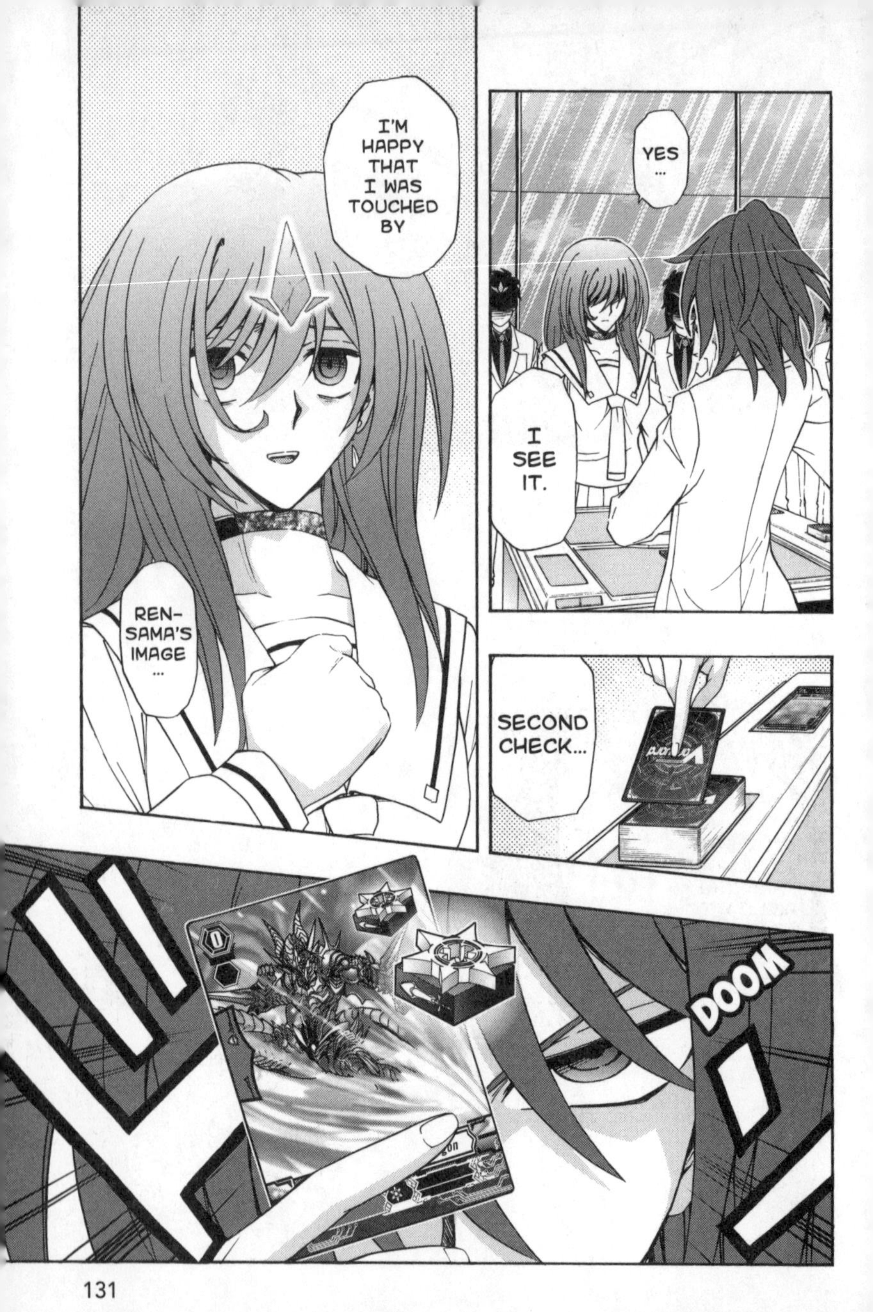
YES ...
I SEE IT.
SECOND CHECK...
I'M HAPPY THAT I WAS TOUCHED BY
REN-SAMA'S IMAGE ...
DOOM

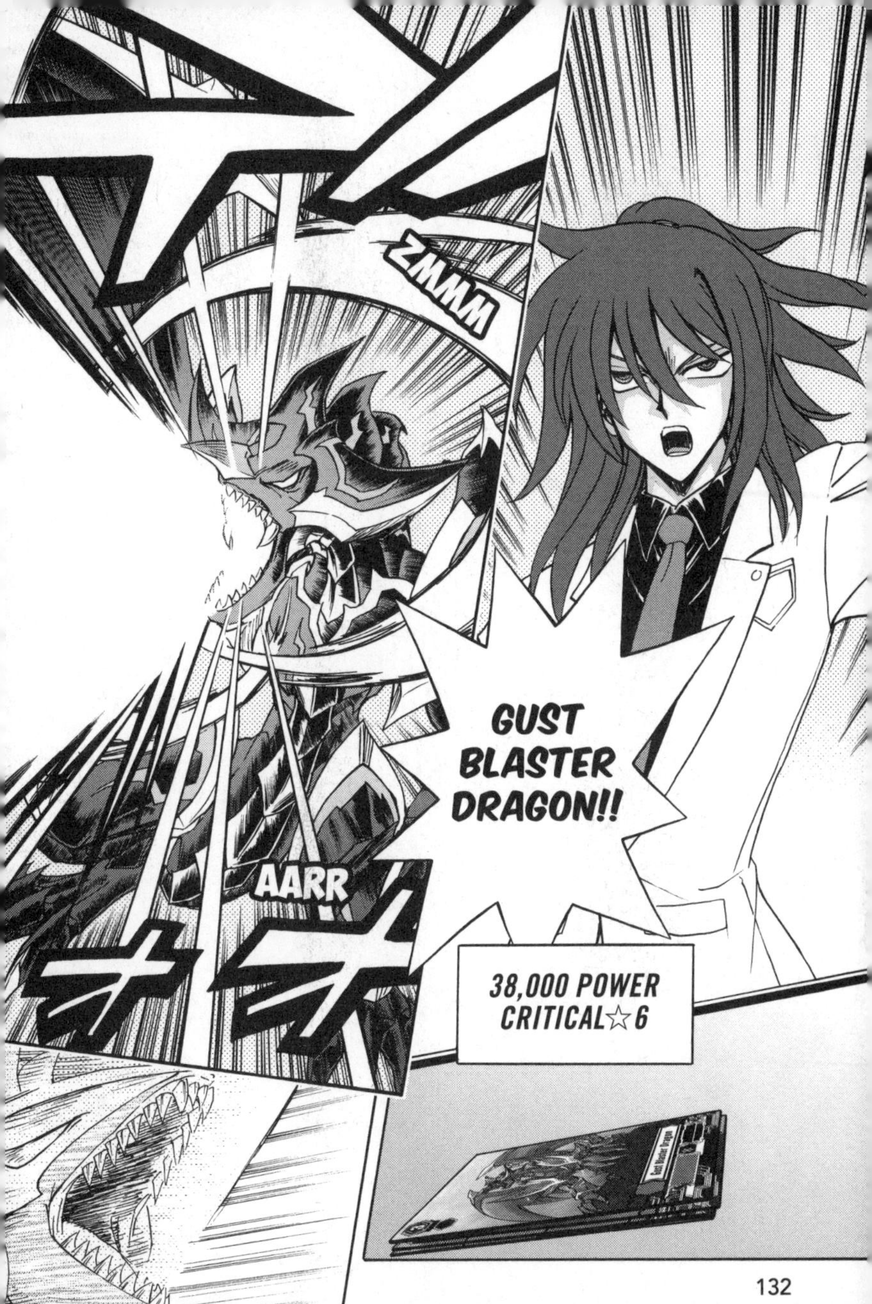
GUST BLASTER DRAGON!!
ZMMM
AARR
38,000 POWER CRITICAL☆6

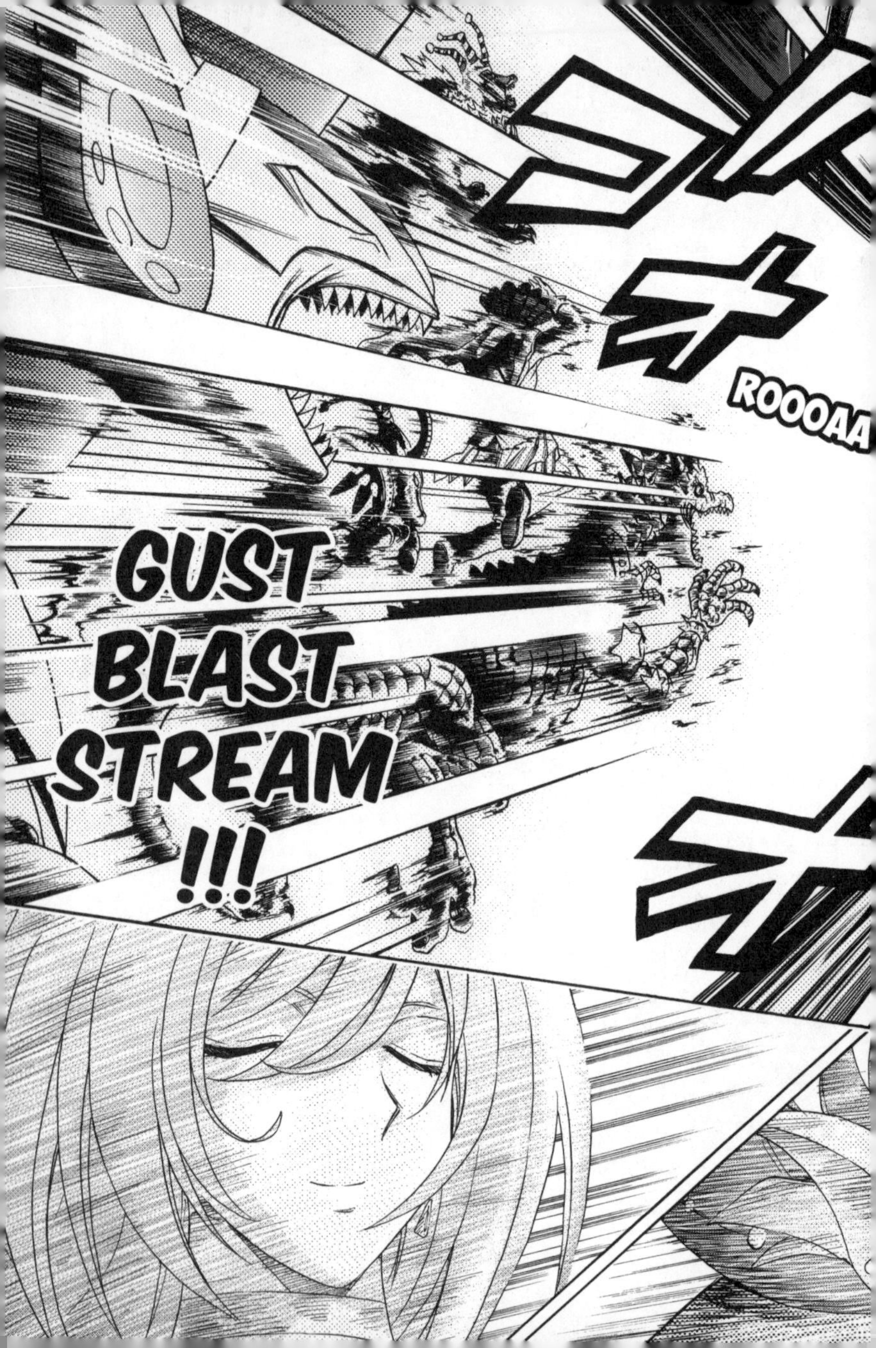
ROOOAA
GUST BLAST STREAM !!!

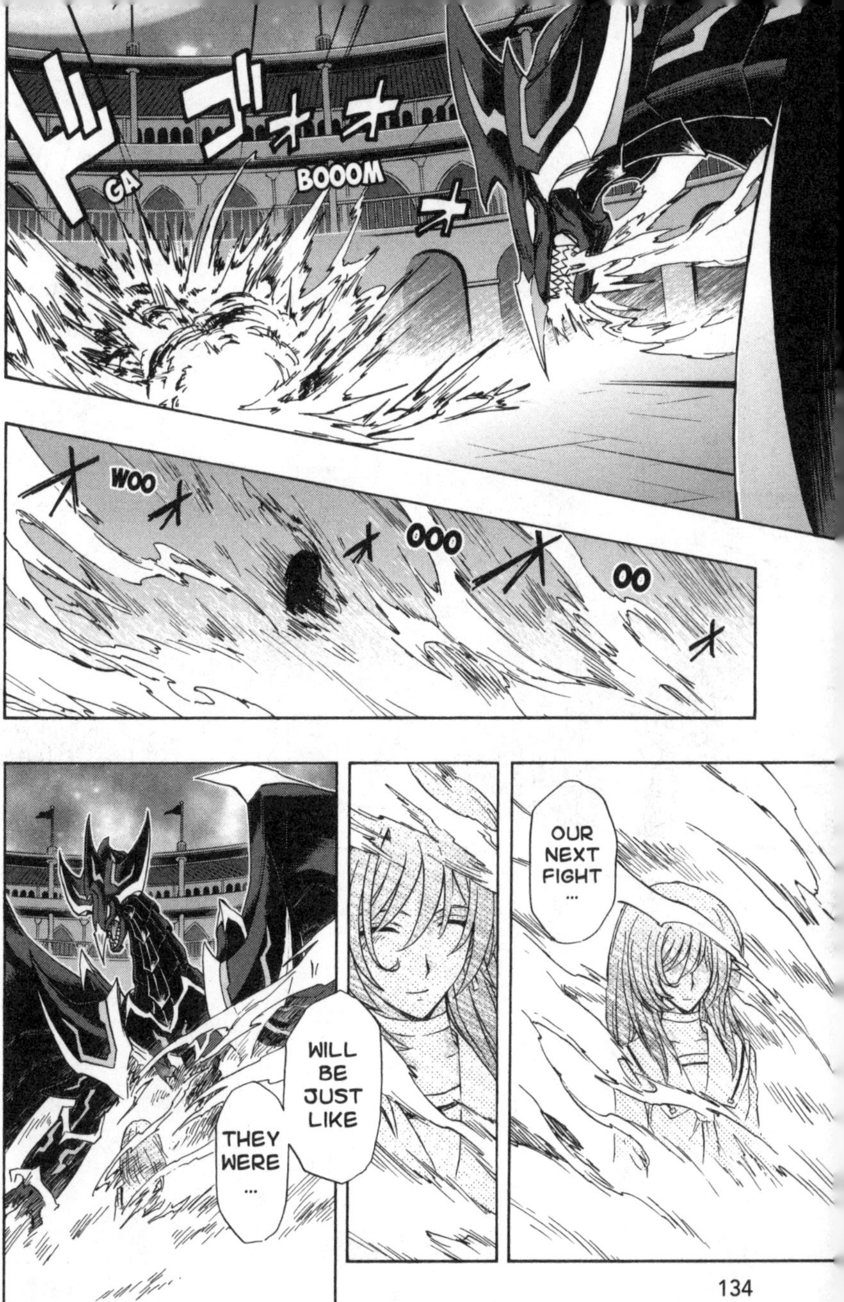

GA
BOOOM
WOO
OOO
OO
OUR NEXT FIGHT ...
WILL BE JUST LIKE
THEY WERE ...

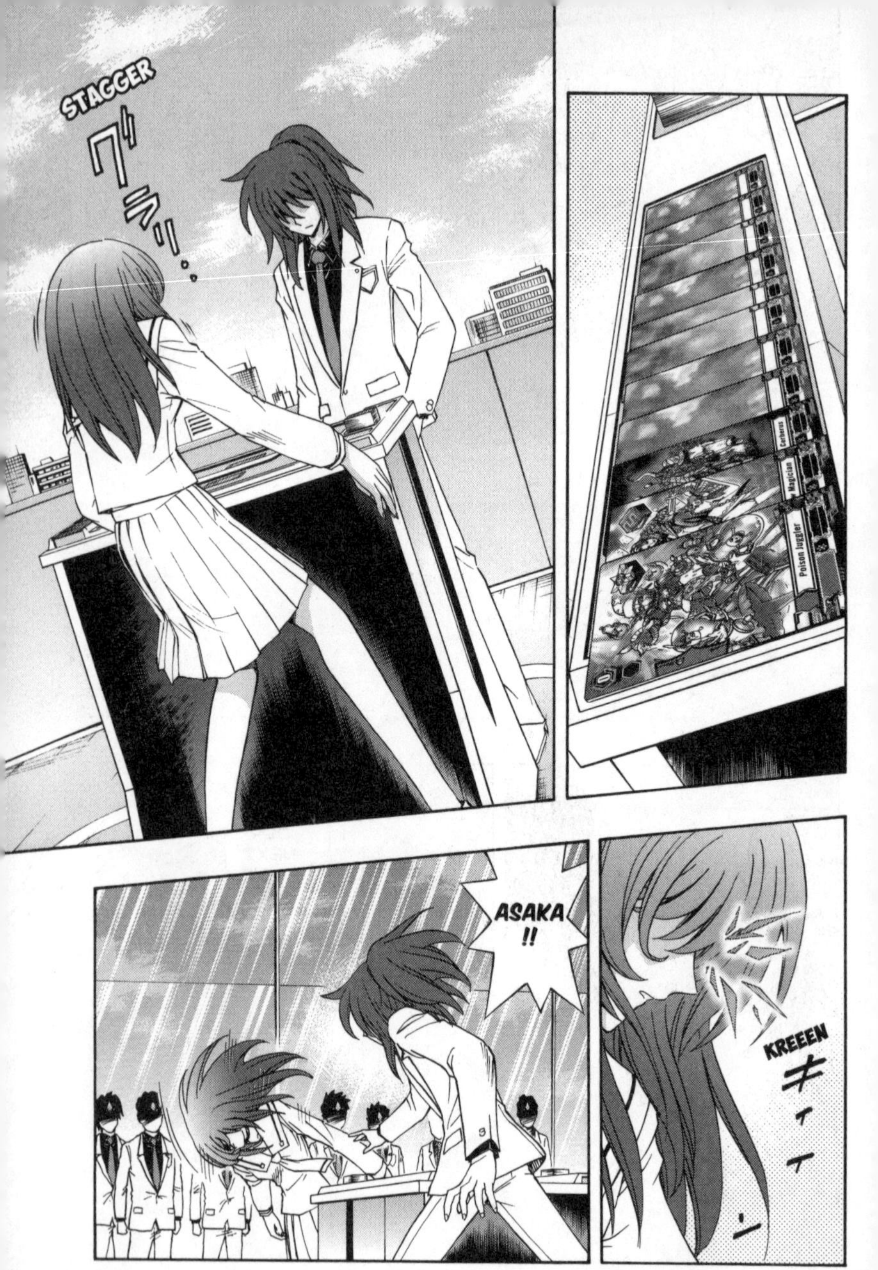
Cerberus
Magician
Poison Juggler
STAGGER
KREEEN
ASAKA !!

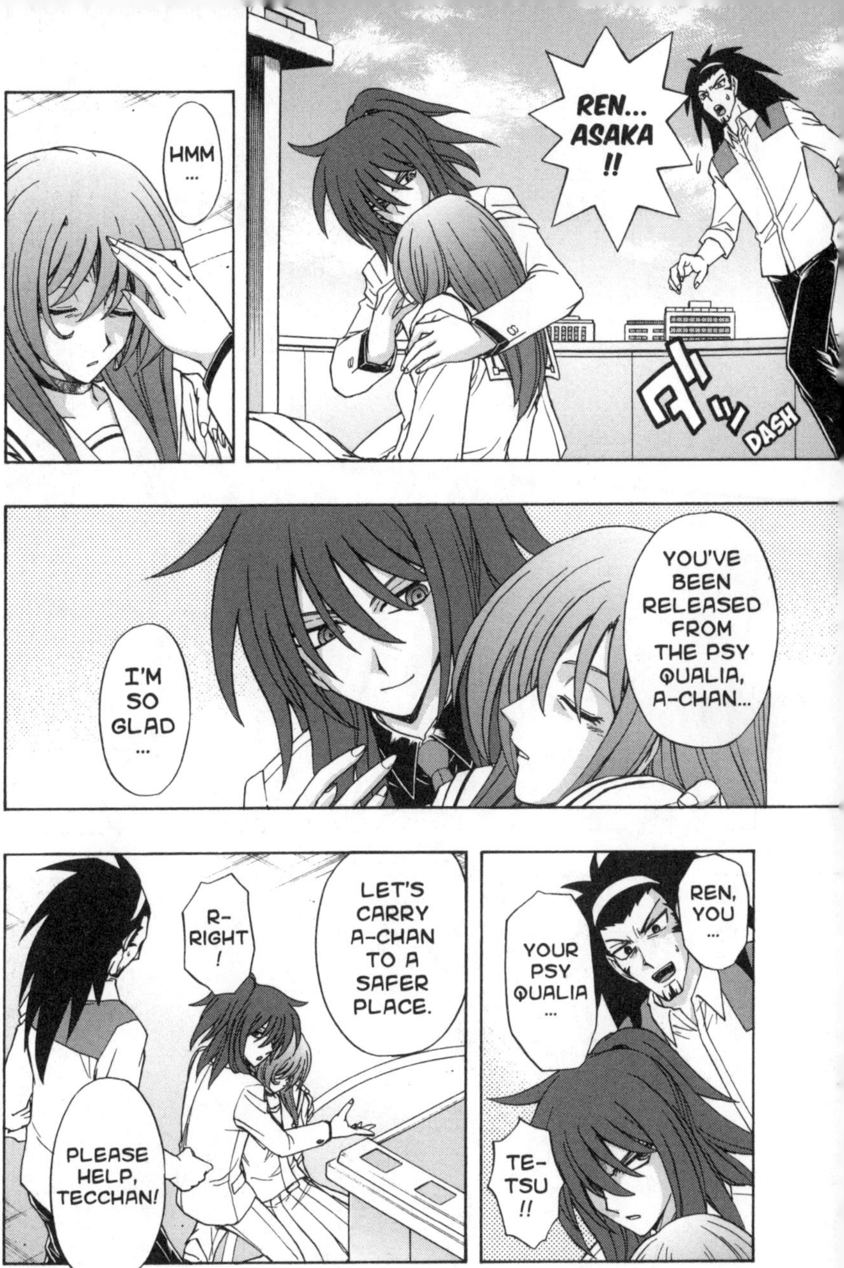
REN... ASAKA !!
DASH
HMM ...
YOU'VE BEEN RELEASED FROM THE PSY QUALIA, A-CHAN...
I'M SO GLAD ...
REN, YOU ...
YOUR PSY QUALIA ...
TE-TSU !!
LET'S CARRY A-CHAN TO A SAFER PLACE.
PLEASE HELP, TECCHAN!
R-RIGHT !

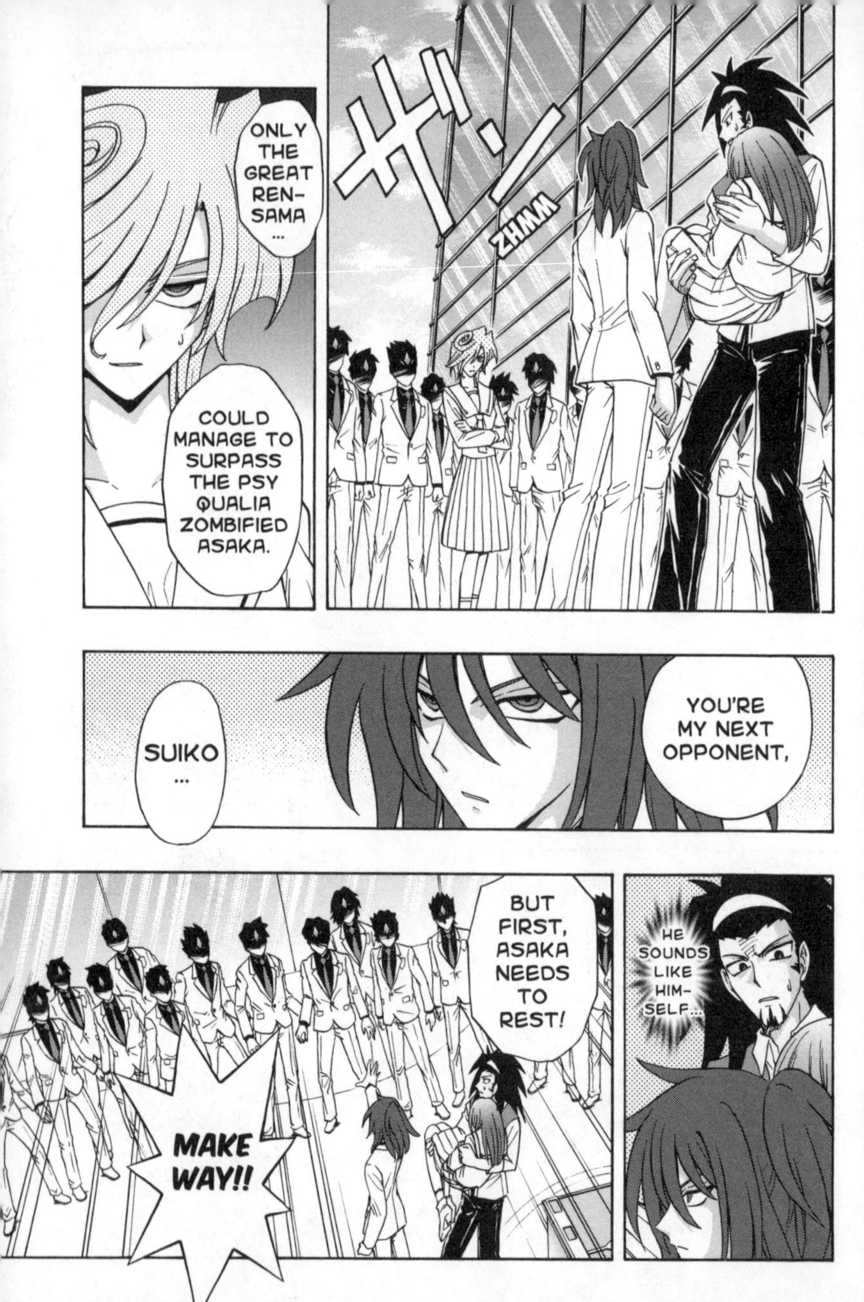
ZHMM
ONLY THE GREAT REN-SAMA ...
COULD MANAGE TO SURPASS THE PSY QUALIA ZOMBIFIED ASAKA.
YOU'RE MY NEXT OPPONENT,
SUIKO ...
HE SOUNDS LIKE HIM-SELF...
BUT FIRST, ASAKA NEEDS TO REST!
MAKE WAY!!

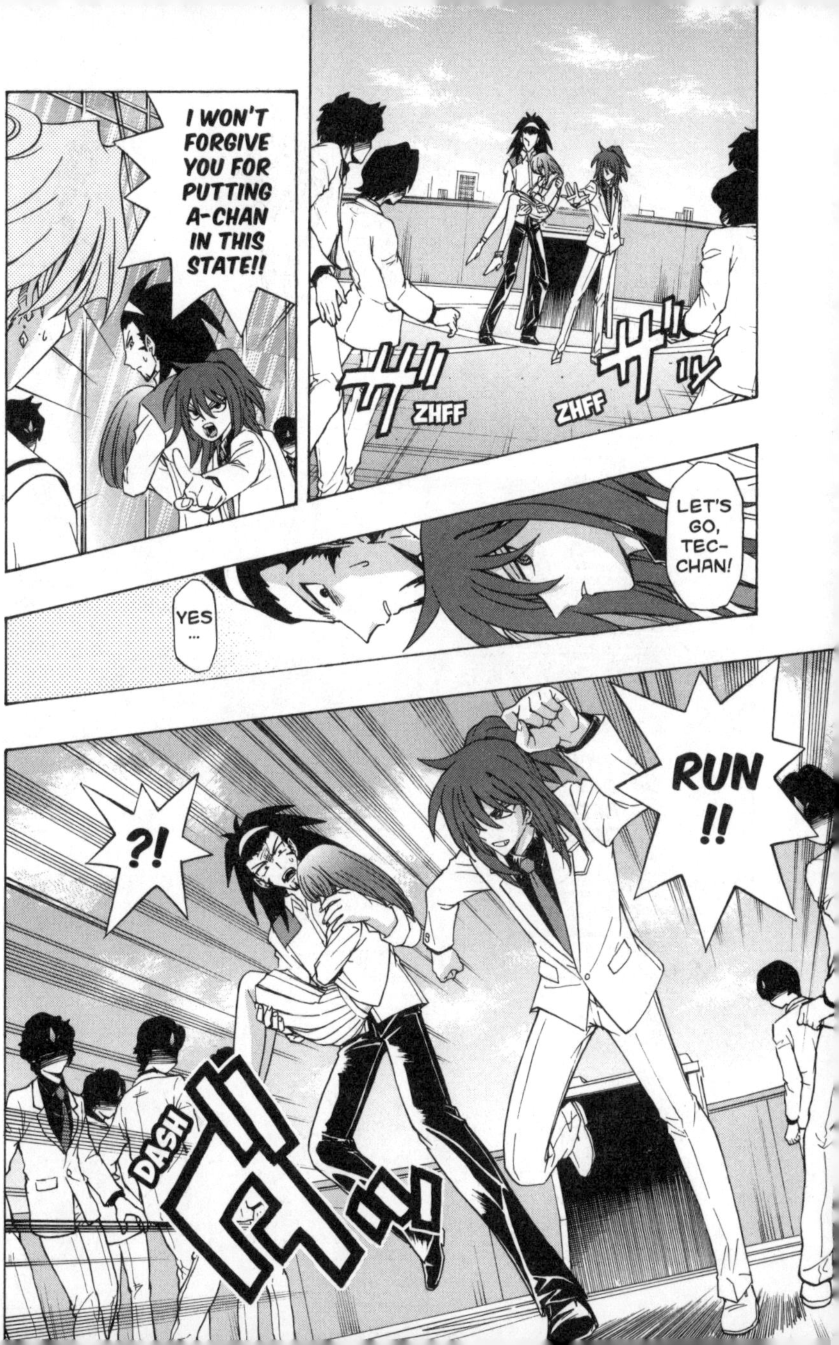
ZHFF
ZHFF
I WON'T FORGIVE YOU FOR PUTTING A-CHAN IN THIS STATE!!
LET'S GO, TEC-CHAN!
YES ...
RUN!!
?!
DASH

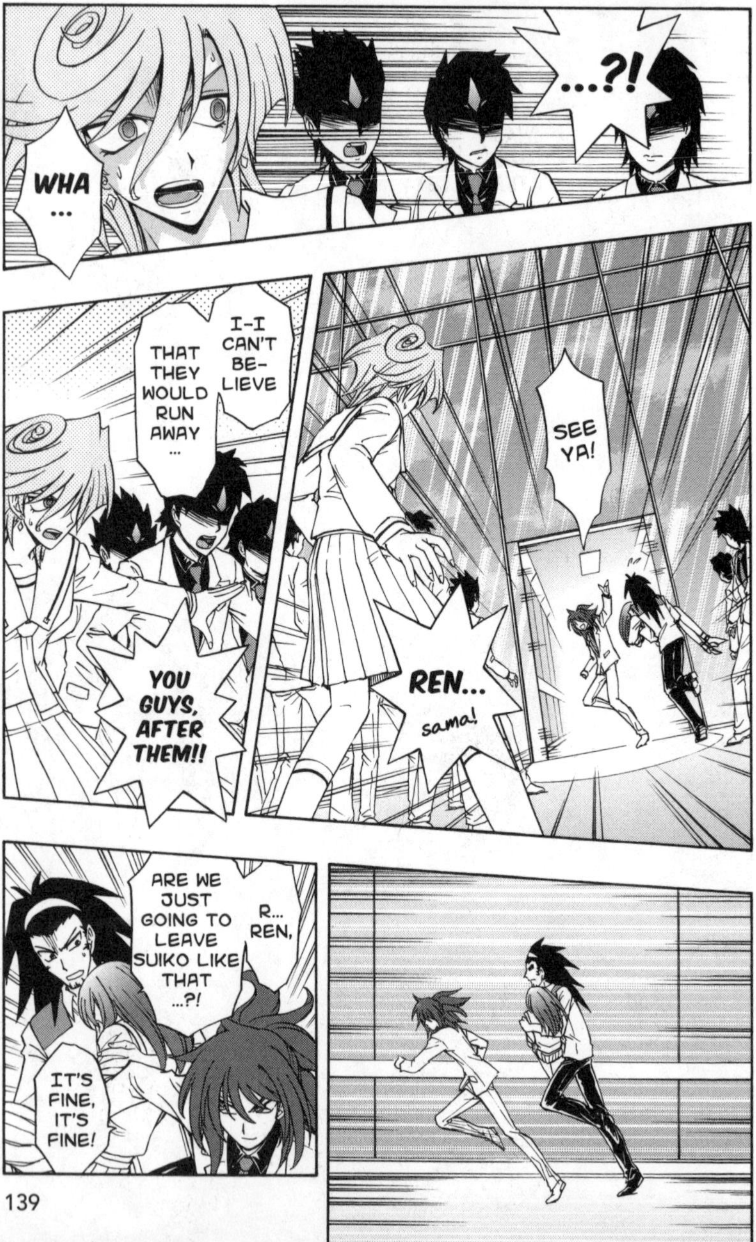
...?!
WHA ...
SEE YA!
REN... sama!
I-I CAN'T BE-LIEVE
THAT THEY WOULD RUN AWAY ...
YOU GUYS, AFTER THEM!!
R... REN,
ARE WE JUST GOING TO LEAVE SUIKO LIKE THAT ...?!
IT'S FINE, IT'S FINE!

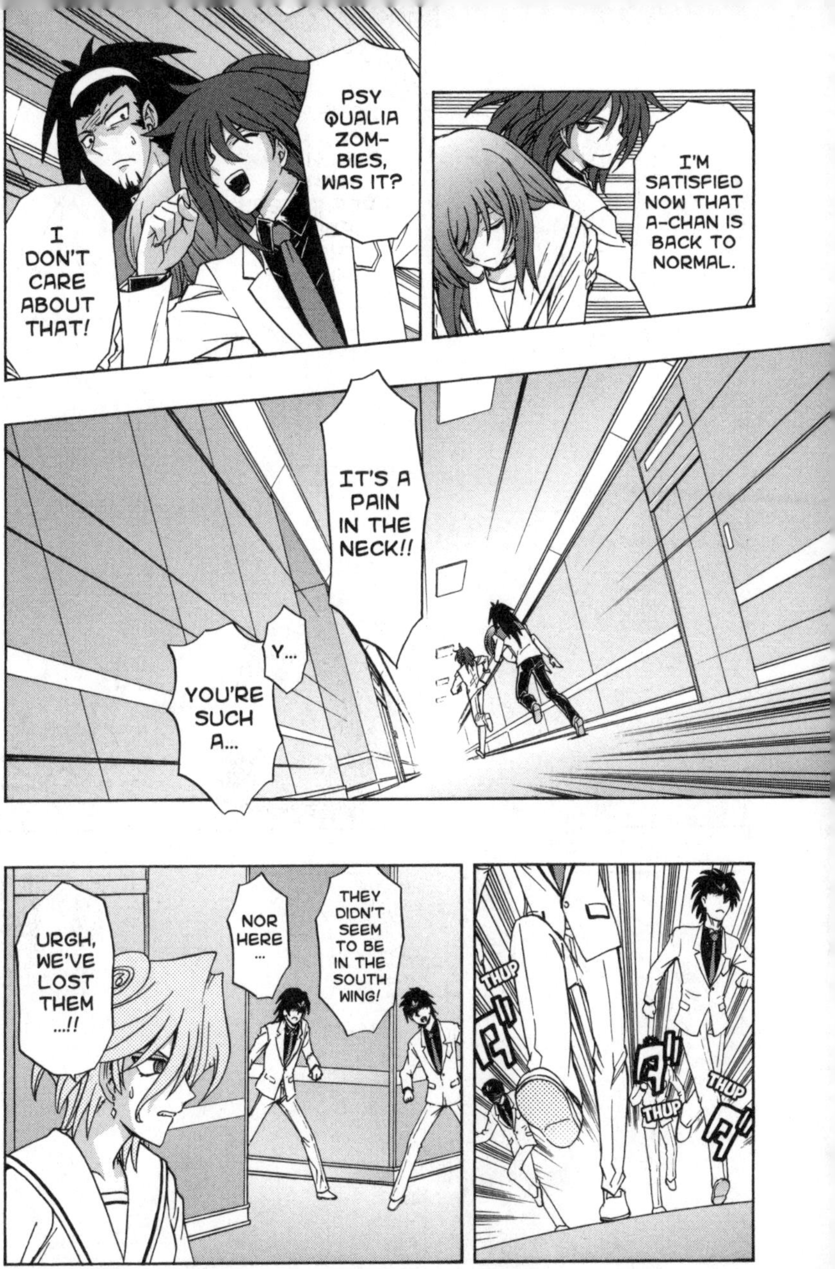
I'M SATISFIED NOW THAT A-CHAN IS BACK TO NORMAL.
PSY QUALIA ZOMBIES, WAS IT?
I DON'T CARE ABOUT THAT!
IT'S A PAIN IN THE NECK!!
Y...
YOU'RE SUCH A...
THUP
THUP
THUP
THEY DIDN'T SEEM TO BE IN THE SOUTH WING!
NOR HERE ...
URGH, WE'VE LOST THEM ...!!

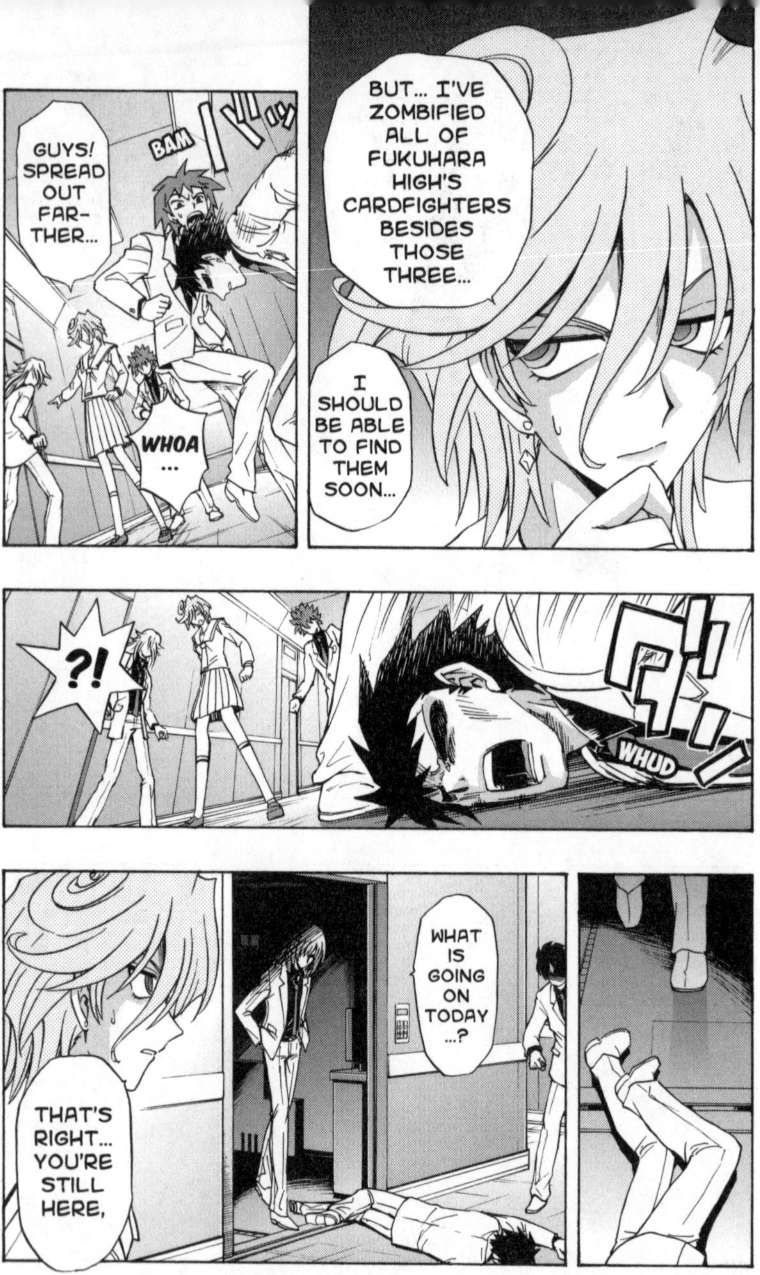
BUT... I'VE ZOMBIFIED ALL OF FUKUHARA HIGH'S CARDFIGHTERS BESIDES THOSE THREE...
I SHOULD BE ABLE TO FIND THEM SOON...
BAM
GUYS! SPREAD OUT FAR-THER...
WHOA ...
WHUD
?!
WHAT IS GOING ON TODAY ...?
THAT'S RIGHT... YOU'RE STILL HERE,

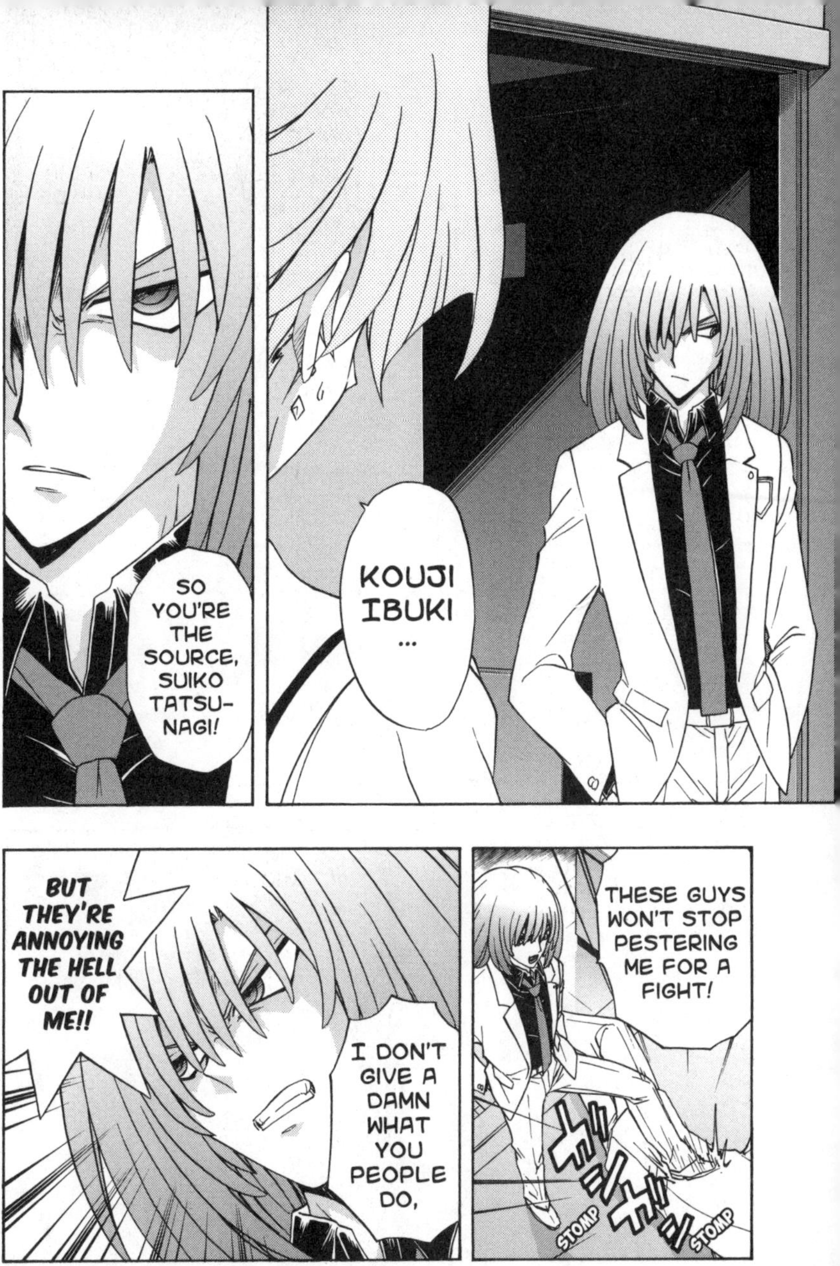
KOUJI IBUKI ...
SO YOU'RE THE SOURCE, SUIKO TATSU-NAGI!
THESE GUYS WON'T STOP PESTERING ME FOR A FIGHT!
STOMP
STOMP
I DON'T GIVE A DAMN WHAT YOU PEOPLE DO,
BUT THEY'RE ANNOYING THE HELL OUT OF ME!!

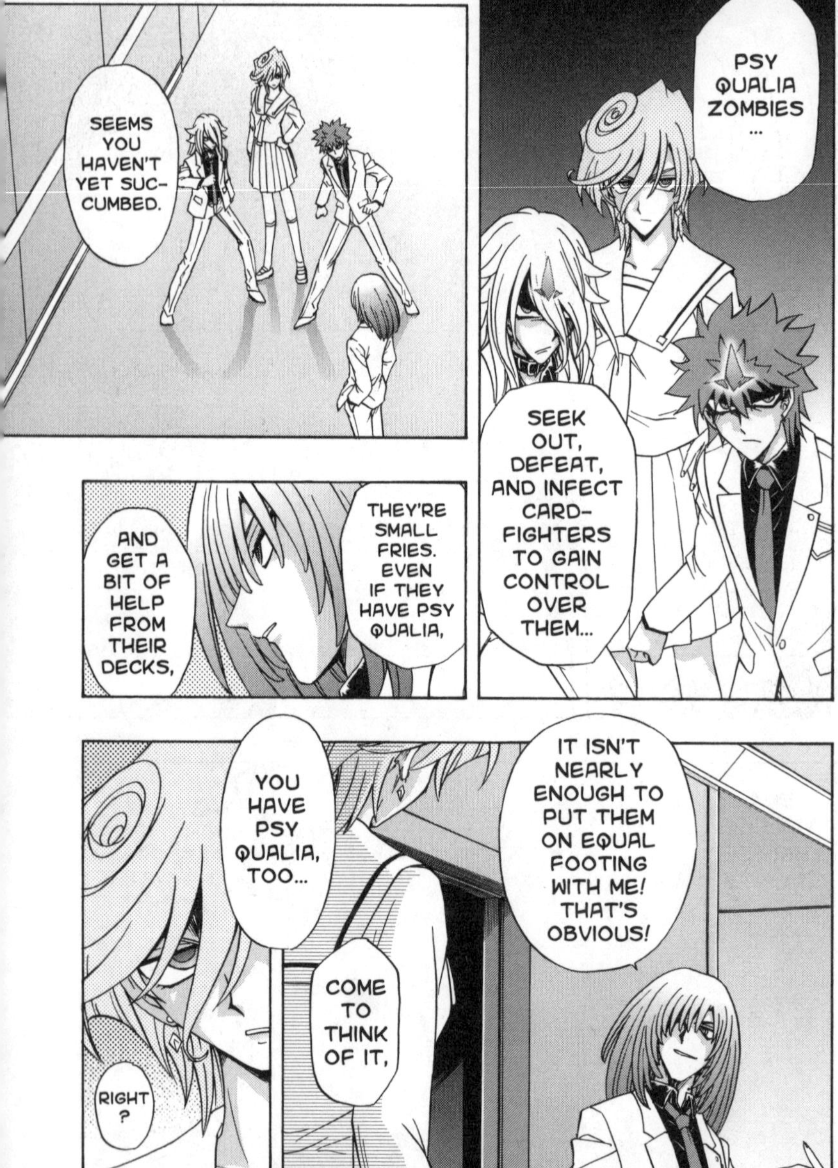
PSY QUALIA ZOMBIES ...
SEEK OUT, DEFEAT, AND INFECT CARD-FIGHTERS TO GAIN CONTROL OVER THEM...
SEEMS YOU HAVEN'T YET SUCCUMBED.
THEY'RE SMALL FRIES. EVEN IF THEY HAVE PSY QUALIA,
AND GET A BIT OF HELP FROM THEIR DECKS,
IT ISN'T NEARLY ENOUGH TO PUT THEM ON EQUAL FOOTING WITH ME! THAT'S OBVIOUS!
YOU HAVE PSY QUALIA, TOO...
COME TO THINK OF IT,
RIGHT?

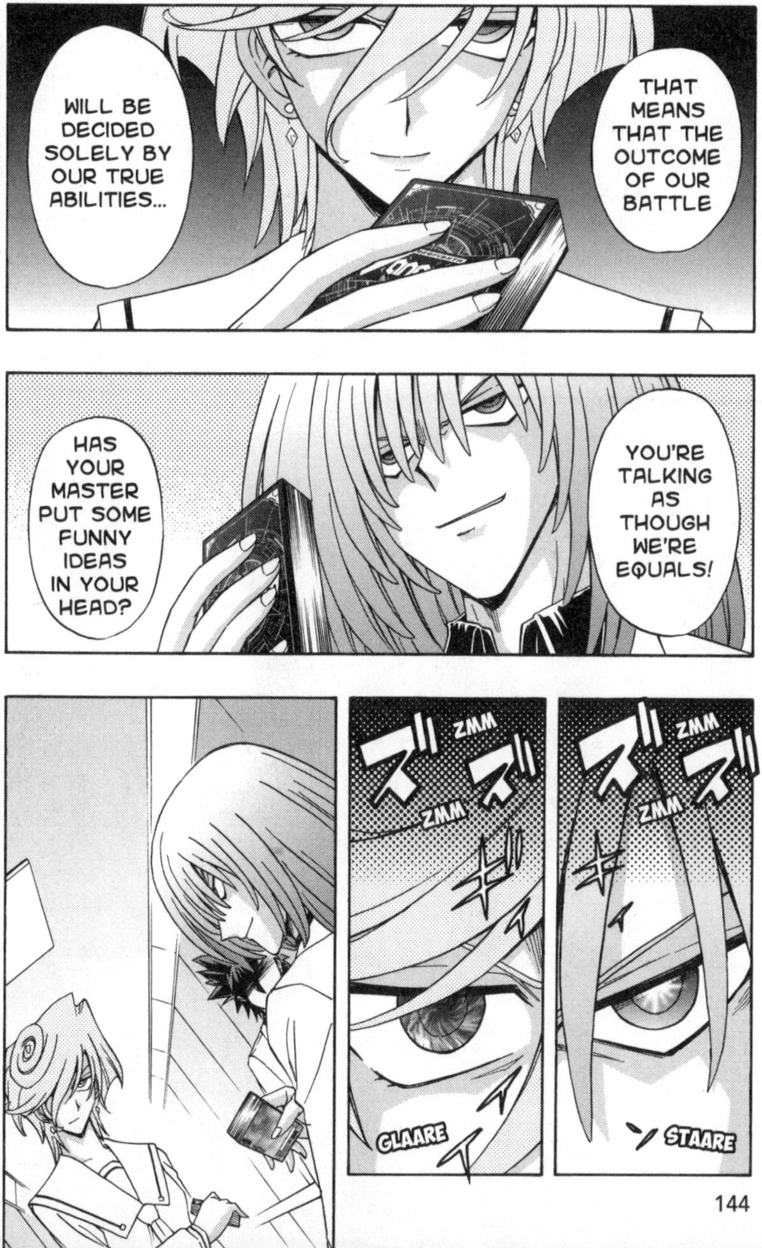
THAT MEANS THAT THE OUTCOME OF OUR BATTLE
WILL BE DECIDED SOLELY BY OUR TRUE ABILITIES...
YOU'RE TALKING AS THOUGH WE'RE EQUALS!
HAS YOUR MASTER PUT SOME FUNNY IDEAS IN YOUR HEAD?
ZMM
ZMM
STAARE
ZMM
ZMM
GLAARE

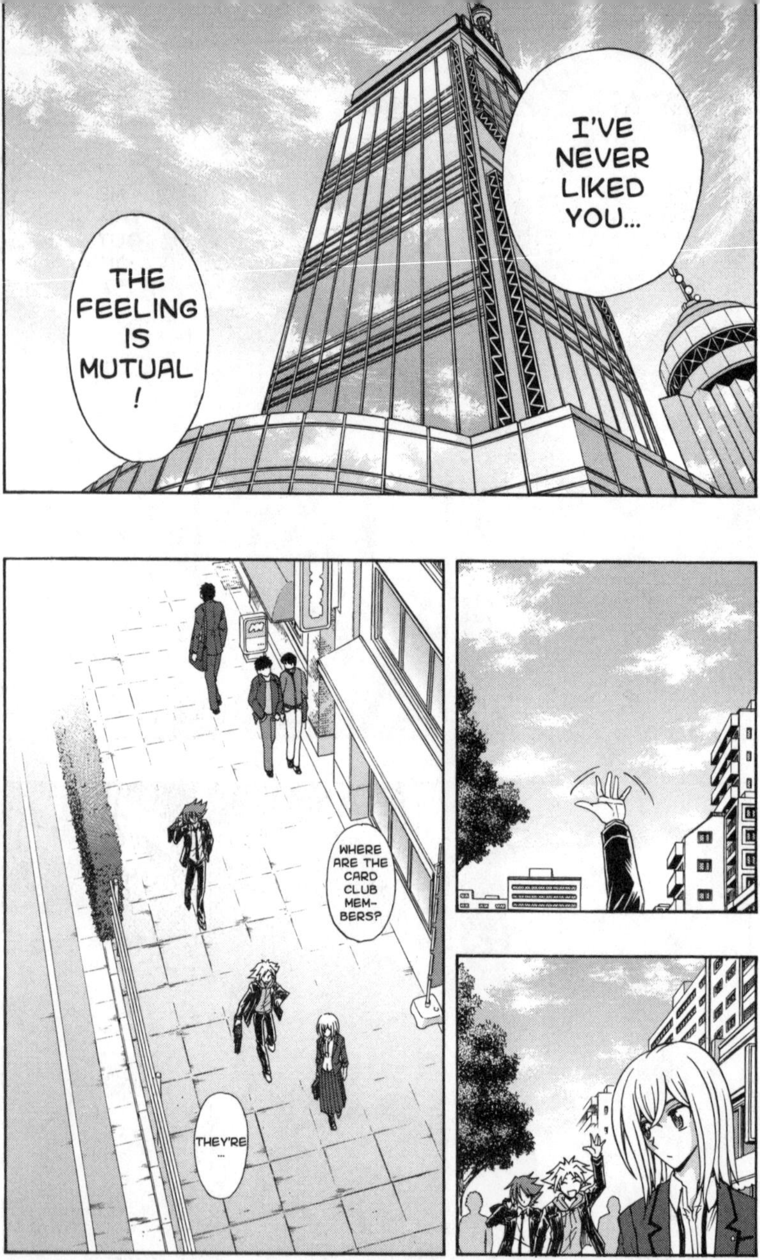
I'VE NEVER LIKED YOU...
THE FEELING IS MUTUAL!
WHERE ARE THE CARD CLUB MEM-BERS?
THEY'RE ...

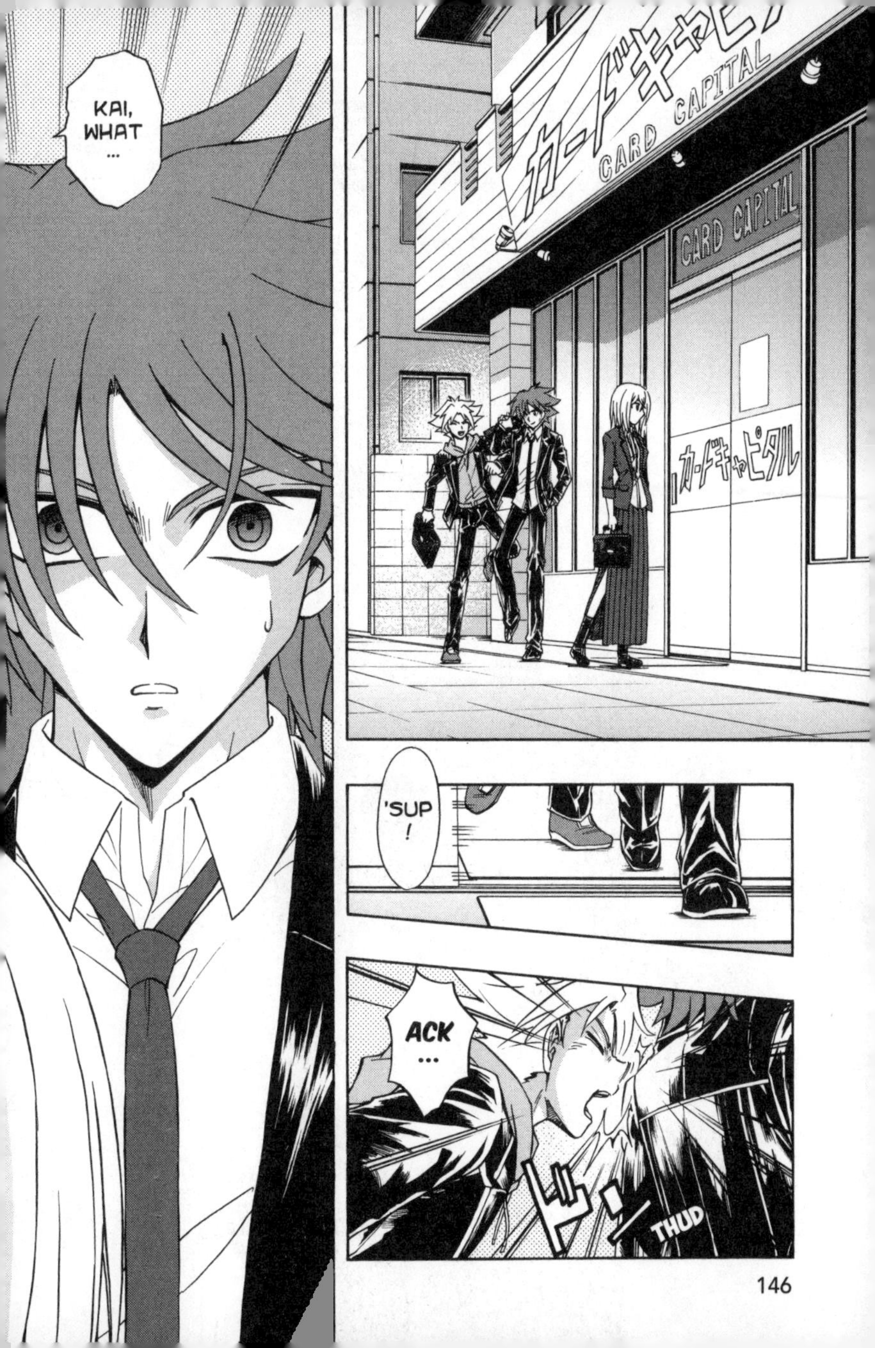
CARD CAPITAL
CARD CAPITAL
カードキャピタル
'SUP!
ACK...
THUD
KAI, WHAT...

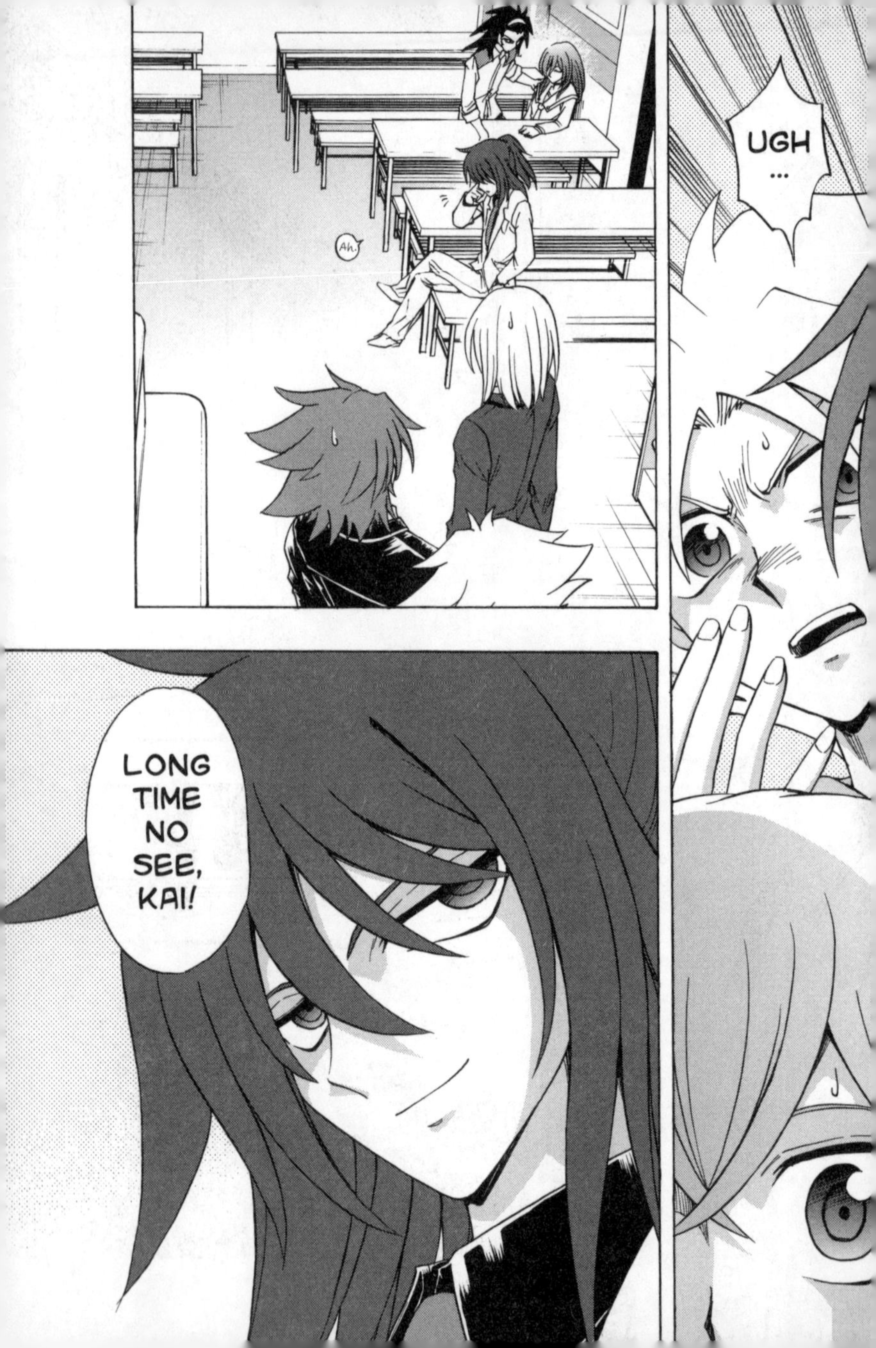
UGH ...
Ah.
LONG TIME NO SEE, KAI!

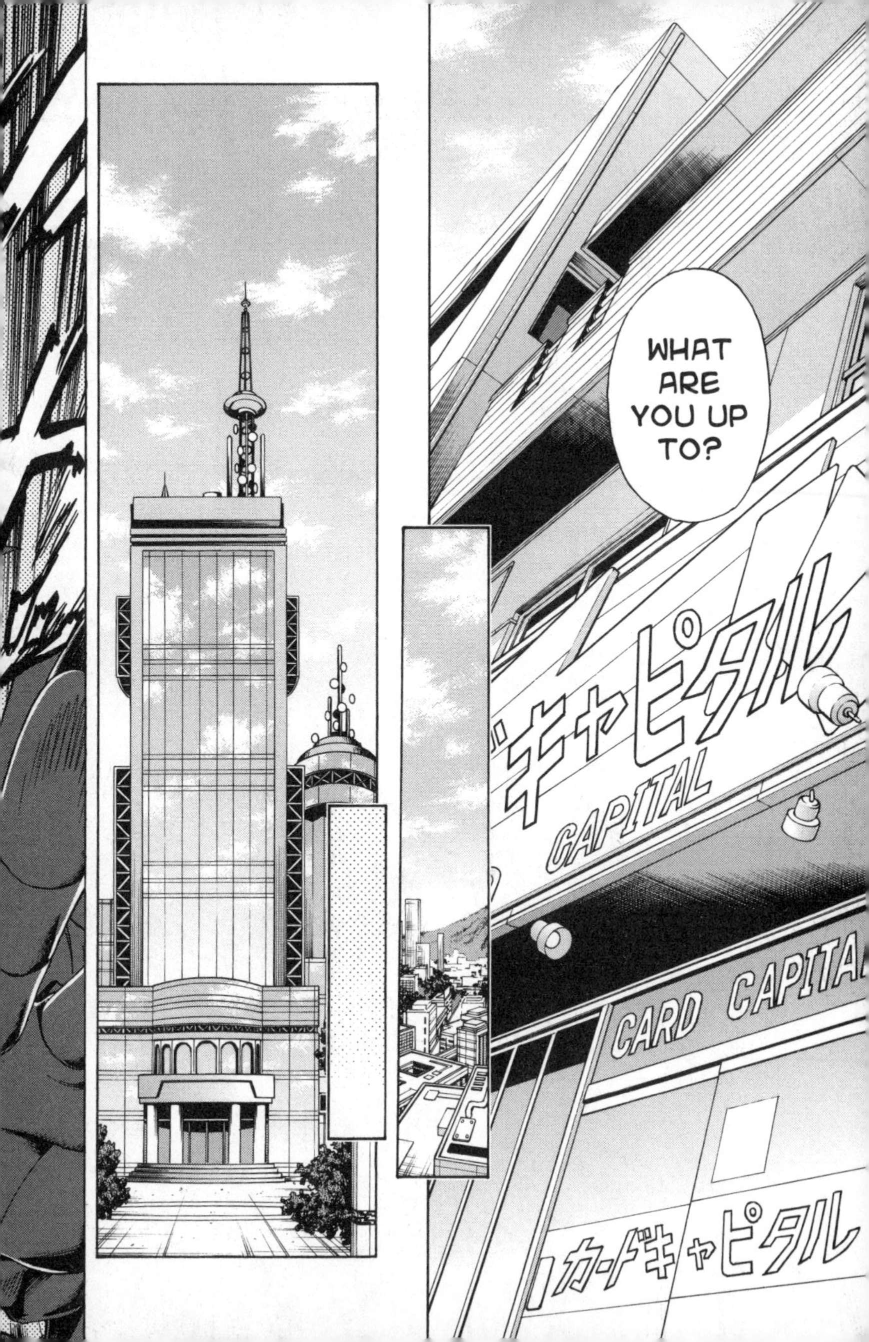
WHAT ARE YOU UP TO?
キャピタル
CAPITAL
CARD CAPITA
カードキャピタル

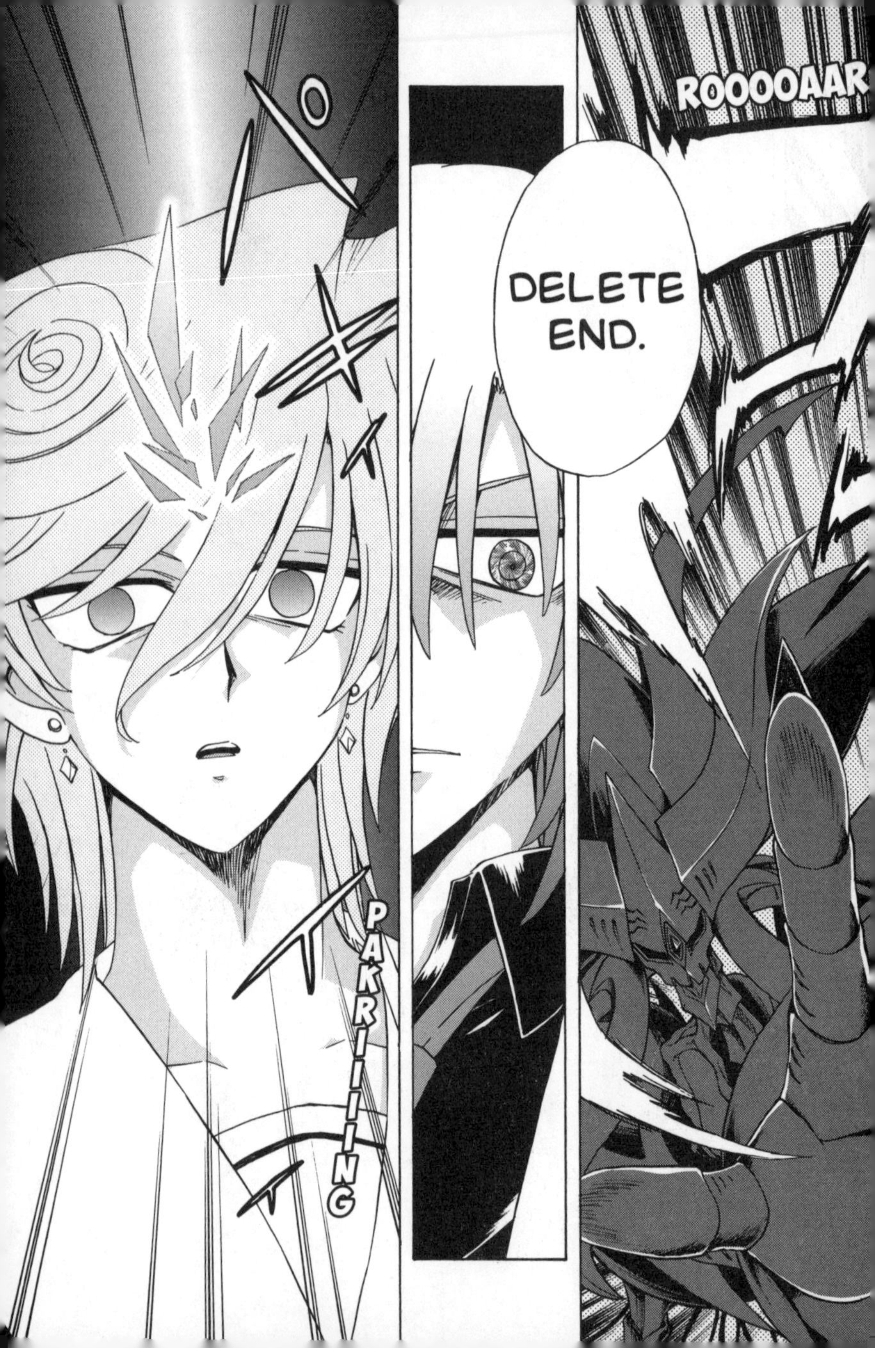
ROOOOAAR
DELETE END.
PAKRIIIING

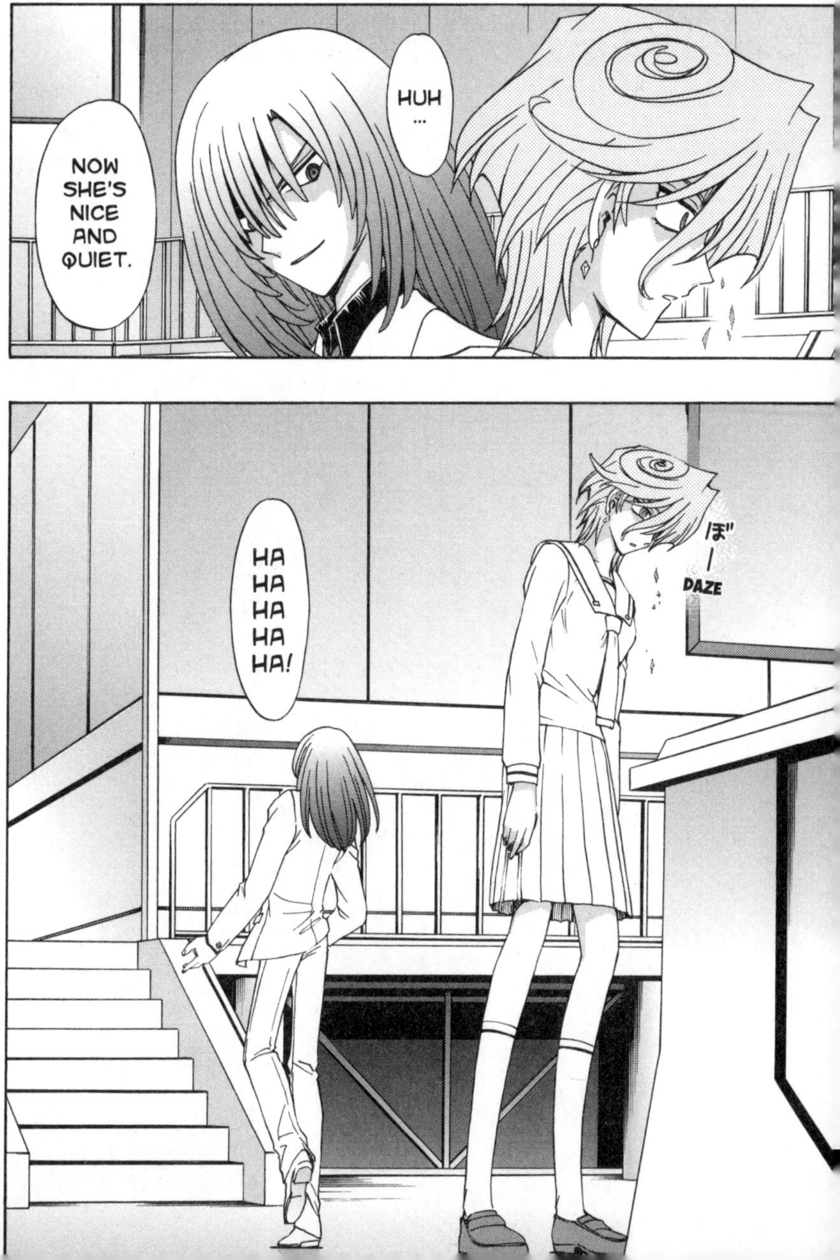
HUH ...
NOW SHE'S NICE AND QUIET.
ぼー
DAZE
HA HA HA HA HA!

BONUS! CARDFIGHT!! Vanguard

BONUS! VANGUARD NEVER-BEFORE-SEEN IMAGE BOARDS

Alfred—Movie Edition

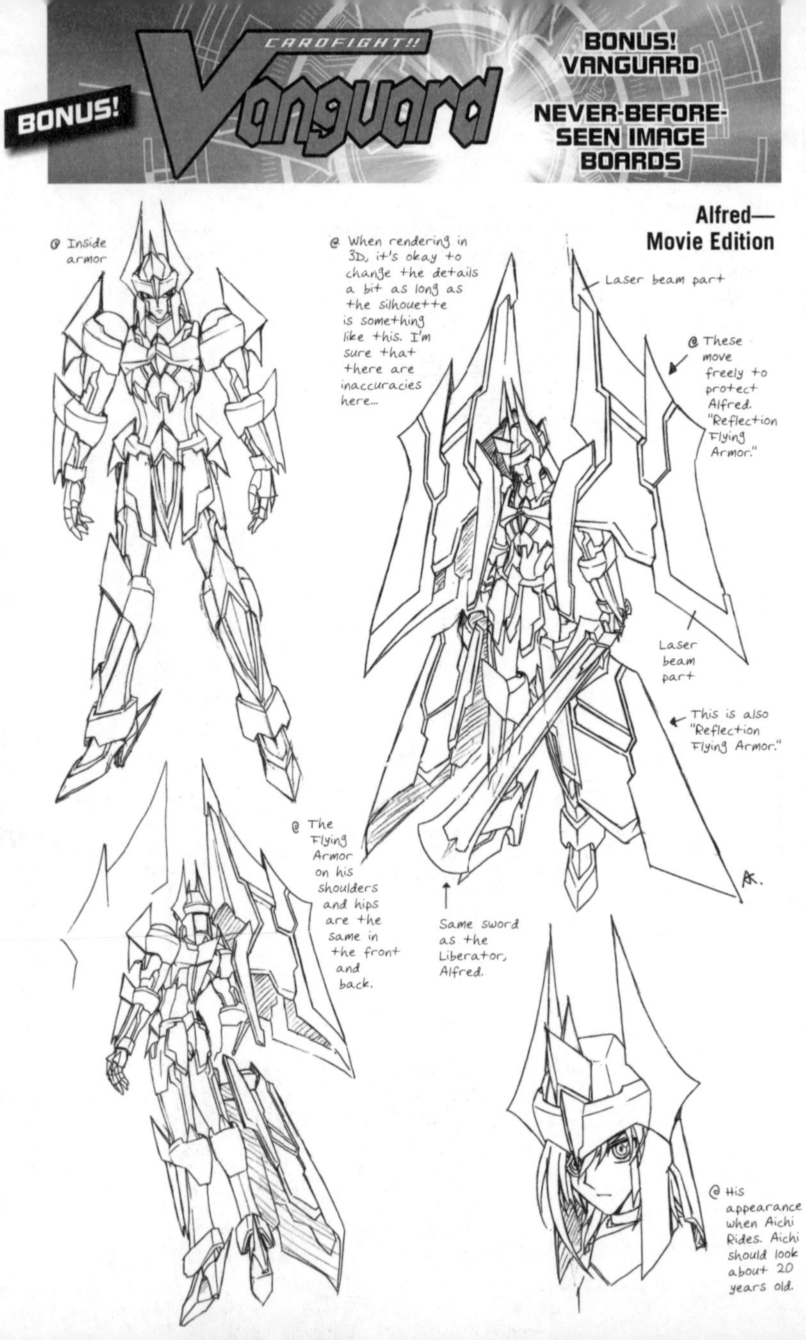

@ Inside armor
@ When rendering in 3D, it's okay to change the details a bit as long as the silhouette is something like this. I'm sure that there are inaccuracies here...
Laser beam part
@ These move freely to protect Alfred. "Reflection Flying Armor."
Laser beam part
This is also "Reflection Flying Armor."
@ The Flying Armor on his shoulders and hips are the same in the front and back.
Same sword as the Liberator, Alfred.
@ His appearance when Aichi Rides. Aichi should look about 20 years old.

BONUS! CARDFIGHT!! Vanguard

BONUS! VANGUARD NEVER-BEFORE-SEEN IMAGE BOARDS

Misaki in casual wear for the opening

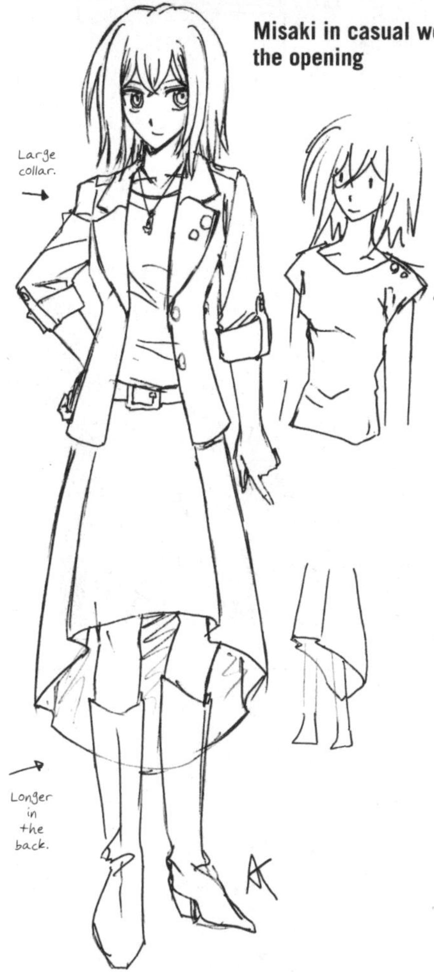

Large collar.
These clothes might be better for Misaki...
Longer in the back.

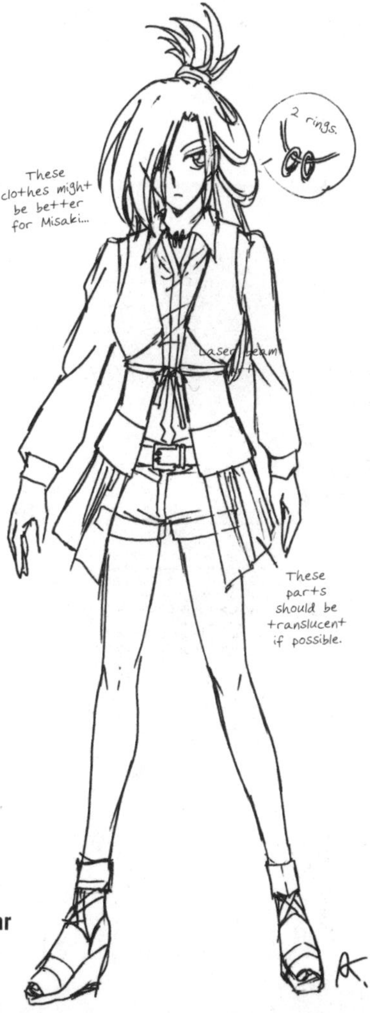

2 rings.
Laser beam
These parts should be translucent if possible.

Kourin in casual wear for the opening

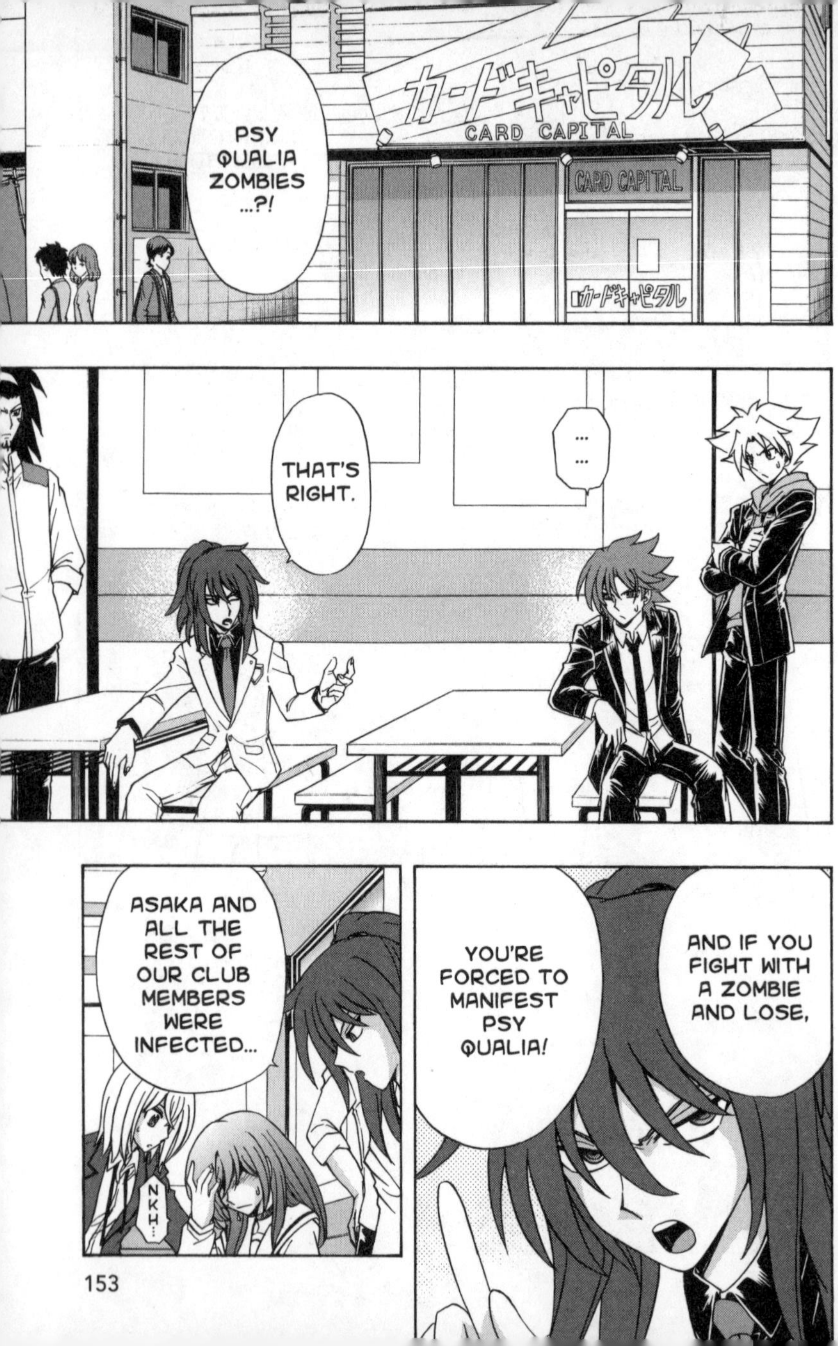
カードキャピタル
CARD CAPITAL
CARD CAPITAL
カードキャピタル
PSY QUALIA ZOMBIES ...?!
... ...
THAT'S RIGHT.
AND IF YOU FIGHT WITH A ZOMBIE AND LOSE,
YOU'RE FORCED TO MANIFEST PSY QUALIA!
ASAKA AND ALL THE REST OF OUR CLUB MEMBERS WERE INFECTED...
NKH...

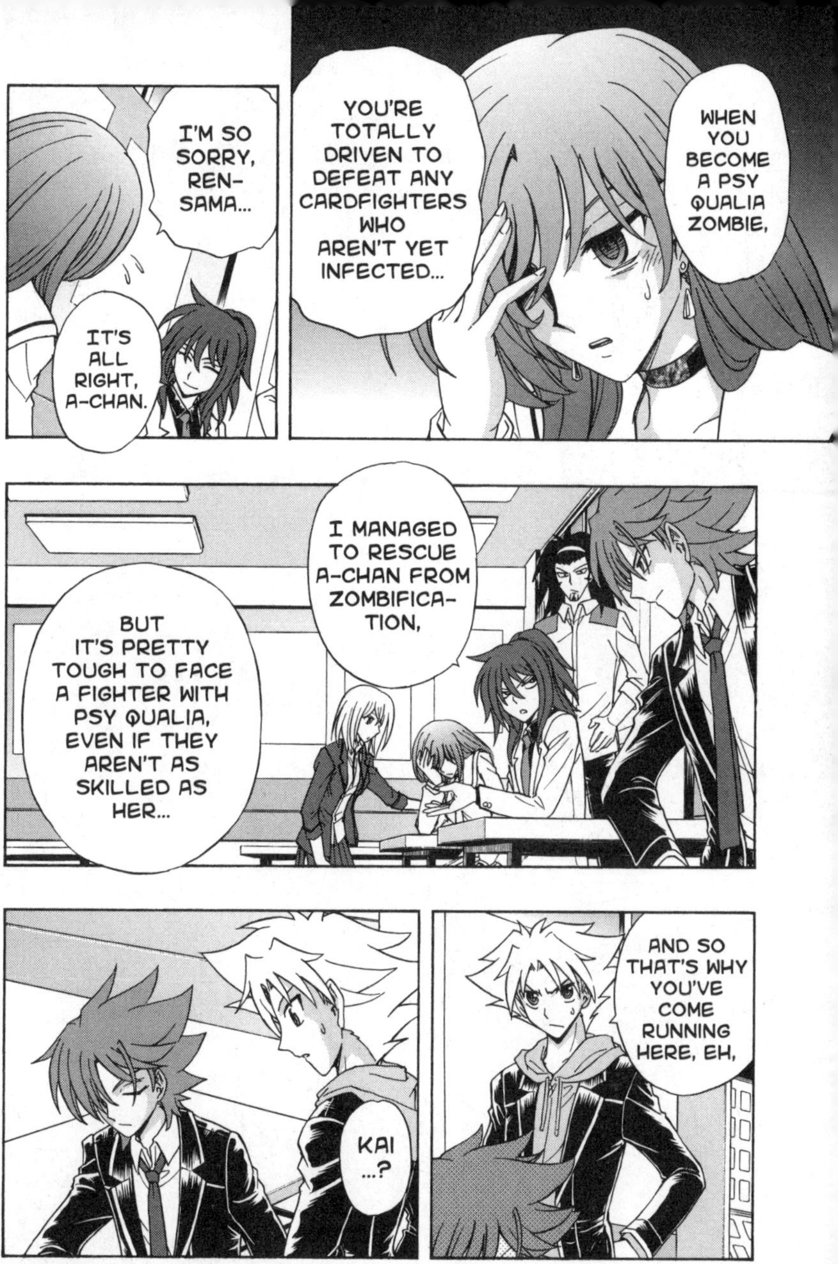

WHEN YOU BECOME A PSY QUALIA ZOMBIE,
YOU'RE TOTALLY DRIVEN TO DEFEAT ANY CARDFIGHTERS WHO AREN'T YET INFECTED...
I'M SO SORRY, REN-SAMA...
IT'S ALL RIGHT, A-CHAN.
I MANAGED TO RESCUE A-CHAN FROM ZOMBIFICA-TION,
BUT IT'S PRETTY TOUGH TO FACE A FIGHTER WITH PSY QUALIA, EVEN IF THEY AREN'T AS SKILLED AS HER...
AND SO THAT'S WHY YOU'VE COME RUNNING HERE, EH,
KAI ...?

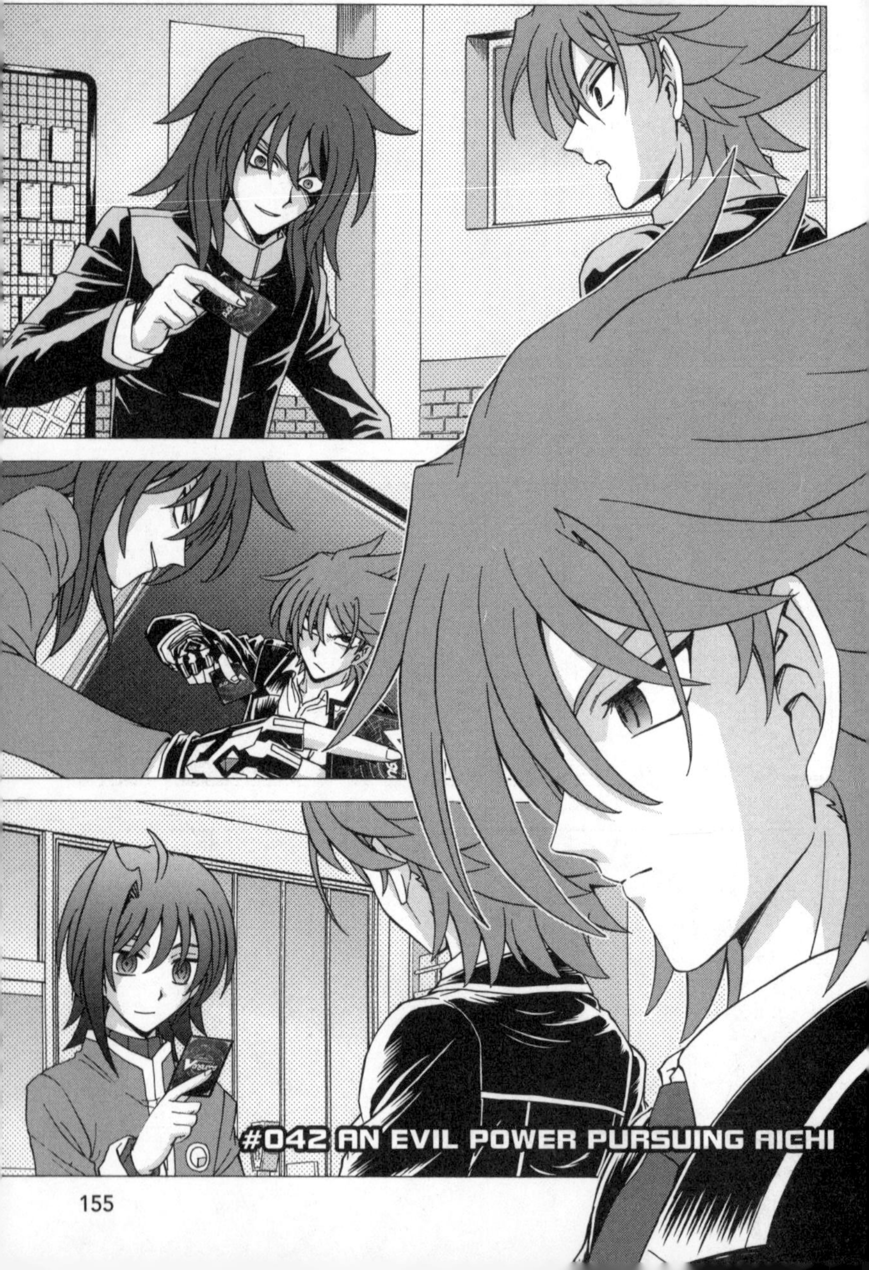
#042 AN EVIL POWER PURSUING AICHI

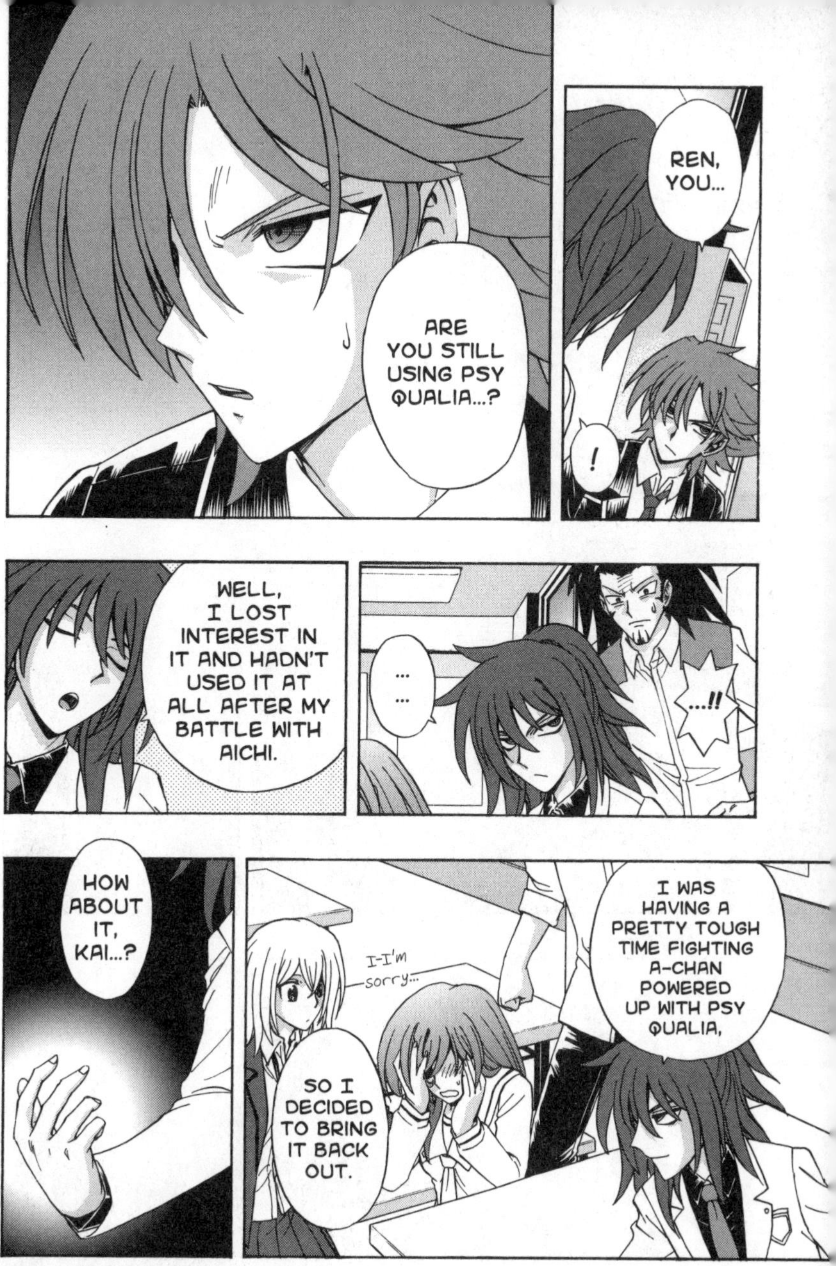
REN, YOU...
!
ARE YOU STILL USING PSY QUALIA...?
...!!
... ...
WELL, I LOST INTEREST IN IT AND HADN'T USED IT AT ALL AFTER MY BATTLE WITH AICHI.
I WAS HAVING A PRETTY TOUGH TIME FIGHTING A-CHAN POWERED UP WITH PSY QUALIA,
I-I'm sorry...
SO I DECIDED TO BRING IT BACK OUT.
HOW ABOUT IT, KAI...?

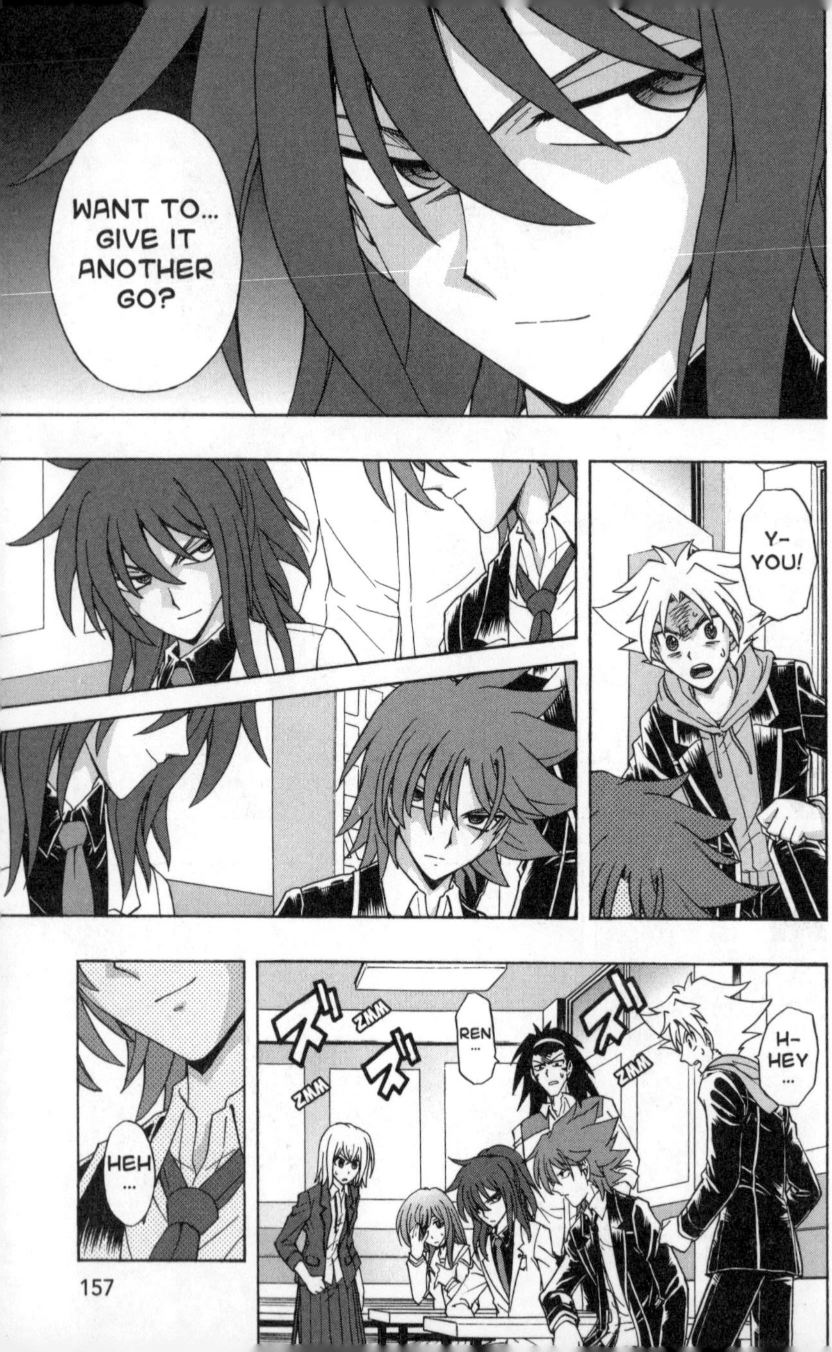
WANT TO... GIVE IT ANOTHER GO?
Y- YOU!
H- HEY ...
ZMM
REN ...
ZMM
ZMM
HEH ...

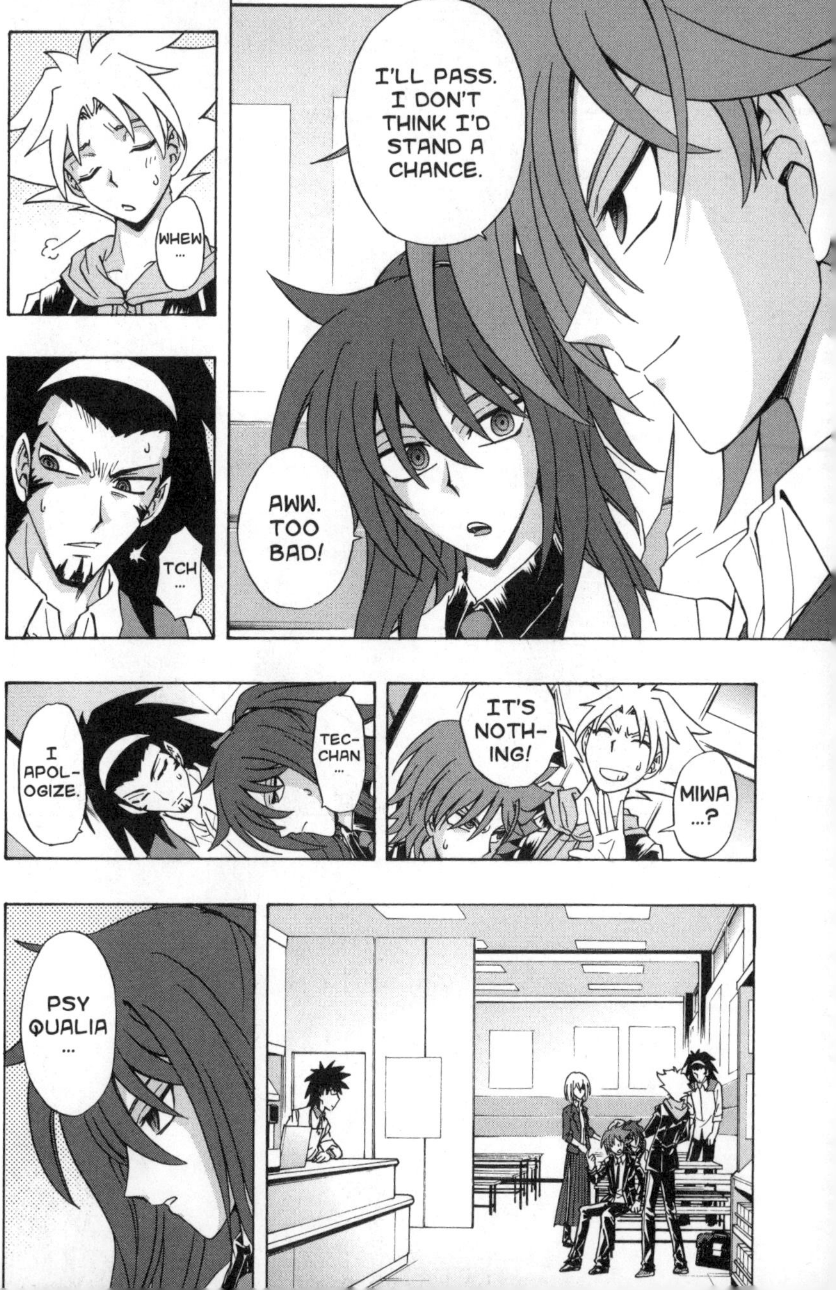
I'LL PASS. I DON'T THINK I'D STAND A CHANCE.
AWW. TOO BAD!
WHEW ...
TCH ...
MIWA ...?
IT'S NOTH-ING!
TEC-CHAN ...
I APOLO-GIZE.
PSY QUALIA ...

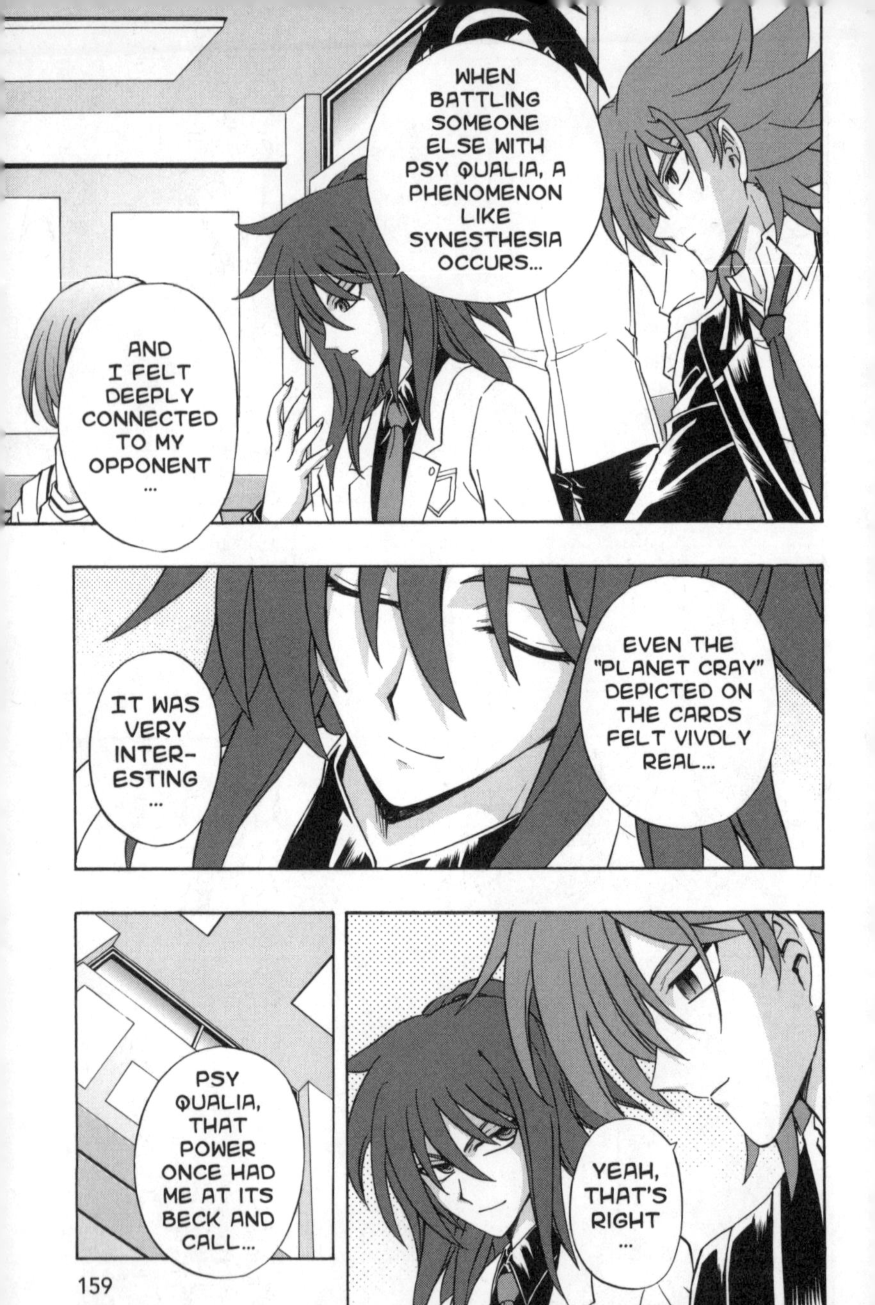
WHEN BATTLING SOMEONE ELSE WITH PSY QUALIA, A PHENOMENON LIKE SYNESTHESIA OCCURS...
AND I FELT DEEPLY CONNECTED TO MY OPPONENT ...
EVEN THE "PLANET CRAY" DEPICTED ON THE CARDS FELT VIVDLY REAL...
IT WAS VERY INTER-ESTING ...
YEAH, THAT'S RIGHT ...
PSY QUALIA, THAT POWER ONCE HAD ME AT ITS BECK AND CALL...

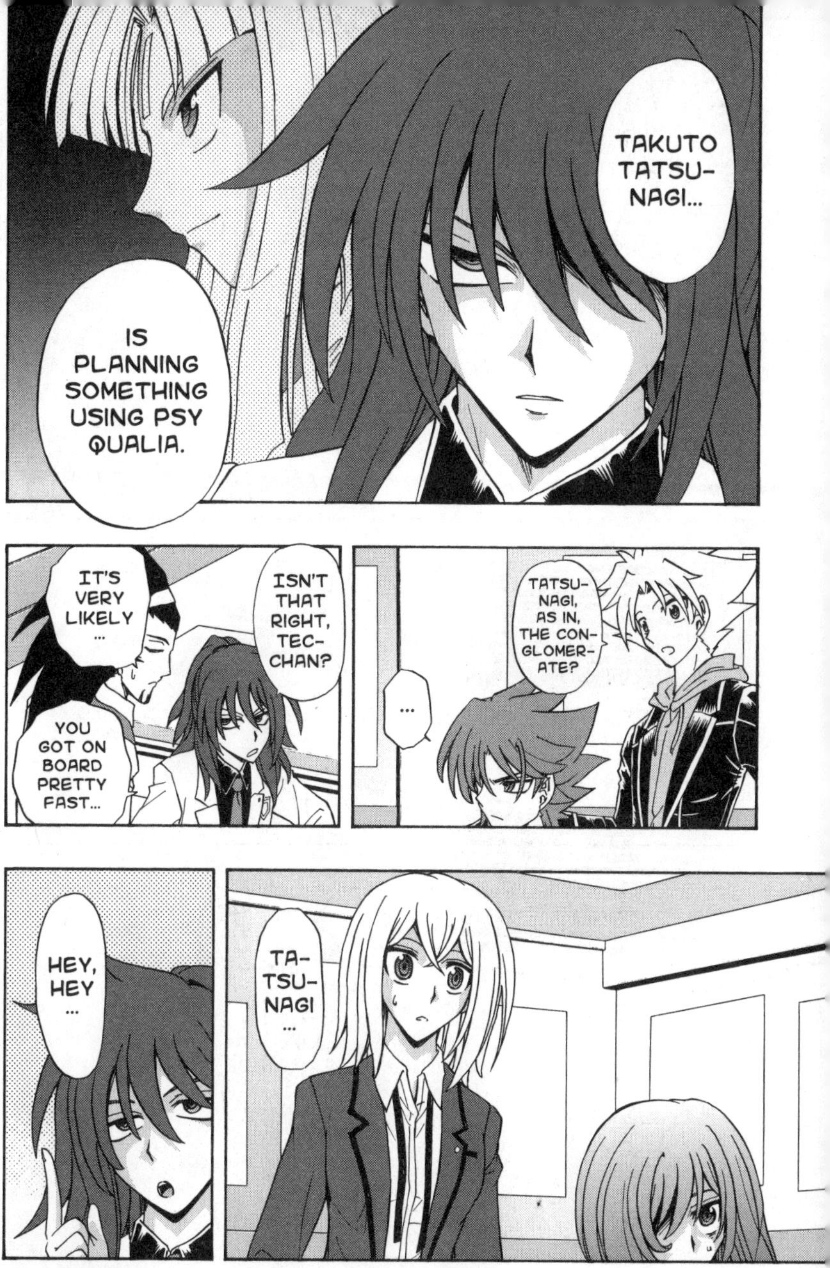
TAKUTO TATSU-NAGI...
IS PLANNING SOMETHING USING PSY QUALIA.
TATSU-NAGI, AS IN, THE CON-GLOMER-ATE?
...
ISN'T THAT RIGHT, TEC-CHAN?
IT'S VERY LIKELY ...
YOU GOT ON BOARD PRETTY FAST...
TA-TSU-NAGI ...
HEY, HEY ...

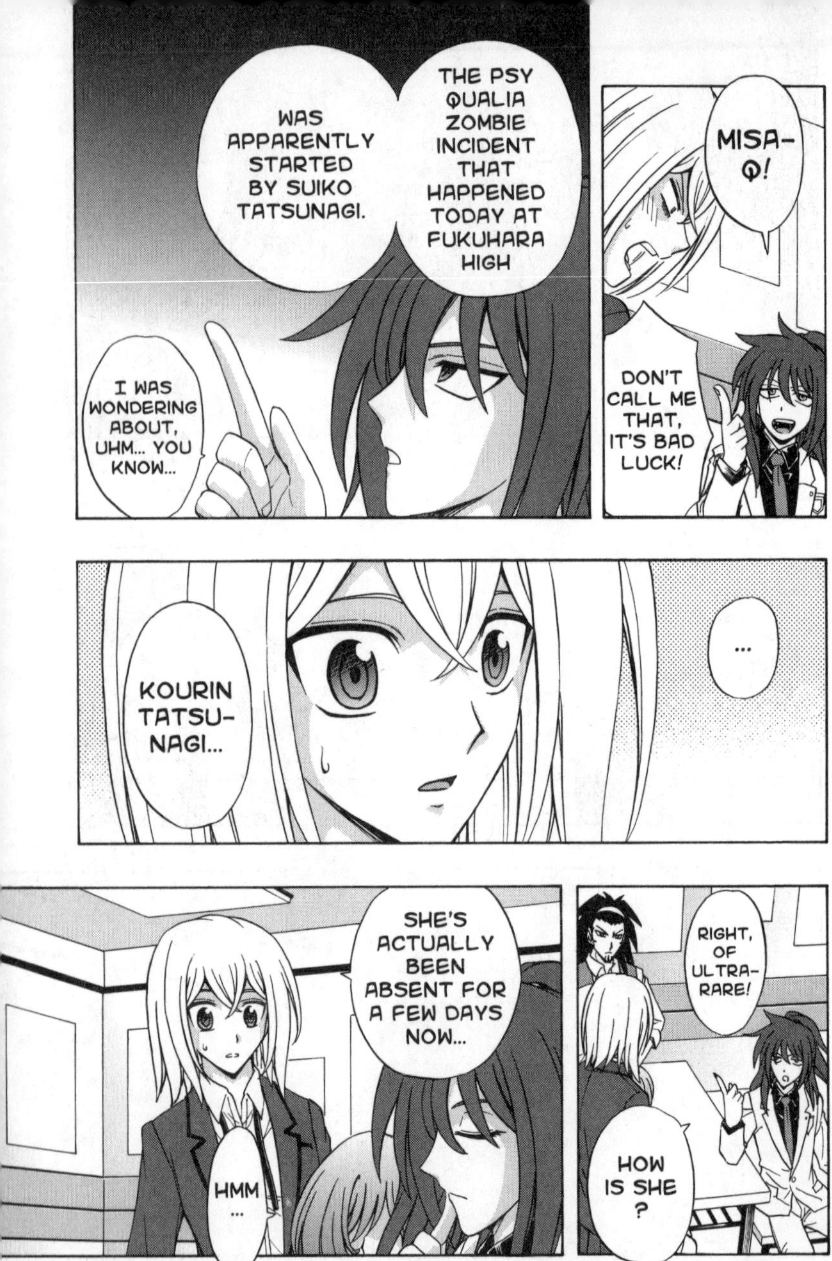
MISA-Q!
DON'T CALL ME THAT, IT'S BAD LUCK!
THE PSY QUALIA ZOMBIE INCIDENT THAT HAPPENED TODAY AT FUKUHARA HIGH
WAS APPARENTLY STARTED BY SUIKO TATSUNAGI.
I WAS WONDERING ABOUT, UHM... YOU KNOW...
...
KOURIN TATSU-NAGI...
RIGHT, OF ULTRA-RARE!
HOW IS SHE ?
SHE'S ACTUALLY BEEN ABSENT FOR A FEW DAYS NOW...
HMM ...

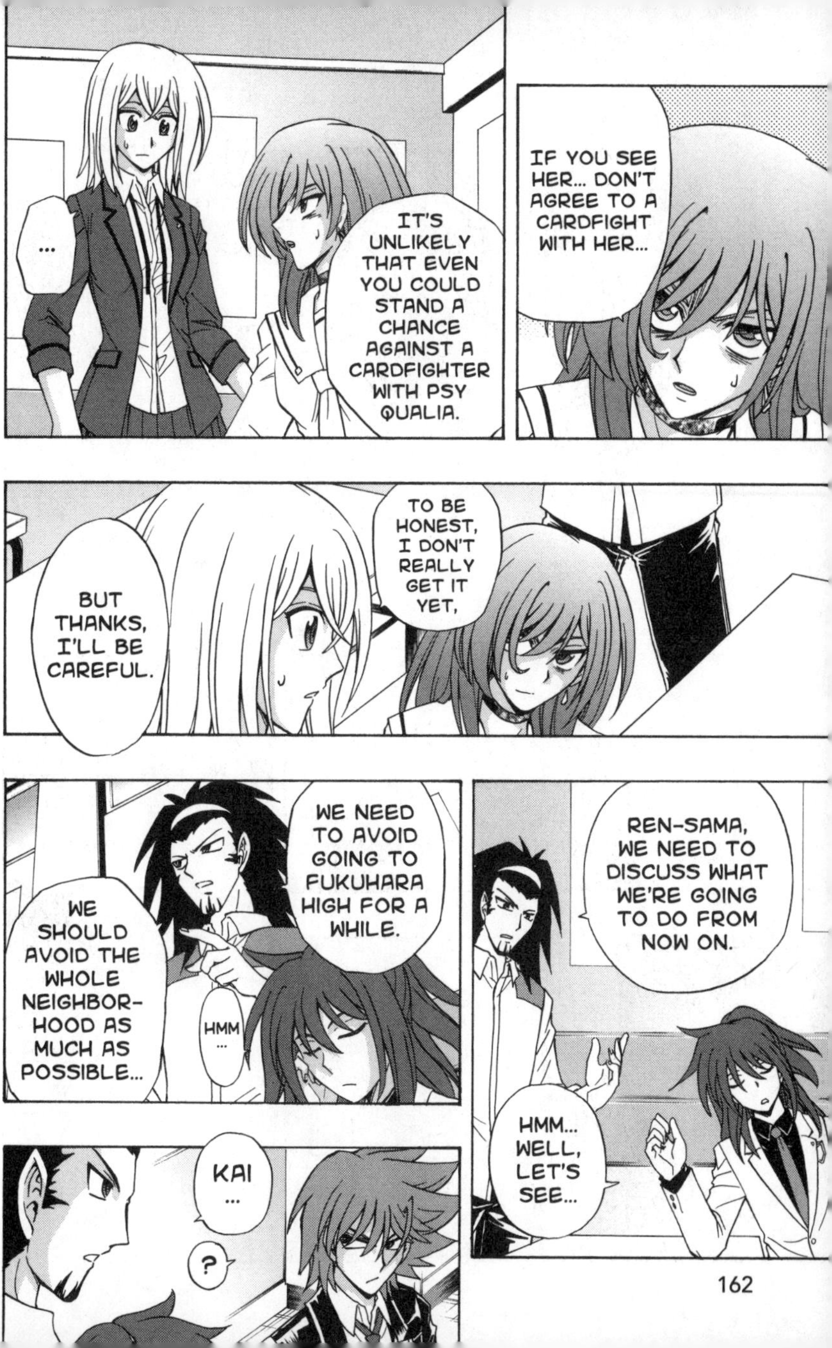
IF YOU SEE HER... DON'T AGREE TO A CARDFIGHT WITH HER...
IT'S UNLIKELY THAT EVEN YOU COULD STAND A CHANCE AGAINST A CARDFIGHTER WITH PSY QUALIA.
...
TO BE HONEST, I DON'T REALLY GET IT YET,
BUT THANKS, I'LL BE CAREFUL.
REN-SAMA, WE NEED TO DISCUSS WHAT WE'RE GOING TO DO FROM NOW ON.
HMM... WELL, LET'S SEE...
WE NEED TO AVOID GOING TO FUKUHARA HIGH FOR A WHILE.
WE SHOULD AVOID THE WHOLE NEIGHBOR-HOOD AS MUCH AS POSSIBLE...
HMM ...
KAI ...
?

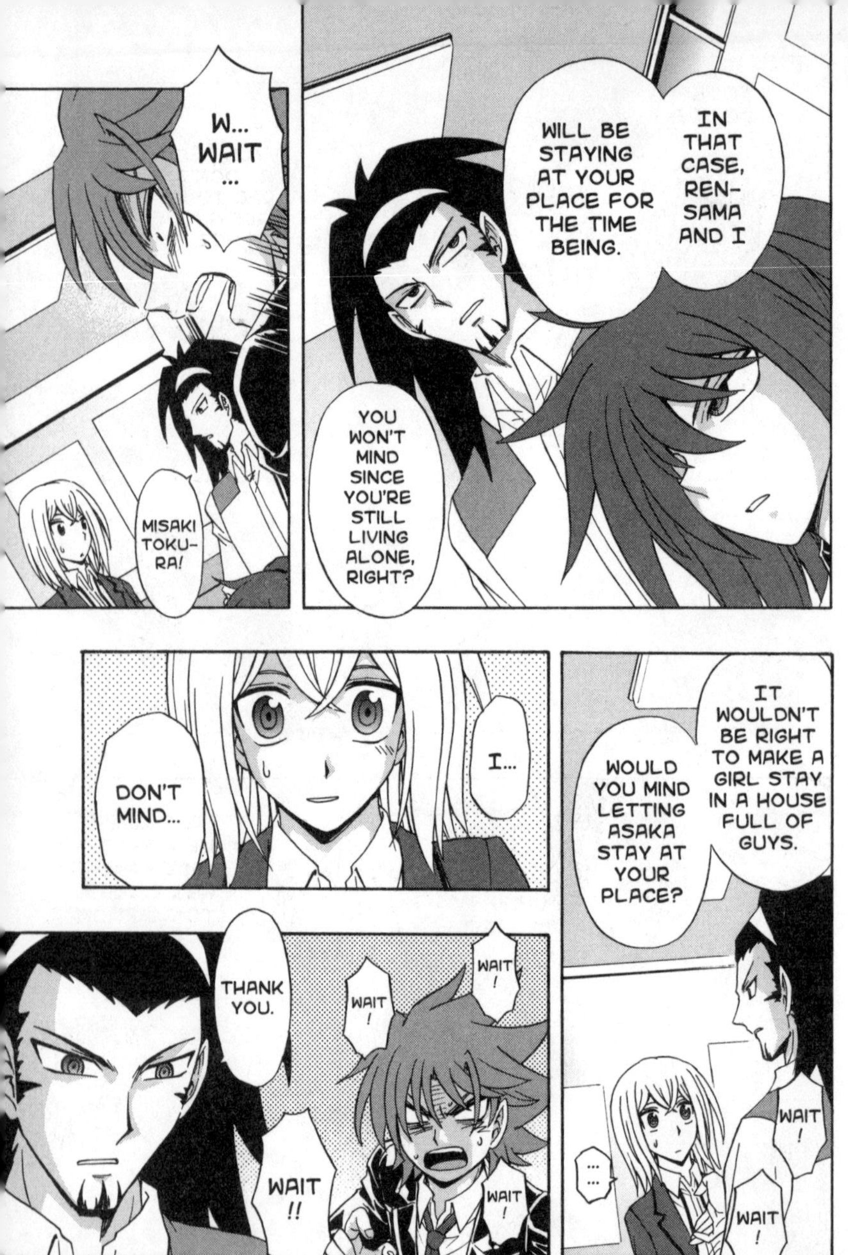
IN THAT CASE, REN-SAMA AND I
WILL BE STAYING AT YOUR PLACE FOR THE TIME BEING.
YOU WON'T MIND SINCE YOU'RE STILL LIVING ALONE, RIGHT?
W... WAIT ...
MISAKI TOKURA!
IT WOULDN'T BE RIGHT TO MAKE A GIRL STAY IN A HOUSE FULL OF GUYS.
WOULD YOU MIND LETTING ASAKA STAY AT YOUR PLACE?
WAIT!
WAIT!
... ...
I...
DON'T MIND...
THANK YOU.
WAIT!
WAIT!
WAIT!!
WAIT!

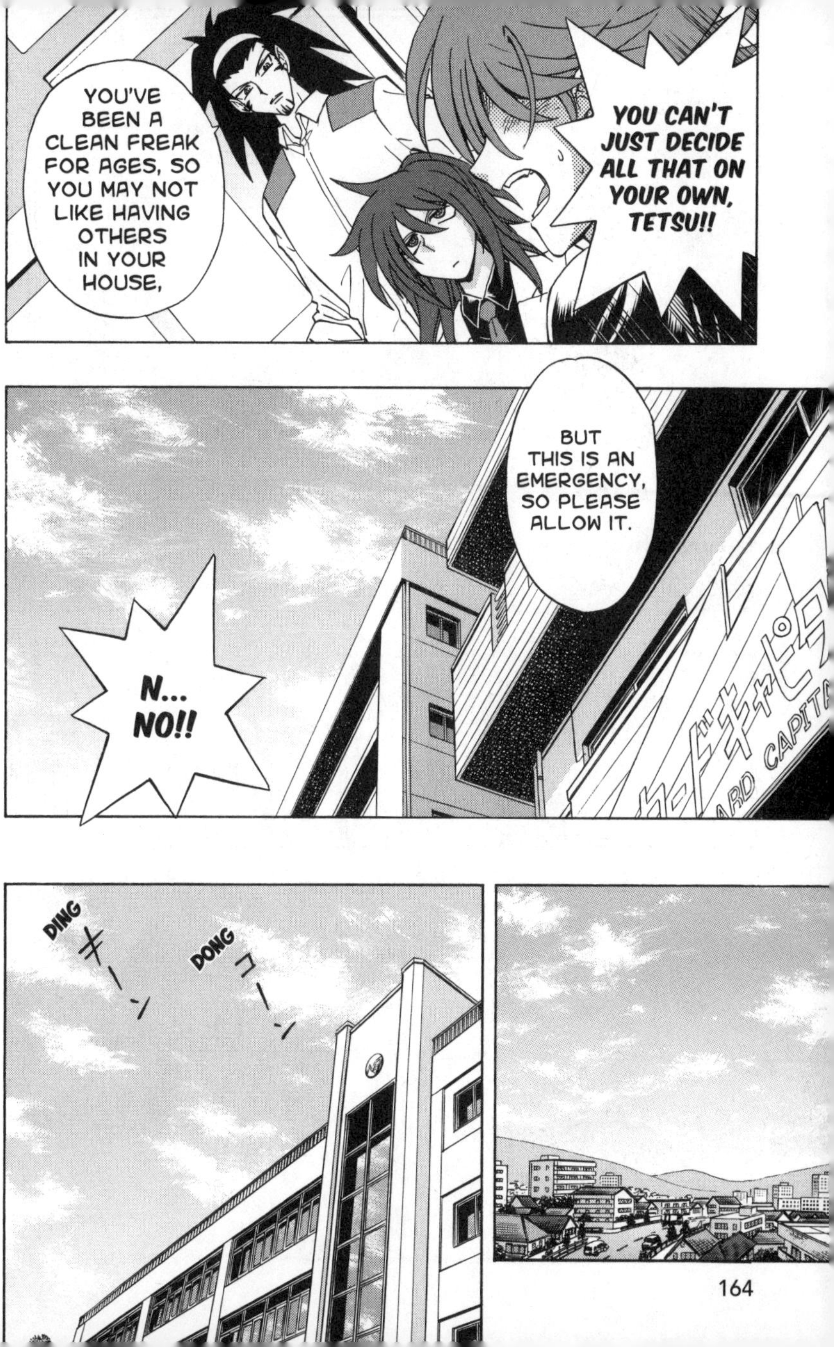
YOU CAN'T JUST DECIDE ALL THAT ON YOUR OWN, TETSU!!
YOU'VE BEEN A CLEAN FREAK FOR AGES, SO YOU MAY NOT LIKE HAVING OTHERS IN YOUR HOUSE,
BUT THIS IS AN EMERGENCY, SO PLEASE ALLOW IT.
N... NO!!
DING
DONG

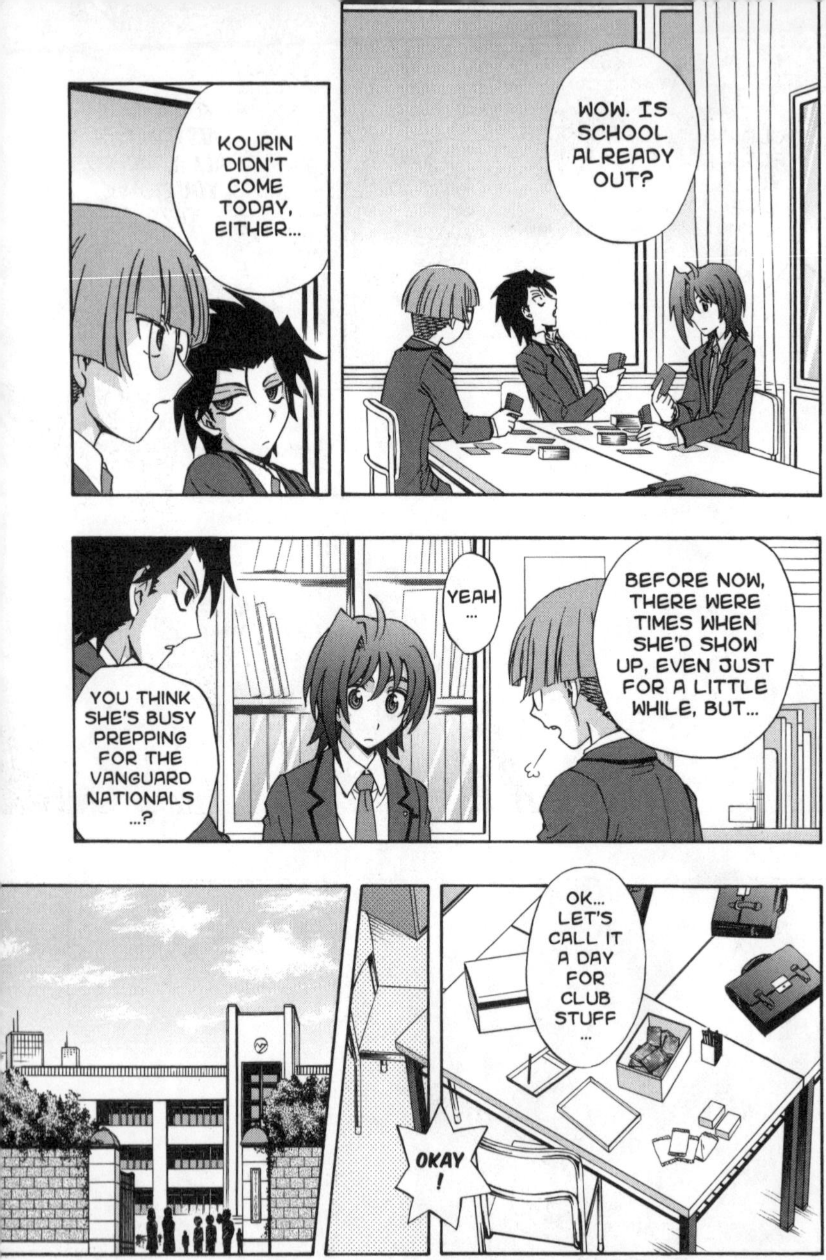
WOW. IS SCHOOL ALREADY OUT?
KOURIN DIDN'T COME TODAY, EITHER...
BEFORE NOW, THERE WERE TIMES WHEN SHE'D SHOW UP, EVEN JUST FOR A LITTLE WHILE, BUT...
YEAH ...
YOU THINK SHE'S BUSY PREPPING FOR THE VANGUARD NATIONALS ...?
OK... LET'S CALL IT A DAY FOR CLUB STUFF ...
OKAY!

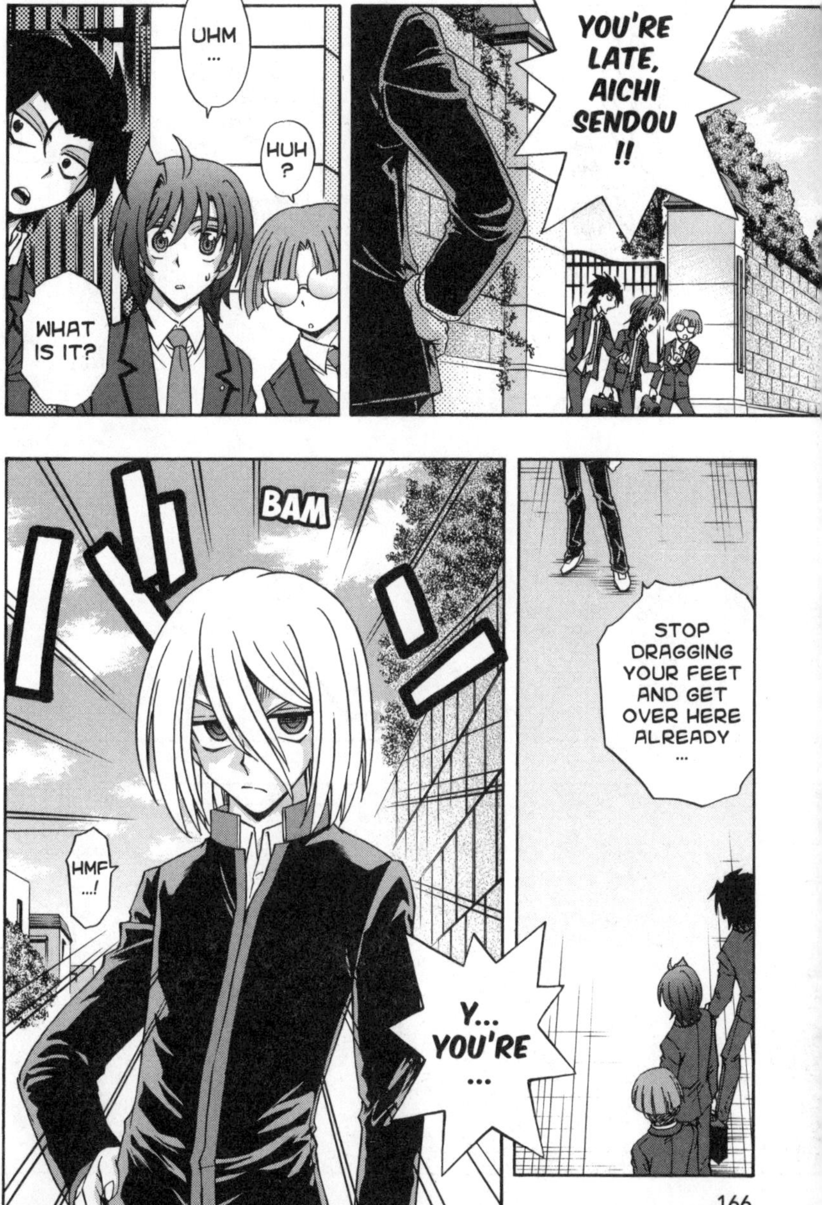
YOU'RE LATE, AICHI SENDOU !!
UHM ...
HUH ?
WHAT IS IT?
STOP DRAGGING YOUR FEET AND GET OVER HERE ALREADY ...
Y... YOU'RE ...
BAM
HMF ...!

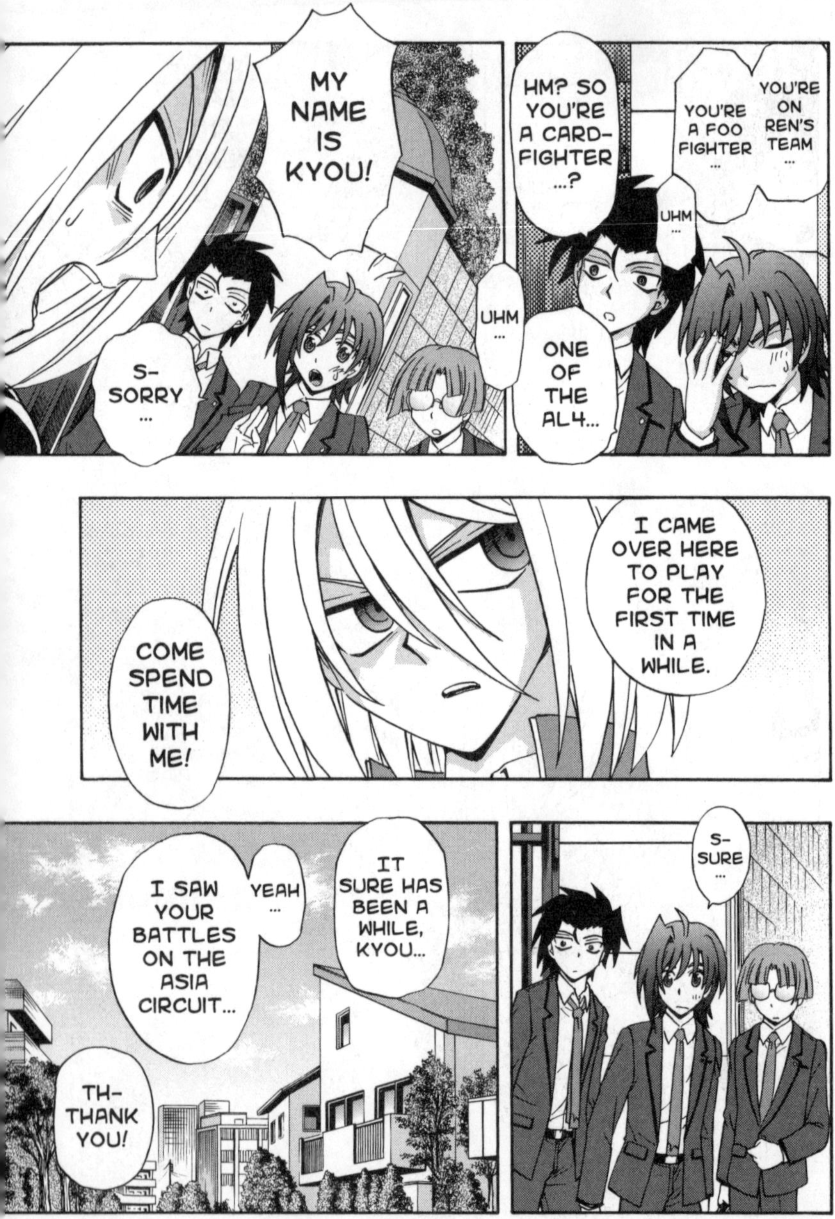

YOU'RE ON REN'S TEAM ...
YOU'RE A FOO FIGHTER ...
HM? SO YOU'RE A CARD-FIGHTER ...?
UHM ...
ONE OF THE AL4...
MY NAME IS KYOU!
UHM ...
S-SORRY ...
I CAME OVER HERE TO PLAY FOR THE FIRST TIME IN A WHILE.
COME SPEND TIME WITH ME!
S-SURE ...
IT SURE HAS BEEN A WHILE, KYOU...
YEAH ...
I SAW YOUR BATTLES ON THE ASIA CIRCUIT...
TH-THANK YOU!

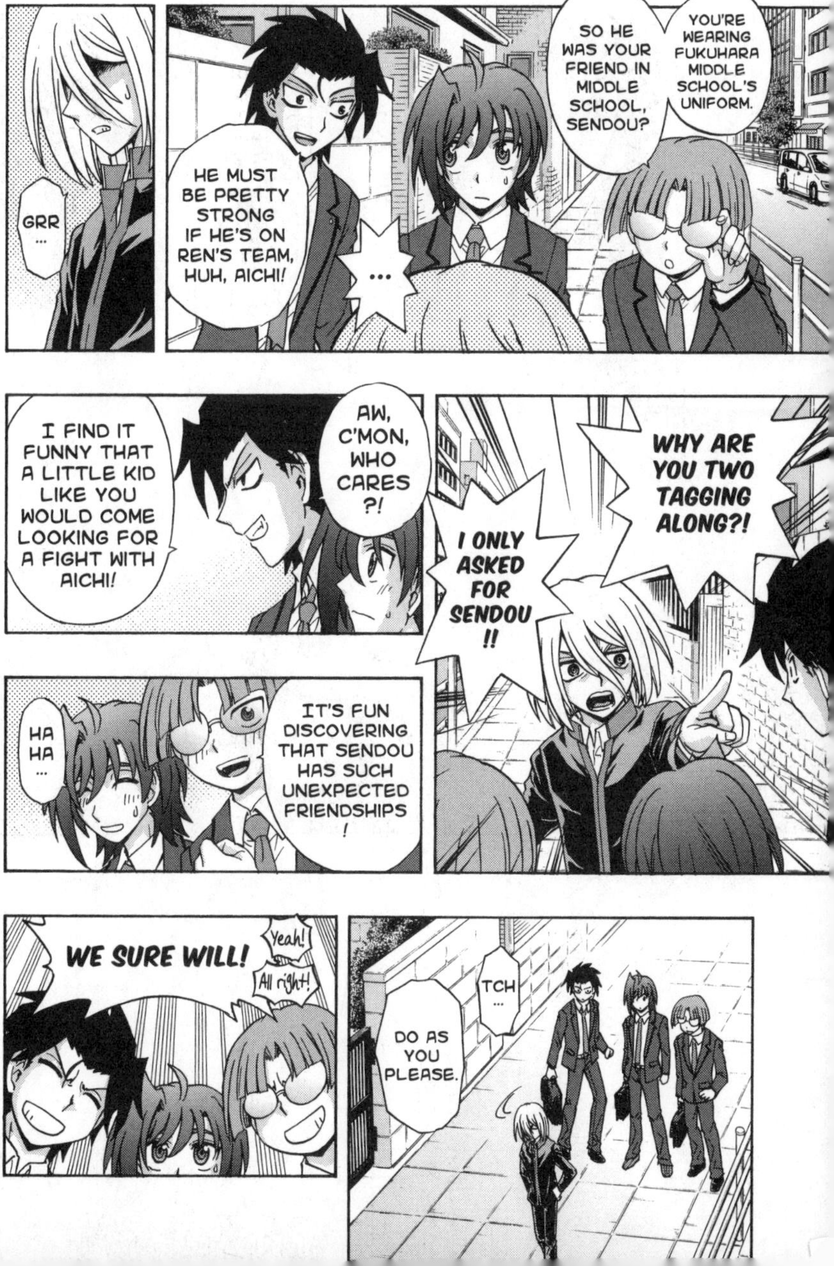
YOU'RE WEARING FUKUHARA MIDDLE SCHOOL'S UNIFORM.
SO HE WAS YOUR FRIEND IN MIDDLE SCHOOL, SENDOU?
HE MUST BE PRETTY STRONG IF HE'S ON REN'S TEAM, HUH, AICHI!
...
GRR ...
WHY ARE YOU TWO TAGGING ALONG?!
I ONLY ASKED FOR SENDOU !!
AW, C'MON, WHO CARES ?!
I FIND IT FUNNY THAT A LITTLE KID LIKE YOU WOULD COME LOOKING FOR A FIGHT WITH AICHI!
IT'S FUN DISCOVERING THAT SENDOU HAS SUCH UNEXPECTED FRIENDSHIPS !
HA HA ...
TCH ...
DO AS YOU PLEASE.
Yeah!
All right!
WE SURE WILL!

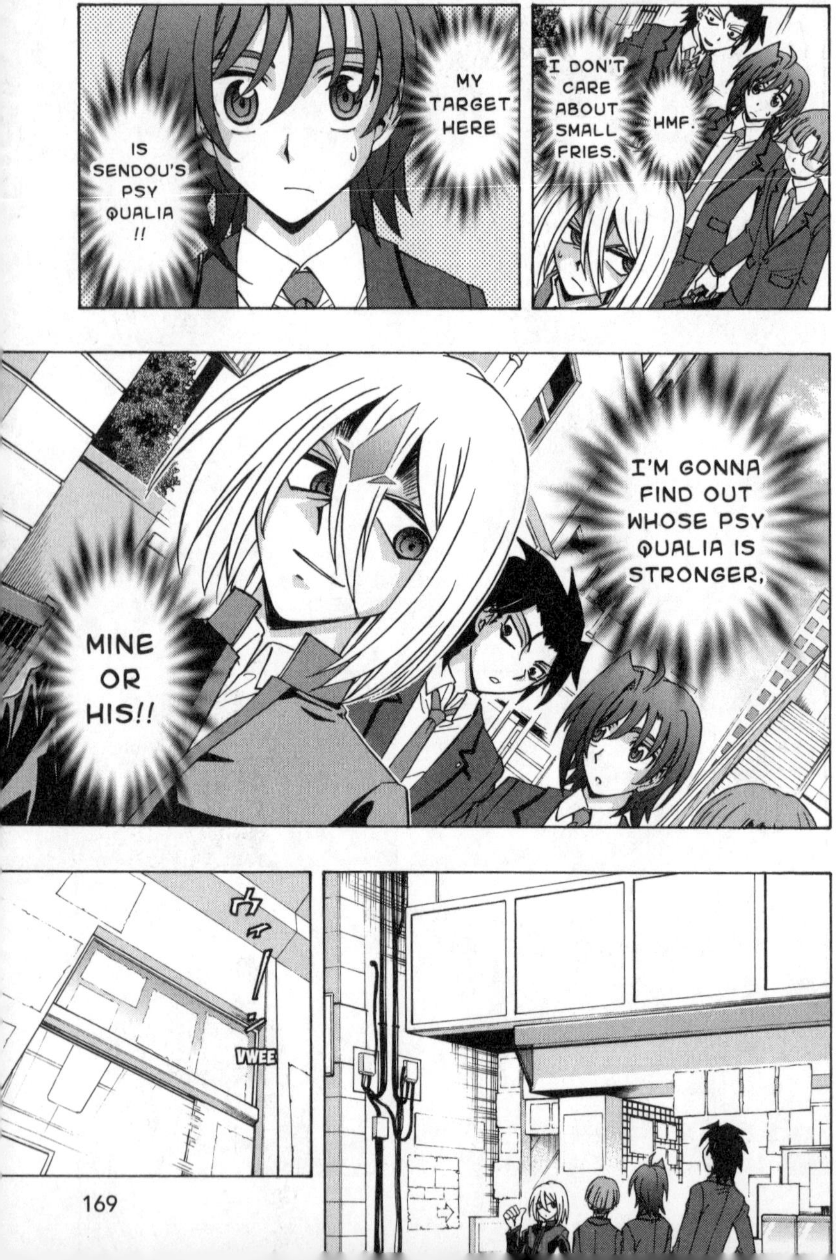
HMF.
I DON'T CARE ABOUT SMALL FRIES.
MY TARGET HERE
IS SENDOU'S PSY QUALIA !!
I'M GONNA FIND OUT WHOSE PSY QUALIA IS STRONGER,
MINE OR HIS!!
ウィー
VWEE

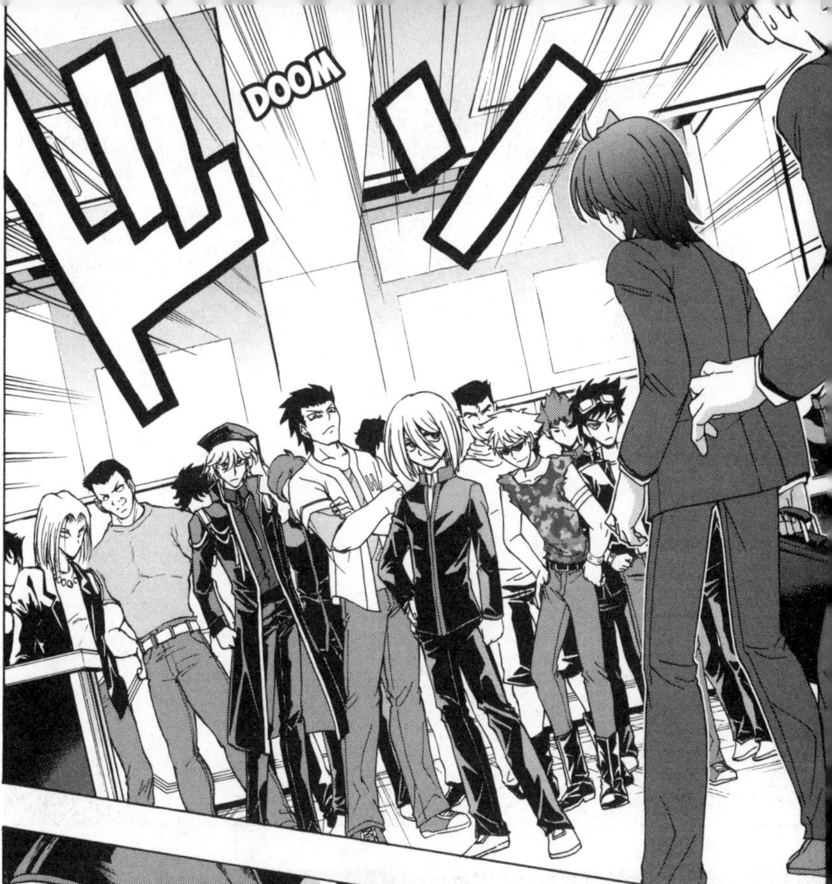
DOOM

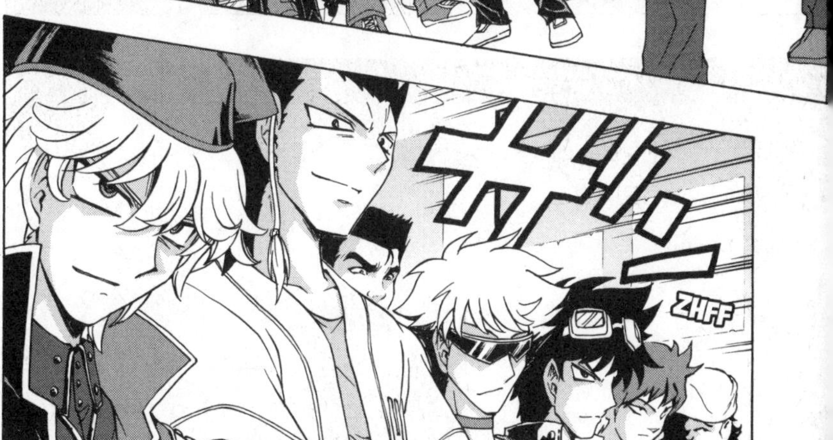
ZHFF

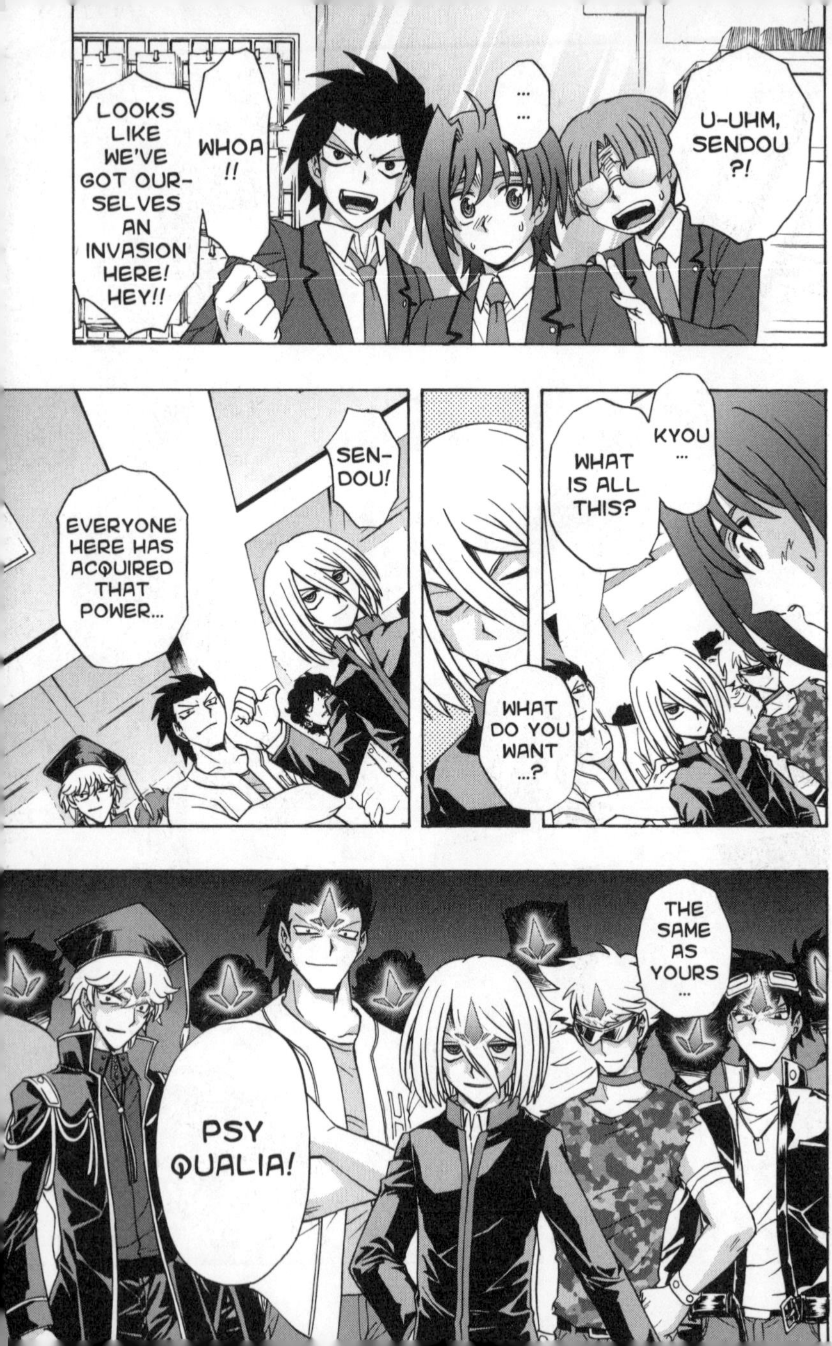
U-UHM, SENDOU ?!
...
...
WHOA !!
LOOKS LIKE WE'VE GOT OUR-SELVES AN INVASION HERE! HEY!!
KYOU ...
WHAT IS ALL THIS?
WHAT DO YOU WANT ...?
SEN-DOU!
EVERYONE HERE HAS ACQUIRED THAT POWER...
THE SAME AS YOURS ...
PSY QUALIA!

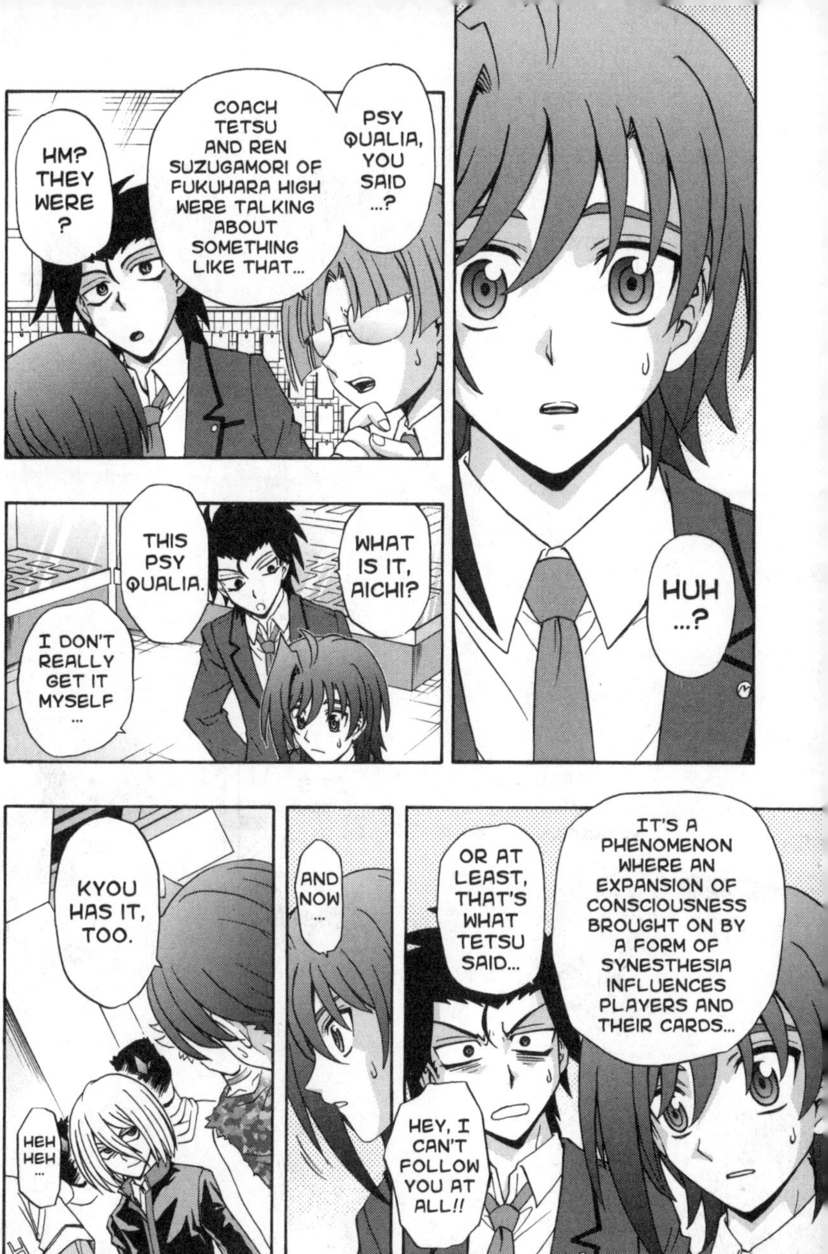
HUH ...?
PSY QUALIA, YOU SAID ...?
COACH TETSU AND REN SUZUGAMORI OF FUKUHARA HIGH WERE TALKING ABOUT SOMETHING LIKE THAT...
HM? THEY WERE ?
WHAT IS IT, AICHI?
THIS PSY QUALIA.
I DON'T REALLY GET IT MYSELF ...
IT'S A PHENOMENON WHERE AN EXPANSION OF CONSCIOUSNESS BROUGHT ON BY A FORM OF SYNESTHESIA INFLUENCES PLAYERS AND THEIR CARDS...
OR AT LEAST, THAT'S WHAT TETSU SAID...
HEY, I CAN'T FOLLOW YOU AT ALL!!
AND NOW ...
KYOU HAS IT, TOO.
HEH HEH ...

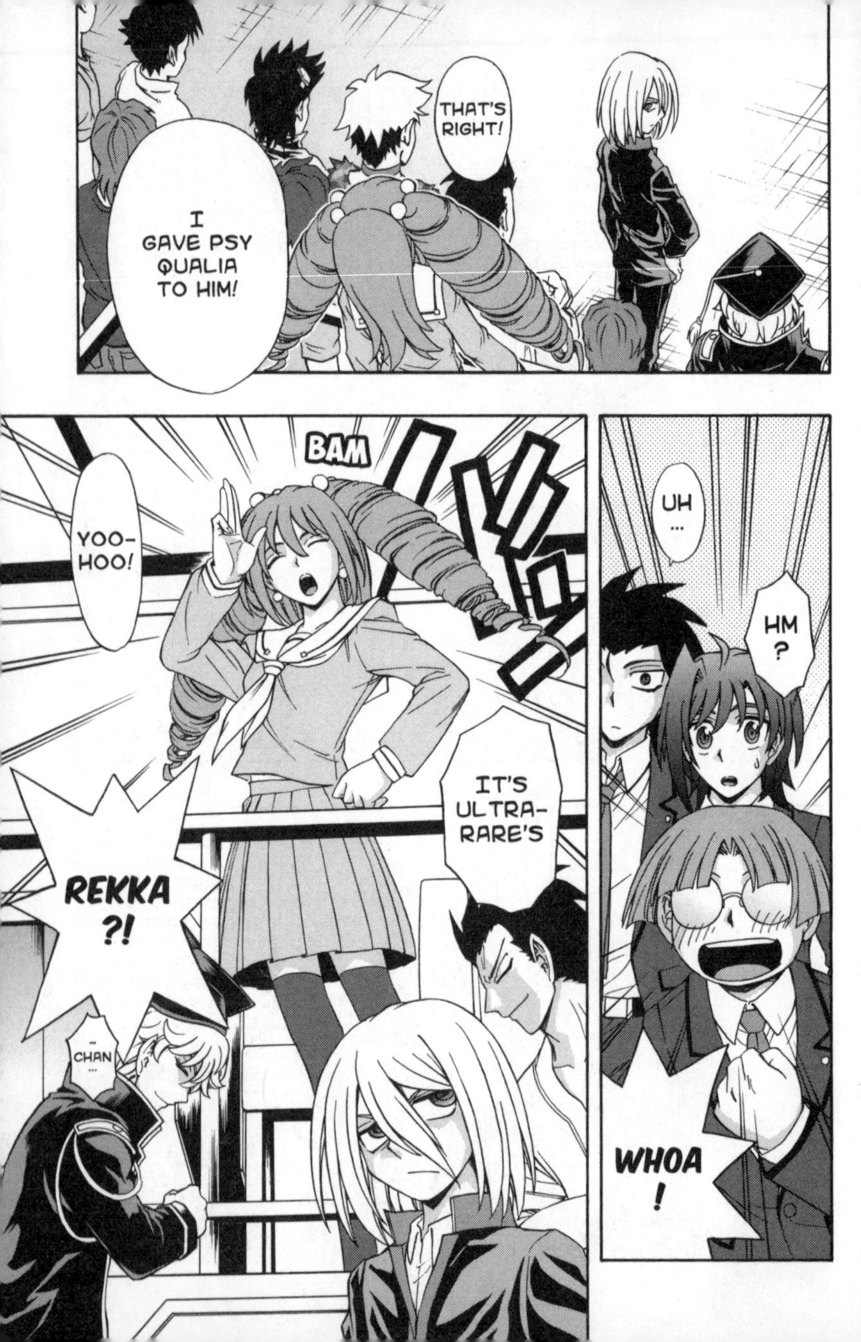
THAT'S RIGHT!
I GAVE PSY QUALIA TO HIM!
UH ...
HM ?
WHOA !
BAM
YOO-HOO!
IT'S ULTRA-RARE'S
REKKA ?!
-CHAN ...

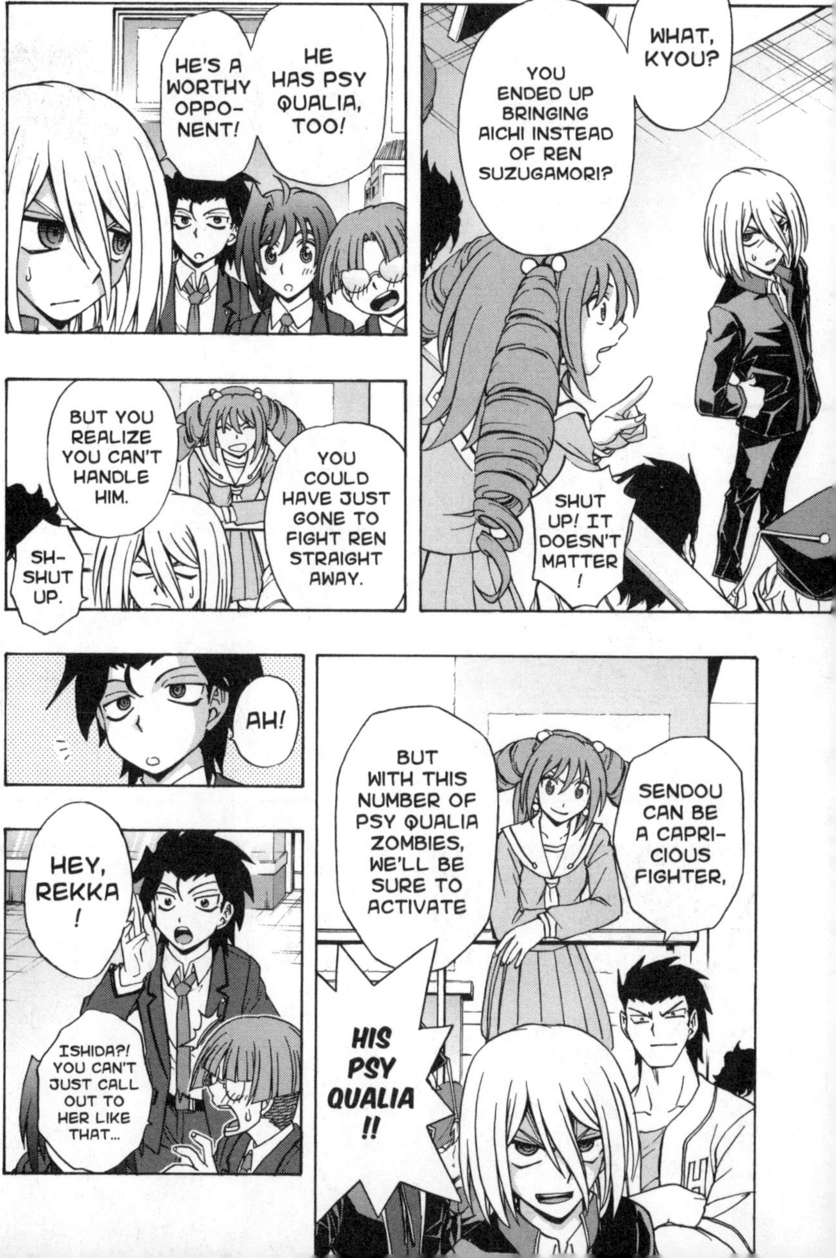
WHAT, KYOU?
YOU ENDED UP BRINGING AICHI INSTEAD OF REN SUZUGAMORI?
SHUT UP! IT DOESN'T MATTER!
HE HAS PSY QUALIA, TOO!
HE'S A WORTHY OPPO-NENT!
YOU COULD HAVE JUST GONE TO FIGHT REN STRAIGHT AWAY.
BUT YOU REALIZE YOU CAN'T HANDLE HIM.
SH-SHUT UP.
SENDOU CAN BE A CAPRI-CIOUS FIGHTER,
BUT WITH THIS NUMBER OF PSY QUALIA ZOMBIES, WE'LL BE SURE TO ACTIVATE
HIS PSY QUALIA!!
AH!
HEY, REKKA!
ISHIDA?! YOU CAN'T JUST CALL OUT TO HER LIKE THAT...

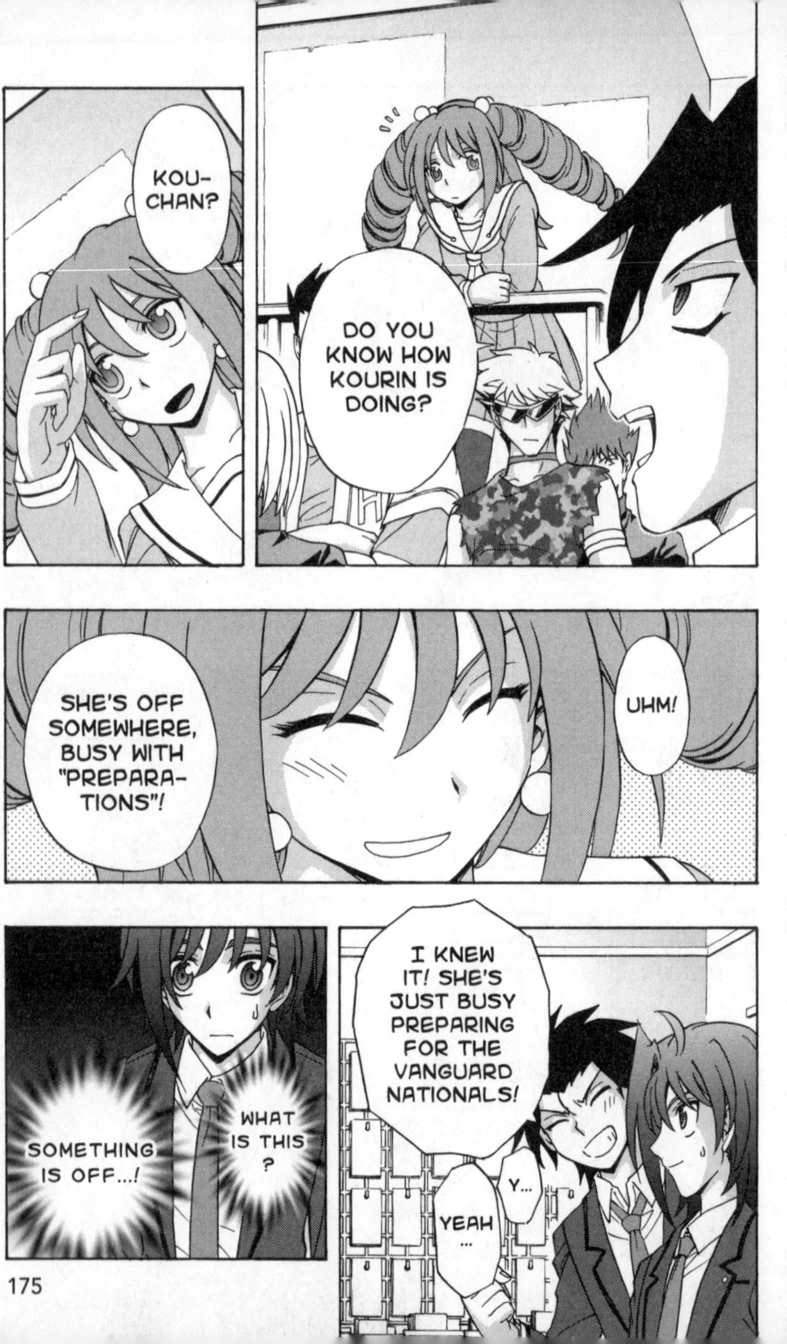
DO YOU KNOW HOW KOURIN IS DOING?
KOU-CHAN?
UHM!
SHE'S OFF SOMEWHERE, BUSY WITH "PREPARATIONS"!
I KNEW IT! SHE'S JUST BUSY PREPARING FOR THE VANGUARD NATIONALS!
Y...
YEAH ...
WHAT IS THIS ?
SOMETHING IS OFF...!

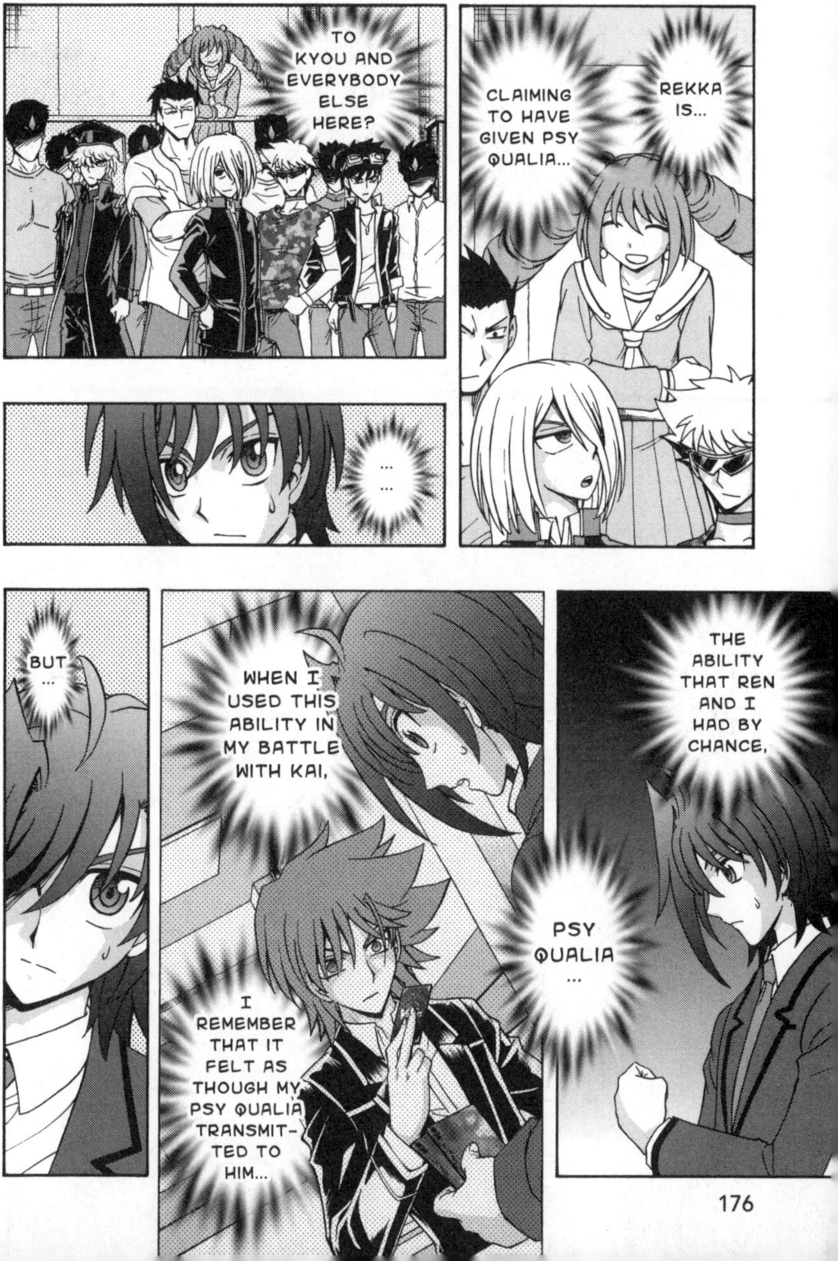
REKKA IS...
CLAIMING TO HAVE GIVEN PSY QUALIA...
TO KYOU AND EVERYBODY ELSE HERE?
... ...
THE ABILITY THAT REN AND I HAD BY CHANCE,
PSY QUALIA ...
WHEN I USED THIS ABILITY IN MY BATTLE WITH KAI,
I REMEMBER THAT IT FELT AS THOUGH MY PSY QUALIA TRANSMIT-TED TO HIM...
BUT ...

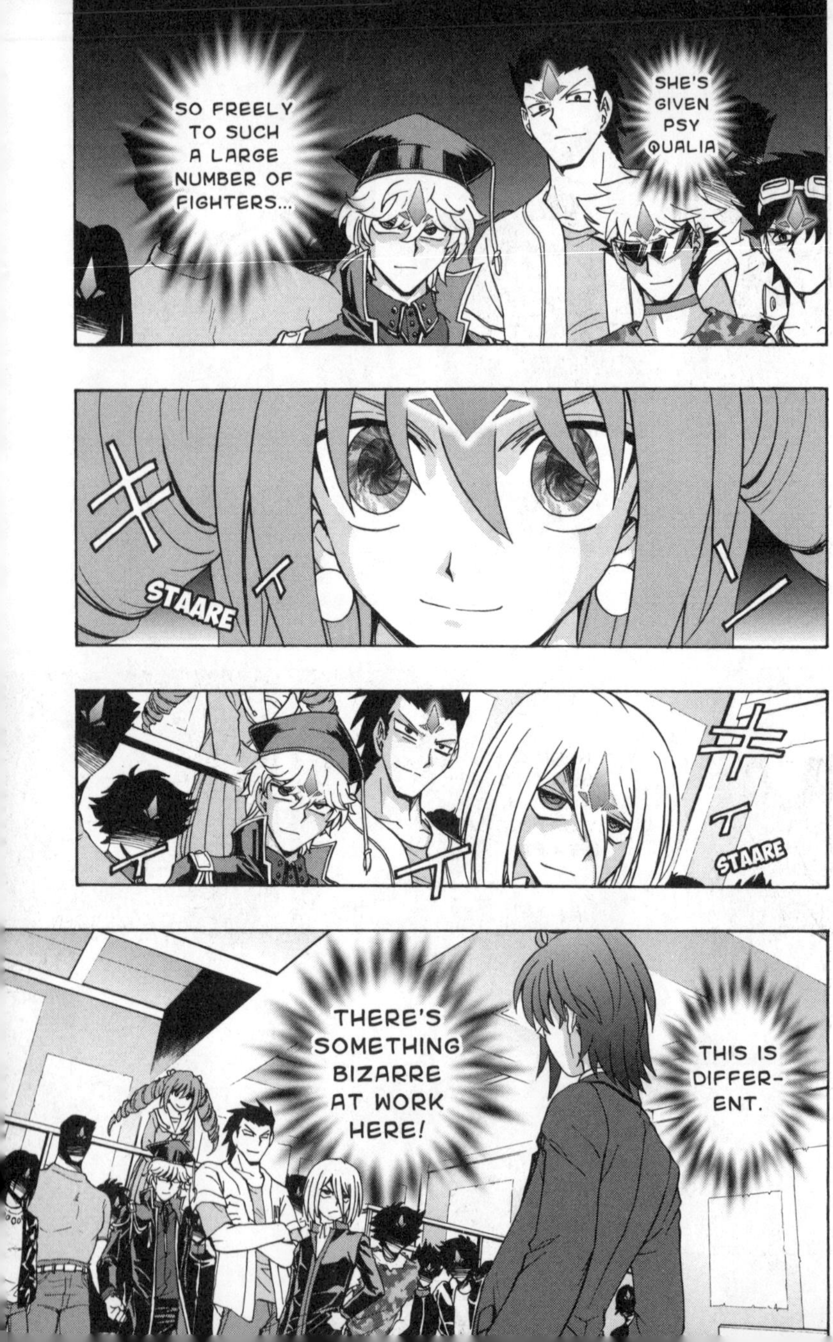
SHE'S GIVEN PSY QUALIA
SO FREELY TO SUCH A LARGE NUMBER OF FIGHTERS...
STAARE
STAARE
THIS IS DIFFER-ENT.
THERE'S SOMETHING BIZARRE AT WORK HERE!

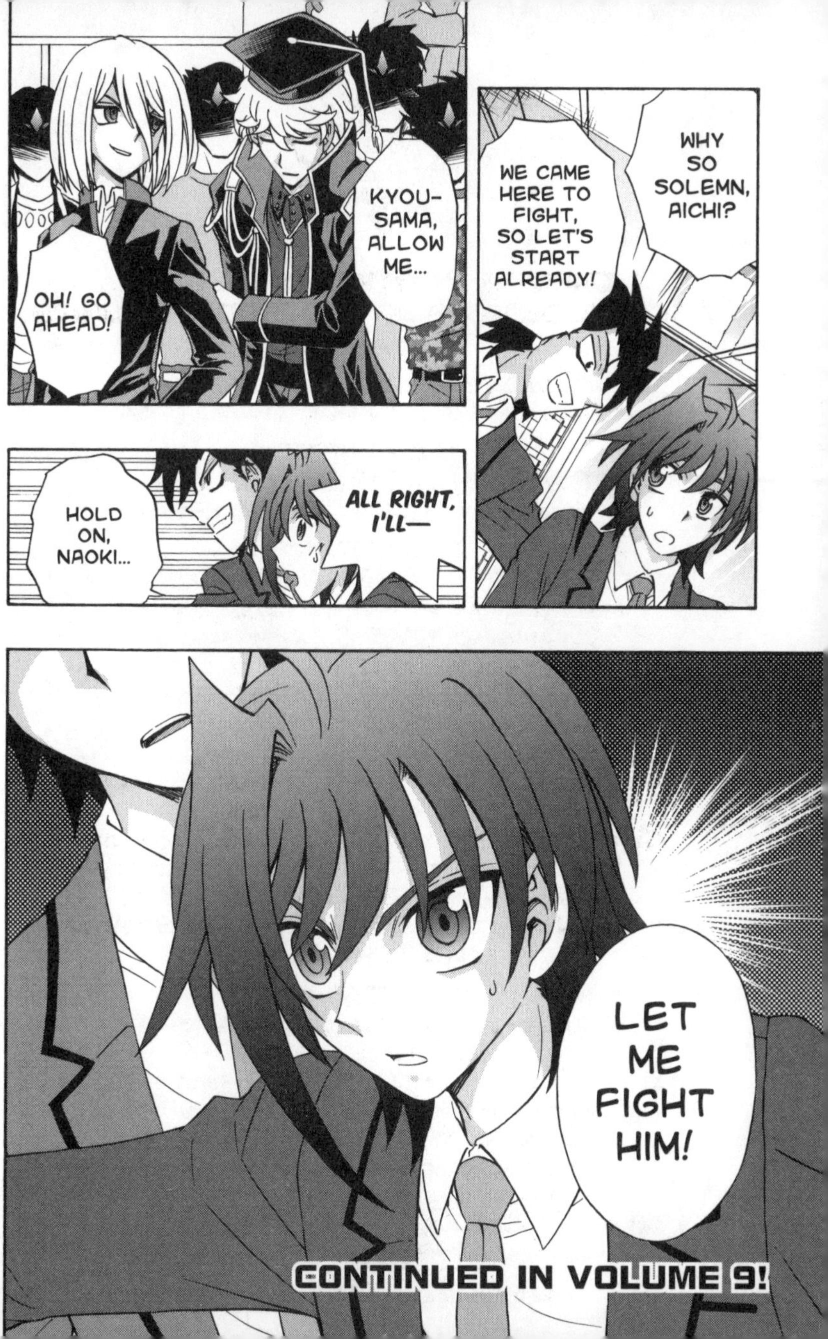
WHY SO SOLEMN, AICHI?
WE CAME HERE TO FIGHT, SO LET'S START ALREADY!
KYOU-SAMA, ALLOW ME...
OH! GO AHEAD!
ALL RIGHT, I'LL—
HOLD ON, NAOKI...
LET ME FIGHT HIM!
CONTINUED IN VOLUME 9!

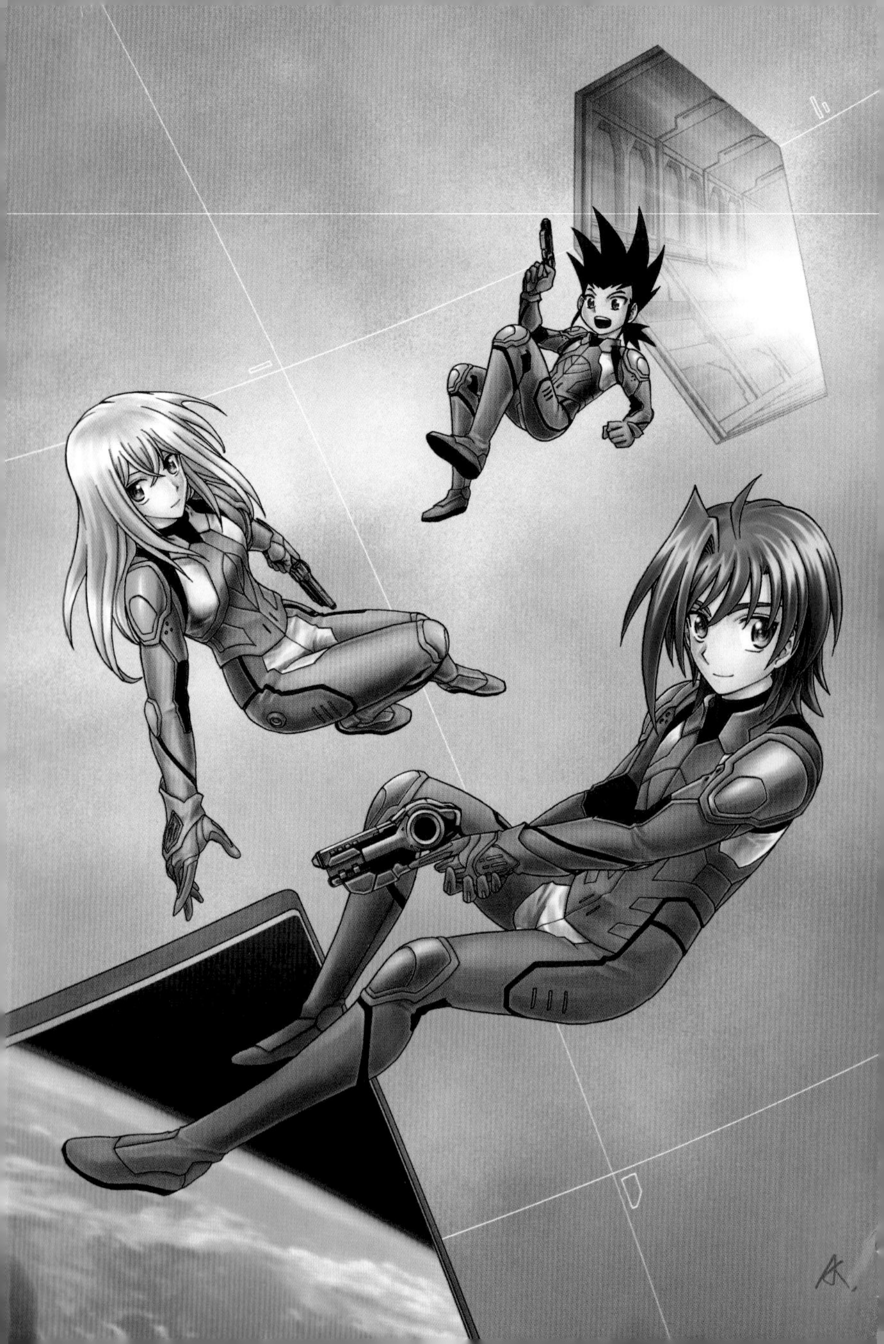

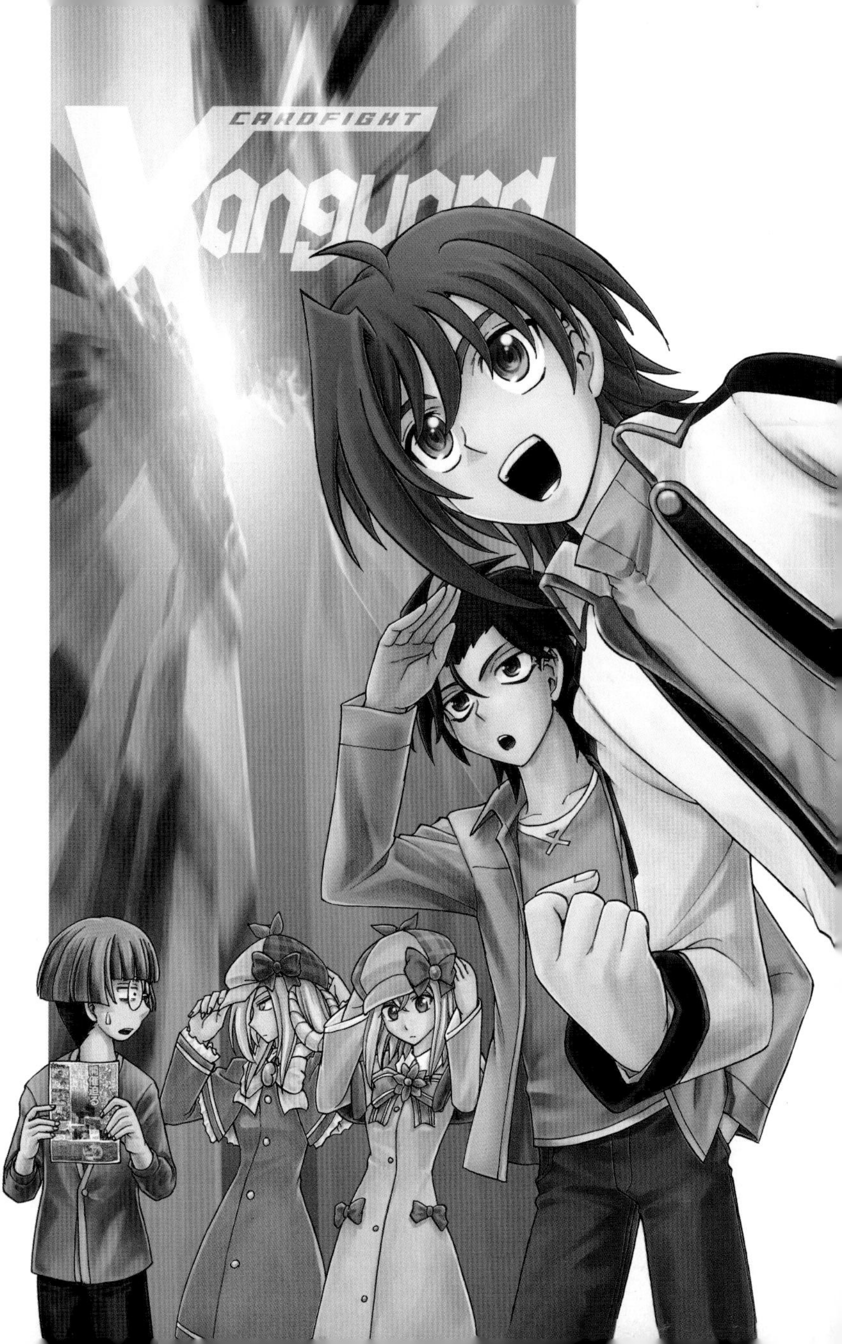
CARDFIGHT
Vanguard

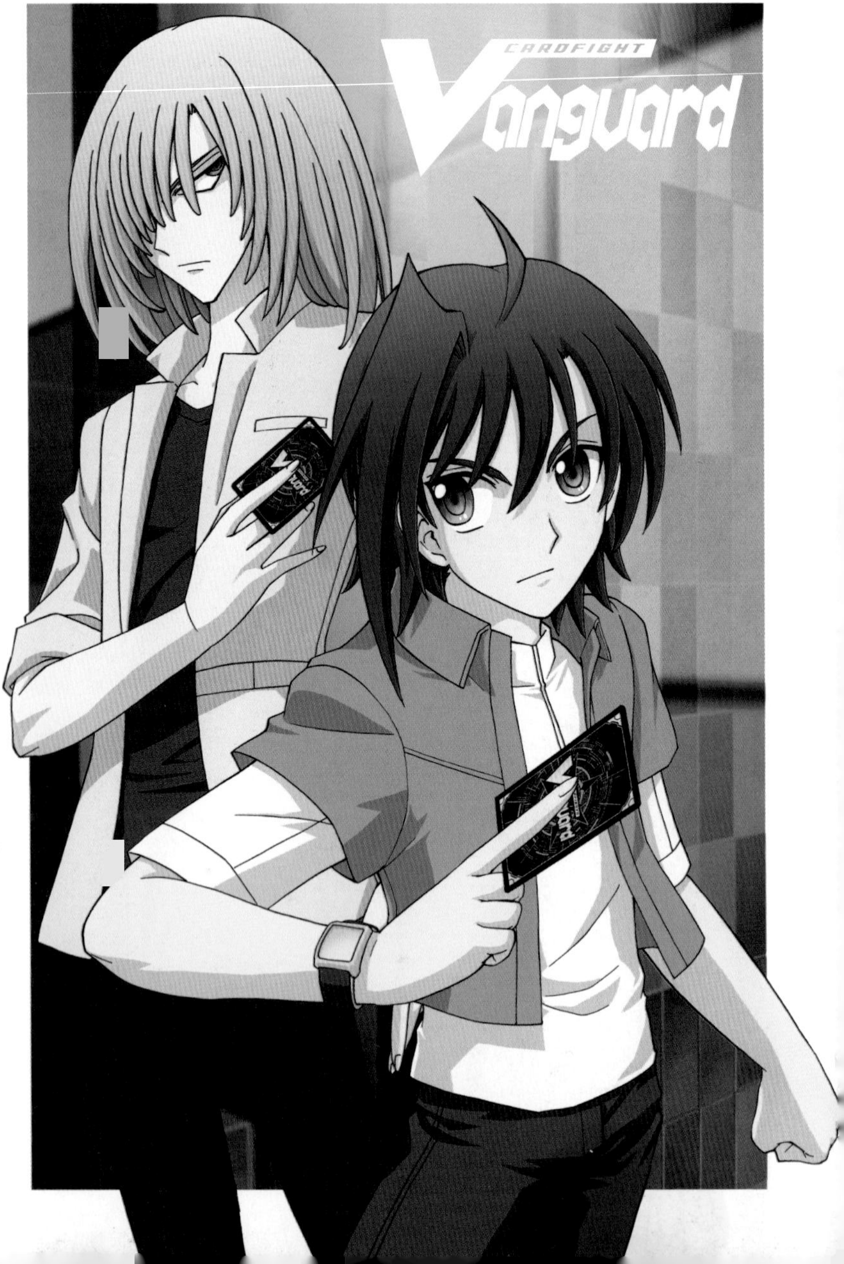
CARDFIGHT
Vanguard

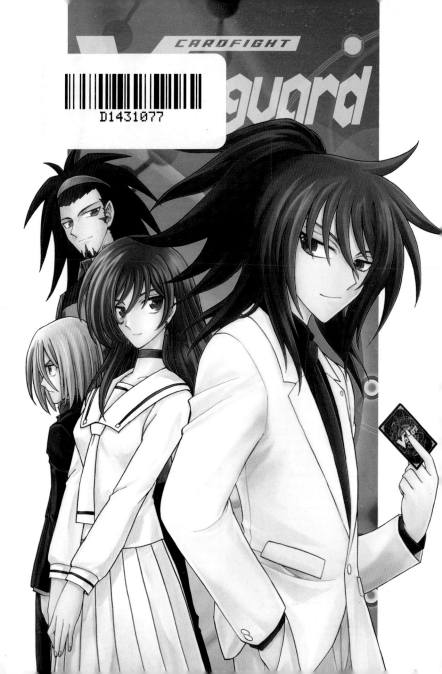

CARDFIGHT

guard